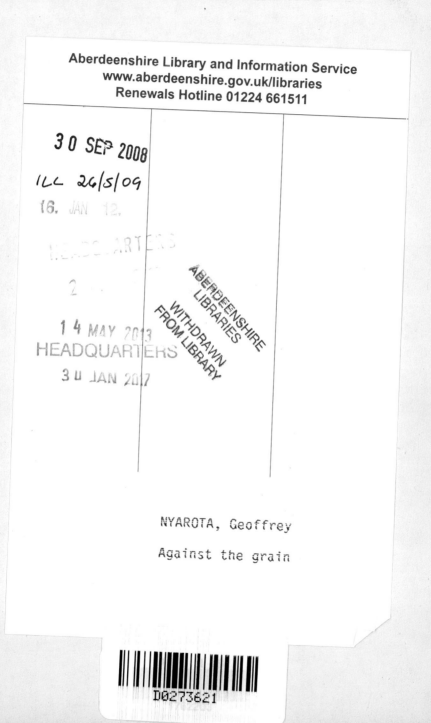

AGAINST THE GRAIN

AGAINST THE GRAIN

MEMOIRS OF A ZIMBABWEAN NEWSMAN

Geoffrey Nyarota

ZEBRA

Published by Zebra Press
an imprint of Struik Publishers
(a division of New Holland Publishing (South Africa) (Pty) Ltd)
PO Box 1144, Cape Town, 8000
New Holland Publishing is a member of Johnnic Communications Ltd

www.zebrapress.co.za

First published 2006

Cover ⌐ ⌐ vspaper stack),

A roduced,
stor any means,
erwise,
wners.

PUBLISHING MANAGER: Marlene Fryer
MANAGING EDITOR: Robert Plummer
EDITOR: Marléne Burger
PROOFREADER: Ronel Richter-Herbert
COVER AND TEXT DESIGNER: Natascha Adendorff-Olivier
TYPESETTER: Monique van den Berg
INDEXER: Robert Plummer
PRODUCTION MANAGER: Valerie Kömmer

Set in 10 pt on 13.6 pt Minion

Reproduction by Hirt & Carter (Cape) (Pty) Ltd
Printed and bound by Paarl Print, Oosterland Street, Paarl, South Africa

ISBN 1 77007 112 1

This book is dedicated to my wife Ursula Virginia, my children
Tafirenyika Julian, Itayi Jethro, Rufaro Thelma and Isabel,
as well as to Chiedza Ruby and Geoffrey Tafara, my grandchildren,
without whose support and personal sacrifice it could not have become reality.
They were, by force of circumstance, individually and jointly denied the
full affection and attention of a husband, father and grandfather.

This book is dedicated to the staff of the Chronicle during my tenure
as editor – fine and courageous journalists who kept a great newspaper going
during a difficult and turbulent period in the history of Zimbabwe.

Against the Grain is also dedicated to all the founding staff of the Daily News,
courageous, selfless and patriotic men and women whose faith in me
I was compelled to betray by the founding fathers of the Republic of Zimbabwe.

Above all, this book is dedicated to the people of Zimbabwe.

Contents

Foreword

O NE OF THE best friends I ever had, now deceased, once said to me, 'John, why don't you coordinate the writing of a true history of Zimbabwe? Do you want the task to be undertaken by politicians who will mangle and distort the facts to suit their political agendas?'

The question was asked in all seriousness, because my friend knew that I had lived through the modern political history of Zimbabwe, initially as a journalist and subsequently as a practising lawyer, from the days of Benjamin Burombo's British African Voice Association in the late 1940s to the liberation of the country by guerrillas of the Patriotic Front.

I wish my late friend was still around, because in this work, Geoff, as he is popularly called, has, in his inimitable style, provided a timely, well-researched, incisive and perceptive account of the latter years of the struggle as he perceived them. With the exception of South Africa, the struggle for the liberation of Zimbabwe was arguably one of the most protracted regional campaigns in southern Africa. What began as a passive, non-violent movement, progressed through militancy and culminated in a formidable armed struggle until victory was achieved in 1980. Geoff's account of the events from the official start of the war of liberation at Chinhoyi in 1966 is a fascinating yet factual story that constitutes a reliable record to which anyone else wishing to write on the subject would be well advised to refer constantly.

Some readers will recall that after Burombo's movement came the militant African National Congress Youth League of James Chikerema and George Nyandoro, Zimbabwe's inseparable lifelong nationalists, political activists, freedom fighters and guerrillas in the true sense. This organisation was followed by the mass movement known as the Zimbabwe African People's Union (Zapu) and its successor, the National Democratic Party (NDP), led by, among others, Joshua Nkomo, Ndabaningi Sithole and Robert Mugabe. After Ian Smith banned the NDP, the party split into the People's Caretaker Council (PCC) and the Zimbabwe African National Union (Zanu).

On the eve of the first one-man one-vote general election in 1980, the Patriotic Front (PF) divided into Zanu-PF, led by Mugabe, and PF-Zapu, led by Nkomo. Zanu-PF won the election and has remained in power until the present day. In December 1987, Zanu-PF and PF-Zapu merged into a single political party and, ironically, adopted the name Zanu-PF. But the merger brought about no change of political dispensation and it was not until 1999 that Zimbabwe had any meaningful opposition to Zanu-PF, in the form of the Movement for Democratic Change (MDC).

I knew that Geoff had won numerous regional and international awards for excellence in journalism. I was pleasantly surprised to learn that although we had worked fairly closely together for a long period before I relocated to another country, Geoff had successfully concealed some of the awards from me. The blame is entirely mine for not keeping up with media issues as diligently as in the past.

I have always been familiar with Geoff's wry sense of humour, but I think that in this book, he has excelled himself. He doggedly traces the fortunes of one of Ian Smith's semi-literate black policemen, who had arrested and tortured him while he was still a schoolteacher in eastern Zimbabwe in the late 1970s, to that character's current position as a director of the national airline, Air Zimbabwe. Typically, Geoff muses ironically that the former policeman's appointment to the board might help to explain why Air Zimbabwe finds it difficult to operate efficiently, if at all.

Geoff has been a powerful influence in the field of journalism throughout southern Africa in general and in Zimbabwe in particular. His outstanding quality as a newspaper editor was that he never sent any of his reporters on an assignment that he was not prepared to carry out himself, and he often did so at great risk to his personal safety, that of his wife Ursula and their children, who have all stood by him through thick and thin. His investigation and courageous exposure of the Willowgate car scandal, the Harare International Airport construction tender scam and other high-profile corruption in Zimbabwe bear eloquent testimony to his ability in, and commitment and dedication to the profession of journalism.

Among Geoff's contemporaries and those who followed him are courageous newsmen such as Trevor Vusumuzi Ncube, publisher of a widely read regional weekly newspaper, and the late Mark Chavunduka, a former Nieman Fellow like Geoff. Ironically, the list of Geoff's former columnists includes none other than Jonathan Nathaniel Moyo, a university lecturer who worked his way up to become Mugabe's spin doctor, until he fell out of favour for allegedly conspiring to defeat Mugabe's choice of vice-president.

A number of texts on Zimbabwe have been published, especially in the last fifteen years or so. But I am convinced that this one stands out as probably the best of the collection. Geoff has truly deserved all the awards he has received for journalism and I believe that more are yet to follow. In the meanwhile, I believe that this book is deserving of a literary award in its own right.

THE HONOURABLE MR JUSTICE JOHN OLIVER MANYARARA
WINDHOEK, NAMIBIA
MARCH 2006

Preface

WHILE MOST OF the research for and the writing of this book was accomplished in the scholarly ambience of Harvard University, *Against the Grain* is by no means an academic or analytical dissertation on the economic, social and political meltdown of Zimbabwe little more than two decades after the country achieved independence from colonial rule.

This is history from a personal perspective – an account of the first quarter-century of the Republic of Zimbabwe from my own close observation and harrowing experience as a journalist. The nature of my hurried and unscheduled departure from Zimbabwe at the beginning of 2003 forced me to leave behind many of my personal documents, which were later hurriedly packed by others and placed in storage. I was thus unavoidably denied access to parts of the manuscript that I had worked on intermittently since 1980. Following my arrival in the United States at the end of January 2003, I was able to resume writing in a more focused manner.

As I worked on the manuscript, Mark Kramer, the writer-in-residence and director of the Program on Narrative Journalism at the Nieman Foundation for Journalism at Harvard, invited me to present a paper at the Nieman Conference on Narrative Journalism in December 2004.

The conference has become one of the highlights of the Nieman calendar.

Kramer asked me to focus on the professional experience of journalists working in environments such as Zimbabwe, where the government of President Robert Mugabe had embarked on a vicious campaign to silence the country's fledgling independent press. After we debated a suitable title, Kramer suggested, *Writing against the grain: Telling stories the government doesn't want to hear.*

His proposal made such an impression that I immediately adopted *Against the Grain* as the working title of my manuscript.

While writing, I relied to a remarkable extent – especially in the chapters on the rise and fall of the *Daily News* – on the painful recollections of my resilient wife Ursula, the meticulous record-keeping of my courageous personal assistant and protector Annie Musemburi-Musodza, and the elephantine memory of my learned colleague Muchadeyi Ashton Masunda. Annie also keyed in corrections in Harare and managed the whole project.

Masunda was the founding chairman and, subsequently, chief executive of Associated Newspapers of Zimbabwe, publishers of the *Daily News*. Latterly, he became the Harare-based editor of my manuscript. I bow to his superior knowledge of Zimbabwe's corporate, social and political worlds and all matters legal. The assistance of my editor in the Diaspora, Eric Meijer, was invaluable. Meijer was my deputy at the *Manica Post* in Mutare in the early days of Zimbabwe's independence. He now lives in Sydney, Australia, and his assignment was to ensure that *Against the Grain* achieved an international appeal.

My son Tafirenyika painstakingly conducted invaluable research on documents at the National Archives in Harare, dating back to the early days of independence. He and Annie also compiled the portfolio of pictures from public records and private collections. In Massachusetts, Victoria Dune-Chari, my dedicated proofreader, burned the proverbial midnight oil to keep chapters moving.

All six men and women made tremendous sacrifices, including many of their weekends, with no promise or guarantee of reward. I owe them a mountain of gratitude.

This project would not have been possible without the wonderful opportunity and research facilities accorded by the Nieman Foundation for Journalism, as well as the Carr Center for Human Rights Policy, both at Harvard University, where I served two fellowships from 2003 to 2005. I must single out Bob Giles, curator of the Nieman Foundation, and Professor Michael Ignatieff, director of the Carr Center, for special mention. Ignatieff was elected to parliament in Canada as this project drew to a close. I wish to thank Ann Cooper and Elisabeth Witchell of the Committee to Protect Journalists, as well as Professor Helge Ronning and other members of the faculty in the Department of Media Studies and Communication at the University of Oslo in Norway for their support and encouragement during the Fall semester of 2005.

It was both a joy and an inspiration to work with publishing manager Marlene Fryer, managing editor Robert Plummer and junior editor Rochelle Solomons, all of Zebra Press, and my manuscript editor, Marléne Burger.

I wish to mention Paul Lewis, my research assistant at the Carr Center, who flew to London to jog Lord Carrington's memory, and to acknowledge the Rev Dr Lawrence Daka at Boston University; Judith Todd in Cape Town; the Rev Gift Makwasha of Boston College; my colleagues at the Carr Center, Tiawan Gongloe of Liberia and Emran Quresh of Canada; Geoff Hill and Tendai Dumbutshena in Johannesburg; Derek Smail, always available to refresh my memory about some of the finer details of ANZ's origins; Wilfred Mhanda and Patricia Mari in Harare; poet Chenjerai Hove in Stavanger, Norway; Florence Mpepo, Charlemagne Chimbangu and Fidelis Kadziyanike in Worcester, MA; Siza and Laura Mtimbiri in New Hampshire; and several others, not mentioned by name, without whose support and encouragement it would not have been possible to complete this mammoth task.

GEOFFREY NYAROTA
WORCESTER, MASSACHUSETTS
UNITED STATES OF AMERICA
APRIL 2006

Abbreviations

ACP: African, Caribbean and Pacific countries
AHT: Air Harbour Technologies
AIPPA: Access to Information and Protection of Privacy Act
AMI: African Media Investments
AMIZ: AMI Zimbabwe
ANC: African National Congress
ANZ: Associated Newspapers of Zimbabwe
BBC: British Broadcasting Corporation
BCCI: Bank of Credit and Commerce International
BSAP: British South African Police
CID: Criminal Investigations Department
CIO: Central Intelligence Organisation
ComOps: Combined Operations
CNG: Community Newspaper Group
CPJ: Committee to Protect Journalists
CPU: Commonwealth Press Union
DA: district assistant
DRC: Democratic Republic of Congo
ESAP: Economic Structural Adjustment Programme
Frelimo: Liberation Front of Mozambique
Frolizi: Front for the Liberation of Zimbabwe
Iana: Inter-African News Agency
IDC: Industrial Development Corporation
IJAZ: Independent Journalists' Association of Zimbabwe
IMG: Independent Media Group
MCI: Makoni Cooper International
MDC: Movement for Democratic Change
MIC: Media and Information Commission
MIPF: Mining Industry Pension Fund
MISA: Media Institute of Southern Africa
MNR: Mozambique Resistance Movement
NCA: National Constitutional Assembly
NDP: National Democratic Party
OAU: Organisation of African Unity

PAC:	Pan Africanist Congress
PF-Zapu:	Patriotic Front – Zimbabwe African People's Union
PISI:	Police Internal Security Intelligence
PLO:	Palestinian Liberation Organisation
POSA:	Public Order and Security Act
RAF:	Rhodesian Air Force
RAR:	Rhodesia African Rifles
RBC:	Rhodesian Broadcasting Corporation
RP&P:	Rhodesian Printing and Publishing Company
SADC:	Southern African Development Community
Samdef:	Southern African Media Development Fund
SB:	Special Branch
TTL:	Tribal Trust Lands
UANC:	United African National Council
UDI:	Unilateral Declaration of Independence
WMI:	Willowvale Motor Industries
WVCF:	War Victims' Compensation Fund
Zanla:	Zimbabwe African National Liberation Army
Zanu:	Zimbabwe African National Union
Zanu-PF:	Zimbabwe African National Union – Patriotic Front
Zapu:	Zimbabwe African People's Union
ZBC:	Zimbabwe Broadcasting Corporation
ZCTU:	Zimbabwe Congress of Trade Unions
ZDF:	Zimbabwe Defence Force
ZDI:	Zimbabwe Defence Industries
Ziana:	Zimbabwe Inter-African News Agency
ZIC:	Zimbabwe Investment Centre
ZIFA:	Zimbabwe Football Association
Zinatha:	Zimbabwe National Traditional Healers' Association
Zipa:	Zimbabwe People's Army
Zipra:	Zimbabwe People's Revolutionary Army
ZLP:	Zimbabwe Liberators' Platform
ZMMT:	Zimbabwe Mass Media Trust
ZNA:	Zimbabwe National Army
ZNWVA:	Zimbabwe National War Veterans' Association
ZRP:	Zimbabwe Republican Police
ZTV:	Zimbabwe Television
ZUJ:	Zimbabwe Union of Journalists
ZUM:	Zimbabwe Unity Movement
Zupo:	Zimbabwe United People's Organisation

Zimbabwe: major towns and cities

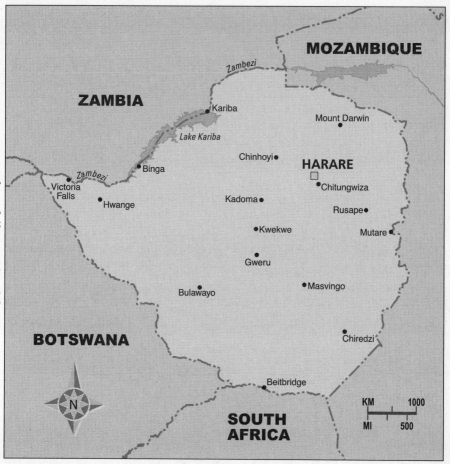

Cartographer: Ryan Africa, copyright © Map Studio 2006

Zimbabwe: eastern districts

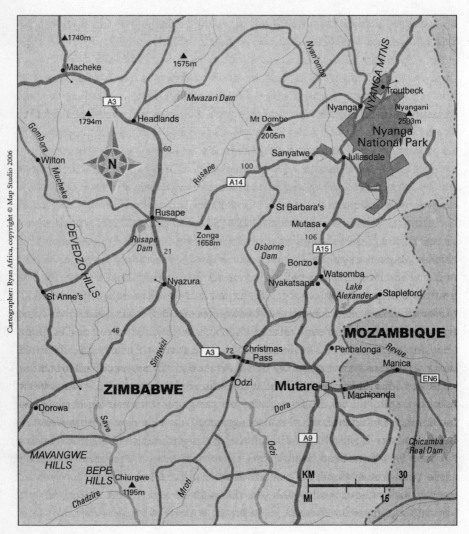

1

Caught in crossfire

THREE MEN IN army camouflage uniform materialised in front of us. They obviously could not be Zanla guerrillas, accounts of whose omnipresence and skirmishing prowess in both combat and ambush generated much excited and occasionally exaggerated debate among villagers living in Rhodesia's operational war zones.

The men approaching us carried FN rifles. This was the regular weapon issued to all army and police units, as well as counter-insurgency operatives, including mercenaries, who fought the bush war against guerrillas infiltrating what was still Rhodesia in the 1970s. Two of the men facing us were white.

They had probably been alerted by our uproarious approach before darting into the undergrowth on both sides of the wide path.

Their rifles were pointed menacingly at us. One of the white men was barely out of his teens, possibly nineteen or twenty years of age. The other, whose demeanour said he was the man in charge, could have been thirty-five or older. While the black man, who was perhaps in his forties, was slightly potbellied, he appeared fit as a fiddle. His shirtsleeves were rolled up to expose muscular arms. What I noticed most about him were his shifty eyes. I never engaged them for more than a fleeting moment in my effort to assess whether he was a friend in uniform or an implacable foe. Many of the black troops serving Ian Smith's regime tended to fall into the latter category.

The leader stepped forward.

'I am Detective Inspector Nigel Spur of the Special Branch in Rusape,' he said, voice cold and barely concealing virulent hostility. His advance towards us was covered by the other men, rifles aimed more menacingly now, or so I thought, at me in particular.

'Which one of you is Geoffrey Nyarota?'

My heart pounded heavily against my ribcage. As I tried to conceal the terror that was building in me, sweat trickled down my face in betrayal.

'It is I.' I spoke slowly to ensure that the grammar of even this three-word utterance was immaculate. I rarely endeared myself to white Rhodesians, especially those of English stock, to whom I obviously sounded like an arrogant upstart. Detective Inspector Spur did not appear to be amused.

'So, it is you?' Spur barked as he savagely whacked me on the left side of the body with his rifle butt. I felt a burning sensation on my face as the weapon crashed into my cheek as well. I tasted blood and spat it out. The sight of red spittle appeared to infuriate the younger white man. He handed his rifle to the black officer and pounced on me. In

1

a frenzy of anger and using the 'clenched fist and booted foot' of Rhodesian police parlance, he unleashed a series of savage blows on every conceivable part of my anatomy. I was taken by such surprise that I did not even think of defending myself.

For some reason that I could not immediately comprehend, Spur and the young man displayed a triumphant attitude that I could not readily associate with their victory over an unarmed man.

My uncle, Cephas Nyarota, and my cousins Cleopas and Cosmas Dzimati, looked on helplessly. All three worked for Rhodesia Railways in Bulawayo, the country's second largest city and headquarters of the rail service. Cosmas, two years my senior, was a general hand, while my uncle and Cleopas, then both aged around forty, were caboose cooks.

The caboose is the kitchen wagon, usually positioned immediately behind the locomotive. In this carriage, the cooks prepared what my uncle assured me were sumptuous meals for themselves before preparing much less lavish fare for the white engineers running the trains between Bulawayo and Johannesburg through Botswana.

By the living standards in Bulawayo's black townships, caboose cooks were well-to-do. For some inexplicable reason, they were always referred to as caboose cooks, never simply as cooks. The sagging bellies of some were ample testimony, even to the most sceptical, of the elevated status of the caboose cook in the social hierarchy of the township.

My three relatives had arrived by train from Bulawayo the previous day. We had arranged that I wait for them at Nyazura Station. I was particularly anxious to show off to them my recent acquisition, the pride of my heart – a 1965 Ford Cortina GT. The car was eleven years old, but to me it was brand new. Members of my extended family were at once proud and amazed that I had bought a car after teaching at a secondary school for little more than a year.

It was a beautiful car, or so everybody said. For most of the eighteen months that I owned the vehicle, I passed through police roadblocks without once being asked to produce my driver's licence. It became a matter of routine for seasoned officers to cheerfully wave me past the barriers, barely able to conceal their open admiration for the car.

If policemen elsewhere waved at me, their colleagues in my hometown, Nyazura, did not share their enthusiasm. Junior officers, in particular, seemed to resent the spectacle of a young schoolteacher driving such a fine car.

I met Uncle Cephas and my two cousins at the railway station in the late afternoon of 31 December 1976. After we squeezed all their luggage into the small boot and my two potbellied relatives negotiated their large frames into the limited confines of the car's interior, we covered the kilometre from the station to the township beer hall at a snail's pace.

The arrival of the car and the sight of its prosperous-looking passengers were cause for commotion among beer hall patrons. Cleopas ordered a round of Castle Lager. Sitting in a corner, not too far away, I recognised two off-duty policemen, both young constables at the local station. They were sharing a mug of Chibuku with two women who were resplendent in brightly coloured miniskirts. Chibuku is a traditional beer, brewed and packaged in a factory, that is popular with the majority of Zimbabweans because it is so affordable.

After we ordered our second round, I observed that the young women appeared to have lost interest in whatever stories the law enforcement officers were trying to impress them with. The policemen sensed the shift in attention and, realising their obvious disadvantage, emptied their beer mugs and stood up to leave. I thought the younger of the two scowled in our direction as they passed.

We decided it was time to depart as well if we were to reach the village before everybody had retired for the night after a busy day in the fields. The two scantily dressed young women did nothing to conceal their disappointment as we walked out in single file. We soon caught up with the police officers, and as the car slowly approached them, the younger of the two flagged us down.

'How dare you drive so fast in a residential area?' he asked.

'The way this car is loaded,' I replied, 'I could not possibly have been speeding.'

'In that case, I will give you a ticket for overloading.'

I sensed that the officers were spoiling for a fight, engaged first gear, waved goodbye and drove off. As we would discover before long, this was a serious error of judgement on my part.

We parked the car overnight at the homestead of an uncle who lived in a village across the Nyamatsanga River from our own. Leaving the luggage in the car to be collected the following morning, we walked in single file in the semi-darkness towards our own village.

In summer, from November to March, when tropical thunderstorms turned even small streams into torrential rivers, it was impossible to drive any vehicle, not even the legendarily robust Land Rover, across the Nyamatsanga. Whenever I visited during the rainy season, I left my vehicle on the Nyazura side of the river at Uncle Timothy Mabika's homestead and walked the three kilometres or so to Nyarota village.

Just after we crossed the river that night, we encountered the most hair-raising sight of my life. A group of about twenty men, all of them heavily armed, suddenly sprang up on both sides of the narrow footpath and surrounded us. I had never seen a freedom fighter before, but stories abounded about the guerrillas of the Zimbabwe African National Liberation Army (Zanla), who had been deployed from Mozambique and had recently infiltrated our Chiduku district. For years their operations had been confined to the north-eastern areas of Rhodesia in the Mount Darwin and Mtoko districts. Now they had set up a main base high up in the awesome Ruwombwe Mountains, some six kilometres south-west of our village as the crow flies. Only the bravest of hunters ventured anywhere near this particular mountain range. The men surrounding us were obviously a detachment of Zanla fighters from the Ruwombwe base, possibly on some important mission.

Zanla was the military wing of the Zimbabwe African National Union (Zanu), a nationalist movement that Robert Gabriel Mugabe would effectively lead in due course. It was one of two groups fighting to emancipate Southern Rhodesia from the racist minority rule of rebel leader Ian Smith.

'How are you, comrades?' one of the men asked.

Before we answered, another question was fired: 'Where are you coming from?'

Then: 'Who are you? How is the situation in Nyazura? Do you have cigarettes?'

The questions rained on us with the intensity of a sudden tropical thunderstorm, and with the same effect. I, for one, was immediately drenched in sweat, but despite their abrasive manner, I sensed that these men were not hostile, only anxious to establish their authority and extract as much information as possible from us before we recovered from the shock of our unexpected meeting.

Assuming leadership of our small group, I answered their questions with an ability that seemed to satisfy them. We handed over the two packets of cigarettes that Cosmas and I had between us. They also relieved us of the case of beer that we had taken turns to carry.

'You must be the schoolteacher?' asked the one who did most of the talking, addressing me directly.

'Yes, I am a schoolteacher,' I responded, heart thumping audibly. I disregarded the hint of familiarity in his question, having long been coached that guerrillas were never to be taken for granted.

'You still teach at Regina Coeli Mission?'

'Yes, I still teach at Regina Coeli,' I answered, filled with consternation at this persistent line of questioning.

'Well, you never met us tonight, did you, comrades?'

'No, we did not meet you,' I assured him.

'*Pamberi nechimurenga*,' he said, raising his AK47 rifle with the left hand while punching the air with his right fist. The Chinese version of the Kalashnikov assault rifle was the weapon issued to the Zanla forces that infiltrated from Mozambique to wage war in the northern, eastern and southern regions of Rhodesia.

'*Pamberi!*' the rest of the group shouted.

'*Pasi ne Mabhunu!*'

'*Pasi!*' This time, we joined in.

Just as mysteriously as they had appeared, they melted into the darkness of the cloudy night and walked briskly towards the river, which they crossed before heading in the direction of Nyazura. Up to the point of this nocturnal encounter we had been suffering the side effects of our late-afternoon conviviality at the beer hall, but by the time we reached the village a few minutes later, we were all stone cold sober.

'*Pamberi nechimurenga*', Shona for 'Hail the revolution', and '*Pasi ne Mabhunu*', meaning 'Death to the Boers', were two of the many slogans adopted by Zanla to galvanise the peasant population in those rural districts that the guerrillas had infiltrated and won over to full support of the liberation struggle. *Mabhunu* was a derogatory word used by the Shona people to refer to Rhodesians of Boer or Afrikaner ancestry. In its wider colloquial sense, the word applied to all white people, including those of British descent.

On arrival in the village, my relatives were greeted with excitement and jubilation. Our nerve-wracking riverside meeting with the heavily armed soldiers remained a closely guarded secret. The visitors from Bulawayo soon feigned exhaustion and enjoined our still excited family members to retire for the night.

Just after midnight, I suddenly sat up in bed. A distant but deafening rumble had awakened me. It sounded like the onset of a thunderstorm.

'What was that?' my young wife Ursula enquired. Before I could answer, the un-mistakable sound of sustained heavy gunfire sent us diving under the sheets. Our baby, Tafirenyika, a little over a month old, started to cry in the darkness. Literally translated, Tafirenyika's Shona name means 'we are dying for the country'. We dared not light a candle. After about ten minutes the gunfire stopped as suddenly as it had started.

As Ursula suckled and rocked the baby back to sleep, I related to her in a low voice details of our encounter with the Zanla guerrillas. I speculated that the same group must have just attacked either the police station at Nyazura or Baker's farmhouse, or both.

'Today there will be no peace in the surrounding villages,' she solemnly proclaimed.

'After we have collected the parcels from the car in the morning, I think we must pack and depart for Salisbury,' I said. 'Smith's soldiers will crawl all over the villages today. They will have a field day, beating up and torturing the villagers and burning houses.'

'This afternoon could be too late, I think.'

'You have a valid point there.'

'By the way,' Ursula said wistfully, 'happy birthday.'

'Oh, thank you, darling, and happy New Year.'

I leaned over the baby in the dark and kissed her.

'What a New Year,' I said.

We settled for the remainder of the night, but I did not sleep again until the wee hours of the morning. The sun was barely up when my three companions of the previous eventful night arrived one by one from their own homesteads, and after we had all wished each other and everybody else happiness for the year that lay ahead, we set off across the river. We walked in silence, not daring to remind one another of our nocturnal meeting, even when we passed the spot where the guerrillas had appeared.

To break our silence we recounted, amid increasing merriment, the dramatic events of the previous day in Nyazura. It was this loud but innocuous banter that Spur and his men must have heard when they set up their ambush.

Nyazura's police station had indeed been attacked. The daring assault, mere minutes into 1977, heralded both the start of what would be a tumultuous year for me and the arrival of the forces of liberation in the Chiduku area of the Makoni district, in the eastern province of Manicaland, home of the Manyika people. Because of its juxtaposition to Mozambique, the springboard of Zanla's insurgency, Manicaland would be one of the main theatres of the guerrilla war that was to force Smith, accompanied by his ragtag team of internally based black nationalist politicians, to Lancaster House by September 1979. There they negotiated the independence of a country that Smith had unilaterally declared independent fourteen turbulent years earlier, on 11 November 1965.

The officer in charge and the police officers at Nyazura had quickly recovered from the shock of being the direct target of an armed attack and discharged a few random volleys of gunfire into the night sky. As the birds broke into melodious song to announce the break of yet another dawn, the policemen took stock of their situation and assessed the damage inflicted on both the station and their egos.

The attack had caused neither death nor injury, as the main office block was deserted at that time of night. However, part of the charge office roof had been blown away and the walls of adjacent buildings were pockmarked by shrapnel. While physical damage was slight, however, a clear statement had been made.

The young policemen who had confronted us in the township the previous day must have somehow concluded that it was I who had organised the attack. Suspicion soon translated to conviction among the traumatised policemen, and in no time Spur and his men from the Special Branch (SB) – the intelligence section of the police force – were called in from Rusape to assess the situation and mount the hunt for me. After the young white soldier had reduced my face to a bloody mess, Spur stepped forward.

'That will be enough, Kevin,' he said. 'Here, Sergeant Mhike, hold Kevin while I talk to our friend here.'

He placed an ominously heavy emphasis on the word 'friend'. I was bleeding through the nose and my mouth was filled with gore. Feigning yet another blow to my face, Spur barked: 'So, where is the car? Where is your bloody car?'

'I parked it at my uncle's homestead last night,' I heard myself lisp. 'We were on our way to collect our luggage from the car now.'

'You mean you parked the car at your uncle's homestead early this morning on your return from launching the attack in Nyazura,' Spur retorted. 'You are a pathetic liar. Tell me, Phillip, why must black people be such insufferable liars? Given a choice between lying and telling the truth, they always opt for falsehood.'

Detective Sergeant Phillip Mhike fell silent, apparently uncertain whether this question required a response or not. When he noticed that Spur was looking at him rather expectantly, he spoke.

'I do not know, sir,' he replied, with what sounded like genuine sincerity. 'But you are aware, sir, that there are some of us who do not always lie.'

'You mean those who lie only some of the time. Well, you had better advise this gentleman, then, that if he wastes my time by subjecting me to falsehoods, he will live to regret it, assuming he lives to regret anything, of course.'

'You are supposed to be a university graduate and to understand English,' Mhike said, looking me straight in the eye for the first time. 'You heard for yourself what Detective Inspector Spur wants.'

'So why did you park your car at your uncle's place?' Spur asked. 'Why did you not drive it to your own homestead?'

'During the rainy season it is impossible to drive even a Land Rover across the Nyamatsanga River.'

'You lie,' he barked again. 'You merely wished to conceal the vehicle far away from your own village after you transported the terrorists last night to attack the police station early this morning. It is so very clear. Anyway, take us to the vehicle.'

We soon arrived at my uncle's surprisingly deserted homestead. We stood in a semi-circle around the car while the SB men inspected it. Spur stared meaningfully, first at Kevin and then at Mhike, as a smile of genuine and, I thought, evil satisfaction spread across his flushed face.

I had insisted on arrival at the Mabika homestead that the car should be parked outside the perimeter fence rather than driven right up to the house, for fear of running over some maize plants that had encroached on the narrow path from the gate to the main house. However, my aunt, Felicity Mabika, would not hear of it.

'You will not cause starvation in this household by running over a few stalks of maize,' she protested. 'The security of your car is more important. There are many stories these days of people who go around in the middle of the night carrying guns. Your car will be exposed to danger if you leave it outside the gate.'

On that logical note, I had driven through the shoulder-high maize to park right next to the house. Now, as he inspected the damage caused to the crop, Spur could reach only one conclusion: he had found the evidence he so much wanted.

'It is quite clear that you concealed the car here after the attack,' he declared triumphantly. 'Why else would you drive over maize plants this size, if not to park the car where it would not be visible from the road? Here, hand over the car keys.'

Turning to his colleagues, he said, 'I will radio for the vehicles to come and pick us up now. Kevin, you will drive the Cortina back to the police station.'

Ten minutes later, two Land Rovers, both in camouflage livery, arrived. My three relatives and I were ordered to jump onto the back of one, beneath a canvas canopy. We set off for Nyazura, the Cortina GT, luggage still in the trunk and with Kevin behind the wheel, leading the way. The second Land Rover, which carried heavily armed soldiers, was at the rear.

The fact that my car was fully loaded in no way dissuaded the SB members that I had transported guerrillas – or terrorists, as Spur insisted on calling them with undisguised disgust – and their weapons to mount a hostile attack on the Nyazura police station the night before.

It was to be twenty-one days before we could remove the parcels, including perishables, which by then had been reduced to a smelly mess, from the boot of the Cortina where it was parked outside the Rusape police station.

At Nyazura, the arrival of the three-vehicle convoy caused a major commotion among the policemen who were milling around their damaged offices and trying to restore some semblance of order.

The member in charge, a white officer of surprisingly diminutive stature for a member of the British South African Police (BSAP), as Rhodesia's police force was called, walked up to us as we alighted from the back of the Land Rover. His face was contorted with anger.

'Which one is it?' he asked of no one in particular, his gaze curiously already fixed on me.

'It is that one, sir,' the young policeman from the beer hall zealously enlightened him. 'The one dressed in denim jeans like a terrorist, sir.'

This time I was prepared, but I was still stunned by the force of the first blow. The member in charge exhausted himself. The young policeman tried but failed to resist the urge to join the fray. He approached me from behind and planted a carefully aimed boot to my posterior in obvious settlement of personal scores arising from our previous encounter.

The member in charge was not introduced by name, but a few months after Zimbabwe gained independence in 1980, I recognised him during a visit to Mount Darwin police station, a two-hour drive north-east of Harare, where he was the senior officer. He had stared at me, recognition momentarily eluding him. By then I was a journalist in Harare, on assignment in the war-ravaged north-eastern border region. Travelling in the company of other journalists, we had stopped at the police station to check on the security situation in the area to which we were proceeding. We left before I could decide how best to turn this sudden encounter with an old foe to my personal advantage.

Three weeks later, however, I telephoned the police station and asked for the member in charge. Much to my disappointment, I was told that he had suddenly left Mount Darwin, and possibly both the police force and Zimbabwe. At the time, there was a general exodus of whites who spurned the hand of reconciliation that their former enemy, Mugabe, had extended to them in his inaugural address on becoming the Republic of Zimbabwe's first prime minister.

At Nyazura on New Year's Day 1977, the member in charge approached Spur, who was standing in front of his vehicle, writing furiously. The two conferred in undertones for about ten minutes, the SB man taking copious notes while the uniformed officer briefed him on the events of that fateful night, stealing occasional glances at me. In due course, the young policeman's moment of glory arrived. He was summoned to where they stood and executed an immaculate salute. I saw him answering the SB man's questions animatedly before he was dismissed. He, too, looked in my direction repeatedly as he spoke. I sensed that our fate had been sealed.

The two officers then toured the damaged offices, occasionally pausing so that Spur could jot down notes as they inspected the damaged roof and pockmarked walls.

Around 11 a.m., Spur and Mhike returned to the vehicle and, standing behind the Land Rover to face us, announced that we were officially under arrest for collaborating with terrorists in the previous night's attack. They were taking us to Rusape, where, unless we cooperated, they had ways of making people – especially terrorist sympathisers like me – appreciate the benefit of cooperating with the security forces in their relentless campaign against the communist insurgents infiltrating from Mozambique to destabilise and undermine the security of Rhodesia and its peace-loving, law-abiding citizens.

In my naivety – perhaps a rare case of sublime optimism – I had somehow assumed that since I had already been subjected to so much physical abuse, we would be allowed to go. I would then drive back to the village in time to pack our bags and depart for Salisbury (renamed Harare after independence), only to return to Nyazura when the security situation had improved sufficiently to be conducive to a safe homecoming. I had never regarded myself as a communist and, indeed, knew very little about the ideology, but Spur's reference to me as someone sympathetic to communist insurgents drove home the gravity of our predicament for the first time.

We were again loaded onto the Land Rover and, as the convoy drove off, I saw the young policeman talking animatedly – about me, I assumed – before he executed an exaggerated kick with his left foot by way of demonstrating whatever point he was making. His antics reduced the senior officers around him to laughter. The chain of events since my encounter the previous day with this particular policeman was to occupy my mind all the way to Rusape, twenty kilometres away. We made the fifteen-minute journey in absolute silence, each of us deep in his own thoughts, but all secretly cursing the day I had bought the Cortina GT.

'Remember, we saw nothing last night,' was all I managed to whisper as we passed through the main gate at the police station. My three companions nodded in silent assent.

Our arrival at the largest police station in the Makoni district caused much commotion among the uniformed police and SB officers. We were ordered to sit on the floor behind the counter in the small charge office before, as if on cue, a stream of officers, both black and white, filed in to satisfy their curiosity about the new prisoner who was said to be both a university graduate and a terrorist sympathiser. To them, it seemed that merely holding an academic degree was a crime.

'That is the graduate,' the new arrivals were informed, 'the one with the little beard and the denim jeans.'

'So you and your terrorist friends think you can forcefully remove the government of Rhodesia,' a man in plain clothes, obviously SB, said with what sounded like a mixture of genuine curiosity and contempt. 'Well, today we will show you who is really in charge.'

The SB man walked around the desk and kicked me viciously in the ribs. Several officers were loitering in the office while discussing the events at Nyazura the night before and congratulating SB, as Special Branch loved to call itself, for remarkable efficiency in making arrests so quickly. A uniformed officer asked for our names and other personal details, then told us to remove our shoes, socks, belts, watches and any other personal effects apart from our shirts, trousers and underwear. As we placed our belongings in canvas bags provided for the purpose, I realised we had reached a point of no return.

An officer led us through a back door to the holding cells located directly behind the offices. A high pig-wire fence, topped by razor-sharp wire coils, surrounded the cells. The officer unlocked the huge padlock on a gate and ushered us through the heavy metal door of Cell 4, the last of four cells in the block.

'Lunch will be served soon!' he shouted, before locking the door behind us.

It was a little while before my eyes adjusted to the semi-darkness, but when I could make out our surroundings, I was appalled. The cell was a solid mass of people, half of them lying on the floor on thin, dirty grey blankets. The disgusting smell of the bedclothes conspired with the pungent stench from a hole in the corner, which served as a toilet, to ruthlessly assail the newcomer's nostrils.

The rest of the occupants were lined up against the walls. A rough count revealed that there were thirty-six people, including the four of us, in a cell designed to hold no more than ten remand prisoners. I was soon to appreciate why half the cell's population leaned against the wall in a vertical position while the rest squeezed together on the floor like skilled contortionists. After two hours or so, the prisoners swapped positions, and those who had been standing gratefully wriggled to find a comfortable position on the lice-infested blankets.

'Welcome to Cell 4,' somebody sitting in the far corner next to the toilet said in a voice that exuded melancholy. Soon the small cell was reverberating to the sound of clapping hands as we greeted the inmates. The Maungwe people of Manicaland's Makoni district are well known for the reverence they attach to the simple process of greeting and asking after each other's health, amid much loud and extended clapping of hands. Visitors to Zimbabwe are often taken by surprise when the tranquil ambience of a debonair venue such as a bar in downtown Harare's world famous five-star Meikles Hotel is disrupted by the rhythmic clapping of cupped hands as company executives in designer suits, especially those from the eastern districts of the country, greet and enquire after each other's health.

Our cellmates asked where we had been arrested and under what circumstances. We explained, and they seemed to find our story satisfactory. The prisoners were fearful of infiltration by SB, and the portly and suave appearance of Uncle Cephas and Cousin Cleopas might have sent the wrong signal to our vigilant companions.

The man who had welcomed us spoke again.

'The toilet next to me here is reserved for the passage of urine only,' he pronounced authoritatively. 'It is not meant for any serious business, except in very exceptional emergencies. There is a toilet outside, and when we go out for meals, we take turns there.'

A volunteer was always positioned next to the hole in the corner to enforce this mutually agreed and exceedingly sensible rule.

The speaker's words were followed by the sound of doors being unlocked and the clang of dishes being arranged outside the cells to the welcome accompaniment of the fragrance of food.

Then the doors of the four cells were opened in turn and we emerged into the blinding sunlight. What had sounded to me like regular food dishes being laid out were, in fact, the upturned lids of huge metal refuse bins. Some of them contained sadza. Others were overflowing with a foul-looking concoction that had tiny pieces of meat floating on top. Sadza is the staple food of the indigenous Shona and Ndebele people of Zimbabwe. It is prepared from ground maize or cornmeal that is boiled and stirred to a thick porridge. A well-prepared meal of sadza can be a delicious feast, depending on the accompanying dish – roast or stewed beef, chicken, fish, sour milk, dried beans, cabbage or rape (a kind of turnip), depending on a family's resources.

The discipline among the prisoners was amazing. They lined up to wash their hands at a huge concrete trough in the corner, before squatting around the metal containers. In no time more than a hundred men and some women had eaten their fill. They ate not with relish, but to keep the proverbial body and soul together. Then they lined up to take their turn in the toilets. An hour later we were back in the cells to begin the long wait for supper, punctuated every two hours or so by what I, in due course, secretly and appropriately named the changing of the guard.

About twenty minutes after lunch, we heard the sound of the huge padlock being opened again.

'Either they are bringing in new arrivals or they are coming to let people out, some for more torture and others to be released in order to create space for new arrivals,' someone announced knowledgeably. 'It is shameful. Most of the prisoners here are innocent …'

The speaker was silenced by the sound of a key being inserted in the lock on the door of our cell.

'Geoffrey Nyarota!' yelled the unmistakeable voice of Detective Sergeant Mhike.

I was standing close to the door and walked out the moment he opened it. Mhike locked the door behind me. I was alarmed that my relatives were not summoned as well. He led me to the office block and into an upstairs room, where Spur and the black officer who had kicked me in the ribs were waiting. The facial expression of the latter sent a shiver down my spine. They went straight to the point.

'We don't intend to allow you to waste our time,' Spur said. 'It is up to you to relate to us in full the events of last night, both before and after the attack, before you are hurt, or to tell us after you are badly hurt. The choice is yours, but eventually you will talk. Stronger men than you have talked. Everybody talks. Even the terrorists eventually talk.'

'I believe those who talk do so because they have something useful to talk about,' I said, trying my level best not to sound confrontational. 'You simply have to believe me, gentlemen, I have nothing to tell you about the attack on Nyazura police station last night and that is the truth.

'I was fast asleep when the distant sound of gunfire roused me. I only realised that

Nyazura police station was attacked when you took me there this morning. In fact, in all my life I have never seen a guerri—'

'Terrorist,' the third officer corrected, swinging into action. His left uppercut rammed into my jaw and I felt my head explode as he repeatedly pounded it and my ribs. I tasted blood in my mouth again and thought I felt some loose movement in a tooth in my upper jaw.

'You can kill me if you wish,' I managed to squeeze in during a temporary respite from the brutal attack, 'but what I am telling you is the absolute truth.'

'Enough, Sergeant,' Spur intervened. 'You may think you can deceive us by playing innocent, but the forensic experts in Salisbury will expose you. We are sending your car to Salisbury for tests at the police laboratory. After the tests have turned up incriminating evidence of your involvement in the attack last night, you will be prosecuted. For your role in the attack, for collaborating with terrorists and for concealing information concerning the whereabouts and activities of terrorists, you will be lucky to get away with anything less than the death sentence. But should you change your mind and decide to assist us in apprehending this gang of vermin, well, of course, your personal circumstances will alter considerably.

'Take him back, Sergeant Mhike. Bring the other three out of the cell, but bring them in here one by one.'

I summoned enough courage to complain about my condition. I said I was feeling severe pain in my ribs and jaws and I suspected a tooth might be cracked.

'Which one?' the officer who had just been ordered to stop assaulting me asked, spitting the words out like venom.

I exposed my dentures and pointed to the relevant position.

'We will be careful not to hit you in the same place,' he said and, by way of a cynically practical demonstration, slapped me on the opposite cheek.

I held my face in both hands as I was led back to the cells. Uncle Cephas, Cleopas and Cosmas were taken out, and they would later tell me that their tormentors said I had already confessed my role and involvement in the attack on Nyazura and that they should do the same. They realised this was a lie meant to trap them, because they knew that I had not been involved or participated in the guerrilla attack on the police station. Their instinct therefore told them I would never have made such a confession, and each of my relatives silently resolved to deny any knowledge of the attack. In any case, none of them had particularly incriminating confessions to make, unless donating a packet of cigarettes was considered a guerrilla attack.

We spent three weeks in the cell at Rusape. After our release, Ursula told me that when the people in our village heard about our arrest and detention, they were frightened and alarmed enough to decide that they should all lie low. They could only have come to check on our circumstances at the risk of being thrown behind bars themselves, so it was decided that Ursula should strap Tafirenyika on her back and visit the police station.

A cousin, Francis Chapeyama, possessed both a motor car and the gift of rare courage.

He volunteered to drive Ursula to Rusape. Their first attempt to see me was unsuccessful, however. On the second attempt, two days later, I was allowed to talk to Ursula in the presence of a police officer. My face was less swollen than it had been, and the police must have prevented the first meeting for fear that my wife would be too shocked by my condition. As it was, tears streamed down her cheeks throughout our ten-minute meeting, while I tried my best to appear brave, which was not easy.

Chapeyama's strength of character and courage in daring to visit me in prison was to provide the foundation for a strong bond of friendship between us until his death separated us two decades later.

Several hours after Ursula's visit, around 10 p.m., there was much hectic activity behind the prison cells. When the noise subsided, we were assailed by an overpowering stench coming from outside. The prisoners were dumbfounded. It was as if rotting meat or decaying animal carcasses had been stacked outside. That night was exceptionally and painfully long, and by the time breakfast was served the following morning, our appetite for it had been totally ruined. But the ghastly sight that met our collective curious gaze along the southern wall of our cell was enough to shock even the most hardened funeral undertaker.

Piled up against the wall were the bodies of more than a dozen dead villagers. We found out later that there had been an encounter between the security forces and a detachment of guerrillas in the Zanla-infested Chigondo area of the Hwedza district. A total of sixteen people had been caught in crossfire, though the SB claimed, predictably, that the majority of the dead were terrorists.

Most of the bodies were those of ordinary villagers. A bullet had ripped open the belly of a boy aged nine or ten, and his intestines protruded from the wound. Rigor mortis had anchored a bright red lollipop firmly between his lifeless lips. Two elderly men, both at least sixty years of age, had obviously been in the wrong place at the wrong time. Judging by their clothing, I estimated that, at most, only two of the bodies might possibly be those of guerrillas.

The dead were the victims of a surprise attack by the security forces, possibly as they attended a *pungwe*. This is Shona slang and, along with many other words, some of Portuguese origin, it was added to the lexicon during the war of liberation.

The literal translation is the period from dusk to dawn. *Pungwes* were all-night rallies organised by Zanla guerrillas for the purpose of indoctrinating the rural population, especially in areas that had been sufficiently liberated for the meetings, usually accompanied by much singing and shouting of revolutionary slogans, to take place without fear of fatal disruption by the security forces.

On occasion there was a breach of confidence, such as when a treacherous or greedy villager passed on to the security forces information about the recent arrival of a Zanla detachment or the exact position of their base. This normally resulted in a surprise attack, as appeared to have been the case at Chigondo.

After breakfast, which we hardly touched, about two dozen strong men were selected from among the prisoners and assigned to dig a mass grave along the road to Nyanga. I was told I'd have a special task. A policeman with a sardonic sense of humour said that as the most educated among them, I was the only prisoner that the police could trust to act as undertaker.

Then came the bombshell. My task, in fact, was to restore a semblance of order to the pile of rotting human flesh for purposes of conducting a headcount as a prelude to burial. Many of the bodies were grotesquely disfigured. A few were headless torsos, while some had broken skulls or bellies that had been slit open to disgorge the bowels. This bizarre exhibition, coupled with the terrible stench and the swarm of huge green flies that had descended on the remains in total defiance of the scorching morning sun, was enough to drive anyone insane.

I was required to match each decapitated head, some reduced to mere shells, to what I assessed to be the correct body. Where the intestines or brains were hanging from the stomach or skull, I was to scoop them up and place them back in the cavity. I was then required to line up the bodies in decent formation along the wall. I surprised both myself and the assembled officers by completing this gruesome task without collapsing or retching.

Fellow prisoners were later to inform me that as my two assistants and I went about our macabre task, the stench inside the cells had become quite unendurable.

My next task as mortician was to record the fingerprints of the deceased peasants and Zanla fighters. Later that day, when the mass grave was ready, the bodies were piled onto a lorry and taken for burial. I lacked the courage to remove the lollipop from the boy's mouth.

That night I did not sleep a wink, but that was only the beginning.

Years after independence, the member of parliament for Makoni East, Didymus Noel Edwin Mutasa, who was independent Zimbabwe's first speaker of parliament, was quoted by the press in reference to the mass grave at Rusape. He said the bodies interred there would be exhumed for proper burial. Like many other official and optimistic pronouncements on the reburial of those who had sacrificed their lives during the liberation struggle and were dumped in mass graves in Zimbabwe, Zambia and Mozambique, Mutasa's proposal seems never to have progressed beyond this initial statement.

After breakfast the following morning, our four names were called out. This was for purposes of release, we speculated, quietly celebrating. But as had become common practice, whenever we tried to guess the intentions of our captors, we were far off the mark. We jumped, as ordered, onto a Land Rover, and with Mhike behind the wheel and Spur in the passenger seat, drove to the Rusape hospital and stopped outside the main entrance to the wards.

Like skilful writers of fiction, the two SB officers had become masters of suspense. They ordered us to jump off the vehicle and follow Mhike into a male ward. Lying on a bed in a far corner, guarded by two armed policemen, was a heavily built and muscular man. Bearded and with long, unkempt hair, he was of fearsome appearance, until one's eyes were drawn to the bottom of the bed, where his badly swollen legs protruded from the red hospital blanket. They were both encased in plaster of Paris.

We were ordered to place the patient on a canvas stretcher and carry him down the narrow aisle between the two rows of beds, as the other patients, temporarily casting their own ills and misery to the wind, lifted themselves up in order not to miss a single detail of this rare event. Once outside, we loaded the stretcher onto the back of the Land Rover and squeezed ourselves in uncomfortably, two on either side of our passenger.

'The man lying on the stretcher calls himself Comrade Seduce Mapondera,' Mhike said slowly, obviously savouring the suspense. 'He is a Zanla terrorist. He was captured by the security forces in the Hwedza district just before Christmas after they shot him in the legs. We are now taking him to Gandanzara in the Makoni Tribal Trust Lands. He has volunteered to make some important indications to us there. We will possibly be gone all day. You will be required to carry Seduce whenever the need arises. As you can see, he cannot walk.'

Mhike then secured the canvas canopy from outside and we set off on the road to Nyanga. Five kilometres before Nyabadza township, the entry point to the Tribal Trust Lands (TTL), we turned left and ascended a steep incline to the flat top of a hill, where a fairly large military cantonment had been constructed. While the camp was quite close to the Rusape–Nyanga road, it was totally invisible from below, so that until this visit, I had not been aware of its presence. There were hurried consultations among the senior SB and army officers, while a stream of Support Unit and Rhodesian African Rifles (RAR) soldiers filed past our vehicle to inspect the dual spectacle of a 'captured terrorist' and a schoolteacher who was a 'terrorist collaborator'.

Then we departed. By peeping through a hole in the canvas, I established that our Land Rovers had been joined by an assortment of other vehicles, including heavily armoured troop carriers and a landmine detector, to make a convoy of nine or ten vehicles in all. The mine detector always travelled in front of such a convoy. It was a strangely shaped vehicle that I thought would not have been out of place traversing the moon's surface.

The design of the various models was a tribute to the inventiveness and creativity international sanctions and the escalating guerrilla war had thrust upon Rhodesian engineers in the 1970s. Mine-detecting vehicles carried an electronic sensor that alerted drivers to the presence of landmines buried in the dust road ahead. The driver would immediately brake to a halt, followed by the rest of the convoy, and soldiers would disembark to take up defensive positions in case Zanla had set up an ambush, as often happened. Occasionally, it was too late to stop and the convoy would only become aware of the presence of landmines when the detector vehicle disintegrated in a massive cloud of dust, smoke, metal and human limbs.

The clear visibility of a long convoy of vehicles such as ours to anyone waiting in ambush in the thick bush that we were destined to travel through heightened my apprehension ahead of a whole afternoon spent in the Zanla-infested Gandanzara area.

As if he had read our collective mind, Mapondera suddenly broke the silence after we had travelled about a kilometre along the narrow dust road, heading south. He informed us that he had operated for months in the area that we were now travelling through. Up to this point, we had not known how to relate to the additional passenger on the back of the Land Rover. He seemed to sense our discomfort and embarrassment and appeared anxious to break the ice.

'How are you, parents?' Mapondera asked politely. Zanla guerrillas always respectfully referred to the adult peasant population in the areas in which they operated as 'parents'.

'We are very well, comrade,' we responded in unison.

'How are your injuries?' I asked after a moment of silence.

'I was in great pain before they brought me in from Hwedza and admitted me to hospital. Now I feel much better,' he said. 'But I feel sharp stabs of pain when my legs are jolted as we drive over the rough dust road, such as now. Before our departure, a hospital orderly gave me painkillers to bring with me, in case I needed them.'

I told Mapondera about my own obviously minor but nevertheless painful injuries. He reached into the pocket of his trousers, the legs of which had been ripped up the side to accommodate the plaster casts, and brought out a bottle of painkillers. He gave me two, which I swallowed without recourse to the prescribed tumbler of water.

Mapondera's right foot was covered in plaster of Paris right up to the toes. The cast on the other leg extended as far as the ankle. I noticed that the sole of the exposed foot was hardened like cement, obviously from walking long distances, all the way from rear bases in Mozambique and over the mountainous terrain of Rhodesia's eastern highlands, then tramping through the bush between camps in the operational area. He appeared exceptionally fit, despite his injuries. Somehow, he looked like a very normal man, nowhere near as fearsome as I had been given to understand guerrillas were.

Ironically, while we had been imprisoned for allegedly collaborating with Zanla guerrillas, Mapondera was the first freedom fighter we had seen at close quarters. Our riverside encounter with the group that would bomb Nyazura police station had been in totally different circumstances.

By the time we reached Gandanzara, Mapondera had loosened up somewhat and now talked about himself. His real name was Sidney Kapumha, he said. He was born at Rukweza, twenty kilometres south of Nyazura. The school and the township at Rukweza were about eight kilometres south-east of our own village, as the crow flies. After attending Rukweza Primary School, the young Kapumha had travelled to Salisbury to seek employment. In 1974, he left the country for Botswana en route to Lusaka, Zambia. Three weeks later he proceeded to Tanzania, where he received military training at Mgagao camp. In January 1976, he moved to Mozambique. Four months later, he had been deployed into Rhodesia through Nyamaropa in a group of eight. Their mission was to mobilise villagers and to arrange food supplies and other logistic support.

Under the *nom de guerre* of Seduce Mapondera, he had operated for a long time as a detachment commander in the Makoni, Chiduku and Hwedza districts.

A few days before Christmas, he and other Zanla men had been drinking in a bottle store at Dendenyore business centre near Mount St Mary's, a Catholic mission in the heart of the Hwedza district, he said. A long-distance bus belonging to Mushandira Pamwe Bus Service was parked outside the bottle store. The government had imposed a dusk-to-dawn curfew in all the operational areas, and any vehicle travelling after dark risked being fired upon by the security forces without warning.

Mapondera said he had asked for the ignition keys to the bus. The driver reluctantly handed them over. Had he dared refuse, he would have been branded a sell-out, with fatal consequences. Villagers labelled as sell-outs were liable for instant execution, their bodies often remaining unburied for days on end. The worst tragedy that could befall a peasant family during Zimbabwe's war of liberation was to have a member marked as a sell-out. The stigma lingered long after the victim's remains were buried, usually at the place of execution, even if this was right in front of the main family dwelling.

Mapondera said he had driven the bus, obviously under the influence of liquor, to Nhekairo, the next township, where the sound of a heavy vehicle travelling at night attracted the attention of soldiers who had camped nearby. They surrounded the empty bus and challenged the driver. Mapondera said he slammed on the brakes and reached for his AK47, but before he could aim in any particular direction, he was shot in the legs and slumped over the steering wheel, blood pouring from his broken limbs.

After his capture, Mapondera said, Sergeant Mhike had promised him freedom if he cooperated with the SB. Mhike pointed out that after he recovered from his injuries, Mapondera would obviously be prosecuted and would, no doubt, be found guilty of engaging in terrorist activities, including multiple murder. His fate would most certainly be the death sentence. However, if he assisted the SB, he would be saved from the hangman's noose. It did not take Mapondera long to decide that his neck was more valuable than the liberation of Zimbabwe. This visit to Gandanzara, his first mission for the SB, was to locate ammunition that his Zanla group had buried high up in the mountains south-east of Rusape.

The convoy turned off the dust road and, following cattle tracks, approached as close as possible to the foot of the mountains. This was obviously a risky manoeuvre, especially if Zanla was encamped in the area, which, Mapondera told us in a hushed tone, was more than likely. We were ordered off the vehicle and, since he could not walk, my relatives and I were assigned the task of being Mapondera's stretcher-bearers.

Carrying the heavy stretcher up the mountainside on our shoulders would be a difficult task in any circumstances, but it was particularly strenuous for my potbellied uncle and one of the cousins. We were soon all sweating profusely, not just from the heat and the weight of Mapondera, but also from a very real fear of a possible ambush.

After an hour of tortuous progress, we reached the flat crest of the mountain and, with the soldiers fanned out behind us in a half-moon formation, we walked more briskly, with Mapondera navigating.

'Slow down,' he whispered after twenty minutes. 'You may now put the stretcher down.'

Spur and Mhike approached us on the double, followed by a few Support Unit men.

'It is hidden there,' Mapondera said, pointing in the direction of a low bush that the SB men approached. They inspected the ground around the plant, then Mhike pointed and shouted triumphantly, 'It must be here!'

Spur called me closer, and I immediately realised the reason for the SB men's excitement. A patch of ground about fifty centimetres square was depressed and had obviously been disturbed. Because of the heavy rains the grass had grown over the spot, however, and to detect it, one needed to be looking for it.

'Mapondera says they buried a box full of ammunition in the ground here,' Spur explained while addressing me. 'You are to dig the soil away, expose the box and then lift it up. If you don't dig, we will not hesitate to shoot you. Then you will become just another villager killed in crossfire.'

As an afterthought, he shouted to Mapondera: 'Is this cache booby-trapped, Seduce?'

Mapondera hesitated before yelling back that he did not remember.

'What that means,' Spur offered by way of friendly advice, 'is that if this box is booby-trapped, there is bound to be an explosion when you lift it up. So you have to be careful. But if they did not booby-trap it, and Seduce clearly does not remember, you should be quite safe.'

Mapondera's stretcher was moved some distance back, and the SB and Support Unit men withdrew as well. Spur, Mhike and a few others trained their weapons on me and signalled to me to start digging.

I realised I had two options: to dig, find the box, pull it up and die instantly in an explosion, or refuse to dig and die in a hail of bullets fired by men who needed only the slightest provocation to kill me in cold blood. If this was the way God had ordained that my life should end, as an innocent victim of the war, blown to countless pieces high up in the sacred Gandanzara Mountains, so be it, I philosophised mutely. I uttered a silent prayer and, looking away from the assembly of military men and my relatives, crossed my heart.

I attacked the bush like one possessed, uprooting the elephant grass. Since I had not been provided with a spade, shovel or any other implement, I used the tools supplied by nature, my bare hands. After I had lifted all the grass from the depression, I scooped out the wet, soft soil. Then I found it. I removed another handful of soil and exposed what looked like greenish metal. Caring little about the risk of being shot, I sprang back with an agility that must have both surprised and amused the onlookers.

'I found something, something that looks like metal!' I shouted across to them.

'You have now reached the tricky part of your task,' Spur shouted back, as though he were a paid consultant. 'Now you need to be cautious as you lift whatever it is that you found.'

For the first time since my initial encounter with Spur and Mhike, I realised that I hated them with a passion. I decided that I also hated all the uniformed Support Unit and RAR men surrounding me.

The object in the ground had obviously come a long way. Most likely a contribution to the war effort from the People's Republic of China, it must have been brought across the border on foot from Mozambique and transported more than 100 kilometres over mountainous terrain before being hidden in the heart of the Makoni TTL.

Mapondera's group would return to this location to replenish their ammunition, only to discover that the enemy had beaten them to their own cache, or perhaps they would assume that another guerrilla group had removed and put the ammunition to good use. And all this was happening because Mapondera had decided to drink too much liquor at Dendenyore instead of remaining vigilant at all times in accordance with his training. He had callously slaughtered villagers accused of being sell-outs, yet here he was betraying the liberation struggle in order to save his own skin.

These thoughts floated through my mind as I scooped out more soil to expose the sides of what turned out to be a box of about twenty-five centimetres square and eighteen centimetres deep. I gritted my teeth, closed my eyes and, denying my tormentors the satisfaction of any cruelly disparaging last-minute instructions, I heaved.

At first I thought I was dead. Then I realised I was alive and holding the heavy box in my hands, while Spur and his men raced towards me from all directions. I carefully placed the box on the ground and, without seeking permission, sat down and started to mop away the sweat that was pouring down my face. I realised I was trembling a little, either from the exhilaration of being alive or from delayed reaction to fear and shock.

The trip back to Rusape was uneventful. On the back of the Land Rover, we lapsed into an embarrassing silence. It was just as well that we limited our verbal communication with Mapondera, since we later discovered that part of his deal with Mhike and Spur was to spy on us.

As we drove out of the hospital grounds after dropping Mapondera off, I convinced myself, being an eternal optimist, that after the psychological torture of the day's events and the physical torture of the beatings over the past few days, we must surely be due for release. So I was elated when our cell door opened before breakfast the next morning and our names were called out once again. But instead of being taken to the front office, we were led to the parking lot at the back.

My heart sank when I saw Mhike and Spur waiting. We climbed back onto one of the two Land Rovers and drove to the hospital, where we again picked up Mapondera. The rest of the convoy was waiting outside the hospital gates, engines running, and after positioning the Land Rovers in the middle, as on the previous day, we set off in the direction of Nyazura. Perhaps we were to be released there, I mused, then realised that if that was the intention, there would be no long convoy. Besides, what about our clothes and the Cortina?

We stopped at the police station and briefly renewed our acquaintance with the member in charge and his staff, including the young constable. On this occasion, to my surprise, there was no violence. Understandably, the focus of attention was Mapondera, who tried his best to reward every officer with a friendly smile, although none seemed keen to reciprocate.

Mhike informed us that we would travel about 100 kilometres west of Nyazura to Hwedza, where Mapondera had an important assignment to perform. The convoy moved out, turning right on the Buhera road to head south. For a military convoy to travel along a dust road that was notoriously prone to landmines and ambushes on the stretch between the turn-off to Makarara and Hwedza was sheer madness, and I sensed Mapondera's growing uneasiness and embarrassment in our company.

Then it happened – much sooner than we expected – in broad daylight and right on the highway.

Shortly after passing Rukweza township, as Mapondera was indicating that his village lay to the left of the road, heavy gunfire erupted from the right. The hail of AK47 automatic fire was coming from the foot of a mountain about 200 metres from the highway. The position of the attackers was camouflaged by huge musasa trees and thick green undergrowth. The Zanla guerrillas had counted on the element of surprise in mounting such a brazen mid-morning attack so close to the recently constructed tarmac highway.

I heard a woman ululate somewhere in the distance after the deafening discharge of a rocket launcher or bazooka, as the devastating weapon was more popularly known in guerrilla ranks. Her eerie intervention was shrill testimony to which of the two warring factions enjoyed the support of the local peasant population. As gunfire crackled insistently from the foot of the mountain, we were ordered off the Land Rover to lie under the heavily armour-plated troop carrier that was travelling immediately behind us. The Rhodesian soldiers took up positions along the side of the road and fired back. The staccato of gunfire rose to a cacophonous crescendo.

Seduce Mapondera was abandoned on the Land Rover. In close proximity to the village of his birth, his people had no idea that their long-lost son lay wounded in the middle of a raging battle. As for young Kevin, instead of responding to the onslaught from Zanla with the zeal and fury that he had displayed when we'd first met, he elected to lie prone in the middle of the road behind our truck, covering us with his FN.

'If you attempt to escape, I will not hesitate to shoot!' he shouted, rather fatuously.

This must surely be the end, I thought, as I lay on my back on the hot tarmac. Perhaps God had ordained that we should perish in these awful conditions in order to spare us from an even more dire dilemma ahead, I consoled myself. I felt particularly sorry for my uncle and cousins. Since our trip to Gandanzara, they had become increasingly uncommunicative. Unable to come to terms with their misfortune, I suspected that they regretted having arranged to be picked up by me from the railway station at Nyazura.

Their predicament was far removed from their normal existence in Bulawayo, where the only reminders that a guerrilla war was raging throughout the eastern and northern regions of Rhodesia were sporadic official casualty reports, broadcast on radio and published in the *Chronicle*, the daily newspaper of which I would become editor a short six years later. The news bulletins were habitually brief, revealing only the number of terrorists killed in a contact or collaborators caught in crossfire, and inevitably claiming 'a few' injuries incurred by the security forces. I wondered what the military spokesmen would say about this particular contact.

From somewhere ahead of us on the road, a man screamed through the din of gunfire. Almost simultaneously, we heard the high-pitched emission of jet engines mingled with the thunderous explosion of bombs that rained down on the mountainside. I peeped out from underneath the truck just in time to see four Canberra jet bombers of the Rhodesian Air Force (RAF) disappear behind the mountain, followed soon afterwards by three Hawker Hunter ground attack fighter-bombers.

The aircraft were approaching from the east, having no doubt taken off a few minutes earlier from Grand Reef Air Force Base west of the city of Umtali, the place of my birth.

About twenty minutes later, two Alouette helicopters – which France continued to supply to the RAF in clear breach of international sanctions against Smith's rebel colony – appeared on the horizon and hovered overhead momentarily, before landing in the over-grazed terrain to the east of the battle raging close to Mapondera's Kapumha village. The helicopters disgorged about two dozen heavily armed troops before quickly lifting off and disappearing in the direction from which they had come.

The firing immediately subsided. Throughout the war, Zanla guerrillas could never sustain pitched battle once air force jets flew over the scene. Half an hour later, we were ordered back onto the truck. I assumed that after this frightening contact with Zanla we would turn around and drive back to Rusape as quickly as possible. But my prognosis was wrong again. Our journey to Hwedza resumed, and as the distance between the convoy and two vehicles that had been badly damaged and abandoned widened, I surmised that proceeding in these circumstances was either a display of utter madness or an act of suicide on the part of our captors.

'They need to be very cautious in the area we are now approaching,' Mapondera volunteered, as if he had read my mind. 'The Mukamba and Chigondo areas are swarming with *vakomana*.'

The word means 'boys' in the Shona language, spoken by about 80 per cent of Zimbabwe's indigenous population, and was used to refer to the guerrillas.

'So why did you invite Special Branch to visit Mukamba and Chigondo if you knew the areas were swarming with Zanla?' I asked, barely able to conceal my antagonism.

'I never imagined they might actually decide to go there,' Mapondera responded. My uncle stared at me meaningfully.

We reached Mukamba as the sun, a fiery red ball in its dying moments, dropped behind the hills to the west of the camp, which was soon enveloped in total darkness. It had not been the intention to stay the night. Mukamba was only a small camp, a mere clearing in the middle of dense bush, but our progress had been delayed by the contact at Rukweza and it was too late to proceed to Hwedza without the risk of running into another ambush in an area where no vehicle travelled after dark.

The atmosphere in the camp was spine-chilling, even without the prospect of an attack by Zanla. Our cell for the night was a tiny pit toilet at the edge of the clearing. Since the structure was too small for the four of us to lie down in, we spent the night in a vertical position. Although we had become used to sleeping on our feet, the night was exceedingly long, both on account of the discomfort and the fear of attack, not to mention the foul stench emanating from the round hole in the centre of the toilet.

But our distress that night amounted to nothing by comparison with the nerve-wracking experience visited on the peasants of Chigondo the next morning. From his base in the surrounding mountains, Mapondera had operated in the Hwedza district for a long time, and his task now was to identify inhabitants who had been in personal contact with him and other guerrillas.

Most vulnerable were the *mujibhas* and *chimbwidos*. The former were young boys, usually recruited from the villages in which Zanla operated, to act as their eyes and ears. They served as scouts and messengers, spying on the movement of government forces.

More ominously, they had become a formidable force in the war-torn rural areas, where they'd acquired a reputation for ruthlessness. They assumed the role of sniffing out and fingering sell-outs, real and imaginary, often for summary execution. *Mujibhas* were fearsome characters, some more so than others. A good number of them exploited their newly elevated status and influence to the full. If a *mujibha* visited a businessman and demanded a sum of money, ostensibly on behalf of the guerrillas, no one dared check on the authenticity of the request.

Nor did any war-wise girl ever turn down the amorous advances of a *mujibha*. Villagers, including their own fathers, brothers and uncles, knew better than to cross the path of the *mujibhas*.

In deference to gender equality, Zimbabwe's liberation war also had female eyes and ears, known as *chimbwidos*. While they were less formidable than their male counterparts, they exploited their proximity to the seat of power at the guerrilla bases to raise their own status in the village. Their role was to ensure that the guerrilla fighters were regularly and well fed and adequately supplied with information, especially about the villagers.

The large number of war children conceived by the *chimbwidos* in the operational zones bore testimony to their less celebrated role as the close companions of the guerrillas, offering them comforts of the flesh that long periods of deployment in the bush otherwise deprived them of. Officially, guerrillas were required to abstain from sexual contact with women or men, but the many female guerrillas and refugees who returned from Zambia or Mozambique with babies strapped to their backs at the end of hostilities in 1980 revealed that the reality of war belied the noble intentions of this edict.

At Chigondo that morning, Mapondera pointed out to Spur and Mhike with ruthless precision all the young men and women who had run errands, provided information, exposed village sell-outs, and brought meals and water to the guerrillas in their bases.

As the terrified villagers slowly walked in single file past his stretcher in the shade of a huge mango tree, Mapondera mercilessly identified all those peasants who had aided and abetted his group of fighters. The mere pointing of Mapondera's finger was like a death sentence passed on the bewildered villagers. Those he fingered were ordered to stand to one side, and included nearly every schoolteacher and businessman present.

Schoolteachers were the backbone of the liberation struggle in the rural areas. They played a crucial role in the process of political indoctrination and were the main suppliers of much needed commodities – clothing, particularly denim jeans, money, food, watches, transport and liquor, especially brandy.

That day, Mapondera destroyed the small world of the peasants. Many of them broke down and sobbed openly. Others flung themselves in the dust, shaking uncontrollably. It was a terrible and pitiful sight. They were puzzled that the popular and gallant Comrade Seduce Mapondera could sell out on such a grand scale. Overzealous soldiers of the RAR and the Support Unit manhandled the perplexed villagers and dragged them to join the growing group of 'terrorist collaborators' standing in the shade of another mango tree, tears streaming down the faces of many, especially the young *chimbwidos*.

What compounded the misery of the captives were the repeated taunts of the soldiers, many of them illiterate and otherwise unemployable school dropouts who were merely exploited by the Smith government.

'You consider the terrorists to be your friends,' they sneered at the villagers, 'but you see what they do to you after we capture them. You hate us, yet we are your genuine friends.'

It was a heartrending demonstration of callousness on the part of Mapondera and his new allies. At the end of the exercise, scores of men and women were loaded onto empty troop carriers, brought along for the purpose of ferrying them back to Hwedza. Those who could not be taken on board because the trucks were too full were kicked, beaten with rifle butts or otherwise assaulted, and left behind to limp back to their village.

This was to be Mapondera's last assignment for the SB. Spur and Mhike appeared to have extracted every ounce of useful information from him in return for the promise of his liberty, and after we dropped him at the hospital on our return to Rusape, I never saw Mapondera again.

Two months later, however, I felt a burning sensation in my eyes when I read a report in the *Herald* at the start of Mapondera's sensational trial. Identified by his real name, Sidney Kapumha, he pleaded guilty to a charge, under Smith's notorious Law and Order (Maintenance) Act, of possessing arms of war. However, he challenged the statement that he had made to the police on the grounds that they had concocted and added several incidents of alleged terrorist activity to those he had outlined. He said he had only made a confession because the prospect of freedom and an opportunity to work for the SB had been dangled before him like a carrot by Detective Sergeant Phillip Mhike.

Mhike denied making any promises to the accused and the court ruled Kapumha's statement admissible. In it, he admitted being involved in numerous acts of terrorism as the detachment commander in the Nyanga, Nyazura and Hwedza districts. The incidents included the burning of buses and trucks, the killing of civilians and a number of policemen, the engagement of government troops in contacts, the burning of council offices and beer halls, and the fatal shooting of a Hwedza businessman.

'I feel very sorry about these things,' Kapumha's disputed statement said. 'I would like to work for you.'

Contrary to his version of events as related to us on the back of the Land Rover, the court heard that Kapumha had been arrested by Detective Section Officer John Gibson at a deserted village in Hwedza, where he was found lying on a bed in a hut with a saline drip attached to his wrist.

'Later, the accused led the police to Makoni Tribal Trust Land and showed them a box of ammunition and told them more was buried in the area,' the *Herald* reported.

Apparently, the police had also unearthed two mortar bombs close to where I had dug up the ammunition box.

I felt sorry for Kapumha as I read the article. At the end of his trial, the Zanla guerrilla who had been tricked into betraying Zimbabwe's liberation struggle was found guilty as charged and sentenced to death.

By 2000, when as editor in chief of the *Daily News* I was branded both a terrorist and an enemy of the state by the government of Robert Mugabe, Seduce Mapondera, the once gallant fighter who had turned traitor, had been dead for more than two decades.

Paradoxically, Mhike had risen through the ranks after independence to become deputy commissioner of the Zimbabwe Republican Police (ZRP). Most of the top officers were former Zanla guerrillas, but Mhike, the ex-SB member, was a single promotion away from assuming control of Mugabe's entire police force.

'Forgive them, Lord, for they know not what they are doing,' I prayed for Zimbabwe's self-proclaimed revolutionary political leadership.

2

A taste of future injustice

I N   T H E   N Y A M A R O P A communal lands of eastern Zimbabwe, seven kilometres west of the Kaerezi River that forms the boundary with Mozambique, lies Regina Coeli, a rural Catholic mission station comprising a secondary school and hospital complex.

Peasants living in the area regularly cross the river, and therefore the border, on their daily chores without the impediment of immigration formalities. In some instances, members of the same extended family live on either side of the river. Both the Nyamaropa irrigation scheme, established by the colonial government to introduce peasants to basic commercial farming, and Regina Coeli Mission were strategically positioned to play a crucial role when freedom fighters began infiltrating the area in 1977. By then, Rhodesia's bush war had intensified along the Mozambican front, especially in the north-eastern districts of Mount Darwin and Mutoko.

The 1974 *coup d'état* by Portugal's armed forces that overthrew the government of Marcello Caetano in Lisbon had sparked the outbreak of protracted civil wars in both Mozambique and Angola. When Mozambique became independent a year later, guerrilla leader Samora Machel was inducted as the first president of Portugal's most prosperous African colony.

After constant feuding in Zambia with the Zimbabwe People's Revolutionary Army (Zipra), the guerrilla army of nationalist leader Joshua Nkomo's Zimbabwe African People's Union (Zapu), Zanla had requested and been offered a rear base in Mozambique by Machel.

By the time I returned to Regina Coeli after being detained in Rusape, Zanla had extended its sphere of operations southwards to cover the Nyamaropa area. While my relatives and I were undergoing the trials and tribulations of our arrest and Seduce Mapondera's treachery, guerrillas had infiltrated the entire area surrounding the mission.

On our return from Hwedza, we had spent an uneventful week behind bars, while Mapondera was transferred to the remand prison in Salisbury. My car had been brought back to Rusape from the capital where, not unexpectedly, forensic tests had proved negative. The bottom had thus effectively fallen out of the Special Branch case against me, and Spur and Mhike had no further cause to detain us. We nevertheless remained in detention for another week, and I was to discover the reason for the extended stay immediately upon our release.

We piled into the Cortina where it stood forlornly in a corner of the parking lot outside the police station. I turned the ignition key and the engine made half a turn, to the accompaniment of a strange hissing sound. Then it stalled. From my knowledge and experience of the internal combustion engine, I knew that the noise was not conducive to a second attempt to start the car. My heart pounding, I lifted the bonnet and was stunned to see the engine spattered in oil. As if to confirm my worst fears, there was a puddle of dirty oil under the car.

The engine had obviously seized.

I rushed back into the police station, taking the steps two at a time, and headed for the SB section, where, after a perfunctory knock, I entered Mhike's office.

'My engine is damaged and the car won't start,' I spat out, my voice shaking with anger.

'Unless you want to go back to the cells,' an uncompromising Mhike replied, 'you will have to remove both your vehicle and yourself from these premises.'

My heart sank. I returned to the car and slid behind the wheel. My uncle and two cousins pushed the crippled vehicle out of the grounds and all the way across town to Vengere township, three kilometres away. Mechanics immediately started to dismantle the engine.

Uncle Cephas, Cleopas and Cosmas caught the train back to Bulawayo that very night. None of them would be seen in the village again until well after independence. Fortunately, they did not lose their jobs. Ursula was elated to see me, as were the rest of our relatives.

We packed our bags and drove, not to Salisbury as originally planned, but straight back to Regina Coeli. The summer holidays were over, and we arrived just in time for the start of the first school term of 1977. It would be a year of severe hardship for the mission schools of Manicaland, and Regina Coeli in particular.

The school was strategically situated at the point of access to and from Zanla's large base camp, Chimoio, in Mozambique's Manica province. Zanla had scored a major publicity *coup* eleven years earlier, on 28 April 1966, which would have profound psychological and political significance for the liberation struggle. The Battle of Sinoia, as it came to be known, was a brief encounter between a guerrilla detachment and Rhodesian security forces in Mashonaland West. A group of twenty-one freedom fighters heading for the Charter district in central Rhodesia – the deepest penetration of the interior by any guerrilla group up to that time – was involved in a fierce battle against government troops backed by helicopter gunships.

Seven of the Zanla fighters – Simon Chimbodza, Christopher Chatambudza, Nathan Charumuka, Godwin Manyerenyere, Ephraim Shenjere, David Guzuzu and a man who was named only as Peter – died in the exchange, and ever since, Zanu-PF has commemorated 28 April as Chimurenga Day, the official start of the war of liberation in 1966. *Chimurenga* is the Shona word for armed revolution.

While the Sinoia contact held deep symbolic significance, a guerrilla attack six years later would mark the beginning in earnest of the war that would culminate in Robert Mugabe being sworn in as Zimbabwe's first prime minister on 18 April 1980.

In the early hours of 21 December 1972, a detachment of guerrillas attacked a farm in the north-eastern Zambezi Valley. The property, 240 kilometres north of Salisbury, belonged to Marc de Borchgrave, whose labour relations reportedly left much to be desired. A Rhodesian security force communiqué stated that one of De Borchgrave's children was injured during the attack, which lasted half an hour.

'As you all know, we have had a few incidents recently in the north-eastern border area,' the official media statement concluded. 'The possibility exists of further terrorist-inspired incidents in border areas.'

This turned out to be an understatement of remarkable dimension. By the time we returned to Regina Coeli Secondary School five years later in January 1977, the operational zone extended from the north-eastern Zambezi Valley through most areas along the borders with Mozambique in the east and Zambia in the north, as well as across a substantial swathe of the hinterland. Zambia was the rear base of Nkomo's Zipra forces, which waged war in the western districts of Rhodesia. By September 1979, when the warring factions sat down to negotiate a peace settlement in London, the entire country had been smothered by the war. To counter escalating guerrilla insurgence, combined operations headquarters in Salisbury demarcated Rhodesia into six operational areas, an implicit admission by the Smith regime that insurgency had spread countrywide.

Security force deployment in the north-eastern region, the original target of Zanla infiltration, was code-named Hurricane. The eastern districts, adjacent to Mozambique and the hottest theatre of conflict, were designated Thrasher, with Repulse covering the southern part of Rhodesia, contiguous to the northern province of South Africa across the Limpopo River.

Military operations against Zipra were designated Tangent in the western districts bordering on Botswana, and Splinter in the Zambezi Valley, across the mighty river from Zambia, the rear base of the Russian-trained army. Operation Grapple covered the Midlands, one of the least infiltrated areas throughout the war.

Rhodesia's third largest city of Umtali (renamed Mutare after independence), the town of Rusape, and the administrative centres of Hwedza and Nyanga fell within Thrasher's ambit, with Regina Coeli situated almost exactly in the centre.

The first school term of 1977 opened on an ominous note. A day after our return to the mission, rumours reached us that John Dembaremba, the headmaster of Kagore Primary School, had been shot dead by Zanla guerrillas. Kagore was six kilometres north of Regina Coeli. Apparently, the guerrillas had accused him of being a sell-out. Like hundreds of others who were similarly executed, Dembaremba was not accorded an opportunity to defend himself.

He was shot at point-blank range in the head as his shocked family and teachers from the school watched. The guerrillas ordered that his body should not be removed from where it had fallen in front of his house. For two days, the remains lay there in a pool of dried blood, exposed to the elements and the sweltering heat. In total contravention of Shona custom, Dembaremba was eventually buried in a shallow grave in the school grounds. Regardless of where death occurs, Shona culture dictates that the body be interred at the deceased's own village and among his or her own people. Kagore School was only Dembaremba's place of employment and he ought not to have been buried there, but throughout the war, not a single voice was raised in protest against such blatant aberrations of cultural mores and the injustice of summary executions such as Dembaremba's.

Those who knew the headmaster well rejected the allegations against him by the guerrillas. Thousands of innocent villagers were fingered as sell-outs or collaborators with the Smith regime and lost their lives in equally brutal circumstances, and in many cases, those who identified them were pursuing personal rather than political vendettas. A businessman would report a more enterprising and thus more prosperous neighbour as being a sell-out or spy for the security forces. A deputy headmaster, impatient for promotion, would name the headmaster as a supplier of information to the police on the movements of guerrillas in the area. A young man, his amorous advances spurned by the village beauty, would point out a rival suitor as a paid security force informant. However spurious the accusations, the outcome was always the same.

If a helicopter or any Rhodesian Air Force aircraft, including the high-flying Canberra and Hawk Hunter fighter-bombers, happened to fly past a village, a vivid description would be rendered by the informant of how he saw the alleged sell-out on board the aircraft, indicating the position of a guerrilla base. Such details were invariably disclosed to the guerrillas in the aftermath of an attack on their base, never as an advance warning, as common sense and truth would more likely have dictated.

The Shona word for sell-out is *mutengesi*, and no worse tragedy could befall a villager during the war of liberation than to be accused of being one.

As a journalist, I flew in helicopters many times on official assignments. Whenever we passed over a settlement, I tried to make out the faces of people on the ground. Even when flying at tree-top level, their features always remained inscrutable to the naked eye above. It was therefore impossible, I surmised, for anyone on the ground to identify a passenger in a helicopter, let alone a jet fighter, even with the aid of binoculars. But anyone daring to dispute such nonsensical claims and allegations would invite calamity upon themselves, so no one did.

The guerrillas, anxious to demonstrate to the assembled villagers the fate of any among them who might contemplate cooperation with the security forces, meted out instant and merciless justice. There was no semblance of a trial or even a kangaroo court, and it did not take the villagers long to realise that the guerrillas were accountable to no one outside of their own immediate command structure.

On a number of occasions, the original informant himself turned out to be the *mutengesi*, and he, too, would be summarily executed. Villagers in any war zone lived in mortal fear of being publicly branded as sell-outs by the freedom fighters or as terrorist collaborators by the security forces. They were forever caught in the deadly crossfire between the warring factions.

The rural peasants were fearful of the guerrillas who descended from their mountain hideouts under cover of darkness to address *pungwes*, have meals prepared by women from the surrounding villages, or mete out instant justice and execution. Morale was usually high at the all-night rallies, which were held against a backdrop of much feisty singing of revolutionary and spiritual songs to the accompaniment of dancing. New tunes and dance steps, imported by the guerrillas from Mozambique and Tanzania, were especially popular. Long after independence, both the music and the dances were popularised by performers such as Simon Chimbetu, Dick 'Chinx' Chingaira and Alick Macheso, who became giants on the Zimbabwean music scene.

By day, the same villagers were terrorised by government forces, who traversed infiltrated rural areas in long motorised convoys or sometimes on horseback if they were a unit of the Grey Scouts. The infamous Selous Scouts were usually dropped off a long distance from a targeted village. Members of this dreaded crack army unit painted their faces black and impersonated guerrillas, carrying AK47s, with their characteristic banana-shaped magazines, and dressed not in their own camouflage uniforms, but in the denim clothing favoured by Zanla. They would enter a settlement on foot while chanting Zanla slogans. Whole villages would be razed to the ground after the poor peasants had fallen for this ruse and openly welcomed these false 'comrades' into their midst.

Such incidents and the element of fear served to buttress the relationship between the peasants and their would-be liberators from both Zanla and Zipra long before Zimbabweans lined up to vote for political candidates representing Mugabe's Zanu-PF and Nkomo's PF-Zapu during the first majority rule elections in 1980.

Dembaremba had been a close friend, and his tragic death had a traumatic effect on me. He was a progressive headmaster, and his school served as a shining example of development and academic and sporting excellence. He had been a regular visitor at Regina Coeli and was popular among staff and pupils alike. On Sundays, he doubled as the official mission photographer, and his arrival each week was met with great excitement by pupils anxious to see the results of previous photo sessions.

Dembaremba's part-time activity was a profitable sideline. I had developed an early affection for photography after my Uncle Arthur, who worked for Television Zambia in Kitwe at the time, presented me with his old Yashica box camera, and although I was not as proficient as Dembaremba, our mutual interest led to a close friendship. After Dembaremba accompanied me to Hwedza to be introduced to Ursula's family, our relationship became fraternal.

Now he was dead, having perished in the most horrendous circumstances imaginable. To complicate matters, I was assured by villagers who had been in contact with the guerrillas since their arrival that a visit to Dembaremba's family to offer condolences was certain to invite a knock on one's own door by guerrillas that very night. As soon as they established themselves in an area, the freedom fighters made it patently clear to inhabitants that sell-outs were not to be mourned.

'If they genuinely believed Dembaremba was a sell-out,' I reasoned silently, 'would they not suspect that a close friend of his was one as well?'

As if in response to my unspoken question, somebody tapped on my bedroom window in the middle of the night a week later, while Ursula and the baby were visiting her parents at Hwedza. I checked the luminous dial of my wristwatch. It was 11 p.m. Sleep did not come easily in those days, so I was wide awake, and by the time the knock was repeated, my heart was pounding from the realisation that a number of people were milling around outside the house.

'Comrade Nyarota, please open the door,' an impatient voice ordered from the darkness. I peeped through a narrow gap in the curtains and my heart almost stopped. The ground in front of the house was swarming with armed men.

'Can you hear us, Comrade Geoff? Open the door.' I detected the mounting impatience in the disembodied voice.

I dressed quickly, tucking my shirt into my trousers as I walked into the living room. With shaking hands and sweat pouring down my face, I slowly opened the door. Two heavily armed figures immediately entered the room.

'Do you always open your door to complete strangers who knock on your window in the middle of the night?' one of them asked. I recognised this as the same voice that had called my name from outside my bedroom window.

'No, that is not my usual practice,' I responded, struggling not to betray my fear. 'You addressed me by name and I assumed you were a friend.'

'*Pamberi nehondo,*' he chanted.

'*Pamberi,*' I responded.

'*Pamberi ne Zanla.*'

'*Pamberi,*' I said

'*Pamberi nekunzwisisa.*'

'*Pamberi!*'

'*Pamberi nevigilance.*'

'*Pamberi!*'

'*Pasi nevatengesi!*'

'*Pasi!*'

These chanted Zanla slogans and many variations became the official form of greeting at thousands of nocturnal meetings in war-torn Rhodesia. What the guerrilla was chanting in Shona was, 'Long live the war of liberation! Long live the Zanla forces! Long live the spirit of understanding! Forward with vigilance!' After each slogan I punched the dark air in front of me with my clenched fist and intoned, 'Long live.'

He concluded his revolutionary greeting by shouting, 'Down with sell-outs!' I responded, 'Down with them!'

'Well, here it comes,' I told myself silently.

'Opening your door to the first stranger to knock on your window in the middle of a black night is not a sign of the vigilance required in the struggle, Comrade Nyarota,' the heavily armed man admonished.

Despite this rebuke, I suddenly felt at ease, perhaps because I was being addressed as a comrade.

'How did you know that we were not Selous Scouts? In future you will have to be more vigilant than that, comrade. Without maintaining extreme vigilance, we cannot win the war of liberation. Without vigilance, it is easy to die in battle. When were you released from prison?'

I had an uncanny feeling that I knew the speaker and that this visit was of a friendly nature. I told them of our release four days earlier, and hastily seized the chance to subtly establish my modest liberation credentials by recounting our ordeal with the car and my return to school the previous week.

'My name is Comrade Batahana,' the man said. 'I am the detachment commander of the group outside. Comrade Mabhunu Muchaparara is our political commissar. We have just moved into this area and we will visit the mission occasionally. We have decided that you will be our contact person among the staff. Whenever we visit the school, we will come to see you first for a briefing and to inform you of our plans and our requirements. Should there be any information or development that must be communicated to us urgently, we will let you know in due course how we can be contacted.

'Now we need to hold a meeting with the rest of the teachers. You will have to summon the headmaster and the other staff. On second thoughts, let me come with you.'

As I walked in front of Batahana towards headmaster Allen Mandisodza's house, I mulled over Mabhunu Muchaparara's fearsome name. My thoughts were interrupted when Batahana tapped me on the shoulder. We both stopped.

'You obviously are not able to recognise my face in the dark,' he said, 'but do you remember Arum Mudzingwa from Nyazura?'

Of course I did, and I realised why his voice had sounded familiar. Mudzingwa had been the proprietor of a private secretarial college at Nyazura for many years. He disappeared suddenly amid rumours that the college had fallen heavily into debt and that he had crossed the border into Mozambique to sign up for the liberation struggle.

The college, which had provided school-leavers, especially young girls from the Makoni district and beyond, with the prospect of a job, a husband and a secure future, had struggled for a while after Mudzingwa's departure, then closed its doors forever. I had not heard of him again.

While we were not exactly bosom buddies, there had been a mutually respectful relationship between the university graduate and the enterprising proprietor of Makoni district's only secretarial college. And now here we were, virtually indiscernible to each other in the middle of the pitch-black night – the schoolmaster and the commander of a heavily armed Zanla detachment.

Batahana and I embraced in the dark, the metal barrel of his rifle cold to the touch.

'Batahana is my Chimurenga name,' he said, as we resumed our walk. 'You are never to call me by my real name or to disclose it to anyone, under any circumstances.'

All freedom fighters had a Chimurenga name or *nom de guerre*. Apart from concealing the real identity of the individual, some guerrillas chose names designed to evoke fear in the hearts of villagers and white farmers, as well as their workers. Some of the more awe-inspiring names were chosen specifically for the benefit of black members of the Rhodesian security forces, who well understood the meaning. Translated literally, Batahana's name meant 'hold your heart', an exhortation to peasants not to disclose any information to the security forces or cooperate with them.

The more ominous Mabhunu Muchaparara was a popular name among the guerrillas. *Bhunu* is a Shona corruption of *boer*, the Afrikaans word for farmer. The term was used in a derogatory sense to refer to all the whites of Rhodesia, including those of British or European origin. Translated into Shona, it encompassed the ominous prediction that all white settlers would perish in due course.

A number of guerrillas adopted the name Mao, in honour of Mao Zedong, chairman of the Communist Party in the People's Republic of China, which supplied Zanla with most of its military hardware. Gaylord Hlatshwayo, a long-standing friend in Old Highfields, quit his job as a salesman with the popular music shop in downtown Salisbury owned by Martin Locke, who would later become a television presenter in South Africa. Gaylord joined the exodus to Mozambique in the mid-1970s to join Zanla. When he returned to Harare at independence in 1980, he was Comrade Mao. He was one of the young guerrilla fighters who acted as Mugabe's personal assistants, and was thus close to the premier. He became a senior official in the prime minister's office, quite an achievement for a young boy from Old Highfields, but despite his elevated status – and unlike a number of returning guerrillas – he retained his humility and was a popular socialite in post-independence Harare. By the time he died, he was a diplomat in Rome.

Another popular Chimurenga name was Bazooka, obviously in veneration of the portable rocket launcher invented by a US Army officer, Bob Burns, in 1941 and used with great effect against the Rhodesian security forces.

The *nom de guerre* that instilled the greatest fear in me was that of Joboringo, though I never found out what it meant. It was not a Shona word, so perhaps it was the man rather than the name that scared me. Joboringo arrived at Regina Coeli in command of a new group of guerrillas from Mozambique about two months after Batahana. By then, Batahana and his men had established a good relationship with the pupils, teachers, hospital staff and, above all, the Irish Jesuits who ran the mission under Father Martin O'Reagan.

As political commissar, Mabhunu Muchaparara had decreed that for their own safety, teachers should never attend the same meetings as pupils. The rule was hailed by the teachers, who were fearful of openly associating with Zanla in front of 240 schoolchildren. Some of the pupils were the children of policemen or other government officials, and there was a great risk that any such association might be communicated to parents – not necessarily with sinister intent – thus prompting a visit to the school by the security forces.

Batahana, Muchaparara and the rest of their detachment treated the mission population with a respect that defied the stereotyping of guerrillas, especially in security force propaganda, as unruly and ruthless terrorists bent on wreaking havoc among rural communities in a bid to subvert government authority.

Although convoys of military vehicles occasionally travelled through the mission within sight and range of Batahana's men, the guerrillas never launched an attack on them. They were mindful of the retribution that would be visited upon the mission by the security forces in the wake of any such attack. Consequently, the guerrilla base in the foothills of a mountain range close to Regina Coeli remained a closely guarded secret for several months.

These sensible strategic arrangements changed dramatically when Joboringo arrived.

He knocked on my door around 10.30 p.m. on another very dark night. His group had just crossed the Kaerezi from Mozambique and they were starving, he said. Food was to be prepared, but while it cooked, Joboringo and his men would proceed to a village about five kilometres beyond the mission and deal, without delay, with a sell-out who had been identified. I cringed.

While Ursula and the wives of other teachers worked out the daunting logistics of preparing a late-night meal for thirty hungry guerrillas, Joboringo and his men disappeared into the darkness.

The mathematics teacher, Everisto Nyamutswa, was a part-time chicken farmer. His supplementary income allowed him to maintain the pride of his heart – a BMW 2000 sedan, whose German manufacturers did not have the roads of Nyamaropa in mind when they'd created it. Nyamutswa constantly faced a pile of repair bills for his car, in addition to dividing his income between the needs of his growing family and his escalating but mandatory contribution to the war effort. That night, his extramural enterprise came to the rescue of our spouses. Five plump chickens squawked as they were slaughtered behind the maths master's residence, and before long our wives were tending to pots of delicious stew and sadza. The food was ready shortly after midnight and the wait began for the return of Comrade Joboringo and his detachment.

Around 12.30 a.m. the distant sound of a single rifle shot broke the silence. We switched off all the lights and continued to wait in the dark. When Joboringo and his group had not arrived by 4 a.m., it dawned on us that they might not return after all, which presented us with a dilemma. Should the security forces receive information about the rifle shot, an early morning raid was a strong likelihood, and we would be hard pressed to explain the large quantity of fine food.

A suggestion that a number of pupils be invited to partake of a sumptuous pre-dawn breakfast was immediately discarded as too risky. Schoolboys would almost certainly be unable to keep such an unexpected feast a secret. Eventually, we decided that each of the five families involved in cooking the meal would take the risk of keeping a share of the stew, while the sadza was buried in a hastily dug hole.

When Joboringo finally returned two nights later, no more than passing reference was made to the uneaten food, with no particular apology being tendered to anyone. To add insult to injury, he informed the teachers that some standing rules about contact with the guerrillas were about to change. For example, his group would address teachers and students jointly at future meetings.

If this left a sour taste in the mouths of Regina Coeli's teachers, the disappearance a few days later of the church catechist, Ernest Mutizamhepo, threw the mission community into a state of bewilderment that bordered on panic.

Aged about thirty-five, the friendly and cheerful Mutizamhepo was a popular man, especially with the schoolboys. Physically fit and of an athletic build, he was the official soccer coach, as well as being in charge of baptism and confirmation classes, with responsibilities extending beyond the mission boundary to the surrounding villages. His wife taught at a nearby primary school, and the two appeared generally happy and got along well with other members of staff.

One evening, a group of guerrillas led by Joboringo departed from their mountain base to visit the school. There was no communication with the teachers that night, but we were informed the next morning that when the group had left the mission, they asked Mutizamhepo to accompany them back to their base. This was a chilling development.

Around mid-morning on the following day, a young *mujibha* arrived at my back door to deliver a message from the guerrilla base. Since the arrival of Joboringo's group, I had regarded the visits of *mujibhas* with growing suspicion and unease. I was therefore less than enthused when this one knocked on my door. His message was that I was to buy provisions for delivery to the base, including two large bottles of brandy. On such occasions, the headmaster allowed me to use his Peugeot station wagon. My own car, with its roaring engine, had long been ruled out as totally inappropriate given the clandestine nature of such missions.

Ensuring that the guerrillas were regularly and adequately supplied was a responsibility thrust upon many mission and business communities in the rural districts. Schoolteachers were frequently forced to deprive their own families in order to meet the financial commitments to the war effort that were simply expected of them.

Having loaded the station wagon with the provisions, some of which were contributed by shopkeepers at the Nyamurundira Business Centre in the middle of the irrigation scheme, I drove past Regina Coeli on my way to the foot of the mountain where the guerrillas had established a new base. Four schoolboys had accompanied me for the purpose of carrying the many cartons up the mountain.

The base was a hive of activity when we arrived. As the *mujibhas* took turns to present their various briefs or reports to Joboringo and his senior men, *chimbwidos* prepared lunch for the forty or so people in the camp. Sitting forlornly on an old log was Mutizamhepo. After we had shouted the necessary slogans and greeted the senior guerrilla officers, I joined the catechist. Joboringo thanked us for bringing the provisions, singled out the two bottles of brandy for special mention and proceeded to open one.

He was tall, muscular and powerfully built. I put his age at about twenty-five. Joboringo pressed the open mouth of the bottle to his lips and took two quick gulps of the potent liquid. He shook his head vigorously, twice, as the dark stuff burned its way down his throat. He took another swig before passing the bottle to a man whom I assumed to be his second in command. This man poured a little brandy into the lid of the bottle and drank from it, much to Joboringo's contemptuous amusement. The commander continued to drink as we were served lunch, each time passing the bottle to a different senior member of the group.

After washing our hands, Mutizamhepo and I started to eat sadza and beef stew from the same plate. I noticed that the catechist's face was slightly swollen. My presence obviously cheered him up. I felt sorry for him, but thought better than to ask any questions. There would be plenty of time for details when he returned to the mission.

Joboringo stood up and approached the log where the catechist and I sat.

'While the teachers and the business community take risks to support the struggle,' he opined loudly, 'this man sells out to Smith's soldiers.'

'I have told you repeatedly, Comrade, that the information which you received is not correct,' Mutizamhepo replied, apparently emboldened by our presence. There was a ring of sincerity in his speech.

'So now you are calling me a liar!' Joboringo retorted, breathing heavily. 'You, a sell-out, dare to call me a liar.'

Joboringo reached for his AK47 that was propped up against the trunk of a huge musasa tree. He released the catch, breathing heavily, and without warning, as we all looked on, frozen in horror, pulled the trigger once at point-blank range, the bullet hitting the surprised catechist right in the centre of the forehead.

Mutizamhepo's head disintegrated before my very eyes. Then he toppled over and fell to the ground, gurgling sounds emitting from the top of his neck where a moment earlier his head had been attached.

After the deafening report of the powerful rifle, a deathly silence fell over the camp. Suddenly I was back at Rusape Prison, behind the cells where the rotting cadavers were piled. I picked up a stick and flicked scraps of the catechist's bloodied brains from my trouser leg, then stood up, bewildered and angry.

As if from a distance, I heard Joboringo shout, 'You can all go. The villagers, the people from the mission, you must all go. Now!'

No one needed any further bidding. I ran down the mountainside, the schoolboys ahead of me, in the general direction of the tree under which we had parked the car. I unlocked the doors with trembling hands and we all piled in. In three dexterous moves, I manoeuvred the station wagon to point back towards the mission. Then I drove like one possessed by evil spirits, the schoolboys holding onto their seats for dear life.

After I had dropped them off behind my house and away from prying eyes, the boys ambled off in the direction of their dormitories. Not a single word had been exchanged since we had witnessed Mutizamhepo's brutal murder. For many months the grisly image of the catechist's broken skull spewing brains and blood onto the grass was indelibly etched in my numbed mind. As was usually the case, we never got to know what crime the catechist was supposed to have committed or who had reported him to the guerrillas.

As I tossed and turned in bed through sleepless nights, I wondered how the Zanla High Command in Maputo would react to information that civilians were being executed in such cavalier and cold-blooded fashion. The culprits were, of course, safe in the knowledge that such information would never reach the ears of the leadership, and that became their shield.

The events of that afternoon, especially when viewed in juxtaposition with my earlier experiences in Rusape Prison, impressed on me how much the war of liberation had diminished the value of the rural peasant's life in the eyes of both the guerrillas – the supposed liberators – and the government soldiers, who claimed to offer protection. To voice such concerns publicly, however, would have been to sign one's own death warrant.

The death of Mutizamhepo, following so closely on that of Dembaremba, was a further demonstration that innocent people – I was not convinced that the catechist had been an informer for the security forces – could be accused of being sell-outs and executed by the freedom fighters just as easily as peasants were massacred when their villages were razed to the ground in aerial bombardments by the security forces on the strength of accusations that they were harbouring terrorists.

I was to meet Mutizamhepo's wife on a regular basis many years later when she transferred to Mupanguri School, close to Gwangwadza township outside Nyazura, where Ursula and I opened a small business after the Mugabe government dismissed me from my job as editor of the *Chronicle* in Bulawayo. Ours was an enterprise in the typical configuration of the Zimbabwean rural business – a general dealer's shop, a bottle store and a butchery. Mrs Mutizamhepo became a close family friend.

Two nights after Mutizamhepo's murder, the silence at Regina Coeli was shattered by a massive explosion. We heard the following morning that a military vehicle had detonated a landmine on the dirt road that ran along the mission's perimeter fence towards the irrigation scheme. Joboringo's men had put the lives of the mission community at risk by planting the explosive device close to the mission, doubtless knowing full well that the security forces would come to investigate the death of the catechist, news of which had spread like a bush fire through the neighbouring villages.

I have occasionally wondered how I would have reacted if I had entered a quiet bar in downtown Harare after independence and sat down close to an immaculately dressed man, only to realise after a while that it was, in fact, Comrade Joboringo, gently nursing a Scotch while stealing a furtive glance at me now and then. But we were never to see Joboringo again. Strangely, I never heard of any Zanla man of that name after the repatriation of guerrillas following the ceasefire that heralded independence. He may have perished in a war that had claimed at least 25 000 lives.

No one from Regina Coeli had the courage to approach the scene of the landmine explosion, but this did not prevent the instant spread of a rumour that a number of soldiers had either died or been badly injured in the blast. As if to confirm this theory, military trucks made a number of trips to the scene of the incident, and, instead of heading east, back to the military cantonment near the irrigation scheme, they travelled west, presumably to Nyanga Hospital or the mortuary.

Later that afternoon, two truckloads of soldiers rampaged through the school grounds in a fit of collective anger. They beat up schoolboys as they quizzed them about the incident. The boys, however, were all aware of the danger and risk inherent in giving valuable or incriminating information to the security forces, even if they had any to give, which they did not. The soldiers left, promising to return. Surprisingly, they made no arrests.

The callous murder of Mutizamhepo and the detonation of the landmine brought home to the mission community the full horror of the war in which they were now embroiled. The average black Rhodesian, especially the enlightened mission populations, supported the guerrilla insurgency against the oppression, discrimination and institutionalised racism of the Smith regime. Many willingly supported the war effort, although they grew increasingly impoverished.

None, however, supported the wanton killing of innocent civilians and the immense power that was vested in and abused by the young *mujibhas*. For me, the dilemma was excruciating. I had been sucked into the war through my identity and my location. The University of Rhodesia was a veritable training ground for revolution, but the bloodshed was now a cause of much inner despair, apprehension and frustration about the independent future for which we all clamoured. Would there be a cut-off point for the bloodletting?

From the safety of the veranda of the bottle store at Nyamusamba township, two fellow teachers and I discussed these issues in muted tones. We watched anxiously as a military convoy entered the mission grounds. The small but busy township comprised a few general dealer's shops, a bottle store, a grinding mill and a restaurant that sustained bus crews, as well as the bachelors among the staff at the mission. The township, situated at the foot of the same mountain that housed the Zanla hideout, offered a bird's-eye view of the entire mission – the school, the church and the hospital.

As we sat there drinking and playing draughts, we finalised plans for my first trip to Salisbury on a Zanla assignment. My mission was to buy blue denim jeans and watches, an order that had long been placed by Batahana's group. Blue jeans were the favoured attire of the guerrillas. Because of the short supply and heavy demand, good-quality jeans could be obtained from only a few shops in Salisbury. Fulfilment of this order meant a visit to the capital, 300 kilometres away. Because of the growing demands on the staff to contribute in various ways towards the upkeep of the guerrillas, it had taken the teachers some time to put the required funds together, but I was to leave the next day.

Most of the staff had grown up in the Nyanga district and had attended a teachers' training college at Gwelo (later renamed Gweru) in the Midlands. I was the Salisbury man, and thus the obvious candidate for the assignment. Ursula prayed that night for divine guidance and protection for me on the perilous trip.

Just before I left the next morning, the headmaster informed us that Regina Coeli had lost its first group of boys to the war. Two dozen pupils had risen in the middle of the night and, under cover of darkness, walked to the Nyamaropa Irrigation Scheme before crossing the Kaerezi River into Mozambique to join Zanla for training. I was headed in the opposite direction and caught the early Mandeya bus to Rusape, en route for Salisbury.

When I arrived in Old Highfields, my mother, who had not seen me since my arrest and detention, broke down in tears as I related my ordeal in Rusape and the subsequent events at Regina Coeli, including the assassination of my friend Dembaremba. She shed more tears when I explained the nature of my mid-term visit to Salisbury and the risk I was due to run, travelling through a military operational area with a carton of denim jeans on the roof of a rural bus and with five wristwatches concealed on my body.

She pleaded with me not to go back. She vowed that she would personally travel to the mission, if necessary, to fetch Ursula and Tafirenyika. Eleven years later, she was to weep again as she watched independent Zimbabwe's minister of defence, Enos Mzombi Nkala, fume and froth at the mouth as he swore on national television that he would have me arrested and locked up. As editor of the *Chronicle*, I had published stories exposing serious corruption involving Nkala and other so-called revolutionary leaders in the new government.

But back in 1977, I convinced my mother that it was imperative for me to accomplish my dangerous mission so as not to endanger the lives of Ursula and the baby, fellow members of staff and the entire mission population.

Realising the helplessness of the situation and my own vulnerability, she eventually relented. Having appreciated the seriousness of the task in hand, she even assisted me in sourcing the required supplies as clandestinely and cheaply as possible. When it was time for us to say farewell, she stripped off her own wristwatch.

'There must be women among these freedom fighters,' she suggested. 'This is not new, but one of them can find some use for it.'

I had not seen a female guerrilla among those who regularly visited the mission, but I gladly accepted my mother's modest contribution to the struggle. Her grudging change of attitude was, in reality, an acceptance of the invidious situation into which the final stages of the struggle for Zimbabwe's liberation had thrust the rural school-teacher. That night, she helped to pack the goods I had bought in a medium-sized cardboard box.

By prior arrangement, my friend Stephen Chingwaru, a beverage manager at the newly opened Monomatapa Hotel in downtown Salisbury, arrived in the morning. We loaded the carton in the trunk of his Ford Anglia, but because of its dimensions, we could not close the lid as we drove first to the centre of Salisbury and then for ten kilometres to the Mabvuku turn-off, east of the capital along the highway to Umtali.

When Chingwaru dropped me at the turn-off, I had reached a point of no return on the first leg of my nerve-wracking trip back to Nyamaropa. I caught a lift in a vehicle driven by one Oliver Tengende, a hefty man who operated one of the many vehicles, mostly Peugeot 404 station wagons, that plied the profitable Salisbury–Rusape route daily as taxis. Tengende had built a reputation as a shrewd operator on this highly competitive route and was to become a famous wrestler in independent Zimbabwe.

He dropped me off in Rusape after an uneventful 170-kilometre journey that took us through two roadblocks. The police did not seem to think much of the fact that I was the only one who sweated profusely as they asked Tengende's passengers to identify themselves. So highly regarded was Tengende by the police along the Salisbury–Umtali highway that travelling in his vehicle was a guarantee of a safe journey in every sense.

My carton tightly secured on the roof of a Mandeya bus, I jumped in and settled down in a seat at the back for the long journey to Regina Coeli. Fifteen minutes and twenty kilometres out of Rusape along the Nyanga road, we ran into another road-block. My heart sank as a young policeman, exuding more enthusiasm than I thought was absolutely necessary, flagged the bus down at the Nyabadza Business Centre. I was reminded of our trip to Gandanzara in the company of Seduce Mapondera, when we had turned off at this junction on our eventful trip to the mountains.

As a senior officer approached and interrogated the driver, the young constable ordered all passengers to disembark and line up along the side of the bus. While a third officer checked the personal particulars of the passengers, his younger colleague clambered onto the roof of the bus to inspect the luggage.

'Whose is this?' he shouted down occasionally. Whoever claimed the item was then asked to join the policeman on the roof and open the carton, trunk or whatever else had drawn the excitable officer's attention or aroused his suspicion. The senior officer finished questioning the driver and, having no doubt received the routine 'money for Coca-Cola' – the amount tendered normally being well above the price of a bottle of the popular soda – joined his colleague, who was inspecting the travellers' identity papers. I stole another glance at the roof of the bus to check on the progress of proceedings there and was panic-stricken when I realised that only two other pieces of luggage stood between the policeman and my carton.

No sooner had the senior officer complained to his colleague about the tardiness of the team that should have arrived thirty minutes earlier to relieve them, than a grey police Land Rover came around the corner from the direction of Rusape. It was travelling at such speed that I imagined it was not going to stop, but with a screech of brakes and in a cloud of dust, the driver brought the vehicle to a well-executed halt alongside the bus.

'That's it, off we go, Constable Takarinda!' the senior officer shouted to the man on top of the bus. As fate would have it, Takarinda required no further prompting. Before this roadside change of the guard was even completed, the passengers were ordered back into the bus, which immediately took off amid a furious changing of gears. I crossed my heart and reached into my travelling bag under the seat for a pint of beer that had grown warm, relieved that my contraband on the roof had gone undetected.

The rest of the journey passed without incident on the twisting road that traversed mountainous terrain through Juliasdale, Rhodes-Nyanga National Park, Nyanga town, up the Nyangani range, past the country's highest mountain peak, and down the other side. The bus arrived at Regina Coeli well after dark, around 10 p.m., as the journey had included the mandatory break of approximately one hour at the Mangondoza Hotel in Nyanga, where the bus crew was fed by management while the passengers kept the tills ringing in the bar and restaurant.

Ursula was immensely relieved to see me back and gave thanks in prayer that night that I had been delivered safely home. My colleagues were delighted that the mission had been a success and impressed by the quality of the goods that I had purchased. In due course the *mujibhas* collected the clothing, now divided into smaller and less suspicious packages.

After the first small group of schoolboys had left Regina Coeli to join Zanla in Mozambique, the trickle of recruits had swelled to a massive exodus. Regina Coeli, Elim Mission to the north, St Mary Magdalene and Marist Brothers, both near Nyanga, St Augustine's and Old Umtali Mission near the provincial capital of Umtali, and other mission schools in Manicaland lost thousands of pupils who crossed the border at regular intervals. The word *kirosa* became the latest entry in the Shona vocabulary, rich with words borrowed from other languages. If someone said, '*Tapiwa akakirosa*,' listeners knew that Tapiwa had crossed into Mozambique to join the liberation struggle.

Most of the recruits were teenagers, many of them with barely an inkling of the political crisis that drew them to undergo guerrilla training. Not even the all-girl institutions such as Kriste Mambo and the elite St David's Secondary School at Bonda Mission near Rusape were spared the ravages of war and the exodus.

As this loss of pupils from schools in Manicaland gathered momentum, I drove to the township in the Nyamurundira Irrigation Scheme one Friday afternoon to refuel the car. It was unbearably hot and I entered a bottle store to order a beer to cool off. A bus from Rusape ground to a screeching halt in front of the shops, and I immediately recognised the second passenger to alight. It was Willard Duri, a first-year student at the University of Rhodesia during my last year there. I knew Duri, because his parents ran a general dealer's shop at Rukweza, a township close to the scene of the attack on our convoy during our second excursion with Seduce Mapondera.

After Duri and I embraced like long-lost brothers, I bought him a beer and we sat down. I was burning with curiosity about his presence in this part of the country and anxious to hear the latest news from both Salisbury and the university, while he wanted an update on the war situation in the Nyamaropa area. I deduced, correctly, that he was on his way to Mozambique. Suddenly, the bus driver started the engine and sounded the horn. He was running late and had just over an hour to beat the 6 p.m. curfew at his final destination.

Duri intended crossing into Mozambique that very night. He had never been to Nyamaropa, so I told him the next stop was not too far away, and that the fast-flowing waters of the Kaerezi were clearly visible from the township. As we embraced, I slipped a five-dollar note into his palm. He jumped back onto the bus, which took off in a cloud of reddish dust and sped its way along the flat fertile lands on the western side of the river.

Duri returned to Salisbury from Mozambique after the ceasefire in 1980, and played a key role in Zanu-PF's election campaign in Manicaland. He had assumed a new name and, as Comrade Zororo, became one of the province's most popular politicians, his youth and energy distinguishing him from the geriatric nationalists who constituted the leadership of Mugabe's party.

Unfortunately, Duri's life was cut short in 1998. He died instantly when his car collided with an army vehicle while he was driving to Rusape from Harare. There was widespread speculation that his death was no accident, and that he had been assassinated because he had become a threat to senior politicians in the eastern province. One version of the rumour even had it that I had been the target and that Zororo had been killed in error. But, like many similar stories on the fertile Zimbabwean political grapevine, no one offered a shred of evidence to sustain these theories, which soon died a natural death.

A new euphemism was coined for such alleged political assassinations – to hit a black dog. A politician who died in suspicious circumstances on the highway was said to have 'hit a black dog' with his vehicle.

I mourned Duri quietly for a long time.

On the eve of the last day of the second term in August 1977, the current local Zanla detachment visited the school to bid the staff and pupils farewell. It had been three or four weeks since the security forces had paid us a call, and the guerrillas now regarded Regina Coeli as a liberated zone, quite often moving from village to village in broad daylight without being challenged by anyone.

On the night in question, there was much revelry in the dining hall. Guerrillas had propped their AK47 rifles against a wall and joined pupils in a dance of reckless abandon as the stereo belted out the latest revolutionary offerings from popular musicians Thomas Mapfumo and Tinei Chikupo. Some of the pupils had decided not to rejoin their families at home the next day, and planned instead to cross into Mozambique and join the liberation struggle later that night.

Ursula and the baby were in Salisbury, so the detachment commander, Comrade Gunner, and three senior officers whiled away the time at my house, sharing a bottle of brandy while I nursed a beer. Seeking to convince me that I should not consider going to Mozambique, Gunner explained in detail the conditions prevailing in the training camps.

'The war effort requires people like you here at the front,' he said. 'The war requires a support infrastructure inside the country. If all the schoolteachers, businessmen and *mujibhas* cross into Mozambique, Zanla will be deprived of its support infrastructure and the war could come to an abrupt end. A fish cannot swim where there is no water.'

As he spoke, I realised that my visitors had emptied the one bottle of brandy I had in the house.

'I am sorry to interrupt you,' I said, 'but we have run out of brandy. I will rush to Father Martin. Maybe he has a spare bottle.'

'I will come with you,' Gunner replied. 'The rest of you, comrades, will remain behind. Vigilance!'

Father Martin, originally from Ireland, was the Jesuit priest in charge of the mission, while Sister Catherine, a Carmelite nun, also from Ireland, administered the hospital. There was a spirit of 'revolutionary understanding' between Regina Coeli's Catholic clergy and the Zanla guerrillas.

As we covered the distance between the house and the church, Gunner continued his admonition. I was never able to ascertain whether he was Comrade Gunner or Comrade Ghana, but he was younger than me and insisted he knew me from Old Highfields.

'What I actually meant about you not coming to Mozambique,' he said in a lowered tone as we walked, 'is something like this. My own observation is that people like you, who are educated, are not too popular with the military high command. Did you not hear about Comrade Dzinashe Machingura who was arrested and is now languishing in prison in Maputo? He is very highly educated and extremely intelligent. They said he was plotting against the leaders and they arrested him along with Comrade Rugare Gumbo—'

He was interrupted in mid-sentence by a burst of gunfire from the direction of the dining hall, followed by screams and what sounded like cries of pain. Then there was more gunfire. The initial burst was unmistakably that of G3 rifles, carried by the security forces. People living in operational zones had long since learned to distinguish the sound of the AK from that of the G3.

Suddenly, the whole mission was plunged into darkness. Gunner and I retraced our steps to my house on the double. By the time we reached my bedroom, where we had left the three other guerrillas, it was empty.

'I must go,' Gunner said, as he made a hasty and unceremonious departure. I was never to see him again. Ten or so minutes later, I heard the sound of footsteps approaching the house. I decided they were not military and opened a curtain slightly to see who was outside. It was a mob of boys and girls running towards the teachers' houses. I opened the door to admit those that I could, while the rest rushed past in the direction of the other houses.

Squeezed into my bedroom, the pupils related in hushed tones what had happened.

A group of government troops, some of them white soldiers with faces painted black, had approached and surrounded the dining hall. Apparently, the Zanla guerrillas had let their guard down and neglected to post sentries while they were dancing and having fun inside. The troops opened fire, killing two pupils and a guerrilla with their first salvo. There was pandemonium as everybody rushed towards the two exits amid much screaming and crying, and more pupils were injured in the stampede. One young girl, Elizabeth, sustained serious back injuries. She was the daughter of Maurice Nyagumbo, a prominent nationalist leader who was languishing in detention at the time, and whose brother had married my aunt, Grace Nyarota.

Mercifully, the electricity had failed or the carnage might have been worse. I don't believe the dozen or so pupils who had found refuge in my bedroom slept at all that night, but daybreak brought greater anxiety and anguish. Deployed at the main entrance to the school was a phalanx of military troop carriers. When they entered the grounds, all hell broke loose. They made straight for the boys' dormitories, where everything that moved was savagely punched, viciously kicked or assailed with rifle-butts. Thankfully, there was no gunfire.

Then the troops moved from one teacher's house to the next, ordering all occupants out, though with less accompanying violence. Either the soldiers were tired or they feared possible repercussions. Once we were assembled, the man who appeared to be in charge addressed us.

'We have always been aware of a close liaison between this school and the terrorists operating in Nyamaropa,' he said. 'We know that Regina Coeli has lost many of its pupils and that your enrolment has declined so much that you should cease to operate as a school. Yet the school authorities have always denied any association with the terrorists. We have known all along that the missionaries were entertaining terrorists on the premises. The death of terrorists and the death and injuries sustained by your own pupils last night should serve as a lesson to you of the capacity of the Rhodesian security forces to deal with any terrorist situation and with those who dare to cooperate with the terrorists.

'With immediate effect, this school is closed. The teachers have today to arrange for the removal of their household goods. When you go, please leave the doors open. By the end of the day, there mustn't be a soul in sight within the school grounds.'

That statement was like a death sentence. It effectively signalled the end of my career as a teacher. I packed what little I could fit into my car, offered three pupils a lift to Umtali and, leaving the doors wide open as instructed, bade farewell to my home of the past thirty months, abandoning the precious household goods that we had accumulated. However, there was so much discipline among the rural population in the liberated zones that not a single item was stolen. The following week, the crew of a B&C Company bus from Umtali bravely entered the house, packed my goods and loaded them onto the roof of their vehicle.

That evening, my possessions were delivered to the Umtali Teachers' College, where I was temporarily camped out at the house of my good friends, Gilbert and Chiedza Musengezi. Gilbert and I had been classmates at Goromonzi High School, while his wife was a year behind us. Their relationship had blossomed at university and they married soon after Chiedza graduated. Gilbert had become a lecturer at the college in Umtali, while Chiedza was a teacher at Sakubva High School. Their house on the college campus was home to us whenever Ursula and I visited the beautiful and picturesque city.

Two days later, Gilbert and I departed for Salisbury in my car. About forty kilometres from Umtali, we heard a loud bang from the engine. The car shuddered as I manoeuvred it to the verge of the road, where it stopped, thick smoke billowing from under the bonnet.

The engine had obviously seized again, but this time I was virtually penniless, having been rendered impecunious by the war's relentless demands and my contributions. We pushed the car a couple of hundred metres to a roadside shop, and there, having ensured that every door was safely locked, I bade farewell to the first valued possession of my life. It was heartbreaking. I remained unemployed for the next five months and was never to drive the car again. It was still on a hire purchase agreement, and in due course it was repossessed and auctioned to settle the outstanding balance.

This was the beginning of what became the first of my three periods of unemployment because of Zanu-PF, the political party which, along with PF-Zapu, spearheaded Zimbabwe's struggle for self-determination. Having endured the trials and tribulations of the war in Nyamaropa for seven months, the events of a single week had ended my promising and fulfilling career as a teacher.

We moved in with my mother in Old Highfields until our own goods arrived in Salisbury, then rented a room in an apartment in the newly built Glen Norah B complex, which had become home to the emerging elite: young doctors, lawyers, insurance salesmen, teachers and nurses. Ursula got a job with a leading private doctor in Old Highfields and we started a new life, with a little help here and there from friends and family.

For me, the change was the beginning of months of anxiety. With neither a job nor the immediate prospect of one and a young family to take care of, I had the reputation of a university graduate to maintain and my pride to protect in a community where the status of an academic education was somewhat overrated.

3

The typewriter beckons

D UE TO A fervent interest in the motor car dating back to childhood, I was an avid reader of the used car sales section in the *Rhodesia Herald* from an early age, for purely academic reasons, of course.

Since returning to Salisbury after the closure of Regina Coeli, I had taken to perusing the 'Situations Vacant' column after going through the news. Frustrated by a lack of the experience that prospective employers always stipulated, even for a gardener's job, I would revert to my favourite pastime and scrutinise the car ads once again.

My only work experience was as a teacher. Not only were vacant positions at schools rarely advertised in the newspapers, there was also an embryonic glut of both teachers and university graduates. Clerical, senior civil service or private sector jobs for which I believed graduates were eminently qualified all demanded experience.

What this really meant, however, was that such jobs were reserved for whites. Black job seekers learned soon enough that when advertisements included the phrase 'experience required', it was a euphemism for 'only whites need apply'.

Early in October 1977, little more than a month after moving back to Salisbury, one advertisement in particular caught my attention. The Rhodesian Printing and Publishing Company (RP&P) was inviting applications from suitably qualified young people wishing to be considered for training as cadet journalists. The course would start in February 1978 and twelve candidates were to be selected.

RP&P was the largest newspaper publishing company in Rhodesia and owned the two major daily newspapers: the *Rhodesia Herald* (as it was then called), which was published in Salisbury, and the *Chronicle* in Bulawayo, of which I would become editor in 1983.

RP&P was incorporated in Salisbury in 1926 as an autonomous organisation, wholly independent of its parent company, the Argus Newspaper Company of South Africa, which held 49 per cent of the shares in the Rhodesian subsidiary. The company had a virtual monopoly in the newspaper industry and, judging by its imposing six-storey headquarters on the corner of Second Street and Gordon Avenue in Salisbury, was an immensely profitable enterprise.

As was the case in the capital, RP&P's premises in Bulawayo and Umtali were situated on prime real estate, with a printing press at each site. The company operated a huge fleet of vehicles – newspaper delivery vans, editorial and advertising saloons, as well as more upmarket sedans for the executives.

As a youngster, I would visit Herald House to see my uncle, Livingstone Mabika. It was at his brother's homestead that I had parked my car on the night of Zanla's attack on the Nyazura police station. Uncle Livingstone walked the streets of colonial Salisbury and post-independence Harare as a messenger with RP&P from 1955 until 2002, when he retired after unbroken service just three years shy of a half-century. After a lifetime of loyal and dedicated service, the company's parting gift was a new bicycle.

This early association with the *Herald* whetted my appetite for newspapers. As I waited for my uncle at the side entrance on Gordon Avenue, I was impressed by the reporters and advertising representatives alighting from company cars before disappearing into the belly of the building. I could soon tell the difference between the ad reps, who were always smartly turned out, and the journalists, who tended to dress rather scruffily and inevitably had cigarettes dangling from their lips.

Many years later, I learned that there was a cavernous garage and a massive printing press in the basement of Herald House.

I had been fascinated by newspapers since primary school. My father Jethro, a postal clerk in Umtali at the time of my birth in 1951, never missed a copy of the *Herald*, even though the cost of his information quest occasionally entailed sacrificing his lunch at work. My mother Ruby, a primary schoolteacher, also read newspapers, and I began flipping through them from an early age. My parents moved to Salisbury in 1956, and a year later I started school at Epworth Mission, a Methodist institution on the outskirts of the city. My parents divorced in 1958, and in 1959 my father took me back to our rural village to live with my grandparents. Both the divorce and relocation were traumatic, but even though the next three years did not include daily access to a newspaper, my zest for education remained undiminished and I read every publication I could lay my hands on.

In 1961, my paternal grandfather and namesake, Geoffrey Nyarota, accompanied me to St Faith's, an Anglican upper-primary school east of Rusape, to take the examination required for admission to what was one of Manicaland's most prestigious educational centres.

We travelled the twenty kilometres from Nyazura to Rusape on the night train from Umtali to Salisbury, arriving at midnight. Along with scores of other passengers and a few semi-permanent residents of the facility, we spent the next few hours in the crowded waiting room at the railway station. Like all the waiting rooms provided for passengers by Rhodesia Railways, the one at Rusape carried the unpleasant stench of urine and was guaranteed to be infested with lice. I was therefore more than grateful when the eastern sky cleared at the break of dawn.

The fifteen-kilometre journey to St Faith's was the longest I had ever walked. Grandfather and I maintained a brisk pace and, without having eaten any breakfast, arrived just in time for me to sit for the entrance exam. St Faith's was the only higher primary boarding school in the Makoni district and competition for a Standard 4 place was intense. I was one of the successful candidates, and in January 1962 I returned to the school as a boarder. In an era when it was not unusual for children to start their education at the age of nine or ten, I had first gone to school when I was six, so, at eleven I was the youngest pupil at St Faith's. By the time I left three years later, some of the older boys in my class had already started shaving and were the proud owners of razors.

My Standard 4 teacher, Oliver Ndora, was a strict disciplinarian who impressed upon his young charges the need for a sound education and repeatedly told us how fortunate we were, not only to be acquiring one at a time when many parents did not appreciate the value of sending their children to school, but to be at so fine an institution as St Faith's. Clara Chavunduka and Arthur Murungu, my Standard 5 and 6 teachers respectively, enjoined us to read newspapers regularly. This was the best way to learn English, we were told. In those days, schools placed far more emphasis on the need to pass English with flying colours than the need to learn, let alone pass, examinations in the indigenous Shona and Ndebele languages. An educated man was measured by how well he articulated the English language. Most pupils had a copy of Michael West's *Students' Companion*, a volume teeming with English idioms, general knowledge and jaw-breakers, which we memorised to impress the girls during debate on Saturday evenings.

It was considered beneath the dignity of a learned upper-primary pupil to speak such humble English as, 'Birds of a feather flock together.' We said, instead, 'Ornithological specimens of identical plumage perambulate in close proximity.' Robert Mugabe, also the product of a parochial school, must have invested a great deal of time studying West's masterpiece, judging by the verbosity of his public addresses in later years.

Clara Chavunduka was the most beautiful woman on whom I had ever laid my juvenile eyes, and she dressed, in the parlance of the period, like a European lady. As a woman in a profession that was still predominantly male, I thought her the ultimate embodiment of success. We learned in a current affairs class that her sister Sarah was the first black Rhodesian woman to graduate from the University College of Rhodesia and Nyasaland, as it was then called. Both Clara and Sarah were sources of youthful inspiration to me, and I vowed to work hard so that I, too, could go to university. This became my burning ambition.

Many years later, Sarah, who lived for a long period outside the country as the wife of Aubrey Kachingwe, Malawi's erstwhile ambassador to South Africa, was appointed permanent secretary in Zimbabwe's ministry of information. Our paths would cross when she was appointed to the board of directors of Zimbabwe Newspapers and I was one of the company's editors. The Kachingwes and my family also became members of the same Anglican congregation at St Luke's in Greendale, Harare.

The Chavundukas, a prominent farming family in the Dowa Native Purchase Lands west of Rusape, were highly educated. The eldest son Gordon was a sociologist who became vice chancellor of the University of Zimbabwe. As part of his work he became heavily involved with the community of traditional healers, the *n'angas*, as they are called in Shona. While he was not one himself, he surprised many when he rose to become president of the Zimbabwe National Traditional Healers' Association (Zinatha), thus boasting the unusual distinction of simultaneously holding high office at Zimbabwe's most senior Western educational institution and in one of the most traditional organisations.

His brother Dexter was the country's first black veterinary surgeon, whose son Mark was news editor at the *Financial Gazette* when I became the paper's editor in 1990. Mark went on to become an editor in his own right, first of *Parade* magazine and then of the *Sunday Standard*, founded while his Aunt Sarah was permanent secretary in the information ministry.

Despite being divorced, my father and mother, as well as my grandparents, continually impressed on me the value of a sound education as the key to a successful life. One of my uncles, Arthur Nyarota, had attended the famous Goromonzi High School and had a well-paying job as a studio assistant with Rhodesia Television in Salisbury. I did not need much convincing, especially after observing, both in Salisbury and the village, the fate of my many cousins and other relatives who had no interest in going to anything beyond the local primary school, or were forced to cut short their education because their parents could not afford to pay their school fees.

Those who lived in the rural areas were restricted to a life of herding cattle, with the highlight of the week being the long trip to the communal dipping tank. Their urban counterparts worked long hours at menial jobs in the industrial areas and drank away their miserable wages on Friday night, only to borrow money for bus fare back to work on Monday morning and start the next cycle of behaviour that ensured they drank and slept like a king for one day each week.

I observed how our teachers, rich by the standards of the time, bought the latest models coming out of the Ford Motors assembly plant at Willowvale in Salisbury. They drove brand new Zephyrs, Cortinas, Corsairs or Anglias. The father of Arthur Makoni, one of my school friends, was a primary school headmaster. He came to visit his son at St Faith's behind the wheel of a majestic Jaguar Mark 10. My own uncle acquired first a Hillman Minx and then a Ford Prefect in quick succession. I required no further motivation or persuasion. If I worked hard, became a university graduate, bought a nice car (maybe a Jaguar) and married a woman as beautiful as my Standard 5 teacher, I would be guaranteed to live happily ever after.

At the behest of my teachers, therefore, I became an ardent newspaper reader. This inculcated in me a keen interest in English, and I always excelled at spelling and taking dictation. Above all, I loved to write essays, both in English and Shona, though I also had a keen interest in all my other subjects, especially history and geography.

After coming top of my class in every examination during my three years at St Faith's, I entered St Mary's Secondary School. Our Class of 1968 would achieve the best O-Level results in Rhodesia, beating the performance of longer-established schools such as St Augustine's Mission, Goromonzi High School, Kutama Mission and St Ignatius College, all of which had a reputation for producing first-rate examination results.

Anglican missionaries had established St Mary's in 1962, and my class was thus only the fourth to take O-Levels at the school. It was situated in the middle of the bush on the edge of the Seke communal lands, south of Salisbury along the road to Hwedza. The school eventually became completely surrounded by the new town of Chitungwiza, sprawling, socially vibrant, politically volatile and mostly poor.

I had trained as an altar boy at St Faith's, helping the priest at mass every Wednesday and Sunday morning. I was the boat-boy. I brought incense to the altar in a silver vessel – the boat – and at the appropriate moment dropped a few grains into the crucible, where it would burn and emit an aroma that wafted down the pews packed with boys and girls.

At St Mary's, I continued faithfully to serve, this time at the altar of the Reverend Zacharia Tekere, father of Zimbabwe's firebrand politician, Edgar, who was the secretary general of Zanu and was detained for a long time before being released in 1974 along with Mugabe. Three months after they were freed, Tekere and Mugabe staged a dramatic escape through the mountainous terrain of Rhodesia's Eastern Highlands before slipping into Mozambique, where Mugabe assumed leadership of the party. After independence in 1980, Tekere served briefly as Mugabe's minister of labour and social services.

My English teacher at St Mary's, Edward Turner, said he saw my potential as a writer and encouraged me to work hard to improve my skills. English literature and language became my favourite subjects as I prepared to write my O-Level examinations in 1968. I also had a fascination for Latin, which most students dismissed as a dead language, unworthy of inclusion in the educational syllabus of a British colony far from Rome.

Our Latin teacher, James Chirwa – or Bo-Bis, as he was fondly or derisively called, depending on whether the pupil's Latin was excellent or a disaster – was another source of inspiration. 'Bo' is the first-person Latin suffix for the future tense 'I will', while 'Bis' is the second-person suffix to convey the same tense, namely 'you will'. Chirwa had obtained a BA degree from the University of Rhodesia, and in my opinion was thus not a man to be taken lightly. He was erudite, yet he remained humble and unassuming, even if he drove a brand new Ford Taunus. Many who drove lesser and much older cars in the townships of Harare (later renamed Mbare) and Highfields considered themselves to be higher class than their neighbours.

I believe that my persistent study of Latin was instrumental in shaping my English, especially since so many of the words in the lexicon of the latter have their roots in the ancient Roman tongue. During my final year at St Mary's in 1968, I was appointed editor of the annual school magazine. Our small editorial team did a fine job and produced an issue that staff members and fellow pupils showered with genuine praise, filling me, in particular, with immense pride.

Yet, when I submitted my application to train as a journalist ten years later, I was not optimistic about the prospect of acceptance. I had fancied a career as either a journalist or a lawyer, both something of a cut above the Chavundukas and the Chirwas, the heroes and role models of my adolescence, but I had not been accepted for a law degree and there had been no opportunity to become a journalist after graduation. From

St Mary's, I had been accepted at Goromonzi High School, which, along with Fletcher High in Gwelo, was the premier government high school for black Rhodesians. Their academic standards were matched only by the recently established A-Level classes at St Ignatius College at Chishawasha outside Salisbury, and St Augustine's, north of Umtali. These were Catholic and Anglican mission schools respectively.

The majority of young black university graduates, most of whom studied the humanities, followed the same career path, unless they were among the few fortunate enough to train as doctors or lawyers. And so, like most of my peers, I became a teacher, treading in the footsteps of my youthful heroes and heroines until the abrupt closure of Regina Coeli terminated my career in the classroom.

The proposed training course for cadet journalists was to take place on the sixth floor of Herald House, situated across the street from Cecil Square, later renamed African Unity Square in honour of the Organisation of African Unity (OAU), a post-colonial initiative aimed at creating a pan-African consciousness. In 2002, the OAU itself was reconstituted as the African Union.

During my time at university, Cecil Square had become a popular venue for student demonstrations, and its lush green lawns were the scene of my first brush with the law. I was one of about a hundred students arrested in 1971 as we demonstrated in support of better salaries for teachers. In truth, however, my seminal taste of protest was as an eleven-year-old pupil at St Faith's.

A few weeks after being admitted to the school as a boarder, I was among a group of pupils who boycotted meals to protest the serving of *nyemba*, or dried cowpeas, as part of our diet. We made our point, and this particularly unpalatable item was soon removed from the school's menu.

Three years later, on 11 November 1965, Rhodesia's prime minister, Ian Smith, issued a Unilateral Declaration of Independence (UDI), thus severing links with Great Britain. I was a Form 1 pupil at St Mary's, and just after midnight the entire student body rose as one to march approximately twenty kilometres to Salisbury to stage a demonstration. Pupils from Goromonzi, St Ignatius College and Nyatsime College, as well as other secondary schools, staged their own marches to Harare. Nyatsime, situated six kilometres south-east of St Mary's, and Bernard Mizeki College outside Marandellas were where wealthy blacks enrolled children who failed to gain admission to more academically demanding schools.

How the protest leaders at the different schools communicated that day has remained a mystery to me. Most schools had only one telephone, usually in the principal's office, yet the organisers somehow managed to stage what appeared to be a well-synchronised march.

The boys from St Mary's got only as far as the Hunyani River bridge, two kilometres beyond the school gate, before a fleet of police vehicles, their searchlights probing the pitch-dark summer night, put paid to our progress. The police escorted us back to school, where the return of the rain-drenched pupils after an absence of more than an hour stunned the headmaster. There were no recriminations, however. The mission staff was not overly fond of Ian Smith.

The university students arrested in Cecil Square six years later were loaded onto police vans and driven to the main charge office at the corner of Inez Terrace and Railway Avenue – later renamed Kenneth Kaunda Avenue in honour of Zambia's first president – a few blocks away. The central courtyard was soon crowded with students singing and chanting revolutionary slogans. Those who had escaped arrest walked across town and poured into the courtyard of their own accord, demanding that they, too, be apprehended. Initially, the police were happy to oblige, but as the size of the crowd swelled way beyond the capacity of the courtyard, the authorities were forced to put an end to the unfolding farce.

We were all hastily charged under the Law and Order (Maintenance) Act, requested to sign an admission of guilt and pay a fine of ten dollars each. Hurried consultation among the now tired and hungry students established that most were in favour of paying the fine, considering that our point about the need for better remuneration and conditions of service for teachers had been made, and that the police had suffered considerable embarrassment by turning away students who demanded that they be arrested.

It was close to supper time at the university residences in the whites-only suburb of Mount Pleasant. We had missed lunch, and the prospect of substituting prison rations for a three-course meal on campus was sufficient deterrent for any further confrontation. In any case, the university authorities undertook to pay the fines on behalf of all arrested students.

The University of Rhodesia was the country's only enclave of multiracial coexistence, but there was little genuine interaction between black and white students. We lived in the same halls of residence – Manfred Hodson, Carr Saunders and Swinton – and shared the same dining facilities, but tables were occupied largely along spontaneous racial divisions. When I enrolled in 1971, whites outnumbered blacks almost four to one. As the number of black students increased, white students took increasingly to living off campus in Mount Pleasant, Avondale and other neighbouring white suburbs.

The Student's Union, the focus of social intercourse, was beyond the financial reach of many black students. Unless they came from other cities and towns or from the rural areas and did not have close relatives in Salisbury, most of them gravitated to the townships of Highfields, Harare, Mufakose and Kambuzuma over weekends. In many instances they returned to campus on Monday morning, just in time for lectures.

In terms of sport, most blacks either played or watched soccer, while a few played tennis or basketball. The major sporting attractions for the majority of white students and the tiny percentage of blacks who attended Rhodesia's few multiracial high schools were rugby and cricket.

However, full integration was enforced in the lecture halls, where aptitude and intelligence were the equalisers.

A number of students from my era became prominent personalities after independence. Witness Mangwende, Samuel Mbengegwi, Simba Makoni and David Karimanzira became government ministers, while Ibbo Mandaza and Iden Wetherell became publisher of the *Daily Mirror* and editor of the *Zimbabwe Independent* respectively.

Charles Marechera became the famous author Dambudzo Marechera, having gained recognition while still a student for staging one-man demonstrations against Smith in downtown Salisbury. He left when he was awarded a scholarship to study at Oxford. Willard Chiwewe, Misheck Sibanda, Joey Bimha and Charles Mashongwa became top civil servants in Mugabe's post-independence administration.

I enrolled for a BA degree in history and Shona. I also studied Latin as a minor subject for two years. Altogether, I spent a total of eight years studying the 'dead language' from secondary school to university, a worthwhile investment for a future career in journalism.

Traditionally, the cadet course for journalists had been confined to whites, but management at RP&P was slowly awakening to the winds of political change sweeping across the Rhodesian landscape, and the previous training group had broken new ground by including Michelle Faul, an exceptionally pretty coloured girl, who became a successful foreign correspondent with Agence France Presse, and John 'Ali Baba' Ndlovu, who hailed from Bulawayo, and was the first black to receive formal training as a journalist in Rhodesia.

After graduation, he worked on the *Chronicle* for a brief period before emigrating to Canada, where he met and married Thandiwe, the daughter of PF-Zapu leader Joshua Nkomo. Ndlovu never returned to Zimbabwe, a foresight for which he must perpetually have congratulated himself. At independence Mugabe offered Nkomo the position of president, but Nkomo turned it down because the position was purely ceremonial. He grudgingly accepted appointment as minister of home affairs, but in due course broke ranks with Mugabe. Zanu-PF, which accused Nkomo's former Zipra fighters of concealing weapons of war in preparation for an uprising against the new government, hunted Nkomo like a rabbit and eventually hounded him out of the country into post-independence exile. Ndlovu would obviously not have escaped the dragnet for people close to the ageing veteran politician.

The advertisement in the *Rhodesia Herald* specified only a minimum of a good O-Level certificate for applicants with a proficient command of English and a keen interest in writing. I had graduated from university *cum laude*, but notwithstanding my apparent overqualification and the obvious handicap of being black, I submitted an application. In their emerging acknowledgement that change was upon the old Rhodesian order, management decided to include four black trainees among the twelve who comprised the class of 1978. I was one of the fortunate four.

However, I was unique as the only university graduate in the group. In fact, I had higher academic qualifications than even the tutor. The rest of the class had O-Level or matriculation certificates, depending on whether they were black or European, as white Rhodesians were officially classified, even if neither they nor their parents had ever set foot on the continent of their ancestry. While my A-Level certificate and university degree would be the source of both problems and advantages in my new profession, they posed no insurmountable quandary to the RP&P management.

In 1970, Rhodesia's currency had switched from British sterling to the dollar (not linked to the US greenback), and at independence in 1980, the word 'Zimbabwe' was appended to the latter. As a teacher, my gross monthly remuneration was the princely sum of $265, a fortune in those days, especially in the hands of a twenty-six-year-old rural schoolmaster. On joining the *Herald* I was offered a starting salary of $240 a month before deductions. Management could not offer me $265 or more without upsetting the company's salary structure. In any case, as I was reminded, the company was footing the bill for my training. Since I was determined to become a journalist and had little prospect of any alternative job, I swallowed my pride and grasped the opportunity of a new career with both hands.

I was convinced that the sacrifice would be a worthy investment in a bright future in a profession of my choice and dreams, until discovering, fairly soon, that the white cadets were being paid a higher salary. Not only were they younger than me, but their parents had invested five years less in their education. While they were all single men and women, I was a married father of one. This became a painful personal manifestation of yet another of Rhodesia's abhorrent racially discriminatory employment practices. Even if they had the relevant qualifications, blacks were excluded from certain job categories, routinely paid less for doing the same work, and required to put in more effort than their white counterparts in order to be recognised or considered for promotion.

Our tutor on the cadet course was Bill Arnold, an unassuming veteran newsman who never tired of teaching us the basics of journalism: the five W's and an H.

'Answering the questions, Who? What? Where? When? Why? and How?,' he preached endlessly, 'is the essence of journalism.'

He also taught us the basic skills of interviewing, story construction, how to establish a comprehensive network of contacts and sources, and how to develop a hound's nose for news. The latter was illustrated by Arnold's variation on the time-honoured example familiar to would-be journalists everywhere:

'A young cadet reporter was assigned to cover a press conference addressed by the mayor,' Arnold told us. 'The reporter returned to the newsroom earlier than expected. "Well," he told the surprised news editor, "a fire broke out at Town House, so the press conference was cancelled and I immediately came back."'

The point, of course, is that the inexperienced rookie had failed completely to recognise the reason for the cancellation, namely the fire, as an arguably more important story than the original mayoral address, and returned to base without any story at all.

'Old Bill', as he was known, drilled us on the elements of municipal, court, sports and economic reporting, coverage of parliament, feature writing and investigative journalism. He emphasised the importance of accuracy, attribution, verification, fairness, balance, objectivity, public interest, human interest, brevity, clarity and social responsibility. He grounded us in the ethics of journalism and in media law, especially as regards defamation.

Arnold believed in practical education. Before the end of our first day, he sent us out on an unspecified assignment. We were to walk around downtown Salisbury and each bring back a story. Emerging from the lift on the ground floor of Herald House, we went our separate ways. I ventured no further than Cecil Square, on the opposite side of Second Street.

Stanley Avenue, now known as Jason Moyo in tribute to the PF-Zapu vice-president who was killed by a parcel bomb in Lusaka in January 1977, was the southern boundary of the central city block that municipal authorities of a generation long gone had devoted to trees, shrubs, beautiful flower gardens, well-manicured lawns and paved walkways. Second Street formed the western periphery, while the south-western corner had been set aside as a flower market that had once been a hive of activity.

It was at this market – inconspicuous to the majority of the city's residents, who had little inclination or resources to invest in such luxuries as fresh blooms – that I found a story for Old Bill.

The flower vendors flocked around me once they got the hang of my mid-afternoon assignment. They vied with each other in an effort to recount their woes about an alarming drop in business. Sales had plummeted over the past year or so, they said, attributing the decline to the departure of many of Rhodesia's white citizens, unsettled by the similarly declining security situation. One man said flowers were now increasingly difficult to acquire, since some of the growers had emigrated, while another told how wholesale prices had escalated to levels where trading in cut flowers had become unprofitable.

After reading my report, Arnold decided it was good enough to publish and sent it down to the newsroom. It missed the deadline for the following day's edition, but appeared on an inside page of the *Herald* a day later under the rather innocuous headline, 'The Blooming Woes of the Flower Sellers'.

I had made it. This was not only my very first story to be published in a mainstream newspaper – and under my name or byline, to boot – it was also the first contribution from our cadet class to make it into print. Seeing my name on a story in a national newspaper was an indescribably exhilarating experience.

Almost three decades later, I was at Harvard University in the United States when the same flower vendors fell early victim to President Mugabe's Operation Murambatsvina – Clean Up the Trash – which left thousands of Harare's residents and vendors homeless and without any source of income. I nearly wept.

During the second week of our course, Arnold assigned us to spend a day in the *Herald* reference library. We were to conduct research on a subject, again of our own choosing, and write a feature article, hopefully for publication. As already mentioned, I had what later became a consummate interest in motor cars and, while still at school, would often walk some six kilometres in the company of my uncle and other youngsters from the outskirts of the poor white suburb of Hatfield, where we lived near Epworth Mission, to the newly established Donnybrook Motor Racing Track near the township of Mabvuku.

I was fascinated by the speed of super-charged racing cars and modified saloons burning rubber around the circuit. I visited my aunt, Bertha Mukwedeya, one weekend in 1958 at the house in Hatfield where she worked as a maid. Her employer had just taken delivery of a gleaming white Jaguar Mark II, 3.4 litre, complete with wire-chrome wheels. I vowed that day that when I grew up, I would become the proud owner of just such a car. In 1987, thirty years later, I indeed acquired a gleaming British racing-green 1965 Jaguar Mark II, 3.4 litre, complete with wire-chrome wheels.

The car was twenty-two years old and therefore nowhere near new. But it was the ultimate fulfilment of a childhood dream. By then, this particular model had become a collector's item. My friends openly discussed my sanity, or absence thereof, when I parked the powerful machine outside the Ambassador Hotel, home of the famous press watering hole, the Quill Club. That afternoon, sinking into the genuine leather seats and surrounded by genuine wood panels, I drove the 330 kilometres to Bulawayo in record time for a car of that age.

I took my pride and joy to a Jaguar specialist in Bulawayo, who resprayed the car a brilliant postbox red. Thereafter, I usually spent the greater part of Saturday afternoons washing and burnishing the bodywork of the magnificent brute to a dazzling shine. After moving back to Harare in 1989, I used to take the car out for a spin along the Mutare highway to the east. Heads turned wherever I drove. Those who knew something about such cars flashed their lights in recognition and appreciation of this specimen of fine British craftsmanship before both Britain and the United States surrendered their pole position in the vehicle industry to the Japanese and the Germans.

Once, I saw in my rear-view mirror a car that I had just observed travelling in the opposite direction execute a swift U-turn to speed after and overtake the Jaguar. The driver signalled and stopped a safe distance ahead of me. When I pulled up, a middle-aged white man, obviously a farmer, approached.

'Are you selling this car?' he enquired, without even extending the courtesy of a greeting.

'Good afternoon,' I said. 'No, I bought the car recently myself.'

On another occasion, as I refuelled the car at a filling station, another white man, also in his fifties, walked up to the vehicle, his wife following closely behind. After inspecting the car and obviously finding it spick and span, he confronted me.

'Is your boss selling this car?' he enquired.

'No, my boss is not selling this car,' I retorted. 'In fact, this is my own car, sir.'

As the powerful six-cylinder motor fired to life, the couple beat a hasty retreat to their Peugeot 504, the man's tail figuratively planted firmly between his legs, or so I thought, while his ears were assailed by the mellifluous purr from the Jaguar's twin exhaust pipes.

In 1984, as editor of the *Chronicle*, I was sponsored to enter the three-hour endurance race at Breedon Evarard Motorway in Bulawayo. My co-driver in a converted Renault Gordini saloon was professional racing driver Yunus Osman. The Renault, which was fitted with a high-performance BMW engine, developed a transmission problem as we drove practice laps around the circuit on the eve of the big day. The car was withdrawn from the race, much to Ursula's relief and, I must confess, my own.

With my abiding love of cars, it was little wonder that I chose my favourite topic for Old Bill's library assignment in 1978. I delved into the history of the motor car in Rhodesia, going back to the first Ford Model T imported into the country. The feature article made it into the *Herald* the following week under the headline, 'All Our Motoring Yesterdays'.

Incidentally, I never lost my passion for cars, and in 1997 launched my own motoring journal, the slick and glossy *Highway Magazine*, of which I was both editor and publisher.

At the end of Old Bill's training course, I was assigned to the *Herald* newsroom as a cadet reporter. In order to prepare them for the diversity of assignments they would encounter, cadet reporters quickly became Jacks of all trades. We covered the presentation of watches and bicycles to long-service workers; traffic accidents; the crime beat; politics; court cases; and soccer matches at Rufaro Stadium. Wherever a newsworthy event occurred and whatever it was, we were sent to do the story, albeit almost always in the company of experienced senior journalists such as Jan Raath, Bill Hipson and Heather Silk, who showed us the ropes in the field and taught us the intricacies of the trade.

'You don't learn journalism on the sixth floor with Bill Arnold, but on the third floor with the journalists,' news editor Brian Streak used to say.

Raath fled Zimbabwe in 2005 after President Mugabe's dreaded Central Intelligence Organisation (CIO) focused its sinister attention on him, accusing him of being a spy. Silk, who was married to long-time BBC correspondent Ian Mills, and Sarah Kachingwe were among the congregants at St Luke's Church in Greendale who prayed for me and my family when I was similarly targeted by government agents from 2000 to 2002 before I, too, fled the country of my birth in 2003.

At quite an early stage of my new career as a journalist, it occurred to me that there was a public expectation of omniscience in those who provided the daily news. Should someone ask a reporter the date of President John F Kennedy's birth or the name of the spaceship in which Soviet astronaut Yuri Gagarin became the first human to orbit earth in 1961, the journalist was simply expected to answer 29 May 1917 or *Vostok 1* without blinking. I therefore read widely, especially magazines, both local and international.

The subeditors' desk on the *Herald* was manned by seasoned journalists who had seen many years of service as senior reporters and were now, depending on their aptitude, either waiting to retire or be promoted to the upper echelons of the editorial department as assistant or deputy editors. The bald-headed and bearded men who sat on the dreaded desk were among the paper's most experienced and knowledgeable journalists.

The 'subs' were the gatekeepers. Spelling mistakes, grammatical errors, poor sentence construction, pompous language or excessive padding of stories by reporters did not normally make it beyond this venerated desk onto the pages of the newspaper. The subs positioned the finished articles on the pages and crafted appropriate and, in their collective view, clever headlines. They also selected, cropped and positioned the pictures that illustrated the stories. That a good picture tells a story better than a thousand words is publishing wisdom the world over. The subeditors worked to strict deadlines and were notorious among reporters for being slave-drivers who routinely threw painstakingly and lovingly crafted stories back at them, dismissing their day's output as rubbish, trash, crap or some other humiliating epithet.

'I want five paragraphs out of this,' a subeditor would shout while throwing back the twenty paragraphs that had taken a reporter most of the day to write with the love and passion of a journalist who has consulted so many reliable or informed sources that he has become an instant expert on the subject of his story. But if a sub wanted an epic cut down to five paragraphs, the reporter had to comply, and within the stipulated five minutes, lest the story be spiked – newsroom parlance for rejected – or risk being responsible for 'the paper coming out in time for lunch tomorrow'.

Junior reporters learned quickly enough that neither was an option and that subeditors did not suffer the presence of fools in the newsroom. They also found out early that newspapers were run on tight deadlines. Cadets approached the subs' desk with a trepidation bordering on terror whenever summoned, but occasionally, in the absence of the overworked duty messenger, it was only to be dispatched to the canteen a floor above to purchase a packet of cigarettes or a cup of coffee.

It was as a reporter on the *Herald* that I began to observe and appreciate that a newspaper, if well packaged and properly marketed in a clearly defined target area, can be a viable product; that news is a profitable, if perishable and somewhat idiosyncratic product. There is a thirst for news, especially when a society is in transition, as Rhodesia was at the time, that renders readers anxious to stay abreast of the latest developments on the local and international scene.

RP&P's target readers were mainly members of the white minority. The editorial content and advertising that filled the columns of the *Rhodesia Herald* and the *Chronicle* were essentially of interest and relevance to company executives, commercial farmers, civil servants, factory foremen, doctors, accountants and other professionals who made up the bulk of colonial Rhodesia's white population. The company also published the *Sunday Mail* in Salisbury, the *Sunday News* in Bulawayo and the *Umtali Post* in the eastern border city of that name. I was to cut my teeth as an editor on the *Umtali Post* in 1982, with a mandate to transform it into a popular paper that would appeal to all sections of the community.

The Argus Group had ventured into Rhodesia soon after Cecil John Rhodes's Pioneer

Column hoisted the Union Jack at Fort Salisbury in Mashonaland, launching the weekly *Zambesian Times* in 1891. The *Rhodesia Herald* followed a year later, and incorporated the *Times*. With the Salisbury market covered, the company shifted its focus to Bulawayo, where the *Chronicle* first appeared in 1894.

As the settler population grew and commerce thrived, RP&P ventured east, adding the *Umtali Advertiser* to its titles. Maurice Henry, a Scottish Jew, launched the paper on 13 December 1893 and sold it in November 1894 to Charles Hancock. RP&P acquired the newspaper in August 1895 and changed the name to the *Umtali Post* on 4 October 1949. The *Post* would undergo another change of name thirty-three years later, when it became the *Manica Post* under my editorship. After independence, Umtali was renamed Mutare, but we opted for a title that embraced all of Manicaland rather than just the provincial capital.

Until Rhodesia shed its colonial shackles, the blacks who formed the majority of the urban population – the factory workers, government messengers and junior civil service clerks, teachers, nurses, railway workers and students who regularly ensured the immense profitability of RP&P – were forced by circumstance to read the company's newspapers.

In their book *Thunder and Silence: The Mass Media in Africa*, D Ziegler and M Asante observe: 'Nothing occurred in the press to indicate that there were people other than the colonial administrators in the territory. The desires and wishes of the African people in social, cultural, economic or political terms were simply ignored. In the old *Rhodesia Herald* not until the 1950s did the editor hint at the possibility that Africans, among whom the whites lived, existed and had ideas and problems of their own.'

The blacks did not find the newspapers particularly stimulating or remotely sympathetic to the cause of majority rule and an end to racial discrimination, which they yearned for. But apart from the African Service of the Rhodesian Broadcasting Corporation, the newspapers were the only regular, if heavily partisan, source of information on the unfolding political landscape in their troubled land.

One major attraction of the white men's newspapers were the classified columns which job-seekers and bargain hunters pored over in search of employment opportunities and cheap second-hand goods for sale. The coverage of soccer, the nation's most popular sport, and the columns devoted to horse racing were added drawcards exploited by the publishers in order to draw black readers. It was the dream of many a township youth to grace the back page of the *Chronicle* or *Herald* in the colours of Dynamos, Highlanders, Zimbabwe Saints, Black Aces or any of the other crowd-pulling soccer teams of the day.

My uncle, George Tumbare, always amazed me. He never missed a copy of the *Herald*, yet he was barely literate. In the early 1970s he was a waiter at the Park Lane Hotel, now Dura House, headquarters of the Grain Marketing Board in Eastlea, Harare. He had waited on the tables of leading hotels in Cape Town and Port Elizabeth in the 1940s, when it was fashionable for Rhodesian blacks to travel – many on foot – to South Africa in search of employment. He returned to Nyazura in 1949 with a bicycle and a suitcase full of the latest fashions. My Aunt Jessica caught the eye of this eminently eligible bachelor and he soon joined the extended Nyarota family.

It was no secret that Uncle George could barely read and always turned to the horse-racing pages, but I remember one especially cruel joke told about him, namely that if he was perusing the front page of the newspaper, Uncle George could easily hold it upside down and not realise his error. As soon as he turned to the racing pages, it was said, he would immediately correct the mistake.

In their editorial columns, the newspapers generally supported the white minority government's policies. Occasionally they adopted a different view to that of Ian Smith's Rhodesian Front, in power since 1962 and more inclined towards the racially dis-criminatory policies of South Africa's Afrikaner-dominated National Party government than those of previous colonial administrations. After Smith declared UDI in 1965, certain issues of the *Rhodesia Herald* appeared with blank columns where the government censor had prevented publication of politically sensitive stories. In protest, the editors refused to place other stories in the empty spaces and the paper frequently hit the streets with embarrassing white gaps in its news columns.

The public thus became aware that the censor had killed an article or two, but never got to know what information they were barred from reading.

One of the dozen cadets in my group, Pascal Mukondiwa, was recruited from an unlikely catchment area, the Rhodesian Prison Service, where he had been a warder. A good writer with a nose for news and a passionate interest in soccer, Mukondiwa had an illustrious career as a sports reporter before becoming the fourth post-independence editor of the *Sunday Mail*, then Zimbabwe's biggest circulation weekly. The turnover of editors between 1980 and 2002 at RP&P's successor, Zimbabwe Newspapers, was the highest anywhere in the media world, and editorship became arguably the most endangered occupation in Zimbabwe.

The legendary Willie Dzawanda Musarurwa was appointed the first black editor of the *Sunday Mail* in 1981. A fiercely independent journalist and a firebrand columnist, Musarurwa ran on a collision course with his new masters, the Mugabe government. He had served as PF-Zapu's pre-independence media spokesman and was fired from the *Mail* at about the same time that Nkomo and other Zapu ministers were sacked from President Mugabe's government of national unity. Musarurwa was one of the first blacks appointed to a senior editorial position following the creation of Zimbabwe Newspapers.

Using a $20 million grant from the government of Nigeria's President Shehu Shagari, which had been at the forefront of the campaign for independence of African countries still under foreign rule, Mugabe's government set up the Zimbabwe Mass Media Trust (ZMMT) in 1981, and bought the 49 per cent of South African–held stock in RP&P, thus becoming the majority shareholder.

The birth of Zimbabwe Newspapers Ltd in 1980 was justified by Zimbabwe's first minister of information, post and telecommunications, Dr Nathan Shamuyarira, a former journalist who had masterminded the takeover.

'Government remains committed to the freedom of the press as stated in its election manifesto,' he declared in a statement. 'We will neither publish nor edit any of the newspapers.'

One of the trustees, Grace Todd, wife of former Rhodesian prime minister Sir Garfield Todd, who was restricted by the governments of both Smith and Mugabe, dismissed what she called 'the fallacy that the ZMMT is a tool, or arm, of government'.

In a letter to the *Herald* she wrote: 'As a trustee I have been impressed by the manner in which the government has distanced itself from the trust and from the press and by the sensitivity on this matter shown by my fellow trustees.'

Events were to prove that both the minister and the trustee were totally off the mark. Setting the trend for the future relationship between government and the editors of its newspapers, the popular Musarurwa was summarily dismissed in 1985 as a result of his uncompromising condemnation of the Mugabe government's abuse of power.

He endured a life of hardship until his death in 1990. He collapsed as he, Steven Rhodes, the newly arrived American ambassador to Zimbabwe, and Andrew Moyse, the editor of *Parade* magazine, were lingering over coffee after lunch at the Courteney Hotel. I had attended the lunch but had rushed off to keep an appointment at the *Financial Gazette* on Simon Mazorodze Way, on the other side of town, where I was executive editor. Musarurwa was rushed to hospital but pronounced dead on arrival. Rhodes, a black diplomat who had not even presented his credentials yet at the time of the lunch, was soon recalled to Washington.

Having castigated and maligned him as an enemy during his term as editor of the *Sunday Mail*, and despite the fact that after being summarily and unjustly dismissed from the paper he led a life of abject penury, Zanu-PF honoured Musarurwa posthumously by conferring on him the status of a national hero. His remains were interred at Heroes' Acre to the accompaniment of eulogies extolling his virtues as a shrewd politician and outstanding journalist. The turnout at the ceremony was both huge and spontaneous, for Musarurwa truly was a hero. Zanu-PF's hypocrisy and perfidy must have caused him to turn in his freshly dug grave.

His successor as editor of the Zimpapers flagship was Egyptian-trained social scientist Henry Muradzikwa. He, too, was summarily dismissed after Mugabe vowed to personally 'get rid of the hand' that had written a story about a group of Zimbabwean student teachers expelled from Cuba amid allegations that they had tested HIV-positive. The Zimbabwe government's official policy was to keep all issues pertaining to the still largely misunderstood syndrome tightly under wraps. What particularly irked Mugabe was the embarrassment of the story being published while a government minister from the 'friendly socialist Republic of Cuba' was visiting Harare.

Charles Chikerema, cynically characterised long after independence as Zimbabwe's only authentic socialist, took over the reins from Muradzikwa. He thus acquired the dubious distinction of being the first and, at the time of writing, last editor of the *Sunday Mail* to leave the paper without being fired. He was promoted to the position of editor at the *Herald*. The dismissal of editors in post-independence Zimbabwe became a ritual that never had any bearing on the performance of the victims.

After four years of loyal, subservient and mostly unappreciated service to the government, my friend Mukondiwa, who had succeeded Chikerema as editor of the *Sunday Mail*, had a rude awakening when he, in turn, was dismissed in 2002 for no apparent reason by the new minister of information, Jonathan Moyo.

Also in my cadet class were Stanley Higgins and Luke Mhlaba. Higgins worked for the *Herald* before being made assistant editor at the *Umtali Post*, then branched out into public relations, where he excelled after setting up his own agency. Mhlaba joined the *Chronicle* in Bulawayo, then quit to study for a law degree. At the time of his graduation, I was editor of the *Chronicle*, and with much cajoling persuaded Mhlaba to return to the paper. As the first qualified lawyer in Zimbabwe to work as a journalist, he embodied my personal vision of starting a newspaper that would be staffed by medical doctors, lawyers, sociologists, economists, politicians, farmers, human rights activists, statisticians, sportsmen and entertainers who had also trained as journalists.

After a second spell on the *Chronicle*, Mhlaba left journalism and Zimbabwe for New York, where he joined the United Nations. By all accounts he had a stellar career as a UN diplomat, serving mostly in the Middle East and Fiji. I believe he had no regrets about quitting journalism.

Had he known, Bill Arnold would have been immensely proud of the fact that, two decades after he had trained us, Mukondiwa and I would both become the editors of leading national newspapers, Higgins a respected public relations executive and Mhlaba a high-ranking UN official, globetrotting from one trouble spot to another.

There was a time, though, not long after we had taken our places in the newsroom on the third floor of Herald House, that I seriously questioned my decision to become a journalist. An incident in the small town of Kariba disabused the few black journalists at the *Herald* of any illusion that our white colleagues regarded us as members of the same professional fraternity, and left me deeply disillusioned.

The mighty Zambezi River forms the natural boundary between Zimbabwe and Zambia, its neighbour to the north. In 1955, a point on the river known as Kariwa – or trap, on account of the water thundering through a narrow gorge – had become a hive of activity as Italian engineers and thousands of indigenous workmen toiled in the sweltering heat to construct a dam wall.

The construction of Kariba Dam, which resulted in the formation of Lake Kariba, in its day the largest man-made freshwater mass in the world, was one of the greatest engineering feats of the twentieth century, but it also became the source of serious conflict with the local Tonga people. They refused to believe that any man could defy their river god, Nyaminyami, by building a structure to stop the natural flow of the great Zambezi's waters.

Folklore has it that when the level of Lake Kariba started to rise and the Tonga were being relocated, they invoked Nyaminyami in a spirit of resistance. Although he was never used as a political symbol, it was generally agreed among the Tonga that Nyaminyami disapproved of the white man's plans to build the dam. In 1957, when a massive flood on the Zambezi halted construction, the local inhabitants are said to have nodded knowingly, and then to have waited for the final onslaught during the next rainy season. And, indeed, the 1958 flood was only slightly less damaging than the first, but the project went ahead anyway.

But the most traumatic event to befall Kariba was the callous shooting down of an Air Rhodesia Viscount by Zipra guerrillas shortly after the aircraft had taken off from the small airport in what had become a popular tourist resort on hilly terrain along the southern shore of the lake.

The catastrophic attack took place in the late afternoon of Sunday 3 September 1978. Flight 825, a four-engined turbo-prop Vickers Viscount, took off at 5.10 p.m. on a scheduled flight to Salisbury. The elderly aircraft was one of the workhorses of Air Rhodesia, an airline reeling under international sanctions. On board were fifty-two passengers and a crew of four. Most of the travellers were returning to the capital after a weekend of fun on the lake. Despite intermittent rocket and mortar attacks launched by Zipra from across the Zambezi in Zambia, Kariba had continued to flourish as a tourist attraction.

The Viscount, the *Hunyani*, had been named after a river that flows all the way from Harare, where it is a major source of water for the city's inhabitants, to Lake Kariba. Five minutes after take-off, while gaining altitude over the remote and sparsely populated terrain, the aircraft heaved violently. There was a loud bang and the inner starboard engine burst into flames. Almost immediately, the second starboard engine also failed, and the crippled *Hunyani* went into a rapid descent.

The stricken aircraft crash-landed in a cotton field, hit an irrigation ditch, cartwheeled and exploded. Miraculously, eighteen of the fifty-six people on board, all of them passengers seated in the tail section, survived the impact.

Moments later, in a scene straight out of a horror movie, as the dazed survivors staggered away from the wreckage, most of them in acute pain, they saw a group of men, armed to the teeth, approaching their position. In an act of cold-blooded murder, the guerrillas opened fire on the helpless and seriously injured group with machine guns, killing ten, including two children. Some were stabbed with bayonets, the *Herald* reported the following morning, quoting some of the eight who had spectacularly cheated death twice within the space of a few minutes. It is rare enough for passengers to walk away from an aeroplane crash, but that some should then also survive a hail of bullets fired at point-blank range is all but unthinkable.

This wicked massacre shocked the entire nation and the world. Black and white united in condemnation of the shooting down of Flight 825 and the senseless loss of innocent lives. Reports that Zapu leader Joshua Nkomo had laughed about the incident when interviewed on television by the BBC were met with utter revulsion.

There was mayhem in the *Herald* newsroom that night. As the gravity of events at

Kariba sank into the minds of the seasoned journalists manning the all-white subs' desk, they rose as one in a storm of protest. They cursed the communist terrorists and everything that was either black or African. I was the duty reporter and the only black person in the newsroom apart from the messenger, who ran endless errands between the subs' desk and the canteen on the floor above, and the night driver, sitting a safe distance away while awaiting instructions to rush out with a reporter and photographer to glean the latest information on the tragedy.

The subeditors were in a vile collective temper. They cursed until their voices became hoarse, threatening dire consequences for all *terrs* and *munts* or *kaffirs*. *Terr* was an abbreviated form of *terrorist*, which became the most common colloquialism used by Rhodesian soldiers to refer to their enemy in the bush war. *Munt* was a derogatory term used by the security forces to refer to blacks. I suspect its origin was the word *umntu*, Ndebele for a person or human being, while *kaffir* derived from the Arabic word for infidel, but had crept into southern Africa's colonial English as an abusive term for blacks. White journalists at the *Herald* and the *Sunday Mail* would pick up these obnoxious words while serving with the Rhodesian Army or as national service conscripts, but under normal circumstances, they never used such terms in the newsroom.

On any other night, the subs' desk was a riotous place after the supper break. Most self-respecting subeditors spent that glorious hour between 7 and 8 p.m. taking what they called a liquid dinner – a few pints of Castle or Lion Lager at the Captain's Cabin, a popular bar a block away at Meikles Hotel. That night, however, the atmosphere on the desk was one of rebellion and extreme anger. Even as they processed the front-page story stating that the cause of the crash was yet to be determined, the subs repeatedly and venomously cursed Zipra's guerrillas and their commander-in-chief, Joshua Nkomo, with the name of rival politician Robert Mugabe occasionally thrown in. It later transpired that it was, indeed, a SAM-7 surface-to-air missile launched by Zipra that had scored a direct hit on one of the ill-fated Viscount's engines.

I sensed that some of the more derogatory remarks made in unnecessarily loud voices that evening were meant specifically for my ears. Notwithstanding the fact that I was as shocked as anyone by the awful news, there appeared to be an assumption that because I was black, I would support the shooting down of a civilian airliner and the even more dastardly act of killing those who had defied the odds to survive the crash.

Few if any blacks hailed the attack on Flight 825, but one of the tragedies of the struggle for Zimbabwe's liberation was the assumption by the white population that all blacks were terrorist sympathisers, and the equally erroneous assumption by the guerrillas that most blacks, especially those living in the cities, were collaborators of the Smith regime.

The fact is that circumstances made blacks wary of openly expressing any opinions about the ongoing war. They tended to keep their thoughts and views to themselves, except in very private conversations, just in case they put themselves at risk by expressing sentiments that might land them in serious trouble with one side or the other. The war engendered a culture of acute fear among the black population.

That night, I wondered how my seniors would have reacted had they known that not only had I been detained by the Special Branch for allegedly transporting Zanla guerrillas in my car, but that such fighters had been regular visitors to my house at Regina Coeli Mission a year before. For the first time, I was frightened to be a journalist and regretted embarking on this career.

While I supported the general thrust of and need for Rhodesia's blacks to wage an armed struggle in order to free themselves from colonial bondage, I could neither accept nor condone that shooting down an aeroplane load of innocent civilians was the right way to go about achieving independence, racial equality and human dignity.

If I had expressed that view at the subs' desk on that September night, no one would have believed me.

Sensing that the newsroom was not the best place for a young black reporter to be in the company of incensed white subeditors, I approached the driver and, after a few quick words exchanged in hushed tones, he stood up and preceded me to a side elevator that was used by the night staff.

When we emerged on the ground floor, I rushed home to the former 'whites-only' suburb of Southerton, recently opened to occupation by blacks. The original residents were low-income whites, mostly artisans and new immigrants who had fled the former Portuguese colony of Mozambique at independence.

In the newsroom, relations between black and white were strained for weeks afterwards. White journalists talked openly of their plans to leave Rhodesia for greener and, more importantly, safer pastures.

By the time Zipra guerrillas shot down another Air Rhodesia Viscount near Kariba on 12 February 1979, there was a steady exodus of whites from the country. In a re-enactment of the *Hunyani* attack five months earlier, *Umniati* took a direct SAM-7 hit in one of the engines, burst into flames and crashed in a ravine in the Vuti African Purchase Area.

This time, there were no survivors.

A few months later, the huge fuel storage depot in the Southerton Industrial Area went up in flames. The fire raged unquenchably. Fire tenders brought in from South Africa battled for a week alongside the local fire brigade before the inferno was subdued. The war had finally encroached on Salisbury.

By September, Ian Smith, accompanied by Bishop Abel Muzorewa, faced Robert Mugabe and Joshua Nkomo across the conference table under the watchful eye of Lord Carrington at Lancaster House to negotiate a peace deal.

4

Embedded journalism

IT WAS COMMON CAUSE during Zimbabwe's guerrilla war that many of the missionaries stationed in infiltrated areas – and the Catholics in particular – were secretly on the side of the insurgents. In some instances, their support arose from a genuine belief in the moral right of a war seeking to liberate the majority black population from the yoke of injustice and racial discrimination perpetrated by a minority white colonial regime.

Some, however, were also motivated by an expectation that assistance to the guerrillas would result in their mission stations being left undisturbed, with staff permitted to carry on with their work. Perhaps support was in some measure perceived as being an investment in the future security of a mission once a black government assumed power.

At Regina Coeli, I had had a rare opportunity to witness first-hand the working relationship between the guerrillas and the missionaries. Groups of freedom fighters had freely entered the premises to organise meetings with both pupils and staff members with the full knowledge and often the blessing of the missionaries. For their part, the missionaries made contributions of money, food and medical supplies to the guerrillas, whose wounded fighters received medical treatment at mission hospitals in some cases.

During 1977, I was witness to atrocities committed by both Zanla guerrillas and the Rhodesian security forces, in most cases against innocent black peasants. While they strenuously denied such allegations, both warring factions were guilty of heinous carnage. When the victims were white farmers, the guerrillas were quick to claim responsibility as part of their psychological warfare. When black peasant farmers fell victim to atrocities, each side blamed the other, except when guerrillas claimed they had killed a government informer or a soldier or policeman on leave in the village. The security forces, on the other hand, accepted responsibility for killing black civilians only when they were said to have been caught in the crossfire of battle against insurgents.

The most sensational atrocities were the brutal attacks on missionaries. While both sides denied responsibility, both the Rhodesian and international media, invariably relying on information provided by Combined Operations (ComOps) headquarters, always pinned the blame on Zanla or Zipra. The war zones were no-go areas for the various military correspondents based in Salisbury, and little effort was made to independently verify information or details. On a balance of probabilities, however, Zanla guerrillas regarded missionaries as essential allies, while to the Rhodesian soldier the missionary was an enemy collaborator, and thus regarded as a foe as well.

The first casualty of any war is, indeed, the truth.

My curiosity about the authenticity of some of the allegations disseminated by the Rhodesian media about guerrilla acts against the missionary community was aroused by one particular incident, long before I became a journalist. It was reported in December 1976 that a lone terrorist had ambushed and killed the seventy-one-year-old former Roman Catholic Bishop of Bulawayo, the Right Reverend Adolf Schmidt. Also killed in the incident were a priest, Father Possenti Weggarten, and a nun, Sister Maria Francis van den Berg. The murders took place on a lonely dirt road near Lupane, in the province of Matabeleland North, an area known to be infiltrated by Zipra guerrillas loyal to Joshua Nkomo's Zapu.

According to initial press reports, the sole survivor of the ambush had been taken to Bulawayo. Sister Ermenfried Knauer had been shot in the left leg as she sought shelter under the bishop's car.

Dr Johanna Davis, the medical superintendent of St Luke's Mission Hospital, who led the police to the scene of the murders and accompanied the surviving nun to Bulawayo, told reporters that the bishop's party had been driving from Regina Mundi, their home mission station, to St Luke's to visit a sick friend. Along the way a single gunman, described as a terrorist, had held them up and demanded money. 'We told him we had no money with us,' Sister Ermenfried said, 'that we were missionaries just out for the afternoon. If he really needed money, he should come back with us to the mission and we would help him.

'The terrorist replied that as we had no money, he would have to shoot us. He began gunning us down, starting with the bishop. He riddled him with bullets. Then he mowed down the others.'

According to Dr Davis, Sister Ermenfried said the gunman was wearing a balaclava and camouflage uniform and carrying a machine gun.

The Catholic Bishop of Bulawayo, the Right Reverend Henry Karlen, said he had told a black man who was returning to Geneva to give the following message to Mugabe and Nkomo: 'Tell those two gentlemen what has happened and that I said, "This is the reward for our work for Africans; for working for them all our lives."'

The murders coincided with the ill-fated Geneva conference, convened as the latest attempt to bring Rhodesian Front leader Ian Smith and the externally based nationalist organisations, Robert Mugabe's Zanu and Joshua Nkomo's Zapu, to the negotiating table. Charges and counter-charges over the killings overshadowed any progress made at the talks. Both Zanu and Zapu and, curiously, Bishop Abel Muzorewa's internally based African National Council as well, blamed the Rhodesian Army's Selous Scouts for the bloodbath, while the government delegation said this terrorist action should be taken as a warning about the future of Rhodesia.

Zanu issued a statement, protesting: 'It is preposterous for us to be accused of murdering civilians.'

One reporter, however, summed up the general sentiment among the press corps covering the Geneva conference: 'Their vehement denial of terrorist involvement and the blame they have placed on Rhodesian security forces are being regarded with utter disbelief by most foreign journalists.'

Sister Ermenfried, meanwhile, added a new dimension to the saga when she revealed details of an offer made by a Rhodesian farmer to fly her to Geneva to give evidence of the attack to any interested parties.

'The wounded nun said she was not in a fit condition to travel at the moment,' the *Chronicle* reported in what was obviously an effort to gain as much political mileage as possible out of a tragedy that had barely been investigated.

'She said there was no doubt in her mind that the attack was carried out by a terrorist. She dismissed out of hand the allegations made in Geneva by the nationalist leaders that the atrocity was carried out by Rhodesian security forces.'

Interviewed in hospital, Sister Ermenfried said the gunman had twice shouted out, 'Missionaries are enemies of the people!' before he opened fire. She said the assailant was unable to look his victims in the eye as he pulled the trigger, and it was apparent that he had been taught anti-missionary slogans as part of his terrorist training.

How the good nun arrived at the conclusion that the utterance of these words stemmed from the military training received by Zipra guerrillas, she was not asked to explain. Neither was she asked to clarify how, in those terrifying and traumatic moments while she lay prone under the bishop's car, she was able to closely study the gunman's eye movement.

Her superior, however, denied Sister Ermenfried permission to travel to Geneva, much to the chagrin of the farmer who had offered to finance the trip.

'We are not going to enter into politics,' said Mother Adelberta Reinhart, Mother General of the Missionary Sisters of the Precious Blood, firmly. 'They have more to do in Geneva now than talk to Sister Ermenfried. I would not allow her to go.'

The benevolent farmer protested vehemently.

'I am very disappointed with the Mother General's decision. Is there no higher authority that can reverse her order? I want this nun to go to Geneva. I want her to confront the people there and tell them the truth about what had happened to her,' he insisted.

I wondered why this unnamed farmer did not have faith in the ability of the foreign press to communicate the essential details of the incident to the delegates attending the Geneva conference, and why he had taken such a personal interest in the murders. Given the obsession in Rhodesian Front circles to link the atrocity and the conference, I pondered whether an attempt to influence the course of events in Switzerland, rather than disappointment that the missionaries had had no money on them, might not have been a more plausible motivation for the attack in the first place.

The conclusion that the Lupane gunman was a terrorist was reached on the basis of Sister Ermenfried's testimony, but she was clearly oblivious to the fact that the Selous Scouts routinely impersonated guerrillas and that one did not necessarily have to train as an insurgent in Russia or China to be able to shout, 'Missionaries are enemies of the people.'

Apart from saying that her attacker wore a balaclava and camouflage uniform and carried a machine gun, Sister Ermenfried did not offer any reason for her categoric identification of the man as a terrorist or guerrilla. A determined investigative journalist would have made some effort to probe further before rushing back to the office to bash out this sensational story.

Events more than four years later were to prove conclusively, to the mortification of both the security forces and the local and foreign press, that the Selous Scouts indeed had had an agenda to undermine the credibility of guerrilla insurgents by launching attacks on religious institutions. In one such attack, the only casualties had been the soldiers themselves.

On Thursday 14 February 1980, during the run-up to the landmark majority rule elections, there was a spate of mysterious explosions in Salisbury. One bomb detonated next to a church in the city centre, close to the Monomatapa Hotel. Another exploded near St Michael's Church, Runyararo, in the populous black township of Harare, now called Mbare. The following day an unexploded bomb was found outside the Roman Catholic Cathedral at the corner of Fourth Street and Rhodes, now Herbert Chitepo Avenue.

The police immediately announced that the bombs formed part of a terror campaign against Christian churches. Bishop Muzorewa and Ian Smith were more forthright. This could only be the work of Marxists, they said, pointing out that Mugabe had once stated that all religious holidays would be banned if Zanu-PF assumed power.

The facts on the ground violently contradicted the assertions of both politicians, however, and in due course it transpired that the bombs were part of a cunning dirty tricks campaign mounted by the Selous Scouts to discredit Mugabe and Zanu-PF ahead of the pending poll.

The explosion outside St Michael's Church had occurred in the back seat of the car carrying the device. The two occupants of the vehicle had died instantly. It turned out that both were members of the notorious Selous Scouts.

They were named by ComOps as Lieutenant Edward Piringondo and Corporal Morgan Moyo. According to the official communiqué, it had been established that 'about fifty-five minutes before the explosion at Harare, the two men had made a telephone report to their duty officer. They had information about the presence of two Zanla terrorists. The men were instructed to follow up their information and to report back when possible.'

No explanation was offered as to how two soldiers came to be tracking two terrorists while in a car carrying a bomb in the back seat, or why, for that matter, they were undertaking police work and taking orders from a police command structure. Nor did the official statement explain why Piringondo and Moyo were roaming the streets of Harare in a bomb-laden vehicle in pursuit of alleged terrorists at a time when, in terms of the ceasefire agreement signed at Lancaster House, they were supposed to be confined to barracks.

Piringondo had been a resident of Harare township, a notorious hoodlum who had dabbled in showbiz, promoting musical shows, before disappearing from the social scene. One of his most bizarre antics was to switch an electric stove on and force a rival in a love triangle to sit on the hot plates, causing severe burns to the wretched man's posterior.

The gruesome campaign mounted by the Selous Scouts against Zanla, especially regarding the unexploded bomb found outside the Roman Catholic Cathedral on Fourth Street, was not without elements of peripheral melodrama. Whoever had planted the bomb had also deposited next to it some posters bearing slogans handwritten in Shona. The posters were supposed to provide a useful link to the identity of the bombers, and many of them sported the words: '*Pamberi neMugabe*'.

This is a common Zanu-PF slogan, the Shona for 'Hail Mugabe'. However, no self-respecting Shona-speaker would utter, let alone scrawl, '*Pamberi neMugabe*'. It is well known that white Zimbabweans – and Rhodesians before them – who have learned the language spoken by the majority of the population tend to confuse the prefix *ne*, meaning 'with an object', and the prefix *na*, which means 'with a person'. To the linguistically astute, this grammatical aberration was sufficient evidence that the bomb concealed on the church premises had not been the handiwork of Shona-speaking Zanla operatives, but more likely that of their military nemesis, the Selous Scouts.

Zanu-PF would never have convinced the local or foreign press that it was not responsible for the bomb explosion at St Michael's if the evidence had not incontrovertibly linked the ubiquitous Selous Scouts to the operation.

The most daring and outrageous episode in the dirty tricks campaign took place in the Midlands city of Gwelo a week before the general elections in March 1980. *Moto*, a vibrant Catholic newspaper printed and published there, had recently resurfaced after many years in mothballs following its ban by the Smith regime. The hard-hitting tabloid had fiercely supported the nationalist struggle with an editorial content that was a blend of religious, ecumenical and political articles.

On Saturday 23 February, an issue of *Moto* hit the streets. Strangely, the date on the masthead read 12 February. Even readers who missed this glaring error were taken aback by the front-page 'scoop'. Under the headline 'Robert Mugabe – Profile of the Man', the writer launched a wicked attack on the Zanu-PF leader, characterising him as having an Oedipus complex and a lust for power that would stop at nothing. While the latter would turn out to be true in later years, no shred of evidence was offered at the time to support the devastating allegation.

'Who is Robert Mugabe?' the writer asked. 'Is he an enlightened progressive Christian leader of a people seeking their destiny, or is he a ruthless, power-hungry Marxist heathen?'

As a parting shot, the profiler suggested: 'One cannot escape the conclusion that he is a psychopath suffering from paranoia – in layman's terms, the man can be considered mentally ill.'

If such a story should have appeared on the front page of a Zimbabwean newspaper at any time in 2005 or 2006, the publication would have sold out in record time. Even in 1980, that edition of *Moto* sold like the proverbial hotcakes. But by mid-morning, word had got round that the publication was a fraud, and Zanu-PF supporters and campaign strategists heaved a collective sigh of relief.

Vengeance was swift, or so it was meant to appear. At 2 a.m. the next day, the printing press at Mambo, where *Moto* was produced, was blown up. The perpetrators sought to create the impression that Mugabe and his men had orchestrated this act in revenge for his vilification in the article.

The plot backfired dismally, however. As fate would have it, the bombers died in the explosion. The charred remains of one were positively identified as those of a white person. Not even the most fervent Rhodesian Front supporter could accept that a white militant would carry out such an iniquitous assignment on behalf of Mugabe. The Selous Scouts had been caught with their dirty hands in the cookie jar again, or, to put it more graphically, with their proverbial pants down, and yet again Zanu-PF was easily able to persuade the press that the bomb had been the handiwork of the Rhodesian security forces or some other white faction that had an axe to grind with Mugabe.

Ironically, two decades into independence, Zanu-PF would resort to the same tactics when the offices and printing press of the newly launched *Daily News* were bombed. By then, the party had become as unpopular as was Smith's Rhodesian Front prior to independence, and Mugabe had shown himself to be a ruthless dictator.

During the war of liberation the Rhodesian security forces had good reason to target missionaries for attack. The Catholics had aligned themselves with the nationalist struggle since the start of the guerrilla insurgency, and the Catholic Commission for Justice and Peace had published a report outlining atrocities committed by the security forces against civilians. Only a few years after independence, the same commission would incur Mugabe's wrath by publishing a damning report on the brutal massacre of an estimated 20 000 Ndebele civilians by the Zimbabwean Army's Five Brigade during the infamous Gukurahundi campaign in Matabeleland.

The case of Donal Lamont, the Catholic Bishop of Umtali, probably best illustrates the love–hate relationship between Rhodesia's Catholic clergy and the Smith regime.

Lamont arrived in Rhodesia in 1946 to establish a Carmelite mission. In 1957 he was appointed Bishop of Umtali, a diocese stretching along the Mozambican border, which would become a hotbed of inexorable Zanla incursion two decades later.

By then, Lamont had become an outspoken critic of the Smith regime's racially discriminatory policies. In an open letter delivered to the rebel prime minister, Lamont wrote: 'Conscience compels me to state that your administration, by its clearly racial and oppressive policies and by its stubborn refusal to change, is largely responsible for the injustices which have provoked the present disorder and it must, in that measure, be considered guilty of whatever misery and bloodshed may follow.'

In 1972, after insurgents had launched the seven-year guerrilla war in earnest, Lamont openly accused Smith of causing the ensuing bloodshed.

'Far from your policies defending Christianity and Western civilisation, as you claim,' he wrote, 'they mock the law of Christ and make communism attractive to the African people.'

To the majority of the white population, this was unadulterated blasphemy. Lamont denounced white people and all aspects of colonial rule, while praising the black nationalist leaders and their 'freedom fighters'. To the whites, Lamont became a traitor and an object of hatred. They accused him of siding with the freedom fighters while ignoring their alleged acts of brutality against innocent people, including priests and nuns.

He was branded Public Enemy Number One, and as Rhodesia's security situation deteriorated, the Smith regime felt obliged to deal with this particular thorn in its flesh.

With the war escalating in 1976 as new fronts were opened along the eastern border districts and the death toll mounted, Lamont was brought to trial. Under the iniquitous and repressive Law and Order Maintenance Act, later to be inherited and used by Mugabe against his political opponents, the clergyman was charged with encouraging nuns and other mission workers to give medical treatment to wounded guerrillas. He was also accused of discouraging them from reporting the presence of Zanla guerrillas to the authorities.

To prevent mission staff from being incriminated by testifying on his behalf, Lamont pleaded guilty. He argued in his defence that Christians should not act as informers for the state or refuse medical aid to anyone 'regardless of religion or politics'.

He was sentenced to ten years in prison, but this was reduced on appeal to four years. In March 1977, Smith stripped him of his citizenship and expelled the fiery Catholic priest from Rhodesia.

Lamont was nominated for a Nobel Peace Prize in 1978 and awarded honorary degrees by several American universities. When Zimbabwe gained independence, Mugabe personally invited him back and Lamont returned in 1980 to a hero's welcome.

But his stay was short-lived. Confronted with rampant corruption under Mugabe and widespread government-sponsored violence in the aftermath of independence, Lamont quickly became disillusioned with the turn of political events in the new Republic of Zimbabwe. Within two years he had resigned as Bishop of Mutare, packed his bags again and returned to Dublin, where he died at the age of ninety-two.

Another Carmelite clergyman, Father Pascal Slevin, was the priest in charge of Mount St Mary's Mission in the guerrilla-infested district of Hwedza. Father Pascal was arrested and eventually deported after being accused of harbouring Zanla guerrillas and recruiting youths for military training. He was also charged with transporting recruits for guerrilla training. Why Zanla would turn on such a benefactor, only ComOps might have been able to explain.

Mount St Mary's was close to where Seduce Mapondera had been captured, and also had the dubious distinction of producing the future commander of the Zimbabwe Defence Force (ZDF), Constantine Chiwenga, as well as Perrence Shiri, the future head of the Air Force of Zimbabwe, who achieved notoriety as commander of the infamous Five Brigade during the Gukurahundi massacres.

While in their third year of secondary school at Mount St Mary's, Chiwenga and Shiri – then known as Bigboy Samson Chikerema – had absconded one night and crossed into Mozambique to join Zanla. Both had been Ursula's classmates at Mount St Mary's. When Father Pascal returned to Zimbabwe for a brief visit in 2002, Chiwenga hosted a sumptuous lunch in his honour, inviting a number of former pupils from Mount St Mary's, including my wife. She and I were thus among the guests at one of the several opulent mansions owned by the ZDF chief in Harare and Marondera.

I did not have the heart to ask Father Pascal whether he could reconcile the sacrifices and suffering of the rural population at the time of his deportation in 1978 with the corruption, bad governance and wanton pursuit of obscene opulence that had become a way of life for the ruling elite by 2002. Some months after the luncheon, Mugabe launched a crackdown on corrupt officials, and the names of our hosts, Chiwenga and his wife Jocelyn, headed a list of thirty allegedly crooked politicians compiled by the police. Approached by a journalist to respond to claims that she and her spouse had illegally exported funds to purchase three houses in South Africa and the United Kingdom, Jocelyn Chiwenga said, 'If you write your nonsense, I will deal with you.' The story was both written and published, but, oddly enough, the military commander's wife never carried out her threat.

During the war, the Selous Scouts would have routinely attacked missionaries as part of their strategy to discredit Zipra and Zanla. Why else would they have impersonated guerrillas if not to carry out covert operations? The insurgents themselves would certainly have had nothing to gain by targeting the rural mission schools and hospitals that formed a vital part of their support infrastructure and offered them both food and medical assistance.

During my time as a teacher at a remote Catholic institution, I witnessed nothing but cordial relations between the missionaries and visiting Zanla groups. Because of their religious convictions, missionaries and their staff members continued to go about their business unarmed, and their quarters, clinics, hospitals and schools remained unprotected throughout the war at their own request, a display of arrogance that was deeply resented by the security forces.

Before Regina Coeli closed its doors in August 1977, the security forces knew full well that the mission was a regular port of call for Zanla groups. They were also aware that pupils abandoned their education in droves to join the liberation struggle. By the time our school was shut down, enrolment had plummeted from 240 to little more than a hundred boys and girls. The bulk of guerrillas infiltrating Rhodesia from Mozambique and Zambia were products of the mission schools.

In my opinion, the bonds between the young guerrillas and their former mentors were so strong that if Father Martin O'Reagan, the priest in charge of Regina Coeli, had been gunned down during the night and posters denigrating Jesus Christ had been strewn all over the mission grounds, I would never have believed it to be the work of Zanla.

About seventy kilometres north of Regina Coeli, in the Katerere communal lands, was Emmanuel Secondary School, a mission station run by the Elim Pentecostal Church. Two of my friends from university, Roderick Chirima and Steen Gumbo, were teachers at Emmanuel, and when I once visited them, they told me how heavily infiltrated the area was and how the security forces rarely ventured there. Soon after the closure of Regina Coeli, the Elim missionaries arranged to relocate the school from what had become an active battleground. They reportedly acted on the counsel of local guerrilla commanders who were anxious to avoid a repetition of the horrific disaster at Regina Coeli.

Elim Mission moved more than 200 kilometres south to the premises of Eagle School, a prestigious institution for wealthy white boys, high up in the scenic Vumba Mountains. Eagle was fifteen kilometres from Umtali and close to the Mozambican border. It had been forced to close as the war escalated. The relocation of Elim to this mountain paradise was an obvious intrusion on the serenity and exclusivity of a white haven, and it has never been ascertained how the move was perceived by the resident farmers and other wealthy whites.

For more than a century, however, the prime real estate of Vumba, with its scenic views and temperate climate, which residents boasted were reminiscent of Scotland, had escaped the presence of mission schools for blacks. To add insult to injury, in an area where every farmstead served as a mini-armoury, where white residents ventured into Umtali with their FNs at the ready and often in military convoys, the missionaries spurned official security protection.

Whether or not the Pentecostal missionaries maintained their established bonds with the Zanla guerrillas after moving to Eagle has never been ascertained, but on the night of 23 June 1978, Elim Mission was subjected to the most gruesome missionary massacre of the entire war. A *Sunday Mail* reporter visited the scene afterwards, courtesy of ComOps, and wrote:

Eight British missionaries and four young children – including a three-week-old baby – were bayoneted to death by terrorists on Rhodesia's Eastern border on Friday night in the worst massacre of whites since the six-year-old war began. Three of the missionaries were men and the others women.

A sixth woman was stabbed and beaten and left for dead. She staggered 300 m into the freezing Vumba bush to spend the night before being found semi-conscious by security forces yesterday. Despite intensive care in a Salisbury hospital she subsequently died.

The gruesome murders, by a group of eight to ten terrorists, happened at Emmanuel Mission School – 15 km southeast of Umtali and eight kilometres from the Mozambique border – once used as the Eagle boarding school.

Even hardened security men were stunned by the bloody scene and stood around silently. 'The quiet is uncanny,' said one. When local and international journalists arrived at the scene of the massacre the mutilated and blood-stained bodies of three men, four women and five children – including a three-week-old baby – were lying as they had been found that morning.

None of the journalists was prompted to ask the obvious question, namely why the bodies of the victims were still lying as they had been found when the press arrived later in the day. One might have thought that the security forces could at least have covered the bodies to accord them a modicum of dignity, given the macabre circumstances of their death.

Nor did any of the reporters attempt to establish whether Zanla guerrillas were known to call at the mission or what the motive for the attack might have been. The official military conclusion that Zanla was responsible for the murders was simply accepted and printed by the press.

In an article written in 1977 in defence of the Selous Scouts, journalist Chris Vermaak, who described himself as a contemporary military correspondent, wrote: 'We find that a number of recent acts of ruthless violence in Rhodesia which were indeed committed by terrorists belonging either to the Nkomo or Mugabe wing of the so-called Patriotic Front, have been consistently attributed to the Selous Scouts. The lie has been spread abroad by both Nkomo and Mugabe, perpetuated by a number of misguided church leaders, gullible journalists guided only by financial preferences and foreign deserters from the Rhodesian forces who should never have been allowed into the country in the first place.'

This passing reference to disclosures made by undesirable deserters was an unwitting admission by an ardent supporter of the Selous Scouts that there was much about their operations that should have been kept under wraps.

Vermaak also referred to the cold-blooded murder of Bishop Schmidt, Father Weggarten and Sister Maria Francis at Lupane in 1976. Regarding Sister Ermenfried's testimony that 'the terrorist denounced the missionaries as enemies of the people before opening fire', Vermaak claimed that one Albert Sumne Ncube, a member of Zipra, had admitted when captured by police that he had committed these and other murders, and that he had undergone military training in Tanzania.

Conveniently, Ncube was said to have subsequently escaped from custody and to have possibly returned to Zambia, which, if true, would make him the only guerrilla to have escaped from security force custody during the entire war!

Coverage of Rhodesia's guerrilla war by both local and foreign correspondents was hampered by restrictions imposed by the security forces. Reports on the externally based nationalist organisations were declared unlawful, and few of the foreign correspondents ventured anywhere outside Salisbury, unless they travelled on facility trips organised by ComOps to cover major Rhodesian Army successes or some gruesome atrocity ascribed to the guerrillas.

Embedded journalism, along with its attendant spirit of patriotism, was entrenched in Rhodesia long before it was adopted and fine-tuned by the US military during the controversial bid to topple Iraqi dictator Saddam Hussein in 2003.

Reports on the bush war were therefore based on information gleaned from press statements released by ComOps and the ministry of information. Press conferences and news releases arranged by the information and publicity secretaries of the internally based political parties also generated much welcome copy for the local and foreign press.

David Mukome of Bishop Muzorewa's United African National Council (UANC) and James Dzvova of veteran nationalist leader the Reverend Ndabaningi Sithole's internally based Zanu faction were particularly enterprising. Mukome found a ready audience among journalists increasingly convinced or secretly praying that Muzorewa was politically invincible and who totally ignored the externally based politicians, Mugabe and Nkomo. A fair percentage of foreign coverage comprised extracts from the *Rhodesia Herald* and radio broadcasts. Some local journalists moonlighted for the international media, writing stories that simply re-angled or incorporated their own copy.

One practical problem faced by foreign correspondents was that even those who had been stationed in Salisbury for years never took the trouble to learn the local languages.

Interpreters are a useful tool for journalists, but in a war situation, they can all too easily convey to reporters the message they themselves want to broadcast rather than what the sources are actually saying. Zimbabwean politicians who want to get a message across to their supporters effectively always resort to speaking in either Shona or Ndebele. When Mugabe addressed his mammoth homecoming rally at Zimbabwe Grounds, Highfields, on 27 January 1980, a recently arrived British journalist attached himself to local reporters, without prior arrangement, and proceeded to pester them with constant and irritating requests for translation of the Zanu-PF leader's address.

'What did he say?' the foreign journalist asked as the stadium exploded with thunderous applause.

'Nothing important,' one of the local journalists coolly informed him.

'Then why are the people applauding?' the visitor enquired innocently as those around him reduced Mugabe's electrifying speech to furious shorthand.

In many instances, coverage of the war and the nationalist struggle was aimed less at informing the public on matters of importance and relevance than on meeting a perceived patriotic need to portray a successful campaign by Smith's illegal regime. In this regard, seasoned journalists set precedents that Zimbabwe's post-independence political leadership would seek to perpetuate in order to entrench themselves in power. Mugabe and the former guerrillas would preach about the need for patriotism just as fervently as had Smith and his cohorts in their day.

The self-serving insistence on partisan journalism and the tendency to want to control the media, spearheaded by Zimbabwe's first minister of information and publicity, Nathan Shamuyarira, was merely a continuation of practices applied during the Rhodesian Front's heyday.

But for post-independence journalists, the expectations of the new ruling elite under Mugabe would create immense practical problems and professional challenges. The demand for loyalty from Zimbabwe's media intensified in inverse proportion to the popularity of Mugabe and Zanu-PF, especially as the new millennium ushered in an era of vibrant political opposition and demand for wholesale change.

5

Media in transition

WHEN THE SECOND Air Rhodesia Viscount was shot down near Kariba, I was working for the *National Observer*, acquired by RP&P shortly after I completed my cadet course. The newspaper had an established circulation among black readers but was suffering from the exigencies of undercapitalisation.

My transfer from the *Herald* to the *Observer* newsroom on the second floor of Herald House opened a new window of professional opportunity. To start with, I was immediately promoted from cadet to junior reporter. Among my colleagues were Giles Kuimba, Lovemore Chiweshe, sports reporter Assel Gwekwerere and photographer Jimmy Salani. One of the *Herald* subeditors, Fred Cleary, was appointed editor and two new members of staff were recruited: political reporter Marion Duncan and ace photographer John Mauluka, arguably Zimbabwe's most enterprising photographer up to the time of his retirement from the *Daily News* in 2001.

Cleary found himself in something of a predicament. He was not a journalist of particularly clear or inspired editorial vision, and it took him a considerable time to come to terms with his transformation from the coalface position of subeditor to that of editor, which required him to make executive decisions. Every edition of a newspaper is the result of decisions taken on the spot, under mounting pressure and against the clock, and the top editorial echelon is no place for vacillation, but Cleary also had another handicap.

Appointed to edit a newspaper specifically aimed at Rhodesia's black population, he had no idea how his readers lived, though the closest of Salisbury's townships, Harare, was a mere five or six kilometres from his office. He was thus almost entirely reliant on the initiative, enterprise and judgement of his staff, and the black journalists in particular, to identify content that would interest the readers.

In the run-up to the 1979 parliamentary elections, which excluded the exiled nationalist parties and resulted in Bishop Abel Muzorewa being sworn in as head of the short-lived Republic of Zimbabwe-Rhodesia, chief reporter Chiweshe came up with a brilliant idea. The *Observer* conducted a national poll to determine which of the three black political contenders was the most popular. The candidates were Chief Jeremiah Chirau, the illiterate leader of the government-sponsored Zimbabwe United Peoples' Organisation, the Reverend Ndabaningi Sithole, a veteran nationalist and president of the original Zimbabwe African National Union, and Muzorewa, the Methodist cleric who was thrust by circumstance into leadership of the United African National Council.

Rudimentary though it was, the poll indicated victory for Muzorewa. Cleary ran the results as the front-page lead, the edition sold out within hours of hitting the streets and management ordered additional copies printed immediately.

The *Observer* was generally regarded as more favourable towards the nationalist struggle and the plight and political aspirations of the majority black population than its sister publications, the *Herald* and the *Sunday Mail*, and it consistently outsold the *African Times*, the Smith government's own 'newspaper for Africans'. Few discerning or self-respecting urban blacks would be seen holding a copy of the ministry of information's propaganda sheet, which was distributed free of charge and claimed an unlikely readership of more than one million. In fact, the bulk of copies was delivered to rural schools and business centres, where bundles, still securely tied with string, lay defiantly in public lavatories until they were shredded for use as toilet paper.

Working on a newspaper where journalists had so much freedom and latitude was an absolute godsend that was unimaginable on the *Herald*. Even as a junior reporter, I was able to develop a fairly flexible work ethic and cultivate fruitful relationships with some of the foreign correspondents covering the story of Rhodesia's protracted struggle for liberation.

The unofficial dean of the foreign press corps in the 1970s was John Edlin, a wily New Zealander who was the Salisbury correspondent for Associated Press. Other prominent and long-term correspondents were Jacques Claffin of United Press International, Ian Mills of the BBC, Matts Holmberg of *Dagens Nyheter* in Stockholm, Christopher Munnion, who reported for the *Daily Telegraph*, Yutaka Shinoda of *Mainichi Shimbun* in Tokyo, Rodney Pinder of Reuters, Martin Meredith of the *Guardian*, and Angus Shaw and Dave Thomas of Argus African News Service. Godwin Matatu, who filed for the London *Observer*, was the only black Rhodesian working for a foreign publication.

These were the big names of Harare's press corps, the journalists who would record the dying moments of colonial Rhodesia and the emergence of the Republic of Zimbabwe. I regarded them with a respect bordering on trepidation. Some of them inspired me with an ambition to make a name as a journalist, as they had done. It did not escape my notice, however, that in covering a nation at war, some among them rarely ventured beyond the outskirts of Salisbury, often even relying on stringers (local correspondents) for details of events taking place in the black townships around the capital.

Having lived and worked in London for many years, the hard-drinking Matatu had returned to Salisbury in 1979. Despite his close association with many in the Zanu-PF leadership, notably Nathan Shamuyarira, who was to become the first minister of information, Matatu failed to secure an appointment at any local newspaper, though he was far more experienced than some of the journalists who became editors after independence. He died a disillusioned man in Namibia.

The number of foreign journalists in Salisbury peaked during the four months from January to April 1980. By Independence Day, 18 April, more than 100 foreign correspondents and photographers were on hand to witness the Union Jack being lowered for the last time and see the red, black, yellow and green flag of the new Zimbabwe hoisted in its place.

Once peace settled over the land, Zimbabwe ceased to be a major story and the foreign journalists left, mostly for Johannesburg, from where they would launch occasional forays north of the Limpopo River, if the story was big enough.

I found the approach of Sweden's Holmberg and Japan's Shinoda particularly impressive, since they tended not to run with the pack or rely on the endless stream of official press conferences and government-sponsored facility trips to anywhere beyond the precincts of Salisbury. Holmberg and I developed a strong professional bond, focusing on the growing number of people displaced by the war and crowded into the sprawling refugee complex in the township of Harare. We also occasionally ventured into the rural combat zones of Chiweshe, Mount Darwin and Mutoko, north and north-east of Salisbury. The articles resulting from these daring weekend sorties took my editor, my colleagues and *Observer* readers by surprise on account of their novelty and bravado. Most of the people in the areas that we covered were happy to talk to Holmberg, because he represented a country generally recognised as one of the major European supporters of the liberation struggle. Shinoda, an unusually hulking Japanese, accompanied us on some of these trips.

Our reports highlighted the plight of the peasants caught in the crossfire. The Smith government removed thousands from their rural homes, and resettled them in hastily established protected villages, where they lived behind barbed wire barricades and were guarded day and night by the notorious district assistants. The government had created the DAs, a paramilitary force, for this specific purpose, as the war escalated. Being mostly illiterate, poorly trained and ill equipped, the average DA routinely abused his newfound power, treating villagers with both brutality and disdain. As a result, they were extremely unpopular and became a favourite and easy target of Zanla guerrillas. The killing or wounding of DAs was a regular feature of ComOps communiqués.

The primary aim of the protected villages was to separate the civilians from the guerrillas. Villagers were not allowed to take any food beyond the perimeter of the settlements, even when they went out to work in their fields. This rule was designed to prevent food from reaching the guerrillas known to lurk in the surrounding mountainous terrain. In order to stop guerrillas from entering the protected villages, peasants were searched each time they passed through the heavily guarded gates.

Women balancing earthenware pots or buckets of water on their heads went down on their knees for the DAs to stir the contents with a wooden rod to ensure that no metal or other object had been hidden in the liquid. It was deplorable practices such as this that exposed the DAs to the hatred and ridicule of the villagers. Shona culture dictates that a woman will kneel only before her husband or elders of his extended family, so the DAs took special satisfaction from the humiliation of women forced to their knees in front of gun-toting imbeciles representing an illegal and despised regime in far-off Salisbury.

During the ceasefire that followed the signing of an agreement between the

Smith regime and the internally based parties, Muzorewa's new Zimbabwe-Rhodesia government launched a massive campaign to entice Zanla and Zipra guerrillas into surrendering. Muzorewa had campaigned on the false premise that he wielded sufficient influence with the guerrillas to persuade them to lay down their arms and join the security forces. So when only a handful of guerrillas responded to his call, he took it upon himself to visit the operational areas and personally appeal to the guerrillas via the villagers, who were known to be in contact with them.

Holmberg and I threw caution to the wind and travelled to the Zanla-infested Mount Darwin district to cover one such rally. Soldiers drove villagers to the venue, where they listened passively as Muzorewa waxed lyrical about the benefits of the peace that had descended on Zimbabwe-Rhodesia. Comrade Max, one of the few Zanla guerrillas who had surrendered and had quickly become the linchpin of the campaign, was paraded as a fine example of what all patriotic guerrillas should be doing.

'You go to the comrades and tell them the peace they have been fighting for has now come to our country,' Muzorewa enjoined the bored villagers. 'Tell them now is the time to come back.'

'You go and tell them yourself,' a villager jibed in an undertone from close to where I sat, much to the suppressed amusement of those within earshot.

'They are not too far away, by the way,' another chimed in conspiratorially. 'In fact, they are observing this circus right now.'

I realised in that instant that Muzorewa and Smith would never win the hearts and minds of the villagers; the guerrillas in the operational zones, which by that time covered most of rural Zimbabwe-Rhodesia, had long secured the support of the peasant population.

Muzorewa was staging his rally in an open space at the foot of a thickly wooded hill, and his security guards scouted the area nervously, doubtless aware that they were probably perilously close to a Zanla base. Much to my relief, the proceedings were cut short in light of the less-than-enthusiastic reception from the crowd.

When a date was set for the first democratic multiparty elections involving Zanu-PF and PF-Zapu after the signing of the Lancaster House Agreement, I sensed instinctively that Muzorewa, Sithole and the much-ridiculed Chief Chirau stood little chance of winning the rural electorate's confidence. Guerrillas were given a deadline of 4 January 1980 to emerge from the bush and turn themselves – and their weapons – in at sixteen designated assembly points. A 1200-strong Commonwealth monitoring force would supervise this process, and Salisbury Airport became a hive of unprecedented activity as a fleet of gigantic C5 Galaxy transports and other aircraft never before seen in Rhodesia disgorged both foreign soldiers and their equipment.

A total of 22 000 guerrillas entered the assembly points after first reporting to a large number of rendezvous points scattered throughout the operational zones, from where they were transported in army trucks and hired buses.

One of the largest assembly points in Manicaland was Foxtrot at Buhera, more than

300 kilometres south of Salisbury. Halfway between the two was St Anne's Mission, one of the rendezvous points for Foxtrot, or Dzapasi, as it was more commonly known among the local population.

Holmberg, Shinoda and I arrived at St Anne's late on the afternoon of Friday 3 January. Our plan was to stay the night and observe events in the makeshift bush camp as the deadline approached. On 11 January, the following story appeared under my byline in the *Observer*:

The moon came out from behind a cloud and suddenly it was midnight, January 3 – the deadline by which the Patriotic Front guerrillas had to move into the various assembly and rendezvous points scattered throughout Rhodesia in the ceasefire exercise.

A few minutes later five Zanla men, heavily armed, filed into the St Anne's rendezvous point in the heart of war-torn Hwedza. They said they had walked a long distance that evening to beat the deadline, but declined to say where they had come from.

Moments later, another three arrived and this became the climax to what had been rather an anxious evening for the 10 British ceasefire monitoring forces stationed at the RV point. With less than three hours to go before the deadline, the monitoring men were becoming rather disappointed at the slow inflow of guerrillas in an area known to be literally swarming with them.

Only 320 Zanla men were in the camp at the time and 300 had been moved out to Foxtrot assembly point in Buhera that morning.

'This area is heavily infiltrated,' said Major Peter Hugh Mills, the monitoring force representative in charge of the RV point. 'There should be hundreds still out in the bush. I suppose we will just have to wait until midnight and see what happens.'

That was at 9 p.m. Exactly 37 minutes later the major was a happy man. For just then 554 returning guerrillas single-filed into the light of the pressure lamp that had been hastily set for them to see their way in.

An hour later another 224 arrived, bringing the total of guerrillas who had arrived by midnight to about 1 100, while others continued to report in small groups throughout the night. A further 167 men arrived at daybreak on Saturday.

There was a total of 1 403 guerrillas assembled at St Anne's by the time I departed at 8 a.m. on Saturday. Fourteen buses were lined up to transport them to Foxtrot and another five were on the way. A total of 1 763 guerrillas had arrived at the assembly point altogether.

'I think we must be the most successful RV point in the whole country,' said Major Mills as 1 500 heavily armed men milled around the mission complex.

The visit to St Anne's about 170 km southeast of Salisbury was not without its hitches. Halfway through, in Marandellas, I met two foreign journalists also bound for St Anne's. [The two journalists, not named in the story, were Holmberg and Shinoda, and our meeting was no accident.]

Seeking comfort in numbers, we decided to go on together in one car. At the back of my mind this became a cause of much concern. What would be the reaction of the villagers or the guerrillas, should we come across any, to my travelling with white men in an area where probably no white man had travelled in a civilian car for the past two or three years?

All went well until we were within 10 kilometres of St Anne's, when a young man suddenly emerged from the side of the road and approached us where we had stopped to drop off a passenger we had given a lift. [It was advisable in the operational zones to pick up local people who asked for a lift. They would alert you to possible danger, especially the presence of landmines.] The young man examined our faces closely and peered into the car. He asked if we could give him a lift to St Anne's. Although he was not armed, my first thought was, with a pounding heart, that he was a returning guerrilla. Trying to be friendly, I offered him a cigarette and asked where he was coming from.

'From around here,' he said, and turned to look out of the window. Could he perhaps be a returning guerrilla on his way to the RV point, I wondered. I later summoned enough courage to ask. He said he was, but in response to a further question, declined to say where he had trained.

Just then, only four kilometres from our destination, we arrived at a township. Sitting next to the road in the shade of a huge tree was a group of 11 auxiliary forces. Particularly unpopular in the operational zones, the auxiliary forces or Pfumo reVanhu, the Spear of the People, were a quasi-military group loyal to Bishop Abel Muzorewa. They were his UANC party's answer to Zanu-PF's Zanla and PF-Zapu's Zipra.

My first concern was what they would do if they realised that we had a guerrilla as a passenger. We stopped the car without being asked. They looked at each of us and asked about our destination. They said St Anne's was quite close now, and bade us farewell.

Sighing with relief, we travelled for another three kilometres before we came to another township. We saw hundreds of people milling around, some of them armed and obviously guerrillas. We approached slowly, uncertain what kind of reception we would get. Three of them suddenly moved and blocked the road and we stopped.

'Who are you and where are you going?' one asked.

We said we were journalists and that we were trying to find our way to St Anne's. We were asked to identify ourselves.

He pointed at the passenger in the back seat and asked if he was also a journalist. I said he was one of them, a guerrilla that we had picked up on the road.

'You, a Zanla soldier?' he asked menacingly as he examined him more closely. 'Under whom have you been operating?'

Our passenger, visibly shaken, confessed that he was not actually a guerrilla, but only a mujibha. He was about to be hauled out of the car when other guerrillas intervened and said he could travel with us for the remaining half a kilometre to the mission. They asked us for cigarettes and directed us to the RV point.

The mission complex was swarming with armed men when we got there. We learned later that there were 320 Zanla soldiers present at the time. We were directed to the monitoring forces' headquarters, a former girls' dormitory.

After introducing ourselves to the man in charge of the RV point, Major Mills, we told him we intended to spend the night. He said he could not say yes or no, but referred us to the Patriotic Front liaison officer, Gerald Sibanda.

Comrade Gerald, as he said he preferred to be called, said he would have to consult the local commanders and would communicate with us within two hours.

We pointed out that this would place us in a quandary, as we could not possibly leave St Anne's after 6 p.m. and travel back to Marandellas after dark, if their answer was negative. 'Well, I cannot hurry them,' he said tersely, 'you need to wait and hope.'

An hour later he came back with the local commander who was introduced as Comrade Kay Kays. The latter said we could relax, but the final answer still had to come.

Thirty minutes and further consultations later, he came back and said all was well, we were free to stay the night, take any pictures we wanted and speak to anyone we wished to interview. An escort was appointed to show us around the complex.

'One thing I must stress to you, gentlemen,' said Comrade Kay Kays, 'is that journalists can either be friends or enemies, good or bad. We do not know you. All we expect of you is to tell the truth as you see it here tonight.'

And that is how we came to spend the night in the midst of 1 000 armed guerrillas. Several hundred villagers also spent the night inside the RV point and they sang and danced the time away.

After the story was published, I received numerous telephone calls from readers wanting to congratulate me. Some were taken aback that I had dared to go where many other journalists did not. Among the callers was Justin Nyoka of the Zanu-PF information department, who said the article was a fine piece of journalism. He was speaking, he said, not as a Zanu-PF representative, but as a journalist of many years' standing.

Space limitations had forced me to omit many details that would have captivated the readers, such as my encounter with Comrade Chinx, whom I had often heard rendering revolutionary songs over the Voice of Zimbabwe. At St Anne's, I had been brought close to tears as I listened to him performing live before thousands of guerrillas and villagers. It was a moving occasion, particularly when Chinx and his choir struck up 'Maruza imi vapambepfumi' or 'You have been defeated, you imperialist exploiters', a mournful but melodious account of ninety years of settler domination, performed by an expert on Zimbabwe's history and a master of song.

Chinx recited the litany of events starting with the arrival of Cecil John Rhodes's Pioneer Column at Fort Salisbury on 12 September 1890 and moving to the First Chimurenga in 1896, when Mbuya Nehanda, Sekuru Kaguvi and Chief Chingaira

Makoni were executed by the settler regime. Chief Makoni, the traditional leader of the Maungwe people, was engaged in battle with a detachment of white invaders at Mount Mhanda, ten kilometres east of the modern town of Rusape. The Maungwe warriors put up a brave fight before being overwhelmed. The chief and a few of his councillors and warriors sought refuge in a cave in the mountain, but he was tricked into emerging from the cave by the settlers, who decapitated him and shipped his head back to England. Traditional leaders of the Maungwe clan still speak proudly about the famous *Hondo Huru yepaMhanda*, the fierce Battle of Mount Mhanda.

As it turned out, the celebrated Zanla singer and I were members of the same clan. Comrade Chinx's full name was Dick Chingaira Makoni, while mine is Geoffrey Nyarota Makoni.

His song chronicled the ravages of colonial subjugation and plunder, the uprooting and relocation of the indigenous Shona and Ndebele people to make way for the white settlers and the upsurge of nationalism in the 1960s, with emphasis on the role of Zanu, and the rounding up and wholesale detention of the nationalist leaders. He sang about the emergence of the guerrilla war in earnest, the harsh conditions in the training camps in Tanzania and Mozambique, the massacre of thousands of trainees and young refugees during aerial attacks by the Rhodesian security forces, betrayal by traitors and the final victory of the guerrilla campaign at Lancaster House.

It was a marathon song, a classic. I had first listened to this and other revolutionary songs composed by Zanla cadres on the Voice of Zimbabwe, broadcast from Maputo. Guerrillas sang both to entertain themselves in camp and to lift their spirits in times of hardship, and during the long marches from bases in Mozambique to the operational zones inside Rhodesia. Because the marches were long, so were the songs.

That night at St Anne's, Comrade Chinx sang for more than an hour, while other guerrillas intoned, *Maruza imi, maruza imi, maruza imi*, in rich male baritones and the refined soprano of female freedom fighters. It was an emotional and heartbreaking performance.

On their return to civilian life, Comrade Chinx and his choir became popular musicians. Their old songs and new compositions were recorded by the Zimbabwe Broadcasting Corporation (ZBC) and played repeatedly on Radio Two, the new name of the former Rhodesian Broadcasting Corporation's African Service. Chinx and his band, the Barrel of Peace, gradually moved into the ranks of Zimbabwe's leading performing and recording artists, with releases that featured prominently in the local hit parade charts.

When Zanu-PF's fortunes began to wane after 2000, Chinx was one of the musicians who remained steadfastly loyal, performing at party and government-sponsored functions and recording songs as part of the propaganda blitz launched by information minister Jonathan Moyo. His continued association with a party that had become somewhat discredited adversely affected Chinx's image and popularity as a musician.

Another familiar face at St Anne's on that balmy January night was that of Rosemary Magara, one of my more brilliant pupils at Regina Coeli, who had simply abandoned a promising education and crossed into Mozambique one night to join the liberation struggle. We would meet again a year after the ceasefire when we were both passengers on a flight to Dar es Salaam. I was travelling with the presidential delegation on a visit to the Tanzanian capital, while Rosemary was among a group of young women selected for training as secretaries in Dar es Salaam. The mass exodus of white office staff from both the civil service and the private sector after independence had created a severe shortage of skills.

After the return of the guerrillas, the tempo of the 1980 election campaign gathered momentum in earnest. Exactly two months later, on 3 March, Holmberg and I flew to Bulawayo, where we hired a vehicle and proceeded to Matabeleland South on a special assignment – to witness the announcement of election results at a unique location, Assembly Camp Juliet.

My editor, Cleary, buried the resultant story on page 12 of the 7 March issue of the *Observer*. I had hoped that the article, which appeared under my byline and the headline, 'Reconciliation Now, Say Guerrillas', would grace the front page, but perhaps it was too positive a portrayal of the guerrillas in the eyes of an editor who was totally opposed to Mugabe, Nkomo and the transfer of political power to the black majority, and had been firmly convinced that Muzorewa would win the election.

Cleary had made it patently clear that if either Zanu-PF or PF-Zapu was victorious, he would resign and leave the country. Many white journalists expressed similar sentiments, as did the majority of the white community. My story read as follows:

There were no wild scenes of jubilation at Assembly Camp Juliet on Tuesday to greet the announcement of the election results.

Juliet is a sprawling complex in the heart of the Siyoka TTL which has had the unique distinction of being the only camp to accommodate both Zipra and Zanla guerrillas since the ceasefire process started two months ago.

Last Friday, a contingent of 50 Rhodesian security forces arrived to join the 1400 Zanla and 980 Zipra guerrillas encamped. On Monday the Commonwealth monitoring forces departed, leaving the former opposing combatants to get to know each other and establish a peaceful and friendly co-existence. There was apprehension and suspicion at first, but relations are now cordial.

'On Sunday, the security forces played a football match against and at the invitation of Zanla,' explained Supt Derrick Kerr, the officer in charge of the security force contingent at Juliet. 'Fortunately, no side was beaten as the ball was punctured before any goals were scored. We have established rapport in the camp.'

So it was that the Zanla men did not openly celebrate the electoral victory of Zanu-PF. The Zanla liaison officer in the camp, Flavian Danga, said his men had celebrated in their hearts.

'Anyway, had this news come to us as a surprise, perhaps we would have celebrated,' he said. 'But we always knew Zanu-PF was going to win, so the victory did not have as much impact on us as it did on the masses.'

The Zipra liaison officer, Velaphi Nyoni, said morale had sagged a little in his camp after the announcement of the election results, but had soon returned to normal.

'In fact, what we have all been fighting for has been achieved, that is majority rule,' he said. 'We will serve under whoever the people have chosen to be their leader.'

Asked if the guerrillas would have adopted that same attitude if one of the former internal parties had won the election, a Zipra commander, Daniel Gambiza, said that would have been the case.

'That would have been the will of the people and their choice,' he explained. 'The motto in Zimbabwe now is reconciliation.'

Eight months later, in November, the Zanu-PF treasurer and government minister of finance, the fiery Enos Mzombi Nkala, addressed a mass rally at Bulawayo's White City Stadium and threatened PF-Zapu with total destruction. For two days Zanla and Zipra fighters exchanged volleys of AK fire on the streets of the city's newly established suburb, Entumbane, where members of the two guerrilla armies had been separately cantoned while awaiting demobilisation or integration into the new Zimbabwe National Army (ZNA).

In due course, the western provinces of Zimbabwe would be plunged into an ethnic conflagration that raged until a unity agreement was signed between PF-Zapu and the ruling Zanu-PF in 1987. By then, many Zimbabweans had been sapped of their enthusiasm for Zanu-PF, particularly those living in Matabeleland and the Midlands, where an estimated 20 000 innocent civilians had been massacred by Five Brigade during the Gukurahundi campaign.

For me, the process of disillusionment began just six months after independence in a rather unlikely setting. Pocket's Hill is the ZBC's headquarters in Highlands, one of Harare's leafier suburbs. The imposing structure stands next to the famous Borrowdale horse-racing track.

At independence, Justin Nyoka of Zanu-PF's information and publicity department was appointed Zimbabwe's first director of information. He was a pioneer black reporter on the *Herald*, along with the likes of Douglas Takundwa, Reuben Nhandara, Phil Nandu and Alan Hlatshwayo. Though my group had included the first blacks accepted for formal training via the cadet course, journalists such as Nyoka had paved the way for integrated newsrooms long before.

His boss at Linquenda House on Baker Avenue, the information ministry's head-quarters, was Nathan Shamuyarira. He subsequently elevated Nyoka to the position of permanent secretary.

Both men were experienced journalists with solid professional reputations. The ministry never had a more formidable and knowledgeable team in charge of its affairs.

The rapid decline of press freedom in Zimbabwe started in earnest after their departure from Linquenda House and cascaded steadily downwards to almost total collapse two decades later under the mercurial Professor Moyo and his information director, George Charamba. For all their erudition and eloquence, the understanding of these men of the media's function and role in a democratic society was somewhat skewed.

Nyoka, or Comrade Soft as he was known among Zanu-PF cadres in Maputo, had resigned from the *Herald* to become a freelance correspondent, mostly for the BBC. In 1978, he disappeared amid widespread rumours that he had been abducted by Zanla guerrillas, resurfacing months later in Maputo as a member of Zanu-PF's information department.

During the Lancaster House negotiations, Nyoka worked closely with the charismatic and eloquent lawyer Dr Eddison Zvobgo to present the Zanu-PF story to the world. Working in tandem with Willie Musarurwa, the PF-Zapu publicity secretary, they became the darlings of the hordes of journalists covering the talks. Zvobgo, in particular, could be relied upon to come up with either a quotable quote or an attention-grabbing headline at every press conference. Immediately after the cessation of hostilities, the party spokesmen returned to Salisbury and braced themselves to lock horns with the government's awesome propaganda machine, headed by Smith's information minister, PK van der Byl. He was a man of prodigious intellect, matched on the Zanu-PF side only by the flamboyant, ebullient and gregarious Dr Herbert Sylvester Masiyiwa Ushewokunze.

The two men breathed fire into independent Zimbabwe's first parliament as they tested each other's wits in English that was way beyond the ken of many backbenchers. Then they would switch to Van der Byl's mother tongue, Afrikaans, which Ushewokunze had picked up while a student in South Africa. They both possessed an uncanny ability to quote Shakespeare and diverse Latin texts liberally. Twenty years later, it was with great nostalgia for those intellectual skirmishes that I perused the lacklustre contributions of Zanu-PF and Movement for Democratic Change lawmakers published in *Hansard*, the official record of parliamentary proceedings.

Shamuyarira had first stepped into the limelight in the late 1960s, when he was appointed editor of the *Daily News*, a popular newspaper that became the mouthpiece of Rhodesia's downtrodden and voiceless black majority. The publication articulated black aspirations and frustrations, reflecting discontent over institutionalised racial discrimination in land distribution, employment and business opportunities, housing, education, health and other social issues. As it did with the Catholic newspaper, *Moto*, the Smith regime banned the *Daily News*.

On his appointment as minister of information in 1980, Shamuyarira invoked the patriotism of journalists, while enjoining them to focus their work on national development policies and programmes. The newly appointed editors responded with enthusiasm, some more so than others. *Sunday Mail* editor Willie Musarurwa and I exchanged meaningful glances during a briefing at which Mugabe bemoaned the repeated use of his image by both newspapers and television. Both ZTV and the *Herald*, under the stewardship of its first black editor, Farayi Munyuki, were particularly guilty of this overzealousness.

'I was invited to a huge gathering of members of the Johanne Masowe religious sect outside the town of Rusape,' said the prime minister. 'The following morning, the *Herald* published my picture on the front page. I believe that a picture of the impressive gathering of members of this religious sect would have better illustrated the story.'

It is interesting to note that, after 2000, thousands of members of the Apostolic Faith Church, of which the Masowe sect was one of the largest, would save Mugabe from the very real threat of political oblivion. Easily identified by the dazzling white dress of female worshippers, the Apostolics inflated attendance at Zanu-PF rallies at a time when support by party members of other religious denominations was on the decline. Their distinctive attire became a regular feature on the tarmac at Harare International Airport, where members turned out in full force to welcome Mugabe home after his frequent visits abroad. Of course, that was before the European Union and the US imposed smart sanctions on Mugabe and scores of top-ranking Zanu-PF and government officials, thus putting paid to the shopping sprees in Europe's capitals for which First Lady Grace Mugabe, in particular, had become notorious.

Following the massive post-independence exodus of white journalists from news-papers, radio and television stations, as well as from the ministry of information, Shamuyarira and Nyoka set about reorganising not only the latter, but the media sector as a whole. The national Inter-African News Agency (Iana) was renamed Ziana and the ZBC was radically restructured. Its predecessor, an enclave of white interests and appointments, had been gutted by the departure of experienced staff for South Africa and beyond, and a massive recruitment campaign was launched.

In September 1980, I was invited to Pocket's Hill in Borrowdale, the ZBC's head-quarters, for an interview as a senior reporter. I emerged from the experience with my faith in our newly achieved independence seriously dented.

The interview was conducted by Comrade Charles Ndlovu, recently returned from Maputo, where he had been a Voice of Zimbabwe broadcaster, and Dominic Mandizha, a doyen of the RBC's African Service. Ndlovu, then known as Webster Shamu, had been a popular disc jockey with the RBC before he suddenly disappeared and resurfaced in Mozambique, where he immediately changed his name. He was alleged to have fled relentless creditors in Salisbury, having fallen hopelessly into arrears on several loan repayments.

On returning to Salisbury at independence, Shamu remained an uncompromising ex-guerrilla. While many fighters dropped their *noms de guerre* and reverted to their real names, he continued to hide behind his jealously guarded persona as Charles Ndlovu, inviting speculation that he sought either to evade identification by his former persecutors or to intimidate them through his liberation credentials.

My job interview took place in an office where Ndlovu sat behind an enormous desk, the affable Mandizha by his side. Pleasantries quickly dispensed with, I settled back in a chair across the desk from Ndlovu, who was, I thought, making a supreme effort to present as stern a countenance as possible. But I had not seen anything yet.

While he stared at me unflinchingly, Ndlovu reached into the top drawer of his desk and withdrew a pistol. Yes, a pistol. As he casually placed the weapon on the desktop in front of him, I went numb with shock. Mandizha avoided my pleading eyes.

'You are one of the sell-outs who wrote terrible stories about us while we were fighting for the liberation of this country,' Ndlovu said. I honestly did not know how to respond. 'Now that we have liberated the country, you come here asking for a job with us.'

'I think you are mistaken, Comrade Charles,' I replied, having rapidly regained some composure as I realised the absolute need to defend myself against the false accusation.

'I am not mistaken,' he retorted. 'Did the *Rhodesia Herald* not call us terrorists when we were fighting to liberate Zimbabwe?'

'You could, perhaps, cite one article in which I personally wrote disparagingly about Zanu,' I responded in desperation, quickly gathering courage.

Ndlovu remained stony-faced for a while. Then a broad smile broke across his features and he stood up to reach across the desk and shake my hand vigorously. I was shocked witless. I had imagined he was rising to shoot me, as Joboringo had stood up to shoot Ernest Mutizamhepo at point-blank range on the mountain at Regina Coeli in 1977.

'It's all right, comrade,' he said, once he had settled back in his seat. 'I wanted to see what kind of man you are.'

I left feeling somewhat relieved, but his assurances did nothing to kindle my interest in a job with the ZBC. A few days later, someone from Ndlovu's office phoned to invite me to a follow-up meeting. I said I had just been promoted to a senior position at the *Herald* and no longer wished to leave the paper. In fact, I had been appointed as the municipal reporter after discreetly leaking the information that I had been invited to Pocket's Hill for an interview. The advent of independence and black majority rule had rendered a newspaper such as the *Observer*, which catered exclusively for black readers, irrelevant and it had been mothballed. Staff members were absorbed by the *Herald* and *Sunday Mail*, and I had returned to the former.

The departure of white journalists had opened several opportunities for advancement. Most of the emigrants went to South Africa and joined the Argus Group, RP&P's parent company, which published newspapers in Johannesburg, Cape Town, Port Elizabeth and Durban. It was ironic that journalists who had supported the Smith regime were thus assured of jobs in South Africa, while their former black colleagues, such as myself, remained behind and were required by the likes of Ndlovu to answer for their alleged professional sins during the liberation struggle.

A few weeks later, in October, the government director of information invited me to his office at Linquenda House. Justin Nyoka said he had been impressed by my work on his return from Maputo and was confident that I had the skills to become an information officer for the new state of Zimbabwe. His department had been woefully denuded of staff following the white exodus to the south.

My salary would almost double to Z$750 a month and, since he was offering me a senior position, I would be entitled to a car loan. Coupled with the abundant prospects of promotion, these were reasons enough for me to resign from Zimpapers at the end of November, having served an exciting two years and ten months as a reporter.

On 1 January 1981, my thirtieth birthday, I became a senior civil servant. Within weeks I was also the proud owner of a Citroën DS 20, that fine example of the eccentricity of French car design. But it was not long before I realised that exchanging the excitement and hurly-burly of the newsroom for the strictures of officialdom had been a grave error of professional judgement on my part.

I was responsible for handling media enquiries, press conferences, and public relations for the ministries of foreign affairs, home affairs, local government and housing, which offered an extensive catchment area for error. When I was summoned to Comrade Soft's office a few months after starting my job, therefore, I was concerned that something was seriously amiss.

However, the director was the bearer of good tidings. My work had been of such a high standard that a decision had been made to transfer me to State House as press secretary to Zimbabwe's first president, the Reverend Canaan Sodindo Banana, a Methodist clergyman who had remained in Rhodesia throughout the struggle, serving long periods in detention.

The promotion was clearly an honour, but I was apprehensive, especially on learning that in addition to handling his media liaison and public relations, I would also be required to draft the presidential speeches.

On arrival at State House, I was relieved to find that the president's secretary was Dr Misheck Sibanda, who had been my senior at university. The comptroller was Clifford Sileya, who was said to be First Lady Janet Banana's relative. Both Sibanda and Sileya welcomed me warmly, but it did not take me long to realise that they were locked in a power tussle. Common sense dictated that my first allegiance was to the president's secretary, and I soon settled into my new post, briefing Banana on significant events of the day, attending to press enquiries and drafting his speeches. He was a prolific writer and also roped me in to edit some of his manuscripts.

One morning, shortly after presenting a speech that I had laboured over for hours, the president appeared in my office doorway, draft in hand.

'Comrade Nyarota,' he said, 'whatever speech you write for me must of necessity include a quotation from the Bible.'

My heart sank. I had dropped Bible study as a subject during my third year at secondary school in a fit of spite against my teacher, Father Cooper. He was also the geography master at St Mary's, and when I scored a mere 65 per cent in an exam, he punished me with a severe spanking and an admonition that he expected at least

80 per cent from me in future. In retaliation, I dropped both his subjects at the beginning of the next term, a decision that I rued at State House.

But, undeterred by Banana's *sine qua non*, I drafted speeches for him that were replete with biblical references, flipping through the holy book at random until I spotted a line that somehow reinforced the point I sought to make.

The best part of my job was the travel for which the president had a yen. He was a non-executive figurehead, but his office constantly demanded that he journey both locally and abroad. For some reason, he was rarely accompanied by his wife.

Most of his internal trips related to the Kushinga-Phikelela Agricultural Institute, Banana's own brainchild, situated about fifteen kilometres from Marondera on the way to Mutare. The president made extensive tours of the industrial complexes in Harare and Bulawayo to canvass for donations of materials, equipment and occasionally cash for the institute, which offered training courses in agriculture and secretarial work. No corporate chief executive targeted by President Banana for a visit ever had the nerve to turn down his requests, and Kushinga-Phikelela prospered.

My first trip outside Zimbabwe was with the presidential delegation that attended King Sobhuza's golden jubilee in Swaziland. It was my first encounter with the traditional Reed Dance, performed annually by scores of young and topless damsels before the monarch. Each year, the king selected one of the girls to be his newest bride. Competition was stiff and the girls spared no effort as they danced and vied to catch the eye of the elderly king. That year, aged eighty-four, King Sobhuza chose a delectable and nubile teenager to join his thirty existing wives.

In Harare, Banana's private life centred largely on soccer, Zimbabwe's most popular sport. After being appointed patron of the Zimbabwe Football Association, the president became a permanent fixture at Rufaro Stadium and the National Sports Stadium, the venues of super league and international soccer matches. Not only was he a registered referee, but Banana had also formed his own soccer team, State House Tornadoes, for which he occasionally donned the Number 9 jersey. As staff members left State House at the end of each working day, a string of young Tornadoes players would arrive for practice sessions on the well-manicured pitch within the grounds, under the watchful eye of Zimbabwe's ceremonial head of state.

In November 1983, two years after my departure from the president's office, Jefta Dube, a youngster who turned out for the police club Black Mambas, caught Banana's eye. An official driver was dispatched to persuade Dube that he should join the Tornadoes, and he needed little convincing. He was transferred to State House as a presidential bodyguard and promptly promoted two notches in rank from patrol officer to inspector.

For the twenty-three-year-old fledging soccer star, it was a dream come true. Having worked as a gardener before securing a police job the year before, thanks to his prowess on the soccer field, Dube's life had undergone a total metamorphosis. Unknown to his teammates, however, the transformation was more profound than anyone realised and, in due course, would plunge him into tragedy.

In 1995, Dube shot a fellow police officer in a bathroom at Gwanzura Soccer Stadium, and a shocked nation learned that the head of state had seen his protégé as far more than a soccer star. To the obvious mortification of Mugabe, who launched an ongoing vendetta against homosexual men, Dube told the High Court in Harare during his trial for murder that Banana had repeatedly raped and abused him over a three-year period. Appeals to his superiors, including the then police commissioner, Wiridzayi Nguruve, had fallen on deaf ears. They were powerless to restrain the president, they claimed.

Dube was sentenced to ten years in jail for the fatal shooting of Patrick Mashiri, who had taunted him as they stood next to one another at a public urinal, calling Dube 'Banana's wife'.

Dube's defence lifted the lid on one of Zimbabwe's juiciest scandals in years. Reduced to a nervous, drug-dependent wreck, Dube became one of the prosecution's star witnesses during Banana's subsequent seventeen-day trial on charges of rape and sodomy, which resulted in the former president serving several months in prison.

Dube told the court that he had first been molested by Banana a few days after arriving at State House. As a result of repeated sexual abuse, he suffered nightmares regularly and was no longer able to have sex with his wife or – as if the scandal was not already juicy enough – his girlfriend.

In December 1983, during Dube's first week as a presidential aide, Banana had invited him to dance to ballroom music in the library at State House, Dube told the court. He declined, saying he did not know how to dance. Undeterred, the president offered to teach him the basic steps. As they waltzed, Dube testified, he felt the erect presidential penis pressing against his thigh.

Banana had then kissed him, placing his tongue in Dube's mouth, before excusing himself. As he left, he patted Dube's buttocks, pronouncing: 'This is the food of the elders.'

On another occasion, Banana had invited him for a drink. Dube told the court he suspected it had been laced with some kind of sedative, because he passed out. When he came to, he realised that his trousers had been removed and felt semen between his buttocks. Banana stood over him, grinning.

'We have helped ourselves,' the president informed the dumbfounded officer.

As the lurid scandal unfolded, it became clear that police and high-ranking government officials had known for years that Banana was a homosexual who had abused several university students, various members of the State House Tornadoes, cooks, gardeners and security guards assigned to State House. One soldier claimed he was raped three times in one night after the president's 1985 Christmas party.

The evidence against Banana caused many to believe that Mugabe himself had known for some time of the president's sexual misconduct, but had done nothing to halt it. It was around the time of Dube's revelations, however, that Mugabe launched his vitriolic anti-gay campaign that angered both international activists and Zimbabwe's small gay community, whom he publicly described as 'worse than dogs'. Peter Tatchell, a British gay activist, twice attempted to effect a citizen's arrest of Mugabe, in London and in Brussels. Despite the fact that the majority of Zimbabweans had come to despise Mugabe as a ruthless dictator by that point, they rallied to his support on the subject of homosexuality, which most of them reject.

I have often wondered whether Mugabe's decision to abolish the position of prime minister and declare himself executive president in 1987 was motivated by a profound hunger for power, or formed part of a cunning plan to effectively put an end to Banana's sexual excesses without firing and publicly humiliating him.

During the six months that I spent at State House, Banana's conduct was still a closely guarded secret. Perhaps it was providential that another summons to Nyoka's office ended my association with the president before the scandal erupted.

In 1981, the last white editor in the Zimpapers stable, Jean Maitland-Stuart of the weekly *Umtali Post*, was summarily dismissed – the first of eleven editors to suffer the same fate during the first two decades of independence. Other victims of what was arguably the highest turnover of editors in the history of newspapers throughout the world were Willie Dzawanda Musarurwa, Henry Muradzikwa and Pascal Mukondiwa, all of the *Sunday Mail*, and Tommy Ganda Sithole, who as editor of the *Chronicle* and the *Herald* enjoyed the patronage of the ruling elite until he was given his own marching orders after eighteen years of loyal service. Also fired were Bornwell Chakaodza, who as director of information was the chief government spin doctor before his appointment to the *Herald*, and Bill Saidi, of Bulawayo's *Sunday News*. My own dismissal from the *Chronicle* in 1988, after I had exposed widespread corruption in the upper echelons of the Mugabe administration, was steeped in controversy.

From the moment he became minister of information in 1981, Nathan Shamuyarira had been unequivocal. The government welcomed discussion and dialogue in the press, and topics such as housing, welfare, the economic system, ideological direction, even the one-party state controversy were acceptable, provided debate took place within certain parameters.

Maitland-Stuart had published an editorial criticising the presence in Nyanga of military advisers from the Democratic People's Republic of Korea. They had been brought to Zimbabwe to train the infamous Five Brigade, the red-bereted troops who, under the command of Brigadier Perrence Shiri, had gained international notoriety for the massacre of an estimated 20 000 people in rural Matabeleland and the Midlands during the Gukurahundi campaign. According to Shamuyarira, Maitland-Stuart's view that 'anyone from a socialist country represents a red menace in the region' reflected racist, neo-colonial and South African thinking.

I had been selected to replace her, and I grabbed the opportunity to become the youngest editor in Zimbabwe. My work at State House was tedious and the move would take me back to Mutare, the city of my birth. The challenge was daunting, but just before leaving the *Herald* I had attended a subediting course, and Maurice Wood, a senior subeditor from the *Herald* who had held the fort since Maitland-Stuart's departure, stayed on for a month while I found my feet.

The journalists were all new, having come from the *Herald*. Senior reporter Eric Meijer and I shared the subediting duties. Max Chivasa handled much of the general reporting, while George Muzimba, who had been on the staff for some time, was our photographer. In due course I recruited Sam Mawokomatanda to cover sport. Geoffrey Hill ran the advertising department. More than two decades later, Hill would publish two books on post-independence Zimbabwe, namely *The Battle for Zimbabwe* and *What Happens After Mugabe?*

We changed the name of the paper to the *Manica Post*, and within a year had raised circulation from some 4000 copies, bought mainly by white readers, to 11000. Continued growth reflected the paper's appeal to new black readers.

Our success did not go unnoticed. In February 1983, I was summoned to head office in Harare, where managing director George Capon told me that, after returning from exile in Zambia to become the first black editor of the *Herald*, Farayi Munyuki was being transferred to Ziana, the national news agency. Tommy Sithole, who had come home from exile in Tanzania to be the first black editor of the *Chronicle* in Bulawayo, would replace Munyuki, while I was to be promoted and become editor of the *Chronicle*, a daily, as of April.

The implications were overwhelming. I had turned thirty-two on 1 January and, after little more than a year as editor of a small weekly, did not believe I was ready for the move to a large daily in Zimbabwe's second biggest city. Furthermore, I was not fluent in Ndebele, the language of the tribe that constitutes 20 per cent of Zimbabwe's population. Bulawayo lay at the heart of Joshua Nkomo's PF-Zapu stronghold, and in the 1980 elections, his party had won all seventeen of Matabeleland's parliamentary seats.

Editing the *Chronicle* would require the skills of a tightrope walker at any time, but never more so than at this delicate point. Serious security problems had emerged in and around Bulawayo, and there was growing evidence of dissident insurgency in rural Matabeleland following an outbreak of fighting between former Zanla and Zipra guerrillas, who lived in separate sections of Entumbane.

That evening, I went to the Quill Club, the popular watering hole of Harare's journalists, situated on the first floor of the Ambassador Hotel in Union Avenue. Far from being congratulated on my new appointment, I was subjected to a barrage of questions, expressions of concern and outright warnings about the wisdom of accepting the job. The outgoing editor, Tommy Sithole, was to spend only one day with me before leaving to assume his own new post.

When I returned home to Mutare, Ursula and I discussed at length the implications of my promotion with the sombreness of a couple facing the sudden dismissal of a breadwinner from work. We had made many new friends, Tafirenyika was in his second year at Mutare Junior School and loved it. Our rural home at Nyazura was only an hour's drive away; my mother's rural home was half as far, up in the majestic Vumba Mountains; and Harare was an easy drive.

Bulawayo was about a four-hour drive from the capital. It was a strange place with an unfamiliar language and was starting to hog the headlines for all the wrong reasons, chief among them the instability caused by the ferocious political rivalry between Zanu-PF and PF-Zapu and the resultant dissident problem.

However, the die had been cast and there was no going back. As if by way of compensation, Bulawayo finally offered me the opportunity to settle an old score, though it would be some time before this came to pass.

Shortly after joining the information ministry in 1981, I was walking up Baker Avenue one afternoon on the way to lunch at the Quill Club. As I approached the Africa Unity Square branch of Standard Chartered Bank at the intersection with Second Street, my heart skipped a beat.

Coming towards me at a brisk pace, wearing a pair of shorts and a colourful short-sleeved shirt and seemingly on top of the world, was none other than Detective Sergeant Phillip Mhike. I had last seen him in Rusape four years earlier. Our eyes locked in mutual recognition before, throwing caution to the wind, Mhike took off like an Olympic gold medallist, sprinting across a Baker Avenue packed with lunch-hour traffic. Onlookers held their breath as Mhike narrowly avoided a taxi speeding towards Second Street. The vehicle screeched to a halt. The middle-aged man in the brightly coloured shirt did not even slow down. On reaching the pavement on the other side of the street, he sped towards OK Bazaars, the huge department store on the corner of Baker Avenue and First Street.

I was obviously the only person who had any idea why the man had fled, and as I proceeded to the club, a sardonic smile occasionally crossed my face. The spectacle of Mhike bolting from a chance encounter on a street 200 kilometres and four years from the prison cells at Rusape evoked feelings of triumph and exultation in me. At home that night, as I shared details of the episode with Ursula, we laughed out loud as we had not done in a long time. The incident was a most welcome fillip.

Four years later, as editor of the *Chronicle*, I received an invitation to a function at Chibuku Breweries in Masvingo, 200 kilometres south-east of Bulawayo. The manager was my old friend Steve Chingwaru, who had ferried my box of supplies for the guerrillas from Highfields to Mabvuku in 1977. I arrived about thirty minutes ahead of time and found that another early guest was the police officer in charge of Masvingo province. Chingwaru introduced him to me as Assistant Commissioner Phillip Mhike.

'Pleased to meet you,' we said at the same time as we shook hands.

I looked him straight in the eye, leaving him in no doubt that I was daring him to repeat his Baker Avenue escapade, but that was as far as I went. He left the function early. But I now knew where to find him, and as luck would have it, our acquaintance would be renewed soon afterwards, when he was transferred to Bulawayo. I occasionally attended functions in the officers' mess at the Stops Police Camp and Mhike could evade me no longer.

Cunningly, he elected to play the perfect host. Fellow officers looked askance as Assistant Commissioner Mhike personally ensured that my glass never ran dry and that the most delectable snacks were always within reach. He once chided me for drinking beer when imported whisky was available in abundance.

'When my companions mix their Scotch with Coca-Cola or orange juice, I usually stick to Castle Lager,' I joked. If he understood the acerbic message, Mhike was not unduly perturbed.

By the time I returned to Harare in 1997, after three years of self-imposed exile in Maputo, Mozambique, Mhike had climbed even further up the police ladder. As deputy commissioner, he was poised to assume overall command of the Zimbabwe Republican Police should Commissioner Augustine Chihuri either retire or be run over by the pro-verbial bus. Chihuri and almost all the other senior officers were former Zanla guerrillas, yet Mhike had not only somehow escaped the post-independence purge of Rhodesian Special Branch officers, but had actually risen through the ranks to the highest echelon of the force and become close to Mugabe, the man he had despised and vowed to defeat.

It could be said that Mhike was walking proof that Mugabe's policy of national reconciliation was working, but, in my opinion, his post-war career served as confirmation that some of the officials surrounding Mugabe had probably not been thoroughly screened.

Mhike and I continued to meet at official functions or when business required me to visit police headquarters, but we never spoke of our initial introduction at Rusape. I continued to allow him to play the role of effusive host in social settings, but knew instinctively that my very silence on our pre-independence encounter was a form of severe psychological punishment.

I came back from Mozambique armed with elaborate plans to launch a weekly newspaper, and registered Landmark Publishing to this end. Dr Simba Makoni, my contemporary at university, was the chairman. He had been appointed minister of energy and technology at independence, and, after being sacked from the post, became the secretary general of the Southern African Development Community (SADC), based in Gaborone, Botswana.

Landmark soon launched *Highway*, a glossy monthly motoring magazine inspired by South Africa's highly successful *Car* magazine. I was both chief executive of Landmark and editor of *Highway*. In a separate venture, working with cartoonist Tony Namate, I produced a compilation of the popular *Nyati* cartoon strip, which I had created at the *Chronicle* in 1983, with another cartoonist, Boyd Maliki. Landmark was grossly under-capitalised, and I was soon buffeted by operational and cash-flow problems. The staff soldiered on, and by September 1997, the second edition of *Highway* had attracted considerable advertising support.

Meanwhile, I was feverishly canvassing funding for the newspaper and finally made a breakthrough. The Johannesburg office of the Open Society Institute, set up by Hungarian-born American philanthropist George Soros, approved partial funding of my venture on the basis of a proposal I had submitted. I would receive $100 000, the equivalent of Z$1 million at a time when Harare had only a handful of Zim-dollar millionaires. I was on cloud nine.

Amid this excitement, I read a newspaper article that upset me more than a little. Senior police officers, only recently allocated Mercedes-Benz C-Class sedans, were to be issued with new official cars, also Mercedes-Benz. They were given the option of purchasing their existing vehicles at book value.

I had already decided that this was exactly the brazen corruption that I was determined to fight through my own newspaper, but when I learned that among the beneficiaries of this generous offer was my former tormentor, Deputy Commissioner Mhike, I cast aside all vestiges of Mugabe's calls for reconciliation.

In one of the cruellest ironies of Zimbabwe's independence, I remained an ordinary citizen who was defenceless against persecution, humiliation and deprivation, notwith-standing any sacrifice during the liberation struggle. While many courageous war veterans were marginalised and treated as enemies by the new political establishment, opportunists such as Mhike, who had deceived a gallant fighter all the way to the gallows, who had put my uncle, cousins and me through weeks of living hell, were gorging themselves on the milk and honey of the very independence they had vowed to thwart.

I had in my files newspaper cuttings about Sidney Kapumha's court case in 1977, replete with irrefutable evidence of Mhike's duplicity. I telephoned the office of the minister of home affairs, Dumiso Dabengwa, and was immediately granted an appointment. Dabengwa, a Soviet-trained former guerrilla, was Zipra's much-feared chief of security in Lusaka, where he was known as the Black Russian. He was arrested by the Mugabe regime in 1982 as a result of a fallout between Zanu-PF and PF-Zapu, following the discovery of arms caches said to have been concealed by Zipra. After a period of detention without trial, Dabengwa was released, and when the two parties signed a unity agreement in 1987, he was reappointed to government.

By 1997 he was minister of home affairs, responsible for the police. We had become acquainted during my sojourn in Bulawayo, his home town, and I had found him an amicable and easy-going politician. I counted Dabengwa and Sidney Malunga, a maverick PF-Zapu politician who had died in a suspicious car accident, as allies of the *Chronicle* during the polarised and troubled 1980s in Matabeleland, but my respect for Dabengwa emanated at least partly from what I regarded as his refined taste in cars. Like Edgar Tekere, his personal vehicle was a majestic Jaguar XJ6.

When I entered Dabengwa's office in Harare, I briefly recounted my personal history during the liberation struggle, highlighting details of my arrest in 1977, my encounter with Kapumha and my subsequent painful ordeal at the hands of the Special Branch. Then I placed before the minister the most detailed cutting of the Kapumha case. I saw his eyes widen and his face tighten as he read the article. When he had finished reading, he stared at me, speechless.

'That man, Minister, arrested and subjected me to untold suffering in Rhodesia,' I said. 'Today in Zimbabwe I continue to suffer while he, as deputy commissioner of the Zimbabwe Republican Police, lives happily ever after. Now he even parks two luxury Mercedes-Benz cars in his garage. Is this the fairness and justice or the vigilance that Zanu-PF preaches about?'

A few months later, Mhike was quietly retired from the police force. Exposing his perfidious past was the right thing to do, but it was not my ticket to a happy ending. By the time Mhike resurfaced as a director of the ailing Air Zimbabwe in 2005, I was yet again living in exile, this time in Massachusetts, USA.

6

From Kutama
to State House

H E WAS BORN in Matibiri village near Kutama Mission, a Catholic institution in the Zvimba district of western Mashonaland. Early in 1980, with little ceremony, he moved into one of two mansions flanking Borrowdale Road, a main artery to the north of Salisbury, soon to be renamed Harare.

The magnificent white structure of Victorian architecture, set in immaculate gardens on the eastern side of the heavily guarded stretch of road. was the residence of the state president, Canaan Sodindo Banana. To the west of the same road lies the sprawling and equally imposing building of similar colonial design. Into this second residence, Prime Minister Robert Gabriel Mugabe, the man in whom executive powers were vested, moved.

Across Fifth Street Extension, to the west of the then prime minister's residence, was situated one of the most distinguished heritages of the capital city's colonial past, the Royal Harare Club.

As the newly elected socialist premier settled into the luxurious ambience of what would henceforth be known as State House, armed soldiers guarding the perimeter of the grounds observed in puzzlement as the capitalist captains of commerce and industry, as well as prosperous farmers from the hinterland, arrived at the club, which remained, for a long time, an enclave of racial supremacy and prejudice.

The favourite garb of both the figurehead president, Banana, and the prime minister was the safari suit, severely styled in the fashion popular with leaders of the socialist world. While Banana favoured open-necked short-sleeved suits in white or loud colours, Mugabe usually dressed in long-sleeved safari suits of grey and navy blue over a matching shirt and tie. In time, Mugabe would abandon safari suits in favour of more formal and expensive designer business suits that transformed his image into one of elderly sartorial elegance.

His epic journey from Kutama to State House had taken exactly fifty-six years and two months.

Mugabe had attended primary school at Kutama, within easy walking distance of his family home. Not much is known about his father, Gabriel Mugabe Matibiri, except that he worked as a carpenter at the mission. It has been widely speculated that he was a migrant worker from Nyasaland (now Malawi), who abandoned his young family in 1934 and went to Bulawayo in search of work.

There, rumour has it, Gabriel met and married a second wife, a common enough practice among men who worked in the cities and returned to their rural families only periodically. But Gabriel never went back to Kutama, and is believed to have made his way south, to become a gold miner in Johannesburg.

Mugabe's mother Bona, for whom he openly displayed affection throughout his time as head of state while almost never referring to his father, was a devout Catholic and devoted mother of four sons – Michael, Raphael, Robert and Donato – and a daughter, Sabina. Robert was ten years old when his father left, and a year later Michael, the eldest child, died, apparently after eating a poisoned cob of maize.

The three surviving Mugabe boys were forced to fend for themselves from an early age, and Robert evidently never forgave his father for deserting the family. According to people close to Mugabe in later life, including some who crossed him in one way or another, he neither forgot nor forgave. To become an enemy of Mugabe was to remain his foe forever. Politicians such as Joshua Nkomo, Ndabaningi Sithole, James Chikerema and Abel Muzorewa, the maverick Dr Eddison Zvobgo and Edgar Tekere, as well as journalists, including Willie Dzawanda Musarurwa and me, would taste his relentless wrath.

Robert was a bright little boy who increasingly came under the care and tutelage of the Jesuit priests at Kutama. The mission was founded by a Frenchman, Father Jean-Baptiste Loubiere, a stickler for religious doctrine, but in 1930 an Irish priest, Father O'Hare, took over the running of Kutama. He introduced a number of progressive changes that set him on a collision course with the colonial authorities, whose official policy was to discourage higher education for blacks. O'Hare set up a training facility for teachers and a technical school, and when the government refused to help him build a hospital for the people of Zvimba, he constructed one himself, using resources provided by his wealthy family in Ireland.

The Jesuit priest's defiant and rebellious spirit did not pass unnoticed by his young disciple who had, O'Hare said, 'an exceptional mind and heart'. At an early age, O'Hare noticed in Mugabe a zest for learning, a seriousness, a certain aloofness of demeanour and a devotion to his mother, whom he always accompanied to church. One of Mugabe's childhood friends was David Garwe, who told biographers David Smith and Colin Simpson: 'We all saw him as a very clever lad. He was by far the youngest boy in his class, and though he was three years younger, he was only one class below me.'

After six years of primary school education, O'Hare offered Mugabe the opportunity to train as a teacher, and in 1945, armed with a diploma, he left Kutama to teach at Dadaya Mission near the Midlands mining town of Shabani (now Zvishavane). The mission had been founded by Sir Garfield Todd, a missionary from New Zealand and a liberal by the white political standards of the day, who went on to serve as prime minister of Southern Rhodesia.

During his brief stay at Dadaya, Mugabe met Ndabaningi Sithole, an aspiring politician who became the founding president of Zanu in 1963, and would most likely have become independent Zimbabwe's first head of state had Mugabe not wrested leadership of the party from him while Sithole was in prison.

Todd and Sithole would ultimately rank among Mugabe's bitterest enemies. The latter was forced to flee Zimbabwe and went to live in exile in the United States, where he told author Geoff Hill in 1985: 'He was so impossibly self-absorbed. You never knew what he was thinking, except that it probably had to do with himself. There was little in the way of team spirit about the man, though I wouldn't call him arrogant; aloof, rather. Sometimes he would discuss things with fellow teachers and, on other occasions, you would ask him something and he would just look at you and not reply, as though your question was not important enough for him to consider.'

In 1949, aged twenty-five, Mugabe won a scholarship to Fort Hare University in South Africa, graduating in 1951. The institution near the town of Alice in the Eastern Cape holds the distinction of producing some of Africa's most important black nationalist politicians, including African National Congress (ANC) leaders Nelson Mandela and Oliver Tambo, Robert Sobukwe of the Pan Africanist Congress (PAC), the Zulu head of the Inkatha Freedom Party, Mangosuthu Buthelezi, and future heads of state Julius Nyerere (Tanzania) and Kenneth Kaunda (Zambia).

It was at Fort Hare that Mugabe was introduced to communist literature and ideas, and he also became familiar with Mahatma Gandhi's ideals. Armed with a BA degree – the first of seven academic qualifications he would acquire – he returned to Rhodesia in 1952, impassioned with a revolutionary zeal not only to free his country from white colonial rule, but also to turn it into a model communist state that would be emulated by other African nations.

He went to teach at Driefontein Mission near Mvuma, in the Midlands, and met Leopold Takawira, who became his political mentor. A spell in Gwelo followed, and in 1955, Mugabe became a lecturer at the Chalimbana Teachers' Training College in neighbouring Northern Rhodesia (now Zambia), while studying part time for his third degree.

When the West African state of Ghana became independent in 1957, President Kwame Nkrumah appealed to educated blacks from other African states to come and work, study and contribute to – while learning from – his country's revolution. Mugabe was among those who responded, arriving in Ghana in 1958 and becoming a lecturer at St Mary's, a training college for teachers in Takoradi.

'I went as an adventurist,' he later said. 'I wanted to see what it would be like in an independent African state.'

As the first African colony to achieve independence, Ghana became an inimitable political experiment, with blacks gaining swift advancement in their own government, civil service, commerce, industry and education. Mugabe's experience and observations reinforced his conviction that his dream for Zimbabwe was attainable.

In quick succession, he embraced the general principles of Marxism and met Sally Francesca Hayfron, a young schoolteacher from a wealthy Ghanaian family. Their relationship blossomed, but in 1960 Mugabe quit his job in Takoradi and returned to

Rhodesia to become a career politician at the behest of Joshua Nkomo's newly launched National Democratic Party (NDP). Following a spate of political violence the party was banned, but a new organisation, the Zimbabwe African People's Union (Zapu), soon emerged in its stead.

However, disenchanted with Nkomo's leadership style and obsession with foreign travel, Mugabe, Sithole, Enos Nkala, George Nyandoro, Maurice Nyagumbo, Chikerema and Tekere broke away from Zapu to form a rival organisation, the Zimbabwe African National Union (Zanu) on 8 August 1963. Sithole was elected the first president.

Meanwhile, unusually late in life for a Shona man, Mugabe married Sally in Salisbury in 1961. He was thirty-seven, she was twenty-nine. Somewhat surprisingly for someone who had remained single for so long, there has never been any evidence that the future prime minister had been a reckless sower of wild oats before he wed.

As Zapu and Zanu challenged one another to become the dominant black party in Rhodesia, wanton violence erupted in the townships of Salisbury, and Ian Smith, leader of the recently launched white right-wing Rhodesian Front party, gained the upper hand. In 1964, he pounced and doused the nationalist threat. The leaders were rounded up and jailed, most of them without trial, for ten years. A year later, Smith issued his Unilateral Declaration of Independence, hoping this would force Britain to endorse white rule of Rhodesia in perpetuity.

Following his release in December 1974, Mugabe remained in Salisbury for only three months while he and Tekere planned their dramatic escape to Mozambique with the assistance of Father Emmanuel Ribeiro, a Catholic prison chaplain who had smuggled letters for detainees.

A white Catholic nun, Sister Mary Aquina, a sociologist at the University of Rhodesia in whom Mugabe had much faith, spirited the two nationalists out of the capital to the eastern highlands under cover of darkness in an unlikely getaway car, a Volkswagen Beetle, much to the embarrassment of Smith's security apparatus. However, they were denied entry into Mozambique on their first attempt in March 1975, and spent the next three months living with Chief Rekayi Tangwena's people at Nyafaru. Somewhat surprisingly, the Zimbabwean police did not detect their presence, and they eventually crossed the Kaerezi River in June 1975.

But Mozambique's new leader, Samora Machel, was suspicious of the academic revolutionary who had suddenly appeared in his midst, and Mugabe and Tekere were whisked north to the port of Quilimane, where they were effectively placed under house arrest for the next few months.

It was an inauspicious start to what would be one of the longest and ultimately most unpopular political reigns in post-colonial Africa, but in fact, Mugabe's ascendancy to the position of Zanu leader and Zanla commander-in-chief was the culmination of a series of events dating back to an uprising at Chifombo in Zambia.

In November 1974, a group of Zanla guerrillas, most of them members of the Manyika tribe, arrested their commanders, seized control of the central command and elected

Thomas Nhari as their leader. He was a schoolteacher who had joined Zanu in 1969. The rebels denounced Zanla commander Josiah Tongogara, who came from the Karanga tribe, as an inept leader responsible for the failures that the guerrillas encountered in the field. Complaints were also voiced about inadequate food and weapons supplies for the bush fighters, while the leaders led an ostentatious life in Lusaka.

On 9 December, Nhari arrived in the Zambian capital with a detachment of twenty guerrillas. They kidnapped Tongogara's wife and brother-in-law, as well as three high-ranking party officials: executive secretary Mukudzei Mudzi, welfare secretary Kumbirai Kangai and treasurer Henry Hamadziripi, all members of the Karanga tribe. The party's information secretary, Rugare Gumbo, reported the abductions to the Zambian police, and Nhari and his men were arrested soon afterwards.

Early in 1975, Tongogara crushed the internal rebellion with reinforcements brought in from Tanzania by Rex Nhongo Mujuru, who as Rex Nhongo would become Zimbabwe's first army chief, and Dzinashe Machingura, who would be a leading opposition figure after independence. Tongogara stormed the camp at Chifombo, leaving forty-five of the rebels dead. On 22 January, a committee of three, headed by Herbert Wiltshire Chitepo, put the rebels on trial at Chifombo, and those found guilty were summarily executed in the bush. Convinced that the Manyikas had launched a tribal war against them and that Chitepo was behind a conspiracy to oust Tongogara, the Karangas embarked on a campaign of retribution. More than a hundred Manyikas were abducted and executed in Zambia and Mozambique.

By February, Tongogara had effectively taken control of Zanu, and on 16 March Chitepo confided in Kenneth Kaunda, the Zambian president, that his life was in danger. Asked who was threatening him, Chitepo is said to have named Tongogara and Hamadziripi. Within forty-eight hours of this meeting, a bomb exploded under Chitepo's car, killing him instantly.

Chitepo was born on 15 June 1923, and became a prominent lawyer after initially qualifying as a teacher in South Africa. He graduated with a BA from Fort Hare in 1949, and was the first black Rhodesian to qualify as a barrister in London. On returning home in 1954, Chitepo set up a law practice, defending many nationalists in court, and became the chairman of Zanu at its foundation. He and Mugabe were the most educated blacks in Rhodesia, Chitepo having obtained his academic qualifications on campus, while except for his initial BA, Mugabe had acquired his by correspondence course while in prison.

Chitepo was assassinated on the morning of 18 March 1975 outside his Lusaka home. Both he and his bodyguard, Silas Shamiso, died in the blast that destroyed Chitepo's VW Beetle. Kaunda immediately appointed a commission of inquiry, comprising officials from fourteen African states, to investigate the murders.

The Special International Commission's report found that Zanu's high command, led by Tongogara, had authorised Chitepo's assassination. Gumbo, Hamadziripi, Kangai and Mudzi were all implicated in the plot.

Immediately after Chitepo's funeral, Tongogara fled to Mozambique and his alleged co-conspirators sought refuge in Tanzania, but they were all extradited to stand trial in Lusaka for murder. Documents released a quarter of a century later, in October 2001, placed the blame for Chitepo's death entirely on Zanu infighting.

Around the time of the Tongogara affair, clear signs began to emerge of Mugabe's ruthless and vindictive quest for power and survival. The inhuman punishment meted out to so-called dissidents who were arrested on his instructions and detained under appalling conditions in northern Mozambique's remote Cabo Delgado province was a pointer long before the post-independence Gukurahundi massacres to the future leader of Zimbabwe's callousness.

Among those who survived Mugabe's early retribution was Wilfred Mhanda, elected leader in 2000 of the Zimbabwe Liberators' Platform (ZLP), a popular alternative to the Zimbabwe National War Veterans' Association (ZNWVA), of which Mugabe was the patron.

Mhanda and I had been schoolmates at Goromonzi, where his academic brilliance was legendary. He scored A grades in three science subjects at A-Level. We were also fellow students at university until 1973, when he abandoned his final-year BSc studies to go into exile in Zambia at a time of political unrest on the campus.

Mhanda had just turned twenty when he left Salisbury by train, travelling through Bulawayo and Plumtree to Francistown in Botswana in the company of a close friend from Goromonzi, Celestine Dembure. Two third-year BA students, Rodrick Musoko and Gorden Zvademoyo, and Kimble Gweshe, who was in his first year, fled Zimbabwe at the same time. Unlike Mhanda and Dembure, however, they had no valid passports and jumped the border. Musoko and Gweshe had previously undergone basic military training in Zambia.

Musoko was a member of the Zanla high command when Rhodesian security forces killed him in a bomb explosion in Botswana in 1975, but he went unrecognised in official Zanu-PF and former Zanla circles and his name was never publicly mentioned during the annual Heroes' Day commemoration.

Dembure and Zvademoyo were both executed during the Nhari rebellion, although Mhanda always insisted there was no evidence linking them directly to the uprising.

'In fact, I was sharing ideas with Celestine in December 1974 on how best to deal with the rebels,' he said. 'I knew him well and I am positive that he was not a conspirator. Quite a number of innocent victims who had absolutely nothing to do with the rebellion were executed. Some senior commanders used the situation as an opportunity to settle personal scores with people against whom they bore grudges.'

Gweshe died in either Mozambique or Rhodesia's north-eastern operational area in 1974, reportedly of thirst.

On arrival in Lusaka as an exile, Mhanda became a teacher and studied economics. However, when Ian Smith haughtily told a journalist that there was no prospect 'in a thousand years' of a black government in Rhodesia, Mhanda was among those who accepted that an armed struggle was the only way to convince Smith that black majority rule was inevitable.

He enlisted for guerrilla training at Mgagao in Tanzania, and soon displayed exceptional qualities as a fighting man. He rose swiftly through the ranks to become first an instructor, then a political commissar and ultimately a Zanla commander. Due to his commitment, aptitude and clarity of vision, the Chinese trainers at Mgagao whisked Mhanda off to Beijing for advanced training.

'China was a strange, closed society and the Chinese themselves were essentially racist,' he told a journalist years afterwards. 'If someone like me appeared on the street there'd be an immediate traffic jam. People queued up to look at blacks like you'd look at monkeys. But I didn't care. The training was excellent and that was what I'd gone there for.'

Despite the insistence of the Chinese instructors that Mhanda was too great an asset to risk his life in the field, his active participation in guerrilla action earned the profound respect of Zanla cadres on the north-eastern front.

For some time, Kaunda had tried to persuade the Zanu elements in Lusaka to accept the leadership of his friend, Zapu leader Joshua Nkomo. While Zanu drew the bulk of its support from the majority Shona ethnic group, Zapu supporters were chiefly found among the smaller Ndebele tribe. Zanu's military wing received logistical support from Beijing, while Zapu was backed by the Soviet Union. In South Africa, Zanu was strategically aligned to the PAC, while Zapu had close links with the ANC.

Bitter political rivalry between Nkomo and Mugabe would endure long after the liberation struggle was over, but in the mid-seventies, the leaders of the Front Line States, including Tanzania, Zambia, Mozambique, Botswana and Angola, insisted on a united onslaught against the Smith regime. Zanu and Zapu's respective military wings, Zanla and Zipra, thus joined forces to form the Zimbabwe People's Army (Zipa) under the command of Zanla's Rex Nhongo. His second in command was from Zipra, while Mhanda filled the third most senior slot. After devising a new military strategy, Zipa launched combined operations in January 1976.

In February 1975, two months after the nationalist leaders were released from prison and the Lusaka Unity Accord was signed, Sithole was rearrested on suspicion of plotting to assassinate his political opponents. When he was released in April to attend an OAU meeting in Tanzania, Mhanda was in detention in Mboroma in the Mkushi area of Zambia.

'We had staged a hunger strike to demand that Sithole come to us. The trick worked, and for the first time the Zanu president had direct contact with his fighters,' Mhanda recalled. 'Over the next three months, however, there was a serious falling-out between him and the guerrillas for a number of reasons, chief among them Sithole's failure to take the Zambian government to task for the massacre of Zanla cadres at Mboroma.'

Mhanda said Sithole had refused to seek permission from the Zambian authorities for wounded guerrillas to receive medical attention or for an investigation into what had happened.

'Sithole clearly supported the Zambian government's action against the Zanu fighters after Chitepo's death. We decided to consult members of the Dare, Zanu's supreme council, who were in prison in Lusaka for plotting to kill Chitepo. They included Tongogara, Gumbo, Mudzi, Hamadziripi and Kangai, and the decision was that Sithole should no longer lead the movement.

'It was the Dare that named Mugabe as the new leader, a choice based purely on the natural line of succession. Zanu's vice-president, Leopold Takawira, had died in prison, Chitepo had been assassinated, and suddenly Mugabe was the most senior available politician,' said Mhanda.

It fell to Nhongo and Mhanda, the two top Zanla representatives in Zipa, to muster support for Mugabe from both the guerrillas and his Mozambican host, Samora Machel. In August 1976, said Mhanda, they spirited first Tekere and then Mugabe from Quilimane to the Zanla camp at Chimoio, without Machel's knowledge, to meet with the guerrillas.

'It was my task to brief Mugabe on our military operations, and I found him both attentive and receptive, a good listener. However, the guerrillas and refugees who met him did not find him an easy man to deal with, and soon formed the opinion that we would not go very far with him,' said Mhanda.

'He was secretive, stubborn and uncompromising, and the more I got to know him, the more I, too, began to fear for the future of the liberation struggle. When Mugabe takes a dislike to someone, he becomes vindictive and never changes his mind,' Mhanda told the BBC in an interview in January 2000.

After he returned to Quilimane, Mugabe was invited to attend a Front Line States summit in Dar es Salaam, where he was officially recognised as Zanu's new leader. From the Tanzanian capital he went to Maputo, where preparations were under way for the Geneva conference aimed at settling the Rhodesian question. In October 1976, Mugabe led the Zanu delegation to the talks.

One of his first acts as Zanu leader was to disband Zipa, fearing that his arch-rival, Nkomo, might gain control of a single, united guerrilla force. This so dismayed Mhanda that he refused to travel to Geneva with the Zanu delegation. Shortly before Mugabe's departure for Switzerland, Mhanda, using his alias, Dzinashe Machingura, told Zanla fighters via a Radio Maputo broadcast: 'We do not identify ourselves with any of the factions trying to lead us.'

For the duration of the talks, Mugabe brooded over what he saw as a threat to his leadership and, on returning to Maputo, heartened by the fact that Machel had finally decided to support him, he persuaded the Mozambican president to act swiftly in order to forestall a military rebellion led by Mhanda.

On 19 January 1977, the Mozambican Army arrested fifty of Zipa's top commanders at Beira, in Mozambique's Sofala province, while they were attending a conference to discuss the reintegration of political and military leaders arrested in Zambia in the wake of Chitepo's murder. Tongogara had been released from prison in Lusaka at

Mugabe's request so that he could attend the Geneva conference, where the two had forged an alliance. In the year that followed the Beira arrests, another 600 'dissident' guerrillas were rounded up at Tongogara's behest in the various training camps.

It was the start of what would be a ceaseless and ruthless campaign by Mugabe to neutralise anyone he perceived as a political opponent or threat to his position.

Among those held were Elias Hondo, James Nyikadzinashe, Bournard Manyadza (alias Parker Chipoera), Dr Stanslaus Kaka Mudambo, Chrispen Mataire (alias David Todhlana) and Dr Augustus Mudzingwa of Zipra. Also arrested were Happison Muchechetere (alias Harry Tanganeropa), who later became the editor in chief of Ziana, Zimbabwe's national news agency, after a stint at ZBC, and Alexander Kanengoni, who worked for the ZBC and wrote a column for the *Herald* after independence.

Mhanda was not among those initially arrested.

'In fact, Mugabe invited me to work with him,' he said. 'We met a day after the commanders were arrested and I was informed of the so-called charges against them. I strongly disputed the claims and protested against this wilful and wanton act of victimisation.

'I refused to cooperate with Mugabe and the new central committee that he had just set up, and demanded that the commanders be released, failing which I would join them. That is how I ended up in prison, too.

'The charges against the commanders were vague, to say the least. They were accused of straying from the party line – *kurasa gwara remusangano*, as they say in Zanu.'

According to Mhanda, nothing more specific was put to the detainees and no evidence was presented against them. There was no trial, or even a hearing in terms of the codes of discipline and conduct applicable to both Zanu and Zanla, and the accused were offered no chance to defend themselves.

'We were held in the basement of the abandoned Grand Hotel in Beira before being taken by road to Nampula province, where we were locked up in a military prison for a week. We were then airlifted to Pemba, the provincial capital of Cabo Delgado in the far north, and confined to our cells for more than seven months,' said Mhanda.

Those arrested in January 1978 were charged with plotting to overthrow the leadership of Zanu.

'They appeared before some form of kangaroo court,' said Mhanda. 'My understanding is that Mugabe was the presiding officer, assisted by Tongogara, Tekere, Herbert Ushewokunze and Emmerson Mnangagwa, who had just joined them in Mozambique after living and working in Zambia since 1970.'

After completing his studies at the University of Zambia, Mnangagwa had served his articles with a Lusaka law firm set up by Enoch Dumbutshena, who would be Zimbabwe's first black chief justice. Mnangagwa arrived in Maputo bearing impressive political credentials, despite not playing an active role in the liberation struggle during his time in Zambia. He had developed a close relationship with Mugabe in detention at Wha Wha, and was married to Tongogara's sister. He went to Maputo at Tongogara's request and was appointed security chief, working out of the military supremo's office. It was the perfect launch pad for his meteoric post-independence rise to minister of state security.

Prominent figures arrested during the second swoop on so-called rebels included Mudzi, Gumbo and Hamadziripi, all previously imprisoned by the Zambian authorities on suspicion of plotting Chitepo's death. Hamadziripi had been a member of the original executive committee when Zanu was formed in 1963. Other detainees were Chrispen Mandizvidza, a founding central committee member, Webster Gwauya, the party's deputy secretary for external affairs, central committee members Matthew Gurira and Dr Joseph Taderera, and Augustine Chihuri, who would profess unflinching loyalty to Mugabe as police commissioner more than twenty years later.

On Chihuri's watch, the standards and performance of the Zimbabwe Republican Police would reach an all-time low, with members being used to carry out witch-hunts against opposition politicians, the press and white commercial farmers. As the beleaguered country's most senior policeman, he was a prime recipient of Mugabe's legendary patronage, including agricultural estates.

Kangai and Richard Hove, who would both serve as cabinet ministers under Mugabe, were also detained. According to Mhanda, they spent several weeks in the Chimoio dungeons, infamous for their execrable conditions, but escaped further incarceration due to their personal connections.

All the prisoners were eventually released as the result of intervention by Nyerere, chairman of the Front Line States at the time. However, Zanu refused to accept them back into its ranks, and Machel, in abeyance to Mugabe, restricted their movements.

'We became free prisoners,' said Mhanda. 'After being confined to Pemba for six months, the Mozambican Army's chief of staff persuaded us to relocate to an abandoned Portuguese military base at Balama, in rural Cabo Delgado. We were free to do whatever we liked, as long as we did not run away. Frankly, it was such a remote area that it would have been suicidal to try and run anyway.

'Mugabe had identified us as counter-revolutionaries and we were anxious to prove to Frelimo that this was not true, so we stayed for two years before we were eventually released.'

They were detained under extremely harsh conditions.

'For the week that we were at Nampula, we were never allowed out of our cells. The lights stayed on day and night, making it impossible to know what time it was. There were twenty-five of us crammed into a cell clearly not intended for so many people,' Mhanda recalled.

Conditions at Pemba were no better.

'We were subjected to painful, cruel and inhuman torture. Our hands were tied behind our backs and we were thrown like bags of maize onto the back of trucks that were liberally strewn with broken glass. The guards derived great pleasure from beating us with anything they could lay their hands on. We were split into three groups of eight and confined to small cells of two metres by two metres.

'We were allowed out of our cells only once every ten days to empty the single bucket in which we had to relieve ourselves. We became accustomed to living with our waste.

'We had no blankets in the winter and our only clothing was a pair of trousers each. Our shirts had been confiscated so that in case we dared to try and escape, we could be easily spotted by our bare torsos. For almost eight months we were confined to our cells in Cabo Delgado, and during that period we were allowed to bath only once, and then without soap. We were so infested with lice that we gave up killing them. We endured all manner of ailments like malaria, high fever and diarrhoea without any form of treatment or medication.

'As for meals, we had rice sprinkled with sand grains, or sadza and beans. Many a time we had nothing to eat for a whole day.'

Tongogara, Mugabe and Nhongo never once visited the prisoners.

'The only person who came, once, was Simon Muzenda, who invited some of us to hold discussions. I refused to attend the meetings and nothing ever came of them,' said Mhanda.

While the 'rebel' commanders were isolated in Cabo Delgado, events in Rhodesia moved inexorably towards a climax. On 3 March 1978, Smith signed a so-called internal settlement in Salisbury with Bishop Abel Muzorewa of the UANC, Reverend Sithole – still leader of an internal faction of Zanu – and Chief Jeremiah Chirau, a traditional leader whose Zimbabwe United People's Organisation (Zupo) had a tiny following.

The agreement provided for qualified majority rule and elections based on universal suffrage. In April 1979, a 64 per cent turnout at the polls catapulted Muzorewa to power as prime minister of Zimbabwe-Rhodesia. The very name of the 'new' country reflected Smith's duplicity and refusal to accept the inevitability of black majority rule. It also underscored the impotence of internal political leaders to achieve the meaningful change for which that black majority yearned.

A group of British observers, led by Lord Chitnis, a special representative of the Liberal Party, travelled to Salisbury to monitor the elections and produced a highly critical report that concluded: 'The recent election in Rhodesia was nothing more than a gigantic confidence trick designed to foist on a cowed and indoctrinated black electorate a settlement and a constitution which were formulated without its consent, and which are being implemented without its approval. We cannot play our appointed role in this process and endorse this blatant attempt to perpetuate a fraud and justify a lie.'

The election had been held while the guerrilla war raged on in many rural constituencies, where voters were subjected to intimidation, especially by the notorious Pfumo reVanhu, or Spear of the People, the military wing of Muzorewa's UANC. The government, in turn, had launched a massive propaganda campaign in a bid by Smith to win international support for the makeshift agreement. The UANC won a clear majority, and on 1 June 1978, Bishop Muzorewa was sworn into office as the first black premier of the deeply divided country.

The credibility of all three black signatories to the internal settlement had long been destroyed. In October 1975, dozens of guerrillas at Mgagao, the largest Zanu camp in Tanzania, had issued a bitter denunciation of Muzorewa, Sithole and Chikerema, the leader of the Front for the Liberation of Zimbabwe (Frolizi).

'These three have proved to be completely hopeless and ineffective as leaders of the Zimbabwean revolution,' the officers wrote in a memorandum to the Organisation of African Unity and the governments of Tanzania and Mozambique. 'They have done everything to hamper the struggle through their own power struggle. They have no interest in the revolution or the people, but only their personal interests. They cherish an insatiable lust for power.'

The government of Zimbabwe-Rhodesia was a coalition between Smith, Sithole and Muzorewa, but the civil war waged by Mugabe and Nkomo raged on unabated. Since 1972, the conflict had claimed more than 20 000 lives, and as long as Britain and the US maintained economic sanctions against the country, there could be no real prospect of peace and development.

In June 1979, African leaders secured a strong condemnation of the internal settlement at the summit of non-aligned nations in Sri Lanka, and in July the OAU summit in Liberia adopted an even stronger position against Zimbabwe-Rhodesia. In London, two days after Margaret Thatcher's Conservative government was elected, the high commissioners of thirty-four Commonwealth countries warned her of the perils of recognising Muzorewa's government and lifting sanctions.

In the face of such widespread and determined opposition and the stark reality that the republic of Zimbabwe-Rhodesia faced an early demise, fresh peace initiatives were proposed.

Britain arranged an all-party conference at Lancaster House in September 1979 to thrash out a workable constitution and basis for new elections. Mugabe and Nkomo joined forces under the banner of the Patriotic Front for the talks, which signalled an end to fifteen years of conflict and paved the way for democratic general elections in March 1980, culminating in full independence on 18 April.

The conference was chaired by the British foreign secretary, Lord Carrington. Smith and his allies – Muzorewa, Sithole and Chief Chirau – sat on one side of the table, Mugabe and Nkomo on the other. After three months of difficult negotiations, the Lancaster House Agreement was signed in December, setting the seal on a lasting peace deal.

At the conference, Tongogara, the tall, bearded and charismatic Zanla commander, towered over everyone, including his comparatively diminutive leader, Mugabe. According to Lord Carrington, Tongogara was a crucial moderating force during the talks.

As a child, Tongogara had worked on the farm owned by Ian Smith's parents. As a young man, he took up arms against the racist regime led by their son. On the first day at Lancaster House, he surprised Smith by recalling how the latter's mother had given him sweets as a child. Such was the influence of the Zanla commander that when an irate Mugabe started telling Carrington to go to hell during a press conference, it was Tongogara who leaned over and calmed him. He became such an icon of Zimbabwe's struggle that virtually every town and city named a street for him after independence. Not to do so was considered unpatriotic.

While he was not entirely satisfied with the ceasefire arrangements made at Lancaster House, since they were heavily weighted against the two guerrilla armies, Tongogara nevertheless believed the causes of the war had been removed. He reportedly held private meetings with Nkomo during the conference and spoke openly in favour of unity between Zanu and Zapu. Mugabe was adamant, however, that Zanu should go it alone in an election, saying Nkomo's Zipra had not shouldered the burden of fighting.

Six days after the agreement was signed, the Voice of Zimbabwe broadcast 'an extremely sad message to all the fighting people of Zimbabwe' from Mugabe in Maputo. Tongogara, aged forty-one, had been killed in a car accident on Christmas Day while driving from Maputo to Chimoio, in the central province of Manica, to brief Zanla commanders about the ceasefire agreement. He never arrived. The vehicle in which he was a front-seat passenger rammed into the back of a Frelimo truck and Tongogara died instantly.

There has been fervent discussion, albeit in hushed tones, ever since about whether the accident was genuine, or whether Tongogara was murdered. It later transpired that he had actually died on 26 December, not Christmas Day as stated officially, and it took two days for his body to reach the mortuary in Maputo. Inquiries launched by the Mozambican government and the Zanu leadership, as well as a report issued by Mashford and Son, the funeral directors flown from Salisbury to Maputo to embalm the body, all arrived at the same conclusion, however, namely that no foul play was involved in the Zanla leader's death.

'The injuries are consistent with a car accident,' said Ken Stokes of Mashfords in a statement released by Zanu.

Never one to ignore an opportunity to undermine his enemies of fifteen years, Smith fuelled speculation that Tongogara was murdered by insisting in his book, *The Great Betrayal*, that he had been killed 'by his own people'. He claimed that Tongogara had confided in him at Lancaster House that his life was in danger.

'I made a point of discussing his death with our police commissioner and head of Special Branch, and both assured me that Tongogara had been assassinated,' Smith wrote. How either official, no matter how enterprising, could possibly have determined with any certainty that Tongogara was assassinated in the Manica province deep inside Mozambique, Smith did not venture to explain. Neither of the two officers independently confirmed Smith's claims.

Mugabe finally arrived back in Salisbury on 27 January 1980, triumph staring him in the face. With the return of the guerrilla leaders from Maputo and Lusaka, Smith's UDI regime, masquerading as the government of Zimbabwe-Rhodesia, was effectively replaced by a colonial authority under Lord Soames, a British governor.

Both Mugabe and Nkomo were given a rapturous welcome by their supporters. On hand to greet *Umdhala Wethu*, Our Old Man, or Father Zimbabwe, as Joshua Nkomo was affectionately known, were thousands of people from all over Rhodesia, many of them elderly. Thousands more, mostly young, thronged the airport to catch a glimpse of Robert Mugabe, who was both a legend and an enigma, reviled by Smith and the white population as a despicable terrorist ogre.

Mugabe's homecoming rally at the Zimbabwe Grounds later that day attracted an estimated 200 000 supporters, the largest political assembly the country had seen. They came by car, bus, train, bicycle and on foot, leaving observers in little doubt as to what direction the election would take. Zanla guerrillas had canvassed massive rural support for Zanu over the years, but this was the first time that Mugabe – charismatic, militant and as eloquent in the Queen's English as in his native Shona – had also demonstrated his urban appeal, thereby instantly enhancing his image and credentials, while effectively undermining the credibility of his main rivals, Nkomo and Muzorewa.

He returned from exile an undisputed national hero among blacks, but what no one had expected was that he would almost immediately set out to woo the apprehensive white population as well. In October 1976, he had told a press conference in Geneva unequivocally that 'none of the white exploiters will be allowed to keep an acre of land in Zimbabwe'.

However, Mugabe's delegation had travelled to Salisbury from London via Maputo, where Machel put a damper on their exultant spirits by insisting that Zanu-PF adopt a pragmatic and moderate approach in drafting an election manifesto.

He proffered advice based on the Mozambican experience and the failure of the Marxist-Leninist revolution that his own Frelimo had embarked on upon assuming power. For Machel, the exodus of a quarter of a million white Portuguese on the eve of independence in 1975 had had disastrous and regrettable consequences on the economic and social fabric of Mozambique.

Maputo had become a dilapidated ghost of its former seaside grandeur. Long queues for foodstuffs and essential commodities available in the few shops that were still operating had become a common sight.

Lack of expertise and equipment had caused production to plummet on Mozambique's newly established collective farms. Huge quantities of basic food were imported instead of being produced locally. Machel's revolution was at a crossroads. Failure of the Lancaster House Agreement would have further exacerbated this crisis.

Machel was invited to address the Zanu-PF central committee on 9 January, and his message was that whatever their racist excesses and shortcomings, Rhodesia's remaining whites had a crucial role to play in building the economy of a new and independent Zimbabwe.

'Cut out the rhetoric,' he told Mugabe and his lieutenants, 'because you will scare the whites away, and you need them. You will face ruin if you force the whites to take flight. Don't try to imitate us. Don't play make-believe Marxist games when you get

The author's grandfather, Geoffrey Nyarota,
with sister, Rusina Chiganze,
and great-grandson, Tafirenyika

The author's father Jethro Nyarota
in Mutare, *c.* 1953

The author as a schoolteacher
at Regina Coeli Mission in 1976

The author's mother, Ruby Mukwedeya,
in Highfields in 1990

The censored front page of the
Rhodesia Herald, 21 September 1966

The author as cadet reporter on the *Herald*
at home with Ursula and Tafirenyika in 1978

The author as *National Observer* reporter, with journalist Matts Holmberg of Swedish newspaper *Dagens Nyheter*, interviewing a villager in a protected village in Chiweshe in 1979. At left is Holmberg's wife, Matissa Vasques

From left: information minister Dr Nathan Shamuyarira, Zimpapers managing director Elias Rusike, Maurice Nyagumbo, minister of political affairs, Zimpapers Bulawayo branch manager Ewart Armstrong and the author watch a lino-type operator at the *Chronicle* in 1986. Nyagumbo was to commit suicide over a *Chronicle* story

In 1985 from left: Bulawayo branch manager Ewart Armstrong, *Chronicle* deputy editor Don Henderson, chief subeditor Ibrahim Jogee, the author as editor of the *Chronicle*, sports editor Shaun Orange, news editor Edna Machirori, and assistant editor David Ncube

The *Chronicle* team after scooping awards at the 1987 National Journalism and Media Awards in Harare. From left: reporter Joseph Polizzi, Costa Manzini (Photographer of the Year), Gibbs Dube (News Reporter of the Year), business editor Jonathan Maphenduka, the author as the editor, David Mazura (Business Reporter of the Year), Ursula Nyarota, features writer Walter Mapango and Andy Hendry, chief photographer

As editor of the *Financial Gazette*, the author interviews Prime Minister Junejo Khan of Pakistan in Islamabad in 1990

The author addresses Malawian dictator Dr Hastings Kamuzu Banda
on behalf of visiting southern African editors

The author chats with newly elected President Bakhili Muluzi of Malawi in Blantyre in 1994.
Looking on, from left, are journalists Ndaretso Mathobo of Lesotho, Karin-Lis Svarre
of Denmark, Peter Chirwa of Malawi and Babbington Maravanyika of Zimbabwe

President Mugabe addresses
a press conference

MDC president Morgan Tsvangirai
and deputy Gibson Sibanda

Professor Jonathan Moyo as
minister of information

Chenjerai 'Hitler' Hunzvi, chairman of the
Zimbabwe National War Veterans' Association

Joseph Chinotimba, one of the leaders
of the 2000 farm invasions

The police confront demonstrators

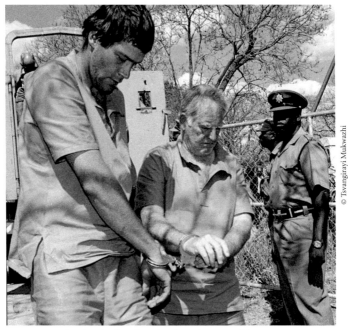

During the farm invasions in 2000, arrested farmers
are brought to court in the town of Chinhoyi

home. You have no Marxist party as yet, so you can't impose Marxism. It's difficult enough in Mozambique, and we *are* a Marxist party.'

In Lusaka, an impatient Kaunda did not beat about the bush either.

'There is no stomach in Zambia, Mozambique or Tanzania for war any more,' he warned both Mugabe and Nkomo.

Machel's counsel had a profound effect on the Zanu-PF leadership and on Mugabe in particular. The election manifesto that went to the printers a few days later was a skilful exercise in compromise between socialist ideology and capitalist reality. It exuded moderation, was purged of all reference to Marxism and paid little more than lip service to socialism.

'In working towards the socialist transformation of Zimbabwean society,' the manifesto stated, 'a Zanu government will recognise historical, social and other existing practical realities. One of these is the capitalist system, which cannot be transformed overnight. Hence, while a socialist transformation process will be brought under way in many areas of the existing economic sectors, it is recognised that private enterprise will have to continue until circumstances are ripe for socialist change.'

The manifesto also addressed the crucial issue of racism.

'Zanu wishes to give the fullest assurance to the white community, the Asian and coloured communities that a Zanu government can never in principle or in social or government practice, discriminate against them. Racism, whether practised by whites or blacks, is anathema to the humanitarian philosophy of Zanu. It is as primitive a dogma as tribalism or regionalism.'

After having faced an unremitting barrage of government propaganda towards the end of the war, even the black population was relieved at Zanu-PF's conciliatory tone. Having personally witnessed some of Zanla's excesses during the bush war, I was no exception. Over the first two decades of independence, the major beneficiaries of Mugabe's policy of reconciliation would turn out not to be the multitude of blacks who had thrown themselves into the liberation struggle, but his sworn enemy, the whites. Those who bore the brunt of his recrimination were those blacks who supported political organisations other than Zanu-PF, entertained political beliefs contrary to his own or dared to criticise him openly, as some journalists did.

Armed with his manifesto of moderation, Mugabe campaigned for an election in which Muzorewa, as the incumbent prime minister, had all the advantage. He had access to and total control of a large share of government resources, including the country's only television channel and the most effective information medium, radio, through the RBC's African Service.

Three Rhodesian Air Force helicopters were at Muzorewa's disposal to whisk him from one election rally to another. At his three-day Huruyadzo (Shona for 'biggest) Rally at Zimbabwe Grounds in Highfields, cattle were slaughtered daily and beer flowed like water. To further ingratiate himself with the voters, Muzorewa awarded hefty salary increments to teachers, policemen and other civil servants ahead of the elections. They accepted what amounted to bribes with delight, but on polling day abandoned their benefactor in droves. When the chips were down for Zanu-PF twenty years later, Mugabe resorted to the same ploy, and suffered similar consequences.

Despite all the resources and financial backing thrown into Muzorewa's campaign, his party scraped through the election with only three seats to its credit. Cynical commentators uncharitably observed that he had won 'a seat for each of the helicopters used to get him to the voters'.

Even more surprising was the fact that Nkomo's Zapu claimed only twenty seats, including all seventeen in Matabeleland, confirming that Zimbabwe's main opposition party was an ethnically based organisation with little following in non-Ndebele-speaking constituencies.

Mugabe, who had entered the race late and was demonised by both the local and international media, scored a landslide victory, taking fifty-seven of the eighty seats that were up for grabs.

On 18 April, the reticent boy from Kutama was sworn in as the first prime minister of the Republic of Zimbabwe. At the stroke of midnight, the heir to the British throne, Prince Charles, watched sombrely as the Union Jack was lowered for the last time and the magical strains of 'Zimbabwe', specially composed and performed for the occasion by Jamaican reggae king Bob Marley, ushered in an era of independence, self-rule and freedom for the black majority. From Rufaro Stadium in Harare to the farthest outposts of the land between the Zambezi and the Limpopo, it was a night of joy and celebration over the fulfilment of a long-standing national dream and the sublime belief that milk and honey would now flow freely over earth still clammy with the blood of thousands.

The optimism was immediately boosted by Mugabe's inaugural address, in which he spoke of turning swords into ploughshares, of reconstructing the war-torn land, of restoring international confidence and internal stability.

'Let us forgive and forget; let us join hands in a new amity,' he said.

His conciliatory tone, coupled with the twenty parliamentary seats that the Lancaster House Agreement had reserved for whites for the next seven years, achieved exactly what Machel had counselled would be needed to set a free Zimbabwe on its way, and elevated Mugabe to the level of statesman in the eyes of the international community.

In one of his early interviews as prime minister, Mugabe explained his apparent transformation from militant to moderate, telling journalist, author and occasional Zanu-PF apologist David Martin:

'The change is not in me. I am not the one who has undergone a metamorphosis. The transformation really is taking place in the minds of those who, once upon a time, regarded me as an extremist, a murderer, a psychopathic killer ... they are the people who have had to adjust to the change. I have remained my constant self. What I was, I still am.'

And, indeed, it wasn't long before his actions began to show that the change truly was in the mind of the observer and not in himself.

Zanu-PF's former detainees at Pemba were rather subdued when they flew into Salisbury from Maputo three months before independence and were whisked straight from the airport to a press conference at the Monomatapa Hotel. The motley band of ex-prisoners presented a pitiful sight. Dishevelled and emaciated, they appeared out of place in the opulent ambience of the majestic hotel, which had risen at the southern end of the luxuriant Salisbury Gardens while most of the assembled guerrillas had been in exile.

The press conference attracted hordes of local and international journalists. Among the men seated in a row facing the assembled journalists, I immediately recognised Mhanda, my erstwhile schoolmate and fellow student. As a child, Wilfred had sustained fairly severe burns in a fire that had left him with shiny bald patches in his hair. His head was now clean-shaven, and he was introduced as Dzinashe Machingura, the legendary figure about whom I had heard much. I could hardly wait for the formalities to conclude so that I could renew my acquaintance with the so-called leader of the dissidents.

Machingura was both eloquent and scathing in his denunciation of Mugabe, the man who had ordered the arrests that had caused untold suffering in horrendous conditions for hundreds of Zanla fighters and perhaps had even prolonged the war. Machel had proposed that repatriation of the prisoners be conditional on them joining Zanu-PF, formed while these very proponents of unity with Zapu were locked up, but this had been rejected by Machingura.

It was with great difficulty that I followed his speech. I had a genuine problem reconciling the legendary Dzinashe Machingura with Wilfred Mhanda, the maths wizard of Goromonzi, who was a legend twice over, as a modern-day Albert Einstein and as a Che Guevara.

'Zanu-PF had stigmatised our group and made life very difficult for us back in Harare,' Mhanda told me twenty-five years later. 'It was not possible to get a job. That is why I had to go and live in Germany in 1981. In fact, eighteen of us were arrested and detained without charge just ten days after independence on 28 April. We spent two weeks in the cells before being released by Nkomo, who had become the minister of home affairs, after we staged a ten-day hunger strike.

'For the sake of sheer survival, people such as Muchechetere, Chihuri, Sam Geza and Alexander Kanengoni sought to rehabilitate themselves in the eyes of Zanu-PF. It's perfectly understandable. It was opportunism for survival. But they never displayed any open antagonism towards people such as me,' Mhanda said.

Three years later, Nkomo himself had to flee arrest by Mugabe's men by escaping across the border into Botswana 'dressed as a woman', as the newly appointed home affairs minister, Herbert Ushewokunze, announced to the shameless amusement of his colleagues in the Zanu-PF leadership, and to the chagrin of Zimbabweans who placed a high value on post-independence unity and reconciliation between PF-Zapu and Zanu-PF.

I was not to meet Mhanda again until 2000, when I was editor in chief of the recently launched *Daily News*. Indomitable as ever, he had just established the ZLP, which brought together war veterans who were disenchanted with and anxious to distance themselves from the excesses, violence and avarice of the discredited ZNWVA, led by Chenjerai 'Hitler' Hunzvi. In the interim, Mhanda and I shared the dubious distinction of having been declared 'enemies of the state' by Zanu-PF.

Based on the twenty-nine years of their acquaintance, I asked Mhanda to characterise Mugabe as a politician.

'He is a remarkably consistent man, with a sharp focus on power. From 1976 he methodically consolidated his position within Zanu, which was to serve as his springboard to state power.

'Whatever he did from that time on was calculated to ensure his ascendancy within Zanu. Once he had secured his position in the party, he consolidated his power by systematically eliminating or neutralising all potential threats. Anything that stood in his way was ruthlessly disposed of. The party's history is littered with Zanu greats who have been methodically eliminated for their perceived or real pretensions to his throne. As Mugabe sought to consolidate his power base, everyone became dispensable.

'Of all the Zanu founding fathers dead or alive, only his long-serving deputy, Simon Muzenda, who was totally devoid of ambition, remained by his side up to the very end of his own life. This was an expedient way for Mugabe to keep the powerful Karangas in check.

'After becoming prime minister in 1980, Mugabe's objective was to entrench his position by progressively eliminating Nkomo and his party, PF-Zapu. He needed Nkomo on his side at first, to confer popular legitimacy on his authority. Once he achieved that, he moved against Nkomo after forging an alliance of sorts with the whites, which he could not have done with justification if he had left Nkomo out in the cold from the beginning.

'He used this alliance to crush Zipra and Zapu's grassroots support in Matabeleland and the Midlands. After Nkomo's defeat and the signing of the Unity Accord in 1987, it was time to direct his focus at Zanu again and eliminate any critical or dissenting voices,' Mhanda told me.

After independence, Mhanda met his nemesis only once, at the Harare Sheraton in 1994 during the world conference of agricultural economists, officially opened by Mugabe.

Mary Chimedza, who was a year behind us at Goromonzi, had organised the conference and invited Mhanda to attend. During a coffee break, Mhanda and a group of delegates were standing some forty metres from where Mugabe was being mobbed.

'I wasn't keen on a face-to-face encounter with him, but Mary insisted that I join the VIPs. She was quite irate and said that this was her conference and she did not care about my personal differences with Mugabe. So I moved closer. Then Kumbirai

Kangai, who was the minister of agriculture, spotted me and dragged me all the way to where Mugabe was.

'He was visibly shaken, and on noticing this, the dignitaries around him drew back tactfully. Kangai then asked Mugabe whether he still remembered me. He shook his head and said, "Not at all."

'Then, speaking in Shona, he said, *Chiso ndinorangarira asi handichazivi kuti ndiani*, meaning he remembered my face from somewhere but could not place it.'

Kangai then introduced Mhanda to the president and, rather mischievously, beat a hasty retreat.

'I sensed Mugabe's discomfort,' said Mhanda. 'He asked where I lived and what I was doing for a living. After about three minutes, I decided I didn't want to prolong his discomfort, so I left. Many, including some of the cabinet ministers who had earlier withdrawn, asked who I was. I wasn't keen to say, and I'm sure they didn't dare ask Mugabe. But I don't doubt that Kangai satisfied their curiosity.'

One of the prisoners from Pemba, Rugare Gumbo, became a cabinet minister in the Mugabe government. His rehabilitation was the result of personal connections with the vice-president, Simon Muzenda, who had initially secured a job for him at Buchwa Mine and then with Wankie Colliery, where he became human resources manager. Government had the majority shareholding in the colliery at the time.

Later, the leading female guerrilla during the war, Joyce Mujuru – appointed as Mugabe's deputy in 2005 – drafted Gumbo onto the ZBC board of governors while she was minister of information.

'All these appointments were a form of apprenticeship to test Gumbo's loyalty,' explained Mhanda. 'With these good references, Mugabe eventually conceded to his cabinet appointment, albeit reluctantly.'

According to Mhanda, the principal factor influencing Gumbo's appointment was that, as deputy minister of home affairs, Mugabe and Muzenda saw him as a counterweight in the Masvingo province to maverick politician Eddison Zvobgo. After both Muzenda and Zvobgo died, Mugabe used Gumbo as leverage against Emmerson Mnangagwa in the Midlands, especially following the so-called Tsholotsho Rebellion of December 2004. Many leading politicians, including Mnangagwa and information minister Jonathan Moyo, were accused of plotting against the president's succession plans.

'In Mugabe's scheme of things, there is always a purpose to everything,' said Mhanda.

When Mugabe and his wife Sally moved into State House, they had little first-hand experience of life in Harare or the rest of Zimbabwe, for that matter. The sum total of his exposure to the capital had been a brief period of hectic political activity between his return from Ghana and his detention at Gonakudzingwa. Strictly speaking, therefore, Mugabe gained a working knowledge of his country only after becoming prime minister. He was rather like Hastings Kamuzu Banda, who in 1963 had assumed the leadership of Malawi, a country from which he had been exiled for forty years, with detrimental results.

But in the beginning, Mugabe personified all the hope and promise that had sustained black Zimbabweans during fifteen years of hardship, sacrifice, tragedy and war.

On 7 June 1980, seven weeks after being sworn into office, Mugabe paid his first official visit to Kutama Mission, the village of his birth and foundation of his intellectual achievement. It was a big occasion. The villagers had prepared for the return of their heroic and long-lost son, while the mission authorities had spared no effort in preparing to receive Kutama's most accomplished and famous alumnus.

The prime minister's long entourage of official cars raised a cloud of dust as it sped into the mission grounds amid much brandishing of AK rifles by the military and shrill ululation from female party officials and Mugabe's relatives. Looking immaculate in his trademark long-sleeved safari suit, he shook as many hands as he could, including mine.

The schoolboys, immaculately turned out for the day, had fashioned a rickety wooden platform with a handle at each corner. The introductory formalities over, Mugabe was led to where the platform had been laid on the ground and asked to stand on it.

Four young boys, resplendent in well-pressed khaki, stepped forward and, each taking hold of a handle, lifted the platform – the prime minister balancing precariously on it – hoisted it onto their shoulders and began moving forward, their hero held aloft. It was a proud and awe-inspiring moment for Kutama, and an award-winning image for the press photographers who had turned out in force on that wintry morning and switched frenetically from one camera to another slung around their necks.

For me, it was a simple moment of proof that the torment and sacrifices of Zimbabwe's people over the years had not been in vain. Here, at last, was a national leader who was truly a man of the people. Fortuitously, as it turned out, I resisted a strong urge to pocket my notebook and take a turn bearing the premier's weight.

Mugabe's knowledge of the country he now led was gleaned in the unnatural conditions under which any head of state must live. Always heavily guarded, he was never free to take an afternoon stroll through Harare Gardens or window-shop on First Street. While he was indisputably a learned man, Mugabe was not a streetwise politician when he assumed leadership of a country and a people that he barely knew. This major liability rendered him prone to being occasionally taken in by supporters and hangers-on of dubious character or questionable intent. As he became more geriatric, many such characters, some of them outright rogues and others simply worthless, wormed their way into positions close to his seat of power.

Throughout his eventful life, including ten years of detention by the Smith regime, Mugabe's greatest asset was an uncanny aptitude for turning adversity to personal advantage. He used his time behind bars to gain several academic degrees and a reputation as an excellent tutor, inspiring leader and organiser, while serving as an executive member of Zanu. On his release he had either propelled himself to leadership of the organisation or it had been thrust upon him by circumstance. Either way, power was within his grasp.

The Lancaster House Agreement had effectively retained the emergency powers used by Smith to rule Rhodesia with an iron fist. This gave Mugabe free rein from day one, with no real checks and balances. The agreement did not prescribe a lasting solution for the vexing issue of equitable redistribution of land in favour of the rural peasant population. More ominously, the state of emergency was to be used with catastrophic consequences when Five Brigade was unleashed on innocent Ndebele supporters of Nkomo's Zapu in western Zimbabwe.

In 1987, as soon as the Lancaster House sunset clause on parliamentary seats for whites expired, Mugabe amended the constitution, abolished the post of prime minister in favour of an executive presidency, and scrapped the upper house, or senate. The portal to absolute power beckoned.

After I exposed the corruption committed by several members of the Mugabe cabinet in what came to be known as the Willowgate scandal in 1988, I was dismissed as editor of the *Chronicle*. Although Mugabe had personally sanctioned the investigation, he went back on his word when he informed the nation that I had been fired from the government-owned newspaper because I was overzealous. He offered no evidence to sustain the allegation, but both my career and my personal life were egregiously disrupted, resulting in long periods of exile in Mozambique and the United States.

Enos Nkala and Maurice Nyagumbo had been the only Zanu-PF leaders who addressed Mugabe by his first name. According to Mhanda, Mugabe took advantage of their fall in the wake of Willowgate to strengthen his own position. Subsequently, he effectively reduced the power and influence of people such as Eddison Zvobgo and Nathan Shamuyarira.

But it was the rise of the first real political opposition in decades, the Movement for Democratic Change (MDC), that would unleash some of Mugabe's most diabolical megalomania. The demise of Muzorewa in 1980 should have served as a lesson for Zanu-PF's future election strategists. Old loyalties can induce voters to suffer much and suffer long, but when they finally become fed up with a political party, their wrath can be terrible.

In the run-up to the 2000 election, the MDC, born of the grassroots trade union movement, potentially threatened something that Zanu-PF had not faced in twenty years: regime change. Mugabe's response, as always, was a systematic assault on anyone and everything that might conceivably contribute to his downfall.

'First it was the whites again, the Rhodesians, hence the invasion of their commercial farms in 2000, and then he targeted the political opposition and the press, especially the *Daily News*,' said Mhanda.

In 2005, I arranged an interview with Lord Carrington, chairman of the Lancaster House conference, in London. At the ripe old age of eighty, he had long since retired, while Mugabe, a year older, was still head of state after twenty-five years in office.

Carrington's recollections of Mugabe's attitude and performance during the negotiations were vivid and unequivocal.

'I never liked Mugabe,' he said. 'He was reptilian. He was a very cold fish. He didn't really want to sign the Lancaster House Agreement because he was absolutely certain that he was going to win, anyway. He could see that the white Rhodesians were on their knees, and they were calling up everybody that they possibly could to fight. The economy was in disarray because seventeen years of sanctions were beginning to bite. And, therefore, he thought he was going to win. And there was no need whatever to compromise. He only signed because of Nyerere and – what's his name – Machel, who were suffering as a result of what was happening.'

Mugabe had never once doubted that he would emerge triumphant, said Carrington.

'Well, the Shona are the majority tribe, his guerrillas were the only ones doing any fighting because Nkomo's guerrillas were sitting in Zambia, rather to the embarrassment of poor old Kaunda, not doing anything very much. And I think Mugabe took the view that the Shona were the majority, they were the people doing the work; he had the support of Nyerere and what's-his-name from Mozambique.

'Muzorewa really was a sort of uncle-whatnot. He was a puppet. He was not going to be accepted by anyone – no African country, other than South Africa, would have regarded it as being acceptable, no country in the Commonwealth. Carter was then president of America – he certainly wouldn't have accepted it. And there was no one in the European Union who would have done so. Therefore, we [Britain] would have been landed with having recognised a Rhodesia – whatever we called it in those days – that was not recognised by anyone else other than South Africa.'

Asked about the pre-election political violence, Carrington waved his hand dismissively, and said: 'Oh, they all did it. It was merely a question of who was doing it more. Yes, I think Mugabe probably was. But the white Rhodesians weren't blameless. Nor was that little bishop. There is no doubt about it. Okay, there was intimidation, but the fact is, there's no doubt whatsoever that the result was what the people of Zimbabwe wanted.'

Carrington and Mugabe first met when the chairman hosted a dinner before the conference began. 'I had already come to know Smith and Muzorewa and Nkomo and various other people, but Mugabe absolutely refused to see me. He was the only one of those people at the Lancaster House conference – the important people – that I hadn't met before.'

During that first dinner, Carrington asked Mugabe if he was bitter at being treated 'violently badly' by Smith, being locked up for ten years and denied permission to attend his only child's funeral. The former foreign secretary said Mugabe told him, 'I am not bitter about the people, I am bitter about the system.'

Mugabe's only child with Sally, Nhamodzenyika, had died in infancy in Ghana, where she had taken the sickly boy for treatment. Prison authorities in Salisbury bluntly denied Mugabe permission to travel to the West African state, even under guard, to bury his son. He and Sally never had another child.

Swedish journalist and author Per Wastberg, once Mugabe's staunchest champion in the international media, no longer talks to the man he used to call a friend. Wastberg first travelled to Rhodesia in 1959 as a student. He struck up a friendship with historian Terence Ranger, who published a news sheet that was extremely critical of the governments headed by Edgar Whitehead and Roy Welensky, and regularly attended debates and meetings on the political situation in Rhodesia.

While Mugabe was imprisoned, Wastberg not only offered support to Sally, but also served as Mugabe's link with Amnesty International. While attending a media conference at Chobe in northern Botswana in 1989, Wastberg and I met and became friends, and I subsequently visited him several times at his home in Stockholm.

On one such visit in 2005, Wastberg spoke frankly about his relationship with the Mugabes and the changes he had observed over the years.

'When I was a student in Salisbury, there were three blacks who always attended our meetings: lawyer Herbert Chitepo and journalists Willie Musarurwa of the *African Weekly* and Nathan Shamuyarira of the *African Daily News*. Nathan struck me as a sly intriguer with a soft voice. The two others were straightforward and honest,' Wastberg recalled.

Later, when Mugabe was in detention, he was anxious about Sally being in London, and wanted her to live in neutral Sweden instead.

'She did, and the Swedish development agency, Sida, sent her around the country, preaching anti-racism in schools. She learned some Swedish and was well liked by everybody for her humour. For some time, on and off, she took care of our two young children. They loved her very much.'

When Mugabe was released, Sally joined him in Mozambique, and then he 'disappeared', said Wastberg.

'I wrote an article expressing fear that he had been assassinated. It was also published in English newspapers, and eventually it turned out that Mugabe was under house arrest in Quilimane, judged by Samora Machel as too immature to lead a guerrilla campaign.

'Mugabe hated Machel. Sally told me that when Machel was killed in October 1986, Mugabe commented: "Good for him, good for us."'

Machel and thirty-three others perished when his aircraft hit a mountain in South Africa's north-eastern Transvaal while on a flight from Lusaka. At a time of growing political tension between Mozambique and apartheid South Africa, foul play was immediately suspected and there were allegations that a decoy beacon had been used to divert the aircraft from its course of approach to Maputo. An official inquiry blamed error on the part of the Russian pilot for the accident, but doubt still lingered over the possible involvement of dirty tricks by South Africa's security forces.

But, as Machel himself had pointed out to Mugabe, post-independence Mozambique was a seriously impoverished country, much of its infrastructure destroyed by a prolonged civil war and lacking even the most basic skills and commodities. Aircraft maintenance was not the highest item on the Machel government's priority list, and prior to the fatal crash, Mugabe and Zimbabwean officials had watched in shocked silence as his Russian-built Tupolev 134 belched ominous black smoke while slowly gaining altitude after taking off from the airport at Victoria Falls.

As late as 1994, when I arrived in Maputo at the start of a three-year period of self-imposed exile, I very nearly caught the next aeroplane back to Harare. Accustomed to the order and cleanliness of the Zimbabwean capital, I was appalled by the squalor and dilapidation of Mozambique's largest city almost two decades after independence. A Danish aid worker once angered me by denouncing Harare as being 'too clean', adding: 'Maputo is the real Africa.'

I suspect Harare would have more than met her standards for 'reality' by 2005, with mountains of garbage, endless queues for sporadic and short supplies of essential commodities, and policemen who offered citizens no guarantee of protection. In the midst of this chaos, compounded by chronic power outages and regular water shortages, the Mugabe government launched its iniquitous Operation Murambatsvina, which saw informal housing and business structures bulldozed and destroyed without warning or compassion, all in the interest of 'cleaning up the trash'.

Street vendors lost their last remaining sources of income and thousands were rendered homeless, forced into 'refugee camps' barely fit for human habitation as Mugabe's security forces moved against the burgeoning urban population that made up the opposition MDC's biggest power base, and tried to force people back to the barren rural areas they had left in search of jobs and food.

If Harare in 2005 represented the 'real' Africa, it might as well have been a foreign country to the well-travelled and big-spending Mugabe.

'His first visit to Sweden was unofficial,' Wastberg told me. 'He stayed in my house and I invited the then foreign minister, Ola Ullsten, to join us for dinner. Mugabe's bodyguard fell asleep at the table, right in the chicken soup. When Mugabe was in London for the Lancaster House conference, I saw him a few times privately at a small flat, where Sally served us breakfast.'

Wastberg had written numerous articles on Rhodesia for the Swedish newspaper *Dagens Nyheter* since 1959, and was included in the official Swedish delegation at the 1980 independence celebrations, most likely thanks to a suggestion from Mugabe to the government in Stockholm.

'I even had a personal bodyguard, who turned out to have been part of Ian Smith's entourage,' he recalled. On a subsequent visit later in the year, however, he arrived at Harare Airport only to be told that he was prohibited from entering the country. A prohibition order issued by Smith's government was still on file and Wastberg had to call Shamuyarira before he was allowed to proceed.

'I went back perhaps every three years until 1997. Each time, I saw Mugabe privately, sometimes even when Sally was hooked up to a dialysis machine. I visited them at State House and remember seeing the Penguin editions of Graham Greene's novels that Mugabe liked to read.

'When he visited Stockholm in March 1986 for the funeral of our murdered prime minister, Olof Palme, Mugabe was down on the floor, playing with my children, laughing, though he was never as naturally relaxed as Sally. To me, he was the ideal university principal, a stern teacher, a man who knew too much from books and too little of reality because of his many years of prison and guerrilla warfare.

'During our last three-hour conversation in 1994, he told me he was dissatisfied with students, mainly black, taking drugs and raping at leisure on the campus. He always did like to tell people how to behave … an extremely intellectual man, determined, but without empathy or insight.

'I remember that he unwrapped a cake, sliced it and then told me what was wrong with the state. I detected no signs of racism, but there were hints of dictatorial tendencies and an unwillingness to be proved wrong. He could afford to behave generously only if he had success, the wind of praise behind him.

'We parted with stiff politeness, well knowing that we now disagreed too much to be able to meet again. I started to write a number of highly critical articles, and commented with indignation on the Catholic Justice and Peace report on the Matabele massacres. His Christmas and New Year cards stopped coming, and so did invitations from the Zimbabwe Embassy in Stockholm.'

In an increasingly democratised world, Mugabe became one of the worst tyrants, according to Wastberg.

'He became merciless, egotistical, always playing for power, sacrificing anything to hold onto it. He could have stepped down years ago and left a fairly good record for history, but he left it too late. He became a freedom fighter who knew not how to guard the freedom once the fight was over; a self-made Roman emperor of the worst kind.'

Mugabe's obsession with keeping the press under strict control was always part of a greater scheme to build and maintain an unchallenged power base. Successive information ministers – the vindictive Shamuyarira, Chitepo's disgruntled widow Victoria, the clueless Joyce Mujuru, the affable Chenhamo Chakezha Chimutengwende and the mercurial Jonathan Moyo – were all merely instruments used to achieve Mugabe's goal. In their different ways, they engaged the emergent private press, the *Financial Gazette* and the *Zimbabwe Independent* at first, and later, more forcefully, the *Daily News*.

Mugabe's actions against Zimbabwe's white citizens long after independence may suggest that he was, indeed, bitter towards them, despite his conciliatory pronouncements in 1980. But he was no less vindictive against blacks who did not share his political views or who questioned his leadership.

Wastberg's experience with Mugabe lends credibility to my belief that, in the eyes of Zimbabwe's president, anyone – white, Shona or Ndebele – who challenged his authority would be unacceptable and thus a target for retribution. I would learn this lesson at enormous personal cost.

7

No quiet on the
Western Front

MY ARRIVAL IN Bulawayo in April 1983 aroused no fanfare. Tommy Sithole, the man I was replacing as editor of the *Chronicle*, was winding up his own affairs before leaving for Salisbury the next day to take control of the *Herald*.

The previous editor, Zambian-trained Farayi Munyuki, had been summarily re-assigned to head Ziana, the national news agency, after publishing an editorial comment that the government deemed to be offensive to its counterpart in Botswana.

The standard of journalism in Zimbabwe was exceptionally high at independence, but the first three *Herald* editors in the Mugabe era had all trained abroad: Munyuki in Zambia, Sithole in Tanzania (where he became sports editor on the *Daily News* in Dar es Salaam) and Charles Chikerema in Cuba.

Manyuki's sudden move left little doubt that neither management nor the board of directors was calling the tune regarding editorial appointments at Zimpapers any longer. They had been usurped by the Mass Media Trust at the behest of information minister Nathan Shamuyarira, former editor of the defunct *African Daily News*.

It was widely speculated in media circles that Shamuyarira's obsession with keeping a tight lid on journalism was initially motivated by personal considerations, with Zanu-PF and government possibly benefiting by default.

Soon after being elected deputy secretary of finance at Zanu's 1964 conference in Gwelo, Shamuyarira had gone to study in the United States and was politically dormant for four years. On his return to Africa, he settled in Lusaka, Zambia, and after Zanu's supreme council, or Dare, was expanded from four to eight members in April 1969, he became the party's secretary for external affairs.

Shamuyarira was an ardent supporter of James Chikerema, the Zapu vice-president, who, in the absence of Nkomo in prison, became the organisation's de facto leader in exile. Chikerema tried to strengthen his position by resorting to divisive tactics. When these failed, he tried to effect reconciliation between Zapu and Zanu, which had broken away from Nkomo's movement in 1963.

The majority of Zanu's leadership, including Herbert Chitepo, chairman of the Dare in Lusaka, mistrusted Chikerema's intentions, but Shamuyarira and others, all of them from Chikerema's Zezuru tribe, rallied to his support. Shamuyarira went a step further by challenging Chitepo's chairmanship, but at Zanu's 1971 review conference, Shamuyarira's group suffered a decisive defeat, with two-thirds of the delegates voting against his clique.

Humiliated, Shamuyarira immediately resigned from Zanu and aligned himself fully with Chikerema. Tribalism not only became rife in the nationalist movements, but also led to the creation of the Front for the Liberation of Zimbabwe, with Chikerema as the leader.

Shamuyarira later became a lecturer at the University of Dar es Salaam, rejoined Zanu-PF and was appointed minister of information at independence, but his association with Frolizi remained an albatross around his neck.

When I reached Bulawayo in 1983, I checked into a medium-sized hotel that would be my home for the next six months, and Tommy Sithole gave me a quick tour of the newspaper, introducing me to staff in the various departments.

After a brief meeting with senior editors, Sithole and I met alone in the editor's office and he gave me a brief rundown on the staff and operations – who the bright sparks were, who to watch out for, what issues were outstanding, which people were useful contacts and so forth. He touched on the deteriorating security situation in Matabeleland and advised that I play it by ear. I sensed that he was relieved to be leaving, which did not make me particularly happy to have arrived.

Pointing to an unusually large chair in a far corner, he said: 'That chair is reserved for Dr Joshua Nkomo. He is a regular visitor, and normal chairs would be too small for his frame. When he calls, there is usually trouble, and he does not phone ahead to make an appointment.'

Nkomo, founder and president of the Zimbabwe African People's Union, was born in 1918 of Ndebele parents, who taught at a mission school. Like Mugabe, he studied at Fort Hare University in South Africa, where he met Nelson Mandela and other future political leaders. On returning to Rhodesia in 1948, he secured a job in the social welfare department of Rhodesia Railways, and later became an official of the black railway workers' trade union.

In the wake of British premier Harold Macmillan's speech about the 'wind of change' blowing across Africa, Nkomo formed the National Democratic Party in 1960. Among the party leaders were the Reverend Ndabaningi Sithole, Robert Mugabe and Enos Nkala.

Zapu was formed in 1962 after Ian Smith had banned the NDP, but no sooner was it established than it, too, was outlawed. Sithole, Mugabe, Nkala, Herbert Chitepo and others broke away from the party to launch Zanu, while Zapu became an essentially ethnic-based Ndebele organisation.

Nkomo was among the black nationalists detained in 1964 and released ten years later after South African prime minister BJ Vorster put pressure on the Smith regime to free them. Nkomo went to live in exile in Zambia, from where Zapu's military wing, Zipra, played its part in the armed liberation struggle.

There was no love lost between Nkomo and Mugabe, but when Zapu captured all seventeen parliamentary seats in Matabeleland and took another three in the Midlands to boot, Mugabe was obliged to include Nkomo in the government of national unity, formed in the wake of the Lancaster House Agreement and subsequent election.

The Zapu leader turned down the ceremonial position of president, accepting a cabinet post instead. In 1982, however, Nkomo was accused of plotting an uprising against the government, and Mugabe unleashed the notorious Five Brigade on the Matabele homeland. The ruthless Gukurahundi campaign claimed an estimated 20 000 lives in Matabeleland and the Midlands. Nkomo was forced to flee Zimbabwe and go into exile again, this time in the United Kingdom. On his return, he and Mugabe appeared to set aside their long-standing differences and bitter rivalry, and in December 1987, PF-Zapu and Zanu-PF merged to become one party, Zanu-PF.

With Gukurahundi's wounds still raw, Nkomo's Ndebele supporters accused him of selling out, but he nevertheless accepted the sinecure of a vice-presidency, shared with Simon Vengesai Muzenda. Broken, humiliated and with his health failing, Father Zimbabwe, as Nkomo was affectionately called by the faithful, died in 1999.

While I was editor of the *Chronicle*, Nkomo visited my office twice, once to make my acquaintance and once to complain about a leading article that suggested he could not expect the newspaper to publish reports of atrocities on the basis of information he provided, without independent substantiation.

'Do you think this a figment of my imagination?' Nkomo asked, pointing at the head of Sikwili Moyo, swathed in bandages after Five Brigade had assaulted the PF-Zapu official.

An abusive tirade against me followed, delivered mostly in Ndebele and punctuated with exhortations to 'go and tell this to Robert'. I protested that I was not Mugabe's messenger and that my comprehension of Ndebele still left much to be desired. I immediately regretted the latter admission, which served only to further infuriate the seasoned politician.

'Is it my fault that you don't even speak Ndebele when you live in Bulawayo?' he demanded angrily.

A few weeks after this, a senior police officer burst into my office one morning. I should leave immediately, he advised. The PF-Zapu leader was tearing up copies of the *Chronicle* and vowing to come and deal with me next.

We had reported that Nkomo had threatened to take physical action against the paper. I protested to the law officer, pointing out that I could not flee my office each time Dr Nkomo said he wanted to beat me up. If he wished to deal with me, in whatever manner, he would find me waiting. Realising that I was going to stay at my post, the policeman left, but as a precaution, posted two of his men in uniform at the building's street entrance as back-up for our own security guards.

An hour later, my visitor telephoned to say I could relax. Dr Nkomo and his entourage had just driven past the small town of Esigodini, forty kilometres south of Bulawayo, suggesting he had either forgotten about or postponed his promised visit.

On my first day at the newspaper, of course, my encounters with Nkomo lay some distance in the future. I was still trying to decide whether or not Sithole's reference to the corner chair was his little joke at my expense or a serious warning, when he suddenly looked at his wristwatch and sprang to his feet.

A short but athletic man, Sithole played tennis regularly and had informed me earlier that we would be lunching at the Bulawayo residence of finance minister Enos Mzombi Nkala, the most powerful Zanu-PF politician in Matabeleland and, *ipso facto*, Nkomo's mortal enemy.

I felt somewhat uneasy. I had not expected that my first official lunch as editor would be with a top government minister, and the fourth most powerful man in Zimbabwe at that. Tommy sought to reassure me.

'He is okay,' he said. 'You will like him once you get to know him.'

In 1974, when Zimbabwe's black nationalist leaders were released, the Zanu luminaries were each assigned an area of the country in which to recruit new members for the party. Zanu had become largely moribund while its leadership languished in detention camps and the official ban on political parties was enforced.

Salisbury and the provinces of Mashonaland, around the capital, were allocated to Mugabe, who, while in prison, had emerged as the likely new leader of Zanu. Edgar Tekere, the fiery politician from Manicaland, was assigned to the Midlands and southern province of Masvingo. He had worked in the Midlands city of Gwelo before his detention. Nkala assumed responsibility over Matabeleland, his home province, while Morton Malianga of Manicaland became responsible for that province. Maurice Nyagumbo, also of Manicaland, was the supervisor of the entire recruitment programme, which encompassed the drafting of young men for guerrilla training with Zanla in Mozambique.

Nkala would hit the headlines six years later during the run-up to the election in the wake of the Lancaster House Agreement. A former office clerk who became Zanu's treasurer at its formation in August 1963, he held a rather unique distinction among the Zanu leadership. The landmark meeting that had heralded the movement's breakaway from Zapu had taken place in his house in Salisbury's black township of Highfields. Subsequently arrested along with the rest of the nationalist leaders, Nkala was to spend ten years in detention. By the time Zanu-PF campaigned ahead of the 1980 election, the boisterous and fiery-tongued politician had acquired both the countenance and the reputation of an inexorable hardliner.

Nkala became Zanu-PF's leading candidate in Matabeleland. Addressing a political rally on Sunday 10 February 1980, he issued an open threat. If his party did not win the forthcoming elections, Zanu-PF would redeploy its 27000 heavily armed guerrillas, now restlessly encamped at assembly points dotted around the country, to launch a new phase of the bush war. Less ominously, he was quoted in the press as saying 'the governor can go hang'.

Nkala was referring to the last governor of Rhodesia, Lord Soames, who had been dispatched to Salisbury by Margaret Thatcher's Conservative government to preside over the transition from Smith and Muzorewa's ill-fated Zimbabwe-Rhodesia to the genuinely independent Republic of Zimbabwe. His major task was to ensure that the first majority-rule elections were held in an atmosphere of reasonable peace and fairness.

Not surprisingly, Soames was incensed by Nkala's insensitive and, in the governor's aristocratic view, particularly disrespectful remark. Soames accused the Zanu-PF finance secretary of incitement. To drive his point home, he immediately banned Nkala from campaigning during the remaining month before the election. There was a common perception that Lord Soames was tougher on Zanu-PF and PF-Zapu during the transition period than he was on the internally based parties. He never proscribed Smith's Rhodesian Front candidates, yet they spoke in similar vein at campaign meetings, even invoking the prospect of South African intervention.

Nkala lost the election. His poor performance at the polls was a devastating blow. His campaign strategy of sustained confrontation and bellicose language had failed to deliver a single seat to Zanu-PF in Matabeleland North and South. His defeat at the hands of a party that he hated with a passion was a particularly bitter pill to swallow. The rivalry between Nkomo and Nkala was said by insiders to be deeply ingrained and to have its roots in their youth. It had something to do – or so it was whispered – with one of them sowing his wild oats at the expense of a young female relative of the other.

As fate would have it, Nkala, Simon Muzenda, vice-president of Zanu-PF, and Tekere, the secretary general, were among the leaders of the victorious party who were with Mugabe, eyes glued to the television screen in tense anticipation, at No. 18 Quorn Avenue, the Mugabes' new residence in Mount Pleasant, Salisbury, as British election commissioner John Boynton announced the election results.

In total defiance of both the odds and predictions by local and foreign journalists and analysts, political pundits and Zanu-PF's array of bitter foes and detractors, the party won by a landslide. Even Zanu-PF's own election strategists were surprised by the margin of its victory. Nkala, however, lost dismally in his own constituency of Bulawayo to Nkomo, his political nemesis. With a heavy heart, Nkala joined his rapturous comrades as they broke into song and dance in the politically inauspicious ambience of Mount Pleasant, one of Salisbury's leafier and most lily-white of suburbs, to celebrate the black majority's victory over settler domination and Zanu-PF's victory over its political rivals.

After two decades of sacrifice and a feisty election campaign, Nkala had been roundly rejected by the people of Matabeleland – his own people. His political future was bleak, and he never forgave Nkomo or the Ndebele for this painful humiliation.

However, Mugabe did not forsake his most senior ally from Matabeleland, although he had now been stripped of any legitimate claim to power. He brought Nkala into the senate before appointing him minister of finance. Apart from having served as Zanu-PF treasurer, Nkala possessed no solid credentials for this post, and his performance as minister of finance was predictably disastrous. Despite his general incompetence, Mugabe kept Nkala in the position until he was replaced by the highly capable but politically inept Bernard Chidzero, who had worked for the United Nations before independence.

After the announcement of Mugabe's victory, Soames invited him to Government House. The prime minister elect was accompanied, rather inauspiciously, by Nkala.

'I don't think you know Mr Nkala,' Mugabe introduced his companion, already warming up to the decorum of his new office.

'Ah, yes, Mr Nkala,' the governor replied. 'I don't think I have heard you make any speeches lately.'

Nkala was stung by Soames's patrician sarcasm. The man whom Mugabe was about to appoint to his cabinet glowered at the Queen's representative. Completely dispensing with the etiquette demanded by protocol on such occasions, Nkala looked the governor straight in the eye and told him in no uncertain terms, 'You cost me my seat.'

It is a matter of conjecture, however, whether Nkala could have won the seat, even if the governor had allowed him to continue preaching his trademark brand of hostile politics, punctuated by the wholesale issuance of dire threats of a return to the bush war. Nkomo's party indisputably enjoyed overwhelming support in Matabeleland. In any case, voters all over Zimbabwe had grown weary of war, and even Zanu-PF supporters had become wary and resentful of politicians who invoked memories of the devastating conflict that had cost 25 000 human lives. And besides, it had not escaped attention that for all his bellicose electioneering, Nkala had not fought in the war of liberation.

On arrival in 1983 at the minister's home in the suburb of Khumalo, Tommy introduced me to Enos and Mrs Nkala, who looked more than two decades younger than her husband. I immediately recognised her, since we had lived in the same suburb of Southerton in Harare. Of course, it was not for me to ask when she had become a government minister's wife.

Lunch was a laboured affair. Tommy did most of the talking, assuring the minister that I was a professional journalist and that the *Chronicle* should be in good hands under me. He spent most of the time informing the minister about his own appointment in the capital city and his plans for the *Herald*. I realised that there was a strong rapport between the two men. I thought the minister regarded me with more than a little suspicion, but I survived the lunch and his constant scrutiny.

The meal over, Tommy wished me well and I drove him to the airport. I was not to have any personal interaction with Nkala again for two years, when we met at the Zimbabwe International Trade Fair, the annual highlight of business and social activity in the city of Bulawayo. The minister was among guests in the lounge of the Lonrho Pavilion, the popular meeting place of government officials during the week-long trade fair. Lonrho executive director Herbert Munangatire wined, dined and kept the high and the mighty of Zimbabwe otherwise entertained in such large numbers that the weekly cabinet meeting could quite easily have been held in the pavilion.

As I entered the lounge where they relaxed while quaffing whisky, Nkala saw me and, without warning, proclaimed loudly enough for many in the large room to hear: 'Aah, Comrade Nyarota, I see you are now a Zapu supporter, a dissident.'

The *Chronicle* had berated him in a recent editorial for ominous threats issued against PF-Zapu. I sat down close to the minister and tried to appease him in a lowered voice. But he was in no compromising mood. He said I was a sell-out, that I had always been one.

I realised I had to do or say something to rescue both myself and my injured dignity in the face of this unwarranted onslaught.

'Comrade Minister,' I said, putting on a brave face and addressing him directly. 'You never seem to have the time to find out anything about the small people of this world. As a result you never get to know who they really are. Meanwhile, the small people are never afforded the opportunity to stand on top of the mountain and shout about their own modest contributions to the liberation of this country.'

He was stunned by this totally unexpected response. He was rendered speechless. I had scored a victory, but I knew that battles lines had been drawn from that day forward.

I was thirty-two when I became editor of the *Chronicle*. The fact that my deputy, Martin Lee, was a good fifteen years my senior did little to console me. The assistant editor, Don Henderson, was more of a contemporary at thirty-five. My new secretary, Elizabeth Louw, was at least fifty-five, very mature, efficient and solid as a rock. Her presence made me feel decidedly uneasy. All three had been with the *Chronicle* for many years. I felt overwhelmed by this wide generation gap, as helpless as an animal caught in a trap. But it was imperative that I stood up to the many challenges ahead. This was certainly not the time to feel sorry for myself.

All eyes were fixed on me. The eyes of the staff were focused on me. My two subordinates were supportive, but I felt they scrutinised my every move and decision. The attention of the *Chronicle*'s readers was riveted on me. Head office was watching me. PF-Zapu scrutinised every article published, every editorial comment for evidence of whether I was a friend or a foe. The eyes of Enos Nkala, and behind him those of the whole Zanu-PF monolith, were transfixed on me. The business community watched the direction of the newspaper for any tell-tale sign of radical deviation from its established course. Journalists at the Quill Club in Harare had more than a passing interest in how I performed, many waiting anxiously for an opportunity to say, 'I told you he would not pull it off.'

Ominously, images of Nkomo and Nkala constantly flashed through my mind.

It was no coincidence that while peace returned to the rest of Zimbabwe and the majority of citizens settled down to celebrate their hard-won independence and start reconstructing and rehabilitating the economic and social structure of the country, the people of Matabeleland continued to lead a troubled existence. Continually harassed and forced to attend vindictive and vitriolic Zanu-PF rallies, villagers and township residents in Bulawayo deeply resented being forced to sing Mugabe's praises and surrender their PF-Zapu membership cards in exchange for brand new Zanu-PF party credentials.

Nkala was the guest speaker at most of the weekend rallies and it could safely be argued that, apart from Mugabe himself, he had to shoulder the lion's share of blame for stoking the tension that would erupt in bloody violence between Zanu-PF's Zanla and PF-Zapu's Zipra guerrillas. They were encamped separately but in close proximity in recently established cantonments in Bulawayo's new high-density suburb of Entumbane.

Rivalry between the mainly Ndebele-speaking Zipra and the Shona-speaking Zanla was nothing new. Throughout the war, Zanla had claimed that it bore the brunt of the fighting, while Zipra waged long-distance attacks from across the Zambezi in Zambia.

The two factions had occasionally turned their weapons on one another long before the ceasefire, and Mugabe's decision that Zanu-PF and PF-Zapu should conduct separate election campaigns had done nothing to improve long-standing differences.

The stage was very much set for confrontation between the dissidents, which some have characterised as ethnic conflict. Some Ndebele analysts argue that in deploying Five Brigade in Matabeleland, Mugabe's agenda had been to wipe out the Ndebele. My own view is that Mugabe wanted to destroy the PF-Zapu political support structure. Once the role played by Nkala is factored in, it becomes difficult to accept that Zanu-PF's most senior Ndebele politician was motivated by a desire to decimate his own people. Nkala wanted Nkomo defeated as much as Mugabe sought to destroy Nkomo's political base.

This argument is reinforced by the fact that when opposition to Zanu-PF surfaced elsewhere than in Matabeleland, the full force of the ruling party's violence was directed there as well – in Harare, Chitungwiza, Mutare, Masvingo and other centres. Shona people, not Ndebeles, then fell victim to ruthless violence. They were assassinated, assaulted, arrested and displaced after their houses and property were destroyed by marauding war veterans and Zanu-PF youth militias from their own tribes.

Mugabe had become obsessed with power, and it is entirely likely that the motive behind the Gukurahundi atrocities was to crush political dissent rather than to launch an ethnic-cleansing exercise, as has often been suggested.

During the 1985 election campaign, Zapu and Muzorewa's UANC were both subjected to violence, while Edgar Tekere's Zimbabwe Unity Movement became the target in the run-up to the 1990 and 1995 elections. While PF-Zapu was Ndebele-based, both the UANC and ZUM were led by members of the Manyika tribe.

If Abel Muzorewa had won all Manicaland's parliamentary seats in 1980 and armed dissidents of the UANC's army, Pfumo reVanhu, subsequently took to the bush in that province, Gukurahundi could just as easily have been a Manicaland phenomenon, with some elements of Five Brigade possibly being conscripted in Matabeleland. Much later, in 2005, there were widespread allegations that Ndebele agents had been deployed in Harare during the iniquitous Operation Murambatsvina, which rendered hundreds of thousands of people homeless when their shacks were destroyed. Mugabe consistently exploited the real or perceived ethnic polarisation between the Shona and the Ndebele to strengthen his own political hand. Zanu-PF successfully used the spectre of ethnicity to undermine the MDC, Zimbabwe's most multi-ethnic political organisation, which drew widespread support in both Matabeleland and Mashonaland.

In 2003, a group of war veterans associated with Zanu-PF kidnapped and assaulted David Mpala, the MDC member of parliament for Lupane. Seith Themba Jubane, Nicholas Minenhle Ncube and Patrick Ndlovu seized Mpala and dragged him into the bush, assaulted and stabbed him until he lost consciousness, and left him for dead. Mpala did die of his injuries, but his attackers were sentenced to a mere two years each in prison for the assault.

Mpala was an Ndebele, as were his attackers.

The popular former mayor of Gweru, Patrick Kombayi, posed a serious electoral challenge against Vice-President Muzenda when they stood for parliament in the same constituency during the 1995 election. Kombayi was seriously wounded in an attack mounted by a CIO agent and a Zanu-PF activist, who shot him in the groin, permanently disabling him. The wealthy Kombayi was a former Zanu-PF official and one of the party's leading benefactors in Lusaka. He received treatment in the UK for a long time before he recovered sufficiently to spend the rest of his life walking with the aid of crutches.

Kombayi was Shona.

One of the victims of the government's campaign against Nkomo and PF-Zapu in the mid-eighties was veteran journalist Willie Musarurwa, the popular editor of the *Sunday Mail*. Before independence, he was PF-Zapu's spokesman in Lusaka and at Lancaster House. Afterwards, he campaigned vigorously against the one-party state and the Gukurahundi massacres. He was summarily dismissed from his post.

Musarurwa was not only Shona, he hailed from Mugabe's own province.

With the emergence of the MDC in 1999, the new party became the focal point of opposition for Zanu-PF. Its leaders and activists were victims of murder, arrest and harassment. Their homes and properties were destroyed.

In one of the most gruesome incidents of political violence in post-independence Zimbabwe, MDC leader Morgan Tsvangirai's driver, Tichaona Chiminya, and a party activist, Talent Mabika, were killed in cold blood and in broad daylight on 15 April 2000.

Chiminya was ferrying MDC youths from a rally at Murambinda Growth Point in the Buhera district of eastern Zimbabwe, Tsvangirai's rural home. Two passengers sat with Chiminya inside the double-cab pick-up truck, including Mabika. A number of other MDC supporters rode in the back.

A vehicle with Zanu-PF emblazoned on the side followed closely behind, until suddenly overtaking the MDC truck and stopping in its path, thus blocking the way. Two men brandishing AK47 rifles and others bearing iron bars emerged from the Zanu-PF vehicle and viciously assaulted the occupants of the MDC truck, before tossing petrol bombs into the vehicle. The doors had been locked, trapping Chiminya and Mabika inside. They eventually managed to jump out of the burning vehicle, but Chiminya was badly burned and died a few metres away. Mabika died later that day in hospital. Eyewitnesses said police officers from Murambinda police station had parked their vehicle about 100 metres away and did not intervene.

The suspects were identified as Kainos 'Kitsiyatota' Zimunya, a war veteran who was an election agent for Zanu-PF, Buhera North MP Kenneth Manyonda, and Joseph Mwale, a CIO agent based in Mutare. They were not brought to court until 2004, when, notwithstanding the testimony of eyewitnesses, they were acquitted and set free.

Neither Chiminya nor Mabika was Ndebele.

Almost from the very first issue, the *Daily News*, of which I was the founding editor, was targeted for reprisal by the government. I was repeatedly arrested, threatened with death and finally forced to flee the country. The man who was Mugabe's most zealous defender and chief spin doctor at the time was Professor Jonathan Moyo. Speaking in his capacity as minister of information on 11 April 2002 about deployment of the army against civilians, Moyo expressed his considered opinion that, 'Where the army is deployed, people should not expect a picnic.'

I am Shona. Ironically, Moyo is Ndebele.

There is an abundance of evidence that Mugabe's political strategy was to emasculate not necessarily the Ndebele, but anyone considered a threat to his political position, regardless of ethnic origin.

Amid strengthening ties between their two countries, Mugabe had signed an agreement with President Kim Il Sung of North Korea in October 1980. The Koreans would train a new brigade for the Zimbabwean army. The agreement was made soon after Mugabe announced the need for a new military unit to 'combat malcontents', though there was little evidence of civil unrest at the time.

The 106 Korean trainers arrived at the new facility established high up in the mountains of Nyanga in August 1981. They immediately set about training a brigade that would, Mugabe said, be used to 'deal with dissidents and any other trouble-causers in the country'.

When Nkomo, who as minister of home affairs was responsible for the police, asked why this brigade was necessary, since the country already had a police force to deal with any insecurity, Mugabe warned that dissidents should 'watch out'. By then the prime minister and his senior officials, especially Nkala, routinely associated Nkomo and Zapu with the dissident menace. Mugabe announced that the new brigade would be called *Gukurahundi*, Shona for the spring rain that washes away the chaff from the previous harvest.

Nkomo expressed fear that Mugabe would use Five Brigade to achieve his oft-stated dream of building a one-party state in Zimbabwe. In order to do so, it would be necessary to neutralise or destroy PF-Zapu, and, in effect, Nkomo's party had already been swallowed by the monolithic structure that Zanu had become. To all intents, Zimbabwe became a one-party state less than eight years after casting off the shackles of colonialism.

The 3500 recruits of Five Brigade were conscripted from ex-Zanla troops at Tongogara Assembly Point in Manicaland. The brigade was granted free reign and total licence to exterminate dissidents from Matabeleland. But they mostly targeted innocent civilians, of whom an estimated 20 000 had been brutally massacred by the time Five Brigade was withdrawn in 1986.

Defence minister Sidney Sekeramayi announced in September 1982 that training of the brigade was complete. The first commander was Colonel Perrence Shiri. This brigade was different from other ZNA units in many respects. Five Brigade was not integrated into the normal army command structures, being answerable directly to the prime minister. Members had different uniforms, codes, radios and other equipment that were not compatible with regular army units. Their most distinctive feature in the field was their red berets.

Wearing this distinctive headgear, the soldiers were deployed to invade and cordon off the two Matabeleland provinces and the Midlands, where dissidents were causing mayhem among the civilian population and the white commercial community. A state of emergency, renewable every six months, was declared, along with a curfew that restricted movement in the affected areas.

Under cover of these measures, Five Brigade troops committed atrocities against the civilian population that they were ostensibly deployed to protect from the dissidents. Five Brigade did not distinguish between dissidents and the peasant population, which bore the brunt of most of the atrocities. In principle, the *Chronicle* and other government media supported the deployment of security forces against the dissidents, but the *Chronicle* did not shy away from voicing concern about atrocities perpetrated against civilians, and opposed the ongoing state of emergency. Journalists were not allowed into the affected areas unless accompanied by the military, and our reporting at the *Chronicle* was thus hamstrung. Because of the restrictions, journalists did not have access to first-hand information about atrocities, but it filtered through nevertheless. However, for the local press to publish detailed accounts on the basis of unsubstantiated reports was to court recrimination from the military and the authorities.

As a reporter with the *National Observer*, I had pursued the big stories of the day, regardless of the location or the risk. My most painful experience as editor of the *Chronicle* during the Gukurahundi era was being blocked by the government from going after what was clearly Zimbabwe's biggest story since independence.

Many years later, my former deputy at the *Manica Post*, Eric Meijer, wrote to me.

'A few months after you left Mutare,' he said, 'I was asked by the sixth form at St Augustine's School to give them a talk on journalism. They were not really interested in my views on journalism as a career and so on, but wanted to hear my explanation for the lack of coverage of events in Matabeleland. I had no exculpatory reason, so I clung with great relief to my explanation that the *Post* was a Manicaland paper, so I had no brief in Matabeleland, and the reason for the lack of coverage elsewhere was a government blockade on the area, which was accepted as reasonable, if not particularly impressive. But this excuse was in truth the drunk clinging to the lamppost for support rather than illumination.'

The predicament of journalists in Bulawayo during the deployment of Five Brigade in Matabeleland could not have been put more succinctly. It was at the *Chronicle* that the real implication of my appointment as Jean Maitland-Stuart's successor finally dawned on me. I had assumed that the posting and my subsequent promotion from the *Manica Post* to the *Chronicle* were recognition by Zimpapers under CEO George Capon of my professional performance. In fact, the new owners of Zimpapers were apparently deploying editors on the assumption that they could be relied upon not to ask embarrassing questions, as Maitland-Stuart had done about the training of Five Brigade by North Korean instructors.

When Capon retired suddenly and prematurely and was replaced by self-proclaimed Zanu-PF activist Elias Rusike, the picture became gloomier. The volume of directives from head office to editors increased ominously, while ministerial briefings to editors, including some by the prime minister himself, became the order of the day. In no time we became hopelessly embedded with government, as it were, while the atrocities committed by government troops raged on unabated in rural Matabeleland.

The government took advantage of the fear and gullibility of the local media, mostly controlled by newly appointed and inexperienced editors, and the inertia of foreign journalists, who almost never ventured out of Harare, in order to literally get away with murder.

'I also think that perhaps more tellingly,' Meijer wrote, 'and this is important, no one wanted to believe that the new government was engaged in such brutal acts of systematic violence. Yes, some bullying, overzealous patrolling, but not systematic torture and murder of civilians. No one wanted to believe it, not the local hacks, not even the foreign hacks, and not the Western governments now supporting Mugabe, and rapidly weaning him back from China and PF-Zapu from the Soviet Union. Exposing massacres and torture didn't sit well with the big aid flows, the state visits, and quietly undermining North Korea, in what was still a Cold War proxy scenario.

'Had the foreign media, through diplomatic briefings if nothing else, and the local media through hearing from local people actually wanted to believe what was said to be happening in Matabeleland, there would have been far more fuss overseas.'

Although government's intentions were quite clear, there had been no public outcry or major international reaction to the takeover of Zimbabwe Newspapers, which was the keystone of government control of major newspapers.

In 1997, twenty years after the Gukurahundi massacres, the Catholic Commission for Justice and Peace released a report that finally made public details of Five Brigade's actions in Matabeleland and the Midlands. Called *Breaking the Silence, Building True Peace: A Report on the Disturbances in Matabeleland and the Midlands, 1980–1988*, the document was compiled in collaboration with the Legal Resources Foundation. It is imperative that a section of the report be reproduced here:

They targeted Zapu officials, government officials, even Zimbabwe National Army regulars on leave. Clinics and schools were attacked, teachers brutalised, medical staff beaten and warned not to treat rising local casualties. They set up permanent and mobile bases, occupied water boreholes, shops – any place people had to go – and they carried lists naming people for assassination. Violence was intentional, systematic and premeditated. It was also random, indiscriminate and meaningless.

Women and children and the elderly were beaten for pursuing their daily lives. People were herded – frog-marched under constant abuse – to all-night indoctrination rallies, sometimes lasting for days, forced to sing and dance, and were beaten or killed for the most trivial 'offences'. They were pulled from buses, forced to dig their own graves in front of loved ones, humiliated and shot. An old man summoned from across a field was beaten for not moving fast enough.

Villages were torched, families burned alive in huts. Bodies were dumped in mine shafts as often as they were left to rot in public. People were killed if they sought to recover their dead, funerals were forbidden. Mass graves proliferated and these remain testaments to the horrible and perverse incidents of violence and torture, geographical apparitions scarring the landscape and haunting the people's psyches, all too real and current.

Government trucks sometimes returned to massacre sites to collect the skeletons and the propensity – if not policy – to tamper with, suppress or destroy evidence persists to the present. While some police and officials worked to shield the populace, most turned a blind eye or participated. Some were targets themselves. Civilians recognised Five Brigade soldiers as the same 'dissidents' that had abused them, demanding food, the night before; people followed 'dissidents' into the bush where they watched them change into government uniform.

The atrocities committed by Five Brigade reached their peak between 1983 and 1985. Massacres were also committed by the Central Intelligence Organisation, Police Internal Security Intelligence (PISI) and Zanu-PF youth militias.

To spare Enos Nkala from further embarrassment and humiliation in the 1985 general election, the Zanu-PF campaign strategists nominated him as the candidate in what they believed to be a safe constituency. He stood for election in the town of Kariba on the Zambian border in Mashonaland West, far from his beloved Bulawayo. While Nkala must have accepted this virtual banishment to a political Siberia with a lump in his throat, he possessed limited options. But in the parliamentary election in question, even the presumably docile voters of the picturesque tourist resort overwhelmingly rejected the nomadic politician from Bulawayo.

Following his political defeat on the shores of Lake Kariba, Nkala returned to Bulawayo with a vengeance. Long after Mugabe had formed Zimbabwe's first majority-rule government, and long after Nkomo and his partners had been expelled from that government, Nkala continued to use inflammatory language and to taunt PF-Zapu at any available opportunity and to hurl abuse at and threaten Nkomo relentlessly, mostly at weekend rallies held in Bulawayo and elsewhere in Matabeleland.

Despite his dismal showing in the 1985 election, Nkala was appointed minister of home affairs. He used his newly acquired power in a vindictive endeavour to crush Zapu altogether. Nkala transformed PISI, a secretive and elite division within the ministry of home affairs, into what amounted to his personal corps. Wearing plain clothes, wielding wide powers of arrest and similar to the dreaded CIO in its operations, PISI members roamed the suburbs of Bulawayo spreading terror.

'We want to wipe out the Zapu leadership,' Nkala declared menacingly soon after assuming office. 'The murderous organisation and its leadership must be hit so hard that it doesn't feel obliged to do the things it has been doing.'

Whatever Nkala lacked in eloquence, humility and magnanimity, he more than compensated for in brusqueness, sheer arrogance and vindictiveness.

Soon after his appointment, five PF-Zapu members of parliament and eight high-ranking ex-Zipra members serving in the national army were detained. Sidney Malunga, the PF-Zapu chief whip and friend of the *Chronicle*, was eventually charged with aiding and abetting dissidents. However, the evidence brought against him was so flimsy that he was acquitted. He and the rest remained in unlawful detention until September 1986. By the end of 1986, there were very few Zapu officials, from the top leadership down to minor office-bearers, who had not been detained, harassed, beaten, forced into exile or killed.

As the press reported hiccups in unity talks between Zanu-PF and PF-Zapu in June 1986, Nkala announced a blanket ban on PF-Zapu rallies. This was followed by closure of the party's offices, and on 22 September, Nkala effectively banned PF-Zapu altogether.

'All Zapu structures will be set aside,' he said, 'and from now on Zapu will be viewed in the same manner as the MNR bandits in Mozambique.'

Afonso Dhlakama's Mozambique Resistance Movement (MNR), the brainchild of the Smith regime and South Africa's apartheid regime, was at the time causing untold havoc in Mozambique while waging a campaign to topple Samora Machel's government.

Mugabe did not reprimand or challenge Nkala, prompting speculation that the ban was part of Zanu-PF's strategy to bring pressure to bear on PF-Zapu. By 30 October, talks between the two parties had resumed, and Zapu offices were reopened on 1 December. Three weeks later, Mugabe and Nkomo ended their feud by signing a unity accord.

The agreement heralded a new era of peace in Matabeleland, with PF-Zapu having effectively been swallowed by Zanu-PF, much to the chagrin of PF-Zapu's staunch supporters and advocates of multiparty democracy. Particularly incensed were those who had lost relatives and loved ones during the Gukurahundi campaign.

On 18 April 1988, Mugabe announced that all dissidents who surrendered before 31 May would receive a full pardon. Nkomo, now a vice-president, called on them to lay down their arms. Amnesty was also granted to various categories of criminals who were serving jail terms, and in June it was extended to all members of the security forces who had committed atrocities and human rights violations since independence.

Sharp-eyed observers were astounded that only 122 armed dissidents emerged from the bush to surrender to the authorities and take advantage of the government's amnesty offer. Nkala had inflated the number of dissidents marauding through Matabeleland each time he tabled a motion in parliament seeking to extend the state of emergency.

At the height of the Gukurahundi atrocities, Nkala had become the self-anointed emperor of Matabeleland, with an idiosyncratic and relentless determination to wrench the region from Nkomo's control and deliver it to Mugabe.

If Nkala felt cockier in the aftermath of the unity agreement, it was out of genuine relief and celebration that his arch-rival had finally been neutralised and his party subsumed, at least on paper, by the ruling Zanu-PF. Unfortunately for Nkala and other politicians who had adopted a countenance of omnipotence and unaccountability bordering on deity since independence, the cessation of hostilities in Matabeleland, the lifting of the abhorrent state of emergency, the return of genuine peace to all Zimbabwe and the accompanying decline in political polarisation spawned a totally unexpected new dimension.

The unity agreement ushered in a period of unprecedented press freedom that saw even the government's own newspapers, and the *Chronicle* in particular, start flexing their muscles after years of blanket censorship.

In December 1988, a year after the agreement was signed, Nkala hit the headlines again as he engaged the *Chronicle* in mortal combat. Linked by the newspaper to serious allegations of corruption, Nkala fought like a fierce Matabele warrior of old. However, the odds were too heavily stacked against him, and the Willowgate scandal would precipitate his downfall. His rapid descent into political oblivion was concurrent with his advent in the realm of born-again Christians.

In the book *Turmoil and Tenacity*, edited by Canaan Banana and published by College Press in 1989, Professor Welshman Ncube deals at length with the government onslaught against the dissidents. Ncube, a leading academic of Ndebele origin and a law lecturer at the University of Zimbabwe, would become secretary general of the MDC when it was formed ten years later. In a chapter of the book, he dwells on the emergence and elimination of banditry in western Zimbabwe:

> After the sacking of Zapu ministers from government in 1982, a number of former Zipra combatants had taken back to the bush. In January 1984, the then minister of home affairs, in seeking a renewal of the state of emergency, informed the House of Assembly that in the preceding six months these armed men had murdered 75 people, carried out 284 robberies and been involved in 16 rapes.
>
> Two years later, in January 1986, the minister ... informed parliament that during the previous six months of 1985 dissidents had murdered 103 people, raped

57 women, committed 263 armed robberies and destroyed property worth millions of dollars.

In material terms the dissident war was devastating, in that virtually all development projects in Matabeleland had been brought to a standstill and that, for example, by early 1984 nearly 500 000 acres of commercial farmland had been abandoned by fearful white farmers in Matabeleland.

In attempting to eradicate banditry and dissidents the government sent the army into Matabeleland. The activities of the army in the process gave rise to accusations of severe brutality by the army against innocent people. The Catholic Commission for Justice and Peace, the Catholic Bishops' Conference, Amnesty International and the Lawyers' Committee for Human Rights all pointed out that the security forces had abused their powers in operations against dissidents.

This reference to the ugly occurrences associated with the banditry problems in Matabeleland and the Midlands ought to be made so that the success and benefits of national unity can be viewed within their proper context. After the signing of the unity agreement and the installation of Robert Mugabe as the first executive president of Zimbabwe, the new president declared a general amnesty and in terms of Section 31(1) of the Constitution of Zimbabwe granted a free pardon to all dissidents who, on or before March 31, 1988, reported to the police in order to claim benefit of the pardon. He also pardoned all Zapu political fugitives who were out of the country to escape prosecution and all persons who had collaborated with dissidents in violation of the laws of Zimbabwe.

Zapu politicians, Zanu-PF politicians, the churches and the press all appealed to dissidents to take advantage of the free pardon and surrender to the police. By midnight of May 31, 1989, virtually all dissidents had reported to the police to take advantage of the pardon. Even the long hunted butcher of the Esigodini missionaries, Morgan Sango, surrendered with a badly broken arm. With the surrender of all the dissidents, peace returned to Matabeleland and parts of the Midlands. The atrocities and brutalities that had been characteristic of dissident activities all came to an abrupt end. For the first time since the liberation war started in earnest in the early seventies, the people of Matabeleland were experiencing normal life.

From Ncube's exposition it is clear that supporting the deployment of government troops to deal with dissidents, as so eloquently outlined by him, cannot be equated with urging Five Brigade to massacre thousands of innocent civilians under cover of the state of emergency.

Some critics have suggested that while the *Chronicle* went overboard in investigating and publishing details of Willowgate, it did not tell the full story of the Gukurahundi massacres. For the record, the paper never made a conscious decision to pursue the Willowgate story at the expense of the atrocities. They were totally different events, occurring in different contexts and at different times.

The Gukurahundi massacres occurred during a period of rigid government control over Zimbabwe's media. Even the operations of the foreign press were restricted. Some critics overlook the crucial fact that the *Chronicle* was a government-owned newspaper. Less concern is expressed about the fact that even though they were not owned by Ian Smith's regime, both the *Chronicle* and the *Herald* were generally supportive of the government before independence.

My deputy Martin Lee and assistant editor Don Henderson had been with the *Chronicle* for fifteen and ten years respectively at the time of my appointment. Senior journalists Jonathan Maphenduka and Saul Gwakuba Ndlovu were well-respected *Chronicle* staffers of Ndebele origin. Ndlovu had been a high-ranking official in PF-Zapu's publicity department in Lusaka, and thus had strong struggle credentials.

But government had enforced measures to ensure there would be no free dissemination of information relating to Five Brigade's activities. Journalists, both local and foreign, risked dismissal or deportation, perhaps even arrest or death, if they entered the curfew areas in pursuit of a story.

Notwithstanding all of this, I accept full responsibility for the performance, including the shortcomings, of the *Chronicle* on my watch.

At least two foreign journalists sneaked into the restricted territory: Donald Trelford, editor of the London *Observer*, and Andrew Meldrum, an American journalist who became the Zimbabwe correspondent for Britain's *Guardian*.

Anyone who suggests that a *Chronicle* reporter, even one of Ndebele origin, of whom there were many on the paper, could have sneaked in likewise and returned to put together a story for publication in Bulawayo, displays a gross misunderstanding of the security situation then prevailing in Matabeleland.

Some media analysts regard Willowgate as a landmark investigation that became the first tangible evidence of the press flexing its muscles after a long period of sustained repression by the Mugabe government. While Zimbabwe's media languished under the repression of both the Smith and Mugabe regimes, it was the *Chronicle* that finally broke the jinx in October 1988. When the government tightened control over its newspapers in the 1990s, independents such the *Financial Gazette* and the *Zimbabwe Independent* intensified their investigations into corruption and other problems.

Much of the criticism levelled in retrospect against the *Chronicle* over its coverage of the Matabeleland atrocities is replete with both the wisdom and the courage of hindsight.

Under the successive states of emergency, the dissident-ravaged area was strictly inaccessible to the press. Assuming a *Chronicle* reporter had braved the consequences and ventured without detection into an area where Five Brigade had committed atrocities, there is no guarantee that the local population would have cooperated with a reporter from a government newspaper, even one who spoke their language fluently.

An editorial that appeared in the *Chronicle* encapsulated the general attitude of the newspaper towards the security situation in Matabeleland at the time. Published on 28 January 1984 under the heading, 'A welcome investigation', the paper argued:

The assurance by the minister of state in the prime minister's office responsible for security that an investigation will be held into allegations that fourteen people, including women and children, were killed by members of the security forces, is most welcome.

In recent months there have been claims of rural dwellers being beaten and harassed by army personnel searching for dissidents.

The investigation to be initiated by Comrade Sidney Sekeramayi will, hopefully, exonerate them. Should it, however, be established that some members of the security forces have overstepped their authority they must be brought before the courts, as would any other offender. There can be no excuse for abusing a position of trust and responsibility.

Weeding out dissidents in vast tracts of Matabeleland is a difficult and unenviable task. Ultimate success can only be achieved by winning the hearts, the minds and the support of the local population.

Antagonising them could have very serious consequences.

In January 1984, a four-man commission of inquiry, led by a senior Harare lawyer, Simplicius Julius Rugede Chihambakwe, took statements in Bulawayo about the atrocities committed in 1983. Hundreds of people turned up to testify before the widely advertised commission and to hear evidence about the burning of houses, mass beatings and executions by Five Brigade.

Chihambakwe was a professional assistant with the legal firm of Gill, Godlonton and Gerrans (GG&G) when he joined the Zanu legal team at the abortive Geneva conference in 1976. He left this firm during 1979 to set up Zimbabwe's first all-black firm of attorneys in partnership with Amos John Chirunda, who had served his articles with Atherstone and Cook. In the run-up to the March 1980 elections, Chirunda, Chihambakwe & Partners were appointed Zanu-PF's election agents. In fact, this became the most sought-after firm of attorneys in Zimbabwe because of its known links with the new regime. Even Tiny Rowland's politically correct multinational corporation, Lonrho, moved some of its work from GG&G to Chirunda, Chihambakwe & Partners.

Chihambakwe, practising as Chihambakwe, Mutizwa & Partners with James Prince Mutizwa, fell out of favour with Zanu-PF after a stint as mayor of Harare in the mid-eighties, but from 2003, he was once again the flavour of the month.

The findings of the Chihambakwe Commission were never released in Zimbabwe. While Mugabe had promised the people the report would be made public, the minister of state security, Emmerson Mnangagwa, announced in November 1985 that this would not happen. The *Chronicle* enquired why the report was not made public, but to no avail.

For the record, both Meldrum and Trelford made contact with the victims of the Matabeleland violence and atrocities. The government took umbrage at their reporting and issued warnings against them. The temporary employment of a *Guardian* correspondent, Nick Worrall, was withdrawn and he was deported. Trelford in particular ventured into a seriously affected area under cover of darkness, but foreign journalists had two distinct advantages over their local counterparts. They could sneak into the country, put their stories together and sneak out again to have them published abroad. The worst risk they faced was having their work permits rescinded while being deported, as was the case with Worrall. The consequences for local journalists were far more ominous.

I have lectured to journalists all over southern Africa and to students in America. I have told them courage is one of the greatest attributes of African journalism. I have also told them that they are more useful alive than dead and warned of the inherent dangers of comparing Western journalism, which is essentially safe, with African journalism, which is often fraught with hazard to life and limb. I have told them how my own experience as an investigative journalist was no incentive for similar enterprise on the part of younger journalists in Africa. When I ask them whether they would die for a story and they answer in the affirmative, expecting to please me, I always tell them: 'Rather than die for one story, live to write two more.'

When the chips are down, no one cares that your children go without food or a roof over their heads, and I speak from experience. Unfortunately, when the trail gets hot on a big story, everything else can pale into total insignificance, including the welfare of one's offspring. What the public sees in many cases is just the downfall of yet another corrupt politician or thieving chief executive; the risks taken by the reporter in bringing the story to light are borne in private, by spouses, sons and daughters.

Black journalists are particularly vulnerable. Foreign correspondents can always catch the next flight to Johannesburg and return to London or New York, while local journalists have their roots in Africa's trouble spots. The risk of an African journalist working on an explosive story is inherently greater than that of a foreign correspondent working on a similar assignment. The foreigner has an array of safety valves. For the local journalist, God may be the only salvation.

Newspapers such as the *Chronicle* and the *Herald* were owned by Zimpapers, a public company in which the government had a majority stake at a time when it was ultra-sensitive to criticism. Mugabe was riding the crest of a popularity wave, wining, dining and being honoured in the capitals of the West.

Meldrum would relate many years later the frustration of foreign journalists being dismissed as liars, even in London and Washington, by a world that did not want to believe at the time that Mugabe, the international statesman, could do any wrong. The world was protective of Mugabe, and, as a result, he committed atrocities with impunity.

The story of Trelford, editor of the *Observer*, who was on the brink of being sacked by Lonrho chief executive Tiny Rowland after he had exposed the Matabeleland atrocities, more than illustrates this point. The story that captivated the imagination of *Observer* readers and those of other London newspapers over a two-week period sparked the brawl between the mogul and the editor. This sensational conflict in London completely overshadowed the original story, the tragic tale of the wholesale massacre of Joshua Nkomo's rural Ndebele supporters at the hands of Mugabe's North Korean–trained Five Brigade. Trelford's story proved that, notwithstanding the risk taken by some foreign correspondents, few in the world's capitals really cared about the mass execution of innocent peasants.

Lonrho, short for London-Rhodesia, had its origins in the former colony of Rhodesia and had major business interests in Zimbabwe. Lonrho and the Anglo American Corporation were the two largest multinational conglomerates operating in Zimbabwe. Lonrho had bought the *Observer* three years before Trelford went to the country. He had informed Rowland of his pending visit as a courtesy, because of Lonrho's interests in Zimbabwe.

'Rowland seized on the opportunity to ingratiate himself with Mugabe and repair relations that had been damaged by Lonrho's long support for the opposition leader, Joshua Nkomo,' Trelford said.

On arrival in Harare in April 1984, Trelford suddenly found himself appearing as guest of the week on ZTV. He was subsequently recognised by a group of black people in the lobby of Meikles Hotel. One of them approached him and said: 'You should go to Matabeleland to see what is happening to our people there. There are terrible things.'

Why this total stranger thought Trelford would be amenable to such a proposal the visiting journalist did not explain. But the instant faith of this stranger in a foreign correspondent with little or no first-hand knowledge of Matabeleland illustrated another dilemma of the African journalist – African news sources seem to prefer foreign correspondents. Accompanied by Godwin Matatu, the *Observer*'s Harare-based representative, Trelford travelled to Bulawayo and Matabeleland South.

'No media had been allowed inside the curfew area for ten weeks,' Trelford said, 'but there were rumours about brutal treatment of the population by Mugabe's soldiers, ostensibly searching for "dissidents" from across the Botswana border.

'We knew we weren't allowed officially into the curfew area, but asked our driver to brave the roadblocks anyway. We passed three without bother, all manned cheerily by policemen in brown boots, then Matatu did some name-dropping to persuade a tough-looking soldier to let us through. We were able to drive through the no-go areas, past Kezi, Antelope Mine, Bhalagwe Camp – all names, I learned later, that filled the Ndebele with dread. We saw nothing unusual.'

I seriously doubt that without Trelford in the car, any amount of name-dropping by Matatu would have seen the Zimbabwean journalist sail through roadblocks manned by policemen in brown boots.

According to Trelford, another stranger delivered a letter to him at his Bulawayo hotel around 10 p.m. that night. He certainly seemed to have an almost supernatural ability to attract mysterious contacts and sources wherever he travelled in Zimbabwe.

'Please accompany this friend,' was all the letter said, according to Trelford.

'Moving quietly to avoid disturbing Matatu next door, I followed the man to the car park, where a headlight beamed in recognition.

'I had no idea where I was going, or who with; and nobody knew where I'd gone. I knew instinctively that I couldn't take Matatu with me. Apart from the Lonrho connection, he was a Shona and close to the government and his presence would have deterred people from speaking honestly,' he later wrote.

This was where the foreign correspondents beat the local reporters hands down – total strangers were prepared to materialise literally from nowhere and without any prior contact, having taken the trouble to make all the necessary arrangements for a massive scoop.

Trelford said he climbed nervously into the car and was driven in silence several miles out of town into the curfew area. There they swapped cars with another man. After another long drive, they arrived at a mission station, where, for much of the night, he was given a series of eyewitness accounts, sworn affidavits and signed statements from victims of the Matabeleland atrocities.

'These were graphic, horrific and profoundly moving,' Trelford wrote.

He said he had earlier met Peter Godwin of the *Sunday Times*, who said bodies had been thrown down a nearby mineshaft owned by Lonrho.

'Godwin had already got some atrocity stories into print, but he was inhibited by the fact that he couldn't betray his presence in the curfew area for fear of being expelled or, as a Zimbabwean himself, suffering even worse retribution,' Trelford said.

'I returned to the hotel at dawn, checked out without waking Matatu, then flew to London via Harare, arriving on Saturday morning with my story written. While in Harare, I had two conversations. One was with a military attaché at the British High Commission, who wasn't at all surprised by the news from Matabeleland.

'My dilemma on returning – should I … tell the truth about Matabeleland, thereby damaging the interests of my proprietor? – has since been written up as a classic case by the Institute of Global Ethics. For me, there was no choice.'

He told Rowland about the story around 5 p.m. on Saturday, 'too late for him to do anything to stop publication, but before he could hear the news from anyone else. He slammed the telephone down after threatening the direst revenge.

'Next morning I turned on the BBC eight o'clock news to hear my story condemned as lies in an official statement by Mugabe, supported by a letter of apology from Rowland: "I take full responsibility for what in my view was discourteous, disingenuous and wrong in the editor of a serious newspaper widely read in Africa."'

Trelford heard himself not only described publicly on BBC as an incompetent reporter, but also threatened with instant dismissal. In 2003 I was to hear for the first time about my dismissal from the position as editor in chief of the *Daily News* during a news broadcast on ZBC. The statement about my dismissal was then distributed to all newspapers in Harare before I saw it. How the normally lackadaisical ZBC reporters had laid their hands on this sensational scoop has remained a closely guarded secret.

Newspaper editors are powerful people. Newspaper publishers are sometimes more powerful and have little respect for editors.

'Rowland wrote me an open letter, which he distributed to all papers before I could see it,' Trelford said. 'He said Lonrho would not go on supporting a failing editor who showed no concern for their commercial interests.'

In fact, the circulation of the *Observer* had actually increased by 22 per cent in the eight years that Trelford had been editor. My own paper, the *Chronicle*, had more than doubled in circulation from 43 000 to 89 000 in five years when I was fired in 1989. The *Daily News* grew from zero to more than 100 000 copies sold each day over a three-year period. That did not prevent my summary dismissal on trumped-up charges. Newspaper editors must be the most vulnerable executives in the world.

To add to Trelford's woes, the British Foreign Office, more concerned about relations with Mugabe than human rights, and sensitive perhaps to the fact that Britain had provided some training for Five Brigade, was briefing against the editor.

'The Foreign Office tell me you were wrong about Matabeleland,' Prince Charles told Trelford over lunch.

The *Observer*'s journalists were highly supportive of their editor – until Rowland let it be known that he was planning to sell the paper to rival publisher Robert Maxwell. A meeting at Claridges was announced for the next day.

'I knew Rowland would never sell to Maxwell and this was just a bluff to frighten the journalists,' Trelford said.

'I was interested to hear an interview with Maxwell about the *Observer* on my car radio. He "greatly admired" me, he said, and would retain me as editor.'

By now, Trelford felt the standoff between him and Rowland was damaging the newspaper.

'I could not allow the paper's future and the prospects of its staff to be jeopardised by my personal position.

'For us and for the paper, that was the end of a remarkable and in some ways entertaining episode. For the people of Matabeleland, however, it provided only brief illumination before the darkness came again.'

The story of Trelford's plight appeared in the *Guardian* in October 2004, twenty years after he had broken the curfew in an effort to bring to world attention the plight of the people of Matabeleland. So powerful was the image of Mugabe that even foreign bureaucrats were scared to cross swords with him. Both historians and human rights activists might suggest that the *Chronicle* should have been more proactive in taking risks and defying the curfew to expose the murderous incursion of Five Brigade in Matabeleland and the Midlands.

As editor of the paper at the time, I plead guilty to lacking the courage of foreign journalists such as Trelford. But in doing so, I remain mindful of the fact that once he'd got the facts together, Trelford took the first aircraft out of Harare. He did not even bother to inform his Zimbabwean colleague that he was leaving. I also remain mindful that, even in the comfort and safety of London, he lost his job once he'd published the story and that, after all his trouble, the massacre of more than 20 000 innocent peasants remained largely shrouded in secrecy.

In 2000, rampaging war veterans and party youths, as well as Zanu-PF's well-heeled leaders in luxury all-terrain vehicles, invaded the huge farming estates owned by Zimbabwe's 4 000 white commercial farmers. The farm invasions instantly sparked an international outcry of unprecedented proportions about human rights abuse and a breakdown in law and order. The invasions signalled the beginning of the final stage of collapse for Zimbabwe's once robust economy. It is very likely that a similar outcry in the 1980s would have reined in Mugabe and forestalled outrages such as the bloody political violence and farm invasions two decades later.

Surprisingly, after Mugabe and Nkomo signed the unity agreement in December 1987, most Zimbabweans, including those who had borne the brunt of the Gukurahundi massacres, appeared content on the surface to let bygones be bygones.

But in 1997, the Catholic Commission for Justice and Peace would finally cry 'foul'.

8

Gods on earth

O N T H E M O R N I N G of Friday 21 October 1988, the *Chronicle* hit the streets of Bulawayo earlier than usual. The engineers had coaxed the paper's antiquated Heidelberg printing press into handling an unusually large print run without a fatal breakdown the night before. The fifty-seven-year-old press was one of only two of its kind still in existence. The other was believed to be in a museum in Chicago.

It was a daily challenge for production manager Weston Mudzengi's team of enterprising engineers to ensure that the newspaper was on the streets each morning. The print quality had become a matter of grave concern to management and a tribute to the ingenuity of the technical staff. A reader with a wry sense of humour penned a letter to the editor suggesting that Zimbabwe Newspapers should consider issuing a pair of reading glasses with every copy of the paper sold.

On that late October morning, the article that our printers had vowed nothing would prevent or delay publication of, ran the full length of the front page. It was a sensational story, with the potential to shake Zimbabwe's powerful political establishment to its very core before threatening to uproot the *Chronicle* itself.

The piece, a well-investigated and thoroughly documented exposé of widespread corruption in the upper echelons of the ruling elite, would bring the political careers of a number of Mugabe's most trusted and powerful lieutenants to an abrupt end. By the time the story played itself out months later, it had brought to a temporary halt the pig-headed self-importance of some cabinet ministers, who had completely dispensed with any sense of probity and accountability, while a few had become a law unto themselves. One politician in particular had conferred upon himself demigod status. Mugabe appeared neither keen nor competent to rein in his errant cronies. The public had become increasingly restless, but in the end the president left the people in no doubt whatsoever that he was on the side of his brazenly corrupt ministers.

The erstwhile Zanu-PF revolutionaries had returned from the war of liberation with nothing material to show for their service and sacrifice. As they gradually began displaying visible opulence, Mugabe challenged critics, including university students, newspapers and his party's secretary general, Edgar Tekere, who complained bitterly about rampant corruption within both party and government, to produce evidence or refrain from making spurious allegations. Vice-President Simon Muzenda chipped in by urging members of the public to report any cases of corruption.

The *Chronicle* had risen to that challenge.

Running under my byline and a massive but not particularly inspired headline, 'Big racket in new cars', the paper broke the story that would have dramatic and far-reaching consequences for Zimbabwe's media over the next sixteen years, and for me in particular. More significantly, however, it would prematurely terminate the careers of the third and fourth most senior ministers in Mugabe's cabinet and cost four other powerful politicians their jobs.

Under the ninety-six-point headline, the paper's subeditors had lined up pictures of four prominent Zimbabweans to strengthen the impact of the scoop. They included a top government minister, his permanent secretary, a prominent Bulawayo business tycoon of Asian origin – well known for exploiting his strong links with Zanu-PF's top hierarchy – and the managing director of the country's largest motor vehicle assembly plant. The businessman, Manilal Naran, owned a number of enterprises in Bulawayo, including Spot-On, a huge wholesale liquor outlet at the corner of Fort Street and Fifth Avenue.

Naran's legendary generosity ensured that his office at Spot-On had become a favourite rendezvous of visiting government officials and local politicians. One government minister could be contacted at Spot-On virtually every Friday afternoon. He had granted at least one press interview there.

There was a public outcry in Bulawayo when the *Chronicle* reported that, on his wedding day, Naran's son was escorted by a presidential motorcade to the family mansion in the suburb of Killarney.

The story that Mudzengi's dedicated team had worked furiously to print that hot October night filled the entire front page of the newspaper before turning onto two inside pages.

'A cheque issued to a client by Willowvale Motor Industries, but sent to a different person in error, has led to the uncovering of what appears to be the tip of a massive iceberg involving the illegal sale of new motor vehicles,' the article began.

It went on to quote well-placed sources at the vehicle assembly plant who had revealed that a network of politicians accessed new vehicles, in contravention of standing regulations, and sold them at huge profit. The politicians, cashing in on a scheme that entitled each of them to one vehicle direct from the assembly plant, had acquired up to six vehicles – in one case, four of them were luxury cars – before adding an extortionate mark-up and selling them in a market that was starved of new cars.

Zimbabwe was faced with a desperate shortage of new vehicles. Motor spares and tyres were impossible to find and exorbitantly expensive. Both private motorists and businesses struggled to keep vehicles on the road. The waiting list was so long that customers could wait up to two years between paying a deposit and taking delivery of a new vehicle. Zimbabwe's vehicle assembly was a protected Rhodesian sanctions-era import-substitution industry, and the import of new and second-hand vehicles was effectively impossible. Only wealthy farmers and industrialists could afford to buy new vehicles. Black people resorted to importing cheap, rundown cars from South Africa and Botswana. Many failed to make the long trip from Johannesburg under their own steam, and desperate owners would hire another motorist to tow the newly acquired pride of their heart all the way to Harare.

By 1988, Willowvale Motor Industries (WMI) and Leyland Motors in Mutare were operating far below full capacity. At only 3 000 units a year, Willowvale, the larger of the two assembly plants, was producing only 10 per cent of the country's demand for new cars.

It was in these circumstances that Zimbabwe's politicians devised a scheme that in due course saw virtually the entire output of cars from the country's two assembly plants being channelled through their hands.

After obtaining the one vehicle to which they were entitled, the politicians and some top civil servants instructed or directed management at WMI to allocate vehicles to other individuals. Some of these third parties merely served as fronts. The government held a controlling stake in Willowvale through its Industrial Development Corporation (IDC). In most cases, the politicians' instructions were conveyed through officials at the ministry of industry and technology.

That Zimbabwe's political leaders had become deeply corrupt in the few years since independence was obvious to all who had eyes to see. However, the *Chronicle* investigation revealed that the intricate web of corruption extended beyond the large circle of Zanu-PF politicians to embrace bureaucrats, captains of industry, the banking sector, and the friends and relatives of the powerful. Some of the latter derived tremendous personal benefit, while others were paid for services rendered.

While Mugabe and his ministers preached hard-line socialist principles at weekend rallies, away from prying eyes a number of his ministers were engaged, virtually full time, in illegal and predatory self-enrichment. By the time the *Chronicle* exposed the graft, it had become apparent that if the politicians did not enjoy their leader's blessing, at the very least they benefited from the blind eye that he turned on their nefarious activities. As for Zanu-PF's strict Leadership Code, it was not worth the paper on which the few available copies were printed.

In terms of the code, adopted enthusiastically at the party's national congress in 1984, leaders would 'not make collusive arrangements with other people or secretly obtain consideration for themselves or other people or fail to disclose the full nature of the transaction to the party or to the government'.

In reality, Zanu-PF's leadership fully exploited the many forms of patronage at its disposal over the years – jobs for the boys, foreign currency allocations, business opportunities, lucrative contracts, farms, scholarships for children and, as it turned out, allocation of scarce motor vehicles.

In a rather absurd political paradox, Mugabe's socialist ministers sold the vehicles they acquired to the capitalist business moguls who were routinely denounced by the head of state.

Most of the vehicles were resold at highly inflated prices. Semi-luxury Toyota

Cressida models, bought at Willowvale Motors for less than Z$30 000, fetched as much as Z$90 000 on the black market. One was sold for Z$115 000.

'Early this month,' the *Chronicle* reported, 'the managing director of a Bulawayo firm, the Zimbabwe Grain Bag Company, a non-constituency member of parliament, Comrade Obert Mpofu, could not believe his eyes when he received an unexpected cheque for Z$3 988.

'His joy was short-lived, however. Closer inspection of the Willowvale Motors cheque revealed that it had, in fact, been made out to one A Mpofu.'

Obert Mpofu contacted the assembly plant in Harare. He was told that he had bought a truck from Willowvale and had telephoned the company asking for a refund after overpaying for the vehicle.

Mpofu, who had been my friend since his days as a line manager at Zimbabwe Newspapers, told me that the factory manager at Willowvale, Dudley Wilde, explained that he had acted on instructions from Callistus Ndlovu, the minister of industry and technology, in issuing the car. When Mr Mpofu telephoned in connection with the refund, according to Wilde, he gave his address as Kezi Shopping Centre, Box 1796, Bulawayo, and his telephone number as 74-622, also in Bulawayo.

'While Kezi Shopping Centre is not listed in the telephone directory,' the *Chronicle* reported, 'the *Boldads Commercial Directory* of Bulawayo lists Box 1796 as being rented by the Wholesale Centre.

'Wholesale Centre (Pvt) Ltd of 62 Main Street is listed in the telephone directory. Their telephone number is given as 74-622. The name and address of the manager are also provided. He is Manilal Naran of 382 Gorebridge Road, Killarney, Bulawayo.'

When the *Chronicle* called the number provided by Mr Mpofu, the phone was answered at Spot-On, the liquor outlet that was also owned by Naran.

Our investigation revealed that the vehicle in question, a Mazda B1800 truck, was collected on 24 August from the Willowvale plant on behalf of not Obert, but Alvord Mpofu, a manager at Spot-On. Alvord adamantly refused to answer any questions from the *Chronicle*, but our investigation showed that a cheque for Z$24 382.80 had been issued in favour of Willowvale Motors for a Mazda B2200 diesel pick-up truck. This particular model was not immediately available, however, and a cheaper B1800 petrol model had been supplied to Alvord Mpofu.

This accounted for the refund that had landed on Obert Mpofu's desk. How the cheque had been wrongly addressed and posted to the member of parliament was never explained. The name Mpofu, which is common among the Ndebele people of western Zimbabwe, was obviously the cause of the confusion.

It was a fairly minor clerical error, but one that almost caused the collapse of Mugabe's government.

The *Chronicle* went on to report that another truck had been collected at the same time, purportedly purchased by Don Ndlovu, an accountant at Spot-On. I knew Ndlovu, and after much persuasion he agreed to help us fit the jigsaw puzzle together and to be identified by name in print. This proved to be a remarkable breakthrough for the *Chronicle*. Ndlovu said that early in August he had received a telephone call from Elias Mabhena, deputy secretary in the ministry of industry and technology in Harare and also chairman of WMI. Mabhena had informed him that his name and that of Alvord Mpofu had been submitted for new car allocations.

'When I asked him under what circumstances our names had been brought forward, he said we were not to worry,' Ndlovu told me. 'All we were required to do was supply personal details about ourselves.'

After doing so, said Ndlovu, Mabhena had advised him and Alvord that Dave Gibson, managing director of Willowvale Motors, would contact them. Gibson subsequently told the two men that their trucks would be ready for collection within ten days.

Their employer, Naran, referred Ndlovu and Mpofu to Ashrat Aktar, manager of the Bulawayo branch of the Bank of Credit and Commerce International (BCCI), which had instructions to issue them with bank-certified cheques to cover the cost of the vehicles.

The BCCI was embroiled in allegations of colossal corruption and eventually closed its global operations in July 1991. The bank had questionable or downright corrupt relationships with government officials in most countries where it operated. Among the thirteen African countries where BCCI had set up shop was Zimbabwe, where cynics commonly referred to it as the Bank of Crooks and Criminals.

Several BCCI officials interviewed by the US Senate committee on foreign relations, which investigated various corruption charges in 1992, stated categorically that bribes had been paid to both Robert Mugabe and Joshua Nkomo when the bank opened a joint venture in Zimbabwe.

'Otherwise, it would not be so easy to get a bank that fast, especially given the opposition of British banks who were already established there,' Nazir Chinoy, BCCI's Paris manager, told the committee.

The committee found that in addition to fraud and money laundering by both BCCI and its customers involving billions of dollars, the bank was also guilty of bribing government officials in many countries in Europe, Africa, Asia and the Americas, smuggling, illicit purchases, and 'a panoply of financial crimes limited only by the imagination of its officials and customers'. While the politicians prospered, some one million small depositors around the world lost their money when the bank collapsed.

After its global demise, BCCI continued to operate in Zimbabwe, where it was renamed the Commercial Bank of Zimbabwe. The name changed again to Jewel Bank under the stewardship of Gideon Gono, a former office messenger who reached the pinnacle of Zimbabwe's financial services sector when Mugabe appointed him governor of the Reserve Bank in 2003.

In 1988, Aktar issued Ndlovu and Mpofu with cheques for Z$28 682 each in favour of Willowvale Motors. When I contacted Aktar, he said that he had a vague recollection of his branch issuing two banker's cheques to Ndlovu and Mpofu after they had brought in the cash equivalent.

'There is nothing wrong with that,' he pointed out. 'It is normal bank practice.'

Although Naran's name was not mentioned during this conversation, Aktar contacted the tycoon immediately to inform him about my enquiries.

When I later questioned him about his phone call to Naran, Aktar responded: 'Do you want to curtail my freedom of association and speech?'

Ndlovu told me he had been given an air ticket from Bulawayo to Harare, where he and a driver, who travelled on the same flight, took a rental car to Willowvale Motors. Ndlovu handed over the two cheques and he and his companion drove away in brand new vehicles.

Like Alvord Mpofu, Ndlovu had qualified for a refund on the original purchase price, but, he told me, he mislaid the cheque when he and his travelling companion went to Meikles Hotel for lunch.

The cheque that had been sent to Obert Mpofu in error was to replace the lost cheque, said Ndlovu. But for this, and the confusion about the names of Alvord and Obert, the Willowgate scandal might never have come to light.

The world-renowned five-star Meikles Hotel, Harare's leading hostelry, has long been favoured by local and international businessmen alike. That Ndlovu and the driver should have lunch at one of the award-winning hotel's well-appointed restaurants before setting off on the road back to Bulawayo was a clear pointer to the sudden prosperity enjoyed by those involved with Willowgate.

In normal circumstances, only Ndlovu would have flown to Harare, while the driver took the overnight train or caught an early morning inter-city bus. Low-income drivers simply did not travel by air, let alone indulge in the gastronomic delights of the Bargatelle, La Fontayne or any other of the fine restaurants at Meikles.

On arriving back in Bulawayo, the vehicles had been handed over to Naran, apparently on the instructions of Callistus Ndlovu.

'That was the last we ever saw of the cars,' Don Ndlovu, apparently no relation to Callistus, lamented. 'In fact, in the case of Alvord Mpofu, I don't think he ever saw his truck.'

In a separate transaction, a registered Bulawayo car dealer received an allocation of three vehicles from Leyland Motors in Mutare. This was followed by a letter instructing him to sell two of the cars to women named by the writer. The letter was signed by Lukas Mahoko, an administrative officer, apparently on behalf of Mabhena.

When I asked Mahoko to explain what circumstances allowed the ministry to prescribe to car dealers how they should conduct their business, he claimed that complaints from official dealers had put paid to the practice of nominating individual recipients of new vehicles in 1986.

'If individuals approach us, we tell them that the ministry doesn't handle cars,' said Mahoko. 'They must approach the dealers directly.'

Confronted with the fact that he had signed a letter in 1987 regarding the sale of cars from Leyland Motors, Mahoko said he had done so on Mabhena's instruction.

'Whenever this has happened we have always been instructed to do so from above,' Mahoko explained innocently. 'Most people who want cars go through Mabhena because he is the chairman of Willowvale.'

Wilde, the factory manager at Willowvale, was not prepared to say anything except that he allocated vehicles on instructions 'from above'.

'I have already received a threat on my life,' he pointed out grimly, 'and I am not prepared to give you anything that goes into the press. All I am doing is obeying instructions given to me. I don't want to get involved. I value my safety and that of my family.'

I overcame an irresistible temptation to ask if Wilde was perhaps suggesting that I did not value my own safety or that of my family. His boss, Dave Gibson, was a little more forthcoming. While he was aware that something fishy was going on regarding the allocation of vehicles, he did not know the extent of the racket, he said.

'We are often asked to assist people who are alleged to have difficulties with transport in their businesses. The ministry of industry and technology asks us to help. It can be any official in the ministry.

'In the case of the minister, he can issue such instructions over the phone. This has happened four or five times. In the case of the vehicles allocated to Mr Mpofu and Mr Ndlovu, the minister contacted us directly. He said these people had a genuine case and he would like us to assist them. The minister said Mr Mabhena was in hospital and that was why he had contacted us himself.'

Mabhena had, indeed, been admitted to Bulawayo's Mpilo Hospital after being injured in a road accident. Speaking in his capacity as chairman of WMI, he denied that the company supplied vehicles directly to individuals. There were, however, special dispensations from the government designed to meet specific or definite needs.

'This is not a general principle,' he said. 'It will never be a general principle. This is why the government introduced certain reforms in 1986. We are aware that some leaders have been involved in some mischief.'

Mabhena paused briefly, then issued a stern warning.

'This is a very hot potato. If you carry on with your investigation you might unearth uncomfortable things.'

He disclosed that he was aware of a number of suspicious car deals, not only in Harare and Bulawayo, but in other centres as well.

Asked to explain his own involvement in the Naran–Ndlovu–Mpofu deal, he said: 'That one I reject in toto. I swear I am not aware of that one.'

The following day, Mabhena relented somewhat and admitted that he did, after all, know something about the vehicles allocated to Don Ndlovu and Alvord Mpofu.

'That one is quite clear,' he suddenly recalled. 'Minister Ndlovu brought their names forward and asked Willowvale to assist his constituents. I telephoned Mr Gibson and gave him their names. I only wish the minister was here himself.'

Callistus Ndlovu was on an official trip abroad. Mabhena went out of his way to assist our futile efforts to contact him by telephone in Romania. Naran refused to discuss anything connected with motor vehicles.

'In fact, the man you want to speak to is Minister Ndlovu,' Naran advised. When I asked why he believed we should speak to the minister, he quickly backtracked. 'I am sorry, I misunderstood you,' he blustered, then promptly hung up his telephone.

By the time Callistus Ndlovu returned from Bucharest, his ministry was engulfed in a crisis of gargantuan proportions. Allegations of sleaze were flying wherever the *Chronicle* circulated, while telephone calls and faxes disseminated the sensational news beyond the newspaper's physical reach. While Ndlovu's name was all over the scandal, government did little to rebut the *Chronicle*'s allegations or anything by way of damage control. It took the embattled Ndlovu and his officials a total of three days to assess the situation before issuing a statement.

Exuding self-confidence and his usual belligerence, Ndlovu called a long-awaited press conference in Harare on Friday 28 October. I had been summoned to the capital for a debriefing with managing director Elias Rusike and Dr Davison Sadza, chairman of the Zimbabwe Mass Media Trust. Both were concerned over the unfolding events, but I assured them I was confident of the veracity of allegations we had already published or were preparing to make. Dr Sadza suggested that I should, perhaps, have informed the president before the story broke, in order to save him the shock and embarrassment of reading such damaging disclosures at the same time as the rest of the nation.

Dr Sadza had been Mugabe's contemporary at Fort Hare University and was one of the few friends he had there.

I stood my ground, impressing upon the chairman and the chief executive that the Willowgate story was watertight. In any case, had they not always preached that press freedom was guaranteed at Zimbabwe Newspapers? I said I was not aware of any special dispensation granting the president advance notification that we intended publishing sensitive stories with the potential to undermine his government's credibility. While the two men seemed somewhat relieved by my confidence, they still could not look me in the eye, especially not the affable Dr Sadza. They must have realised, however, that they were on very shaky ground. Rusike in particular had enjoined editors from time to time to expose corruption 'so long as you have copper-bottom evidence'.

Both the *Herald* and the *Sunday Mail* in Harare and the Zimbabwe Broadcasting Corporation dutifully ignored the story that was causing a major upheaval. As a result, sales of the *Chronicle* boomed in Harare, multiplying tenfold from 300 flown by air to more than 3000 copies delivered by truck and sold out every day over a month-long period. Long queues of readers anxious to secure a copy of the *Chronicle* formed in both Bulawayo and Harare every morning. In October the print run was around 89000. By December we were printing and selling more than 100000. A maximum of 115000 copies were printed and sold out on Wednesday 14 December. The cover price of the paper was fifteen cents. In Harare, second-hand copies were changing hands at Z$2.00 or more, depending on the front page.

Only a serious shortage of newsprint and the unpredictable state of the Heidelberg press mitigated against more ambitious production runs.

After my meeting at head office I proceeded to the Quill Club. As I entered, silence descended on the mixed gathering of local and foreign journalists, the odd politician and other regular hangers-on, mostly drawn from the ranks of the Central Intelligence Organisation. The latter acted as *agents provocateur*, either openly denigrating the government or making half-hearted and often ridiculous attempts to defend even its most indefensible mistakes or shortcomings.

Either way, journalists, in many instances responding under the influence of the popular Castle Lager, fell for the bait, and by the end of the day the CIO agents had compiled adequate material for their morning reports.

I gathered that the commotion at the bar had been generated by the prospect of Callistus Ndlovu addressing a press conference immediately after lunch and joined the exodus from the club to the ministry of industry and technology.

Sitting side by side in front of the packed room, Ndlovu and Mabhena were combative as the minister proceeded to read from a long-winded prepared statement that vehemently denied all the allegations published against him, his fellow ministers and government officials.

'The *Chronicle* of October 21 carried a headline story from none other than the editor himself,' Ndlovu began, as he stole a ferocious glance at me sitting there, pen in hand. 'He alleged a massive racket in the distribution and selling of newly assembled vehicles by officials of my ministry and Willowvale Motor Industries.'

In fact, we had published no such allegation against ministry officials and WMI management, but notwithstanding the false premise on which the minister had elected to build his defence, he proceeded 'in the interests of balanced journalism and the need for the public to know the true facts' to issue the statement.

'To start with,' Ndlovu told bemused journalists, 'there is no massive iceberg involving illegal sales of assembled cars by either staff of the ministry or those of WMI.

'What the *Chronicle*'s investigation brought to light were nothing more than optical illusions where an individual would swear that the tracks of a railway line actually meet on the horizon because, empirically, this is what is observable. In reality, of course, it is a well-known fact that the tracks will never converge, but continue to run parallel to each other.'

Ndlovu paused for effect, then asked: 'How else could the trains run on the rails?'

To the accompaniment of frequent sniggers and muted laughter, the minister plodded through thirty paragraphs of contrived, mostly irrelevant and wholly unconvincing argument. He failed dismally to address the specific and detailed allegations published by the *Chronicle*. Essentially, Ndlovu explained that in view of the scarcity of new vehicles in Zimbabwe, the cabinet had devised a scheme whereby each government minister or member of parliament was entitled to one new vehicle to facilitate their travel, especially to rural constituencies.

Of course, the average rural voter would have happily testified at the time that the last glimpse of any honourable MP had been during the 1985 election campaign. As for the Toyota Cressida being the ideal vehicle to travel the dilapidated roads of rural Zimbabwe, suffice it to say that for months after Ndlovu addressed the press, people were still laughing at the suggestion.

The railway tracks used by the minister to dismiss the 'illusion' of wrongdoing would soon defy the odds and prove that they could, after all, meet in certain circumstances. The result was that Ndlovu's tenure in Mugabe's cabinet was derailed. The political whirlwind that followed also swept a number of other cabinet ministers and a provincial governor out of office.

Jacob Mudenda, the governor of Matabeleland North, and Michael Ndubiwa, the town clerk of Bulawayo, were among the many fine gentlemen with whom I interacted as editor of the *Chronicle*. Ndubiwa was later appointed to the board of the ZMMT, and it is my belief that the media generally benefited from his wise counsel.

We received information that the governor had taken delivery of a thirty-ton Scania truck from Willowvale and instantly sold it to Treger Industries, one of Bulawayo's larger enterprises.

On Monday 7 November, I visited the premises of Monarch Products, a luggage manufacturer and Treger subsidiary, to investigate a recent delivery of Toyota Cressidas. I was accompanied by *Chronicle* chief photographer Costa Manzini. From our vehicle parked across the road from the company's premises, and using a telephoto lens, he shot several frames of the Cressidas, parked in all their mid-morning glory outside the office block.

As Manzini happily snapped away, a monster truck, a spanking new dolomite-coloured Scania P112, emerged from behind the factory and tore towards the main gate. Barely slowing down, the mechanical horse, without trailer, turned right into Khami Road, grinding through multiple gears as the driver put the machine through its paces.

'The Mudenda Scania!' I shouted in triumph, hardly believing our good fortune, as we set off in pursuit.

Manzini took several pictures from behind as we gained on the truck, from the side as we drew level with it and from the front after we had overtaken it. Realising he was the centre of photographic attention the driver waved his hand, grinning widely with the boundless ecstasy of a child playing with a new toy. We waved back before turning into a side road to head back to our office. An hour later, Manzini dropped a dramatic selection of Scania and Cressida prints on my desk as I was briefing my deputy, Davison Maruziva, on our sudden windfall. Displayed on my desk was a consummate example of how a good picture can tell a story better than any thousand words.

We drew up a plan of action.

Maruziva had only recently joined the *Chronicle* on transfer from Harare. I telephoned Mudenda's office to schedule an appointment to introduce the deputy editor to the governor. The next morning, we were ushered into the governor's tastefully furnished office, Maruziva carrying a bulky but innocuous brown envelope under his left arm. The governor emerged from behind an enormous desk to greet us and showed us to the lounge section of his vast office, where we all took our seats.

'Comrade Governor, this is Davison Maruziva, the new deputy editor of the *Chronicle*,' I said once we had dispensed with the greetings, discussion of the weather and the prospects of a good rainy season. 'Mr Maruziva was assistant editor of the *Herald* in Harare before his recent transfer to Bulawayo. Davison, this is Comrade Jacob Mudenda, the governor of Matabeleland North. We have developed a very good working relationship with his office. He understands the role of the press and often anticipates our needs, which is very useful to us.'

Zimbabwe's government and its newspapers have an irritating habit of referring to politicians and other government officials as 'comrade', while the rest of the population is Mr or Mrs – yet another indication that Mugabe's regime merely paid lip service to the socialist notion of egalitarianism that it propounded.

The politician and the journalist shook hands as we settled down to discuss a few general matters. The subject of Willowgate, the burning issue of the day, was carefully avoided. Then we rose to leave. As the governor escorted us to the door, Maruziva suddenly opened the brown envelope and removed a thick wad of large pictures.

'By the way, Comrade Governor,' he said, ever so politely, 'have you seen this vehicle before?'

In addition to photographs, we had obtained copies of documents showing that the governor had paid Z$338 952 for the truck in June and promptly sold it for Z$450 000, or Z$100 000 more than the controlled retail price. The transaction had completely bypassed Tandem Zimbabwe, the official Scania franchise holder. While management at WMI stated categorically that instructions to allocate the vehicle to Mudenda had been received from the ministry of industry and technology, both Ndlovu and Mabhena had refused to answer any questions pertaining to this particular vehicle.

Confronted with photographic proof of the truck that he had briefly owned, Mudenda's mouth fell open, then slowly closed as rivulets of perspiration began trickling down his face.

'I believe we should sit down again,' he suggested, when he eventually found his voice.

While he did not dispute our findings, Mudenda said he preferred not to comment 'at this stage'.

'You see, there is a racket. I might find myself using careless language that might impinge on other people.'

He promised to issue a press statement on the issue later in the day, but around 5.30 p.m. he called me to say he was, after all, going to say nothing.

Maruziva put the story together for publication on Wednesday 9 November, under the front-page headline 'Mudenda in vehicle racket'.

The governor was to generate much mirth among *Chronicle* readers when he subsequently claimed that he had originally purchased the truck for his father's garbage removal business in Dete, the small town of his origin on the road to Hwange National Park and Victoria Falls. We immediately dispatched business editor Jonathan Maphenduka to investigate Comrade Mudenda Senior's refuse removal operation, which was apparently so successful that his son had sought to invest Z$338 952 in it before temptation and greed scuppered his noble plan.

Maphenduka called triumphantly from Dete to report that the Mudenda garbage removal venture did indeed exist, but its entire transport 'fleet' comprised a single donkey-drawn cart.

Throughout the Willowgate investigation, the question was often asked why the editors rather than the reporters had produced the stories. Initially, the task had been assigned to Tichaona Mukuku, our crime reporter, who was briefed to probe the Nkala–Ndlovu–Naran links. Enthusiastic at the outset, the young reporter had evidently developed cold feet by the time Maruziva joined the staff a few weeks later.

He came to see me and asked to be taken off the investigation. No amount of reasoning could persuade Mukuku to change his mind, so, acting on a hunch, we investigated our ace sleuth. To our horror, we found that Mukuku (may his soul rest in eternal peace) had become a regular guest in the Nkala household, where he and his wife were wined, dined and showered with gifts. He resigned from the *Chronicle*, and we decided that all further investigation into Willowgate would be conducted by the most senior editorial staff who were not vulnerable to temptation.

From the time the first story appeared on 21 October, our switchboard was jammed every morning with calls from readers wanting either to congratulate and encourage us or feed us with more information. Then disaster struck.

Towards the end of November a rumour began circulating that Mugabe was extremely upset because the *Chronicle* had dared to publish such serious allegations of corruption within his government without the courtesy of warning him. In due course, the tenor of the speculation doing the rounds of Harare's hyperactive rumour mill changed. It was now suggested that a decision had been taken to fire me for my alleged impudence. My heart sank when Rusike, the managing director of Zimbabwe Newspapers, telephoned and told me to drop whatever I was doing and travel to Harare for an urgent meeting the following day.

The president had requested an audience with all editors, he said. 'Well, this is it,' I told myself with utter resignation. I broke the news to Ursula that night. She tried her best not to show any sign of panic, but we immediately started making plans to relocate to Harare, where I would doubtless face the very real prospect of unemployment.

Ever the pillar of moral support, Ursula prayed hard that night and wished me all the best when I departed in the morning. The driver who met me at Harare airport was not his usual jovial self, I noted.

I reached the sixth floor of Herald House just in time to join my colleagues, Tommy Sithole (editor of the *Herald*) and Henry Muradzikwa (editor of the *Sunday Mail*) on their way to State House. I felt somehow betrayed by my two Harare colleagues. They had refused to publish any detail of the Willowgate scandal. In terms of Zimbabwe Newspapers' inter-branch service, the *Herald* and the *Chronicle* exchanged all news items and rarely was a major story filed by one paper not published in the other.

I genuinely believed that if the two Harare newspapers had carried the Willowgate stories, our collective hand would have been strengthened and my own future made more secure. Their decision not to touch the story had cast aspersions in government circles on the *Chronicle* investigation. In fact, in a spirited bid to counter our disclosures, the *Herald* had reported on 9 November that 'dozens of brand new cars and trucks are sitting in several Harare showrooms, but they belong to the fortunate few with external funds who placed orders for them some time ago'.

The report did not explain, however, why the 'fortunate few' were not collecting their new vehicles. I decided that it would be foolhardy to challenge Sithole on this matter as we drove to State House. It was obviously not in my best interests to create any new enemies when I could not handle existing ones, and I was clearly on my way out, anyway.

Trying their best to sound sympathetic, the Harare editors confirmed that officials at the ministry of information had said that the president was greatly annoyed with the *Chronicle*. They also confided that my chances of returning to Bulawayo as editor of the newspaper after that day's meeting were extremely slim.

On that grim note we stopped at the State House security checkpoint. It was my first visit since quitting Canaan Banana's staff in January 1982. The editors of all the government-controlled newspapers and other media, including Ziana and ZBC, filed into the huge and ornately furnished main lounge, along with senior officials from the ministry of information. President Mugabe entered as we settled down to tea and biscuits, and we all rose to our feet.

Wearing what seemed to me to be a stern countenance, he waved us back into our seats. After dispensing with preliminary formalities, the president launched into a wide-ranging briefing, as was his custom, touching on the general situation in the country, corruption, demonstrations by university students, the need for patriotism and national unity, and the peace and general progress since the unity agreement had been signed almost a year before. I began to feel more at ease as the occasion assumed some semblance of a routine briefing for editors.

The president's eyes slowly wandered over the assembly of media executives and then, without warning, he asked, 'Which one of you is Comrade Nyarota?'

My heart thumped. I nearly spilled my cup of tea as I answered, while struggling to control my voice, 'It is I, Your Excellency.'

'Aah, Comrade Nyarota,' said Mugabe, his gaze now fixed on me. 'So what is this story about corruption at Willowvale Motors?'

While the sudden turn of events took me somewhat by surprise, I had not gone to State House unprepared. This was a matter of professional life and death, and I had decided, between the prayers and falling asleep the night before, that if I was forced to leave the *Chronicle*, I would do so with honour and dignity, even if I was publicly humiliated.

For the next fifteen minutes, Mugabe sat back and listened as I explained the major facets of our investigation and the circumstances leading to publication of the first instalment of the Willowgate scandal on 21 October. I explained that we had received an overwhelming amount of new information or details since then from patriotic citizens who were anxious to see corruption stamped out before it became entrenched in Zimbabwe. I also made the point that I sincerely believed the *Chronicle* had risen to the challenge of both the president and his deputy, Simon Muzenda, in urging the nation to desist from making spurious allegations of government corruption.

'Your Excellency,' I said in conclusion, 'I believe a number of your ministers have betrayed the faith that you placed in them. We have in our possession an abundance of evidence to that effect.'

For the first time, I realised that I was perspiring profusely – and I did not have a handkerchief. I did the only thing I could in the circumstances and wiped my face on the sleeve of my Pierre Cardin jacket. As I waited for judgment to be passed, I felt completely at peace, even though I had no inkling that Mugabe was already familiar with most of the details I had just disclosed. Unbeknown to me, the list of those involved in Willowgate that the police had compiled on the basis of their own investigations since October had been drawn up at Mugabe's request and was already in his possession.

When he finally spoke, the president said he was not entirely certain that the *Chronicle* had chosen the most appropriate route to make public such serious allegations against cabinet ministers.

'Having said that, Comrade Nyarota,' Mugabe continued, 'I cannot, in any way, prevent your paper from publishing the outcome of its investigations. I have one request to make, however. It is that you do not publish falsehoods about any of my ministers.'

I could not believe my ears.

'I will personally make every effort to ensure that no falsehood is printed about any government minister, Your Excellency,' I replied in a barely audible voice. As I mused over the realisation that, to a man, all the editors in the room were avoiding eye contact with me, the president suddenly sprang to his feet with an agility that belied his sixty-four years. He moved among the editors, shaking hands, making a personal enquiry here and cracking a joke there. I felt like one who had been rescued from the jaws of a very hungry crocodile.

At that moment, I secretly vowed to dig all the way to the bottom of the Willowgate scandal, not only out of a journalistic commitment to expose the rest of this particular iceberg, but also because I realised that my whole future hung precariously on the outcome of the investigation.

One of the rumours that had been circulating was that the First Lady, Sally Mugabe, was involved in Willowgate. Our own investigations had unearthed no evidence to substantiate this, but I have often wondered whether Mugabe had summoned me to State House to ascertain whether his wife was, indeed, among those we were probing and, having established the contrary, was only too happy to let events take their natural course.

At one point, my chairman, Dr Sadza, asked me straight out if it was true that I was about to expose alleged corruption by the First Lady. He said he had information that the finished article was in one of my desk drawers and that I was waiting only for the most appropriate moment to unleash the sensational story. There was fear in his eyes and he was obviously terrified by the prospect of lurid details of Sally Mugabe's wrongdoing being splashed all over the *Chronicle*.

'Dr Sadza,' I responded, 'let us call Patience Ncube, my secretary, right now and ask her to go through my drawers. She will read out to you the subject of every document she finds there.'

That seemed to pacify Sadza. I later learned that in a bid to whip up emotions against the *Chronicle* and incite Mugabe to silence the newspaper, one of the ministers under investigation had started the rumour about the First Lady.

The gossip was so strong that I was accused of covering up for Sally, who was certainly not above controversy on occasion. When I requested that my accusers furnish me with evidence of her involvement, however, they could not.

Totally undaunted by Callistus Ndlovu's feisty but incoherent denials and buoyed by Mugabe's assurance of non-interference, the *Chronicle* probe gathered new momentum. Unsolicited information continued to pour in, especially details that helped us track down vehicles that had been resold. Readers generally love to sink their teeth into a salacious account of official transgression, and some relish being able to tell their friends that they had contributed to the big picture.

Willowvale employees and sources elsewhere in the motor industry continued to be a bountiful and reliable fount of information. Increasingly, we also received information from disgruntled buyers who had been coerced to pay up to more than twice the market value for their new vehicles. Most importantly, we eventually received cooperation from the police, as some of those involved in the official investigation had found their efforts blocked by bureaucratic intervention.

The *Chronicle* received unequivocal support from an unlikely quarter – Didymus Mutasa, the parliamentary speaker. On one of my many visits to Harare I attended a function hosted by him at the Park Lane Hotel in Eastlea (now Dura House, head-quarters of the Grain Marketing Board). Mutasa was Manicaland's second most senior politician and a former schoolmate and close friend of my uncle, Arthur Nyarota, parliament's deputy secretary. During the function, he pulled me to the side and asked conspiratorially: 'So, what is all this commotion about the car racket?'

Careful not to reveal any unpublished names, I gave him a brief rundown of the raging scandal.

'Let me assure you that your investigation has my personal support,' he said. 'The country could do with some cleansing right now.'

As an afterthought, he added jokingly, 'Of course, I personally will not be caught in your net. If you want me in your net, you will have to divert your attention to the affairs of politicians.'

I assumed he meant love affairs, but did not pursue the matter.

Given his encouragement, I was disappointed that Mutasa stayed silent when I got into trouble over Willowgate two months later. In fact, far from being my protector, he would become one of my greatest adversaries, especially after the launch of the *Daily News* in 1999. He personally orchestrated the seizure of copies of the new newspaper by Zanu-PF activists in Rusape in 2002. The police stood by, hands folded, as bundles of the *Daily News* were carted away while our young newspaper vendor, Patrick Maguranye, was kidnapped. On one occasion I retrieved a bundle of newspapers from the Zanu-PF office and rescued another vendor from the war veterans' office in Rusape.

The police referred me to Mutasa, who did not mince his words when I visited him at home.

'The people of Rusape don't want your paper in this town,' he said. 'As a politician I respect the will of the people.'

I told him that all the newspapers recovered from the Zanu-PF office had quickly been snatched up by those same people. As I drove away, I observed in my rear-view mirror the spectacle of Mutasa and his bodyguards happily thumbing through the copies of the *Daily News* that I had left for them.

By the beginning of December 1988 we had collected masses of documentary evidence and a long list of names of politicians, mostly government ministers, who had made multiple purchases of vehicles from Willowvale Motors. We had made a major breakthrough by persuading senior police officers to part with a copy of the official list of people who had been allocated up to six vehicles, in one case.

The list read like a who's who of the top echelons of Zanu-PF and government. Our police sources released the list on condition that we alter the order of the names so that our list could not be identified as a replica of the one sent to Mugabe. As it happened, the official list essentially matched the one we had compiled from information supplied by workers at Willowvale.

We then embarked on the painstaking task of compiling a database that included the date of purchase, and the engine and chassis numbers for each vehicle. We traced the vehicles to their current locations, noting the identities of the individuals or companies that had bought them, the exorbitant prices quoted and the dates of the transactions.

The investigation then entered its most daunting stage: verification by means of confronting the alleged culprits in each instance. Predictably, cooperation was minimal. Many of the politicians, especially the cabinet ministers, refused outright to engage in any discussion with the *Chronicle*. Typically, telephone receivers were slammed down as soon as Maruziva or I identified ourselves.

Among those listed as having received one or more vehicles were higher education minister Dzingai Mutumbuka, minister of state for political affairs Fredrick Shava, Simbi Mubako, the minister of national supplies, and Justin Nyoka, his permanent secretary. At the end of 2005, Mubako was in Washington, DC, as Zimbabwe's ambassador to the United States.

Apart from the Scania P112 allocated to Mudenda, Elias Mabhena's name was linked to a number of vehicles, including some issued to transport minister Simbarashe Mbengegwi, defence minister Enos Nkala, finance minister Dr Bernard Chidzero, and Emmerson Mnangagwa, minister of justice, legal and parliamentary affairs. On Mabhena's instructions, vehicles had also been allocated to army commander Solomon Tapfumaneyi Mujuru (formerly known as Rex Nhongo of Zanla), deputy political affairs minister Oppah Muchinguri and deputy information minister Kenneth Manyonda.

The tentacles of Mabhena's burgeoning benevolence reached beyond the corridors of power to include a doctor in Bulawayo, as well as Mercy Sidile, a company executive in the city. Mabhena later testified under oath that Sidile was his girlfriend. Mabhena's boss, Callistus Ndlovu, had arranged for vehicles to be allocated to Naran, the Bulawayo business tycoon, through his two employees, Don Ndlovu and Alvord Mpofu.

New vehicles had also been allocated to two members of parliament, Dr Edward Pswarayi, a former deputy minister of health, and Martin Simela, a non-constituent MP from Bulawayo.

When I spoke to Simela, he admitted without hesitation that he had sold his new Toyota Cressida. However, he expressed distress at being asked by the *Chronicle* to account for the car, since the police had already interviewed him on the matter.

'I feel I have no obligation whatsoever to cooperate with stories that are selective in character and directed at the Ndebele Zanu-PF leadership in Matabeleland,' he said. 'If your car racket stories are national in character, then your interviews must be national.'

I asked Simela if he knew of anyone outside Matabeleland who was involved in any fraudulent car deals. He said, again without vacillation, 'Yes. Why don't you expose them too?'

I felt under no obligation to explain to Simela that the *Chronicle* investigation was, indeed, nationwide and had targeted politicians belonging to tribes other than the Ndebele. In fact, the accusation about ethnicity was, in my view, a red herring aimed at diverting our attention from the real issues.

Simela certainly did not have the last laugh. The *Chronicle* published his objections on 14 December as part of a comprehensive story that was devoid of any ethnic connotations. For the record, apart from Nkala, Ndlovu and Simela, who were all Ndebele, three months of intensive investigation had led us to Maurice Nyagumbo, Oppah Muchinguri and Kenneth Manyonda, members of my own Manyika tribe; Shava, Mubako, Mbengegwi and Vice-President Muzenda, all Karangas; Jacob Mudenda, a Tonga; foreign affairs minister Nathan Shamuyarira, Nyoka and Mujuru, who all stemmed from Mugabe's Zezuru tribe.

A Harare doctor's name was on the list as the recipient of a vehicle through Muzenda's intervention, while Shamuyarira had assisted a white farmer to obtain a vehicle. Ethnic loyalties played no role in Willowgate, but the apparent focus on Matabeleland was inevitable, given that the *Chronicle* was published in the provincial capital of Bulawayo. However, the newspaper could not be blamed for the fact that the major players in the scandal – Callistus Ndlovu, Enos Nkala and Elias Mabhena – all hailed from Matabeleland. In Zimbabwe, as in the rest of the world, corruption benefited those closest to the perpetrators – the brothers, sisters, cousins, friends, acquaintances and business associates of the corrupt officials. This was particularly true of Willowgate.

In December, we received information that apart from the single car on the official list, Nkala had taken delivery of several more vehicles from both Willowvale and Leyland Motors. Most of them had been delivered to Zidco Motors, one of Zanu-PF's trading companies, of which Nkala was chairman.

The defence minister had been as slippery as the proverbial eel despite our repeated attempts to solicit some response to the growing number of allegations against him. On 13 December, Maruziva struck gold. Nkala answered his office telephone himself when my deputy editor called and, after hearing why we wanted to speak to him, he agreed to answer our questions. However, Maruziva and I would have to travel to Harare and meet him face to face.

That afternoon, all hell broke loose. Nkala, possibly the most feared politician in Zimbabwe at the time, often exuding more power than Mugabe himself and arrogant to boot, phoned Maruziva, and this time his disposition was vile.

By the time the third most powerful politician in the country hung up on the deputy editor of Zimbabwe's second biggest newspaper, he had issued a threat reminiscent of those he had hurled with reckless abandon at Nkomo and PF-Zapu.

Maruziva and I were to present ourselves at Nkala's office in Harare, 440 kilometres away, the following morning. Failing this, he would dispatch soldiers from One Brigade at Bulawayo's Llewellin Barracks to arrest and detain us. Alternatively, he would order the police to arrest us.

After Maruziva had spoken to Nkala earlier in the day, I had telephoned the office of Jayant Joshi, managing director of Zidco Motors, a subsidiary of Zidco Holdings, Zanu-PF's major commercial enterprise. Sources had informed us that Joshi was conniving with top politicians, and Nkala in particular, to channel new vehicles illegally acquired from Willowvale and Leyland Motors to the black market through Zidco.

After identifying myself, I explained to Joshi that the purpose of my call was to obtain an explanation for various fraudulent car deals that he had allegedly processed on behalf of the minister of defence. Joshi was polite, but firmly refused to be drawn into any discussion. He relented somewhat when I bluffed that the *Chronicle* was in possession of well-documented information that could be published without any great risk of legal repercussions, and suggested that it was in his best interest to respond to questions or at least attempt some damage control.

Joshi said he needed to consult – his alleged conspirators, no doubt – and would call me back that afternoon. I never heard from Joshi again. Nkala called instead, fuming with unbridled anger as he issued threats to Maruziva. It seemed that Joshi had contacted Nkala and conveyed to him the gist of my enquiries.

'Where did you get that information?' Nkala demanded when Maruziva answered the telephone. 'That information is supposed to be with the police and the president. I want that information here in my office. Who do you think you are? If you do not travel here I will teach each of you a lesson. I will use the army to pick you up; then you can ask your questions. I do not care. I can instruct the commissioner of police to pick you up. Do not play that kind of game with me; I am not Ndlovu.'

There had been bad blood between the *Chronicle* and rank-and-file members of the police force in Bulawayo since the paper had published a front-page picture depicting several police officers in uniform drinking beer at a popular shebeen while they were supposed to be patrolling one of the city's working-class townships. Leaning against a wall were their AK47 rifles. There was a public outcry, and the police never forgave the newspaper. Lower-ranking officers would have welcomed any opportunity to settle personal scores with the paper, while seeking reparation for their tarnished image. Ironically, however, as Nkala was threatening to dispatch the police commissioner from Harare to arrest Maruziva and me, the police officer commanding Matabeleland North, Senior Assistant Commissioner Silas Moyo, was having a cup of tea in my office while we discussed totally different and more mundane matters.

'I am not the kind to play with,' Nkala barked into the phone. 'Play with anybody else. I am giving you an ultimatum. If by tomorrow you do not come back to me to say you are coming, then you will come by other means.

'I have that power. I will lock you up, along with your editor. Who gave you that information? That question must be answered. I am the acting minister of home affairs and I am instructing the police to search your offices and you can write that.'

Fearful that if we did not act at once to publish the results of our investigation so far we might be locked up, the *Chronicle* granted the minister his wish.

The following morning the newspaper carried not only a full account of Nkala's threats, but also the full list of vehicles supplied to government ministers by Willowvale Motors, each one matched to the name of the recipient and the engine and chassis numbers. We reported that the list had been supplied by employees at Willowvale Motors who called themselves 'revolutionaries who want this corruption brought to an end'.

While Nkala was officially listed as having obtained only one vehicle, our information was that he had, in fact, been allocated up to six vehicles from Willowvale. His nervous disposition, public display of hostility and state of panic, far surpassing that of any other official allegedly involved in the scandal, suggested that he had something big to hide.

A close ally of Nkala, Maurice Nyagumbo, had the dubious distinction of appearing at the top of the list of beneficiaries of Willowvale Motors' clandestine transactions. Between October 1987 and August 1988 he had issued instructions for the allocation of six vehicles, mostly luxury Toyota Cressidas.

Nyagumbo, the most senior politician in Manicaland, was the fourth-highest-ranking Zanu-PF politician and an immensely powerful man. In June 1986 he had surprised many, both within and outside Zanu-PF, by stating publicly that despite claims to the contrary, Zimbabwe did not have a socialist government, 'as we now appear to have adopted capitalism, become property owners, and be deceiving our people'.

After admitting that he had bought a huge farm after independence and had sold it only recently, Nyagumbo proposed an emergency conference of Zanu-PF at which members should decide whether or not to replace the party's leadership. Not a word was ever heard again about his amazing proposal.

At a fairly early stage of our investigation, I had been startled to receive a telephone call from Nyagumbo one Friday afternoon. He was in Bulawayo for the weekend, he told me, and his regular tennis partner was out of town. Did I play and would I care to join him for a game at the Holiday Inn, where he was staying? My heart pounding, I explained that I had last played tennis at secondary school two decades earlier, hoping this would put him off.

'That is good enough,' he said. 'I play regularly. All I need is a little exercise.'

The following morning found me sweating it out on the tennis court with a man whose name would subsequently crop up repeatedly in connection with the vehicle fraud. Fortunately, there was no one around to witness the spectacle of the young newspaper editor being thrashed five games to one by a politician old enough to be his father. The exercise was good, though, and I vowed to take up tennis seriously. I am still to do so.

I informed Nyagumbo that a cousin of his who lived in Bulawayo had lost a child during the week. The minister did not know about this bereavement in his family, and, in due course, I drove him to Pumula, a township west of the city, where his cousin lived. After we paid our condolences, I took Nyagumbo back to his hotel, relieved that he did not seem to have got wind of our investigation. I refrained from seizing the opportunity to ask about government ministers and new motor vehicles.

On a subsequent visit to Bulawayo, Nyagumbo agreed to see me in connection with the allegations against him, but he failed to keep our appointment.

On 14 December, the *Chronicle* published details of the four large sedans he had allegedly facilitated on behalf of a newly established company in Harare's Southerton industrial area. A senior manager at Pamberi Marketing confirmed that the company had, indeed, taken delivery of the vehicles in question, which, he claimed, had been allocated to branch managers in rural areas.

It was not possible to confirm this peculiar allocation of resources, but it sounded highly unlikely that the most luxurious cars available would be used to negotiate Zimbabwe's long-neglected rural roads. It was also exceedingly suspicious that against the backdrop of a public hue and cry over the severe shortage of new vehicles, Pamberi Marketing had been able to buy two in a single day!

Another new company, Mereki Enterprises, and one Michael Nyabadza of Harare, had been the recipients of two trucks allocated on Nyagumbo's instructions. The address that Nyabadza gave Willowvale Motors was the same as that of Pamberi Marketing, but the manager denied that anyone of that name was employed by the company. It transpired that the Nyabadzas, who hailed from the Makoni district, were related to Nyagumbo.

The day after publication of the latest revelations of rampant corruption and deception, Nkala called a press conference in Harare. That night he appeared on TV, all but choking on his words as he spewed out venom in anger.

It was a cabinet decision that government ministers should be allocated vehicles directly from Willowvale Motors rather than join long queues with ordinary citizens at the car dealers, he said sombrely. A similar decision had been taken in respect of members of parliament.

'Then Nyarota came out with allegations that there is a car racket involving government officials and ministers,' Nkala said, eyes flashing ferociously. 'When Nyarota's statement came out, the president instructed the police to check on that allegation and they had to check with Willowvale. So a list of cars supplied to ministers, government officials and MPs was prepared by Willowvale and, through the medium of the police, delivered to the president. The police over the weeks have been checking what happened to those cars and they are still checking.'

Apparently, Nkala was unaware that by the time the list arrived on Mugabe's desk, the police had completed most of the checking necessary to form the basis of a prosecution. Frustrated by the president's lack of action and fearful that the list, like other sensitive or incriminating documents before it, might find its way to oblivion under the proverbial carpet, they had leaked it to me.

'Then Nyarota keeps on pestering ministers, phoning daily, phoning houses, wanting to know whether ministers, particularly in my case, still have their cars,' Nkala ranted.

'I object very strongly. Who is Nyarota to ask me that question? The only person – there are two agents of government that can ask me that question – the president himself and the police, in wanting to establish whether or not I sold the car. At about 3 p.m., when I wanted to leave the office, I wanted to be sure whether they were going to come. So I phoned back to find out whether Maruziva and his editor were going to come to put the question they wanted to put to me in my office.

'He said, "no", and then I said, "You don't play games with me because I play games with nobody. You can play games with everybody else in terms of what you publish." I was angry and I am still angry that I should be pestered by little Nyarota about a car. I didn't steal this car. I paid money for it and I see nothing wrong with me having that car and giving it to my wife to drive or my son or any other person to use.

'What corruption is there in a car that I bought with my money for which I worked? We are looking into the possibility of preferring criminal deformation [*sic*] charges against Nyarota collectively because the ministers must be defended. Their dignity and esteem must be defended.'

Nkala presumably hoped that he could use national television to incite other cabinet ministers to institute legal proceedings against me for criminal defamation, rather than the 'deformation' that he suggested. Any attempt at criminal deformation would, of course, have resulted in disastrous consequences for my physique.

'The ministers are not going to let Nyarota character-assassinate everybody,' Nkala said, 'ministers in particular. If he knows of ministers who have committed an offence he should report about those ministers, not lump us together – we are in a racket, we are in a Willowgate scandal, all of us lumped together.'

A reporter interjected: 'Comrade Minister, it was reported in yesterday's *Chronicle* that you had actually threatened to send the army to pick up Nyarota. What is the position now?'

'Forget about that,' Nkala responded. 'Something is being done. We are looking at all possibilities of bringing Nyarota to book.'

Reporter: 'Some of the allegations published in the *Chronicle* were that ministers were tending to abuse their privilege to get cars by giving cars to their friends and relatives while members of the public are struggling to get cars.'

'That's not my problem,' Nkala snapped. 'Nyarota should go to those ministers who have abused the privilege. I have not abused my privilege. I know of no minister who has abused that privilege, but I am not going to speak on their behalf. Even if they had made it possible for their relatives to buy cars from Willowvale, what is wrong?

'I only know about my car and I am not in a car racket. So that's all I wanted to say, that we are working on all possibilities of bringing Nyarota to book. Only through a court can Nyarota make all the allegations he wants to make.'

My mother called me immediately from Old Highfields, in tears. She pleaded with me to leave Zanu-PF's politicians alone. They were too powerful for anyone to fight, she said, asking in obvious distress: 'Do you not care about your family?'

My mother-in-law, Katherine Muzenda, wept when she called from Chivhu. She was surprised I had not been arrested yet. Ursula was in tears as well. I was almost in tears myself.

My son Tafirenyika, who had just celebrated his twelfth birthday, watched awestruck as the fiery politician raved and ranted on the screen.

'Are they going to arrest my father, Mummy?' he asked, tears welling in his eyes.

I found myself wedged between the proverbial rock and a hard place. I was convinced, however, that our only salvation was perseverance. Going back would have been a betrayal not only of all the sources who had risked their lives to give us information, but also of all law-abiding citizens who detested corruption and counted on the *Chronicle* to spearhead an anti-graft campaign on their behalf.

While his embattled ministers celebrated what must have been a bleak Christmas, Mugabe reviewed the unfolding Willowgate saga with growing consternation. Ndlovu's spirited denial of any wrongdoing, reinforced by Nkala's self-righteous huffing and puffing, apparently made little impact on the befuddled president. It was now quite apparent that Elias Mabhena had spoken with characteristic bureaucratic understatement when he invoked the prospect of a 'hot potato'.

On Thursday 28 December, three days before the close of what had been a politically turbulent year, Mugabe called a press conference to announce a course of action that was totally without precedent in the seven years of his increasingly authoritarian rule. Succumbing to a mounting public outcry, Mugabe announced the appointment of a judicial commission of inquiry, Zimbabwe's first, to investigate the allegations published by the *Chronicle* against his ministers over a period of fifty-four days.

The president told a hushed nation: 'Following recent reports concerning the direct sale to members of the public, including employees of the state, of newly assembled motor vehicles by Willowvale Motor Industries, and, given the questions which have been raised in many quarters as to the legality and propriety of such sales, I have in accordance with the law decided to institute a judicial inquiry for purposes of investigating all the relevant aspects of this matter.'

By referring in general terms to 'questions raised in many quarters', Mugabe was attempting to deny the *Chronicle* any credit for its thorough investigation.

Headed by the respected judge president, Wilson Sandura, the commission of inquiry included prominent lawyers Robert Stumbles and Vernanda Ziyambi. The commission's secretary was Diana Mandaza, wife of the chairman of the Parastatals Commission, Dr Ibbo Mandaza. Then known as Ibbotson Joseph, Mandaza had been my senior at university, where he was uncharacteristically politically conscious for a young coloured student. More than a decade after the Willowgate scandal, he would emerge as a prominent publisher, launching two independent titles – the *Daily Mirror* and the *Sunday Mirror* – at a time when Mugabe was cracking down ruthlessly on Zimbabwe's independent press.

The deadline for the Sandura Commission to submit its report was 15 March 1989. 'Beware the Ides of March,' Mugabe appeared to be warning his delinquent ministers.

Within days, it became clear that politicians would not be the only casualties.

9

The taming of the shrewd

During a church service on Sunday 18 December 1988, the priest prayed for my family. Afterwards, in keeping with Nyarota custom, we had breakfast in our beautiful garden.

Gardening was the favourite pastime of both Ursula's and mine. Much of my free time was spent either sitting and enjoying the many fragrances and hues of the roses, chrysanthemums, antirrhinums, hydrangeas and carnations, or tending to the flower and vegetable beds.

Two gardeners who could not come to terms with the spectacle of their employer working with and alongside them had resigned. They were accustomed to employers who walked around the garden, hands in pocket, while either praising their good work or telling them what they were not doing well.

One horticulturist informed me that, in the eyes of the average gardener, an employer who donned overalls and gumboots to dig in the soil was criticising his work. Each time I employed a new gardener, therefore, I set the record straight at the earliest opportunity by explaining that any occasional activity on my part, spade or rake in hand, should in no way be seen as criticism, but as my only form of very necessary exercise.

Ursula and I sat for a while as we finalised our plans for Christmas 1988, which was exactly a week away. We were to depart from Bulawayo on Thursday, drive to Chivhu and spend the night, while reassuring her parents that all was well. They were still reeling from the shock of an enraged minister of defence berating me on national television. We would then proceed to Harare, likewise to pacify my mother in Highfields, before driving to Nyazura to spend Christmas with my grandparents. They particularly loved their great-grandchildren and could not understand why we did not allow Tafirenyika to live with them in the village and help with the cattle. He was already a junior at Plumtree High School on the border with Botswana, Zimbabwe's neighbour to the west. While Plumtree was a government school, it had the excellent standards of some of Zimbabwe's finer private academies.

One of the more lasting legacies of colonialism in Zimbabwe is the omnipresence of the Christian faith. The black population generally venerates Christmas Day. Urban dwellers undertake an annual pilgrimage to the village of their origin to spend this or the Easter holiday with their folk. When they visit for Christmas, they take loads of presents, clothing and delectable groceries, much to the delight of family members, whose staple diet is sadza and an assortment of vegetables.

Depending on the family's means, a plump chicken, fat goat or even a young heifer is slaughtered to celebrate the occasion. Family members partake in a day-long banquet, with friends and relatives dropping in to greet the visitors from the city. No invitation is required for them to join the feast. They eat to their heart's content, the food washed down with traditional beer from huge earthenware pots for the men, and large metal pots of tea and coffee or bottles of Coca-Cola or Fanta for the women. The bottles are refrigerated in a bucket of cold water, unless the city folk have brought ice with them for their Scotch and soda.

As the hot sun dips low in the summer sky, hopefully clear of rain and thunder just for that one day, and a mixture of the best village brew and the finest malt from Scotland starts taking its toll on revellers, spirited singing and rhythmic traditional dancing keep the growing crowd entertained. Among the Shona, the knowledge that visitors have arrived from the city is sufficient invitation for members of the extended family to descend on a homestead. The persistent beating of the drum is an even more urgent summons to all within hearing to join the merriment. At night, the sound of the African drumbeat can travel surprisingly far.

After breakfast that mid-December morning, Ursula took the utensils and cutlery back into the house, while I remained behind to read the *Sunday Mail* and the *Sunday News*. Both were delivered at dawn – one of the many perks of being a newspaper editor. Somehow, I could not concentrate. My mind kept drifting back to the tumultuous events of the week, especially since Wednesday, when the big story had broken.

I had a presentiment of impending catastrophe. On Thursday and Friday I had received several telephone calls from Zimbabwe Newspapers' managing director, Elias Rusike, as well as the chairman, Dr Davison Sadza. They both expressed concern about my safety. Dr Sadza was especially apprehensive and suggested that I leave Bulawayo until the storm had subsided. There was no doubt that an ominous situation was brewing and was likely to sweep me away. However, I stood my ground, pointing out that I could not abandon my post. What impression would that create among the staff and our supportive readers, not to mention the politicians?

What would the staff say if the editor took flight at the first sign of serious trouble? Would they not say that I had sought only to save my own skin after placing the entire newspaper at risk? Maruziva, especially, would be exposed to recrimination from the powerful politicians who had been named and shamed. For three months I had reflected at great length on the likely consequences of our course of action, and I was thus more than prepared to face them.

My thoughts were abruptly interrupted by the ferocious barking of our two dogs as they scurried towards the main gate. No amount of cajoling from where I sat would silence them, and I was forced to approach the gate to investigate the cause of their frenzied excitement.

My heart sank. Three Peugeot 504s were parked in front of our property. For many years after independence, the 504 was the car routinely allocated to senior government officials.

It was the colour of the car in the middle that set my heart pounding. It was the distinctive dark-green livery of Zimbabwe National Army vehicles. The driver of the lead car had emerged and was standing at the gate. It was he who had sent the dogs into a demented frenzy.

I recognised him immediately as the police officer commanding Matabeleland North, Assistant Commissioner Silas Moyo. Without a word, I shushed the dogs and opened the gate. The cars, each carrying a single occupant, all huge men, entered the driveway. I recognised a senior official from the Central Intelligence Organisation, and I had previously seen the army man at an official function at One Brigade headquarters in Bulawayo. I greeted them each in turn. From their very presence and general demeanour I was left in no doubt whatsoever that the game was up, much earlier than I had anticipated. I led them back into the garden, and Ursula re-emerged from the house to greet the visitors. Noting the expression of consternation on her face, they tried to display a friendly countenance. She offered them something to drink, but they declined. Sensing that they might want to speak to me alone and responding to a meaningful stare from me, she retreated into the house. She told me later that she went to sit on the bed in our room to observe the scene in the garden through the window. She had quickly explained to Tafirenyika that I was attending to some important visitors and we were not to be disturbed. Our second son, Itayi, six years old, and our daughter Rufaro, the youngest at four years of age, were blissfully unaware of the calamitous events unfolding in their father's and, indeed, their own small world.

I discussed the weather with the visitors. Inevitably, we talked a little – suspiciously too little, I thought – about the story that had virtually brought Zimbabwe to a standstill. I sensed that my visitors were a trifle embarrassed, then silence fell over us. The lull before the storm, I surmised. Assistant Commissioner Moyo, normally affable and very unlike the tough cop he was supposed to be, cleared his throat.

'Comrade Nyarota,' he said, speaking slowly while looking me straight in the eye, 'we are here on an unhappy mission. We have instructions to arrest you.'

He spoke so calmly that his message induced no sense of panic in me. He pulled out a handkerchief and wiped his brow.

'The minister of defence, Comrade Nkala, who as you know is also the acting minister of home affairs responsible for the police, has instructed that you be arrested at once.'

'On what charge?' I immediately butted in, my voice rising.

'Please, allow me to finish,' he pleaded, his hand raised. 'That is exactly the reason why this delegation has visited you. Junior officers could have easily carried out this simple assignment.

'We are not ourselves entirely convinced that valid reasons exist to warrant your arrest. But the minister is not interested in the validity of any grounds for arrest. He merely wants you locked up. You have already published his threats to lock you up. The heads of the different services in Bulawayo, however, held a meeting and we came to a decision.'

The other officers stared ahead of them stony-faced, avoiding eye contact with me.

'The decision, however, places us at great risk. The minister is expecting to receive confirmation by tomorrow that you have been arrested. We decided to inform him that you were not to be found; that you had travelled out of Bulawayo. That means, unfortunately, that you must leave Bulawayo immediately.'

As I reeled from the impact of what Moyo was saying, the three men stood up to leave. After they departed, I rushed back into the house and broke the news to Ursula. She took it very bravely. We were both overwhelmed by the compassion of the three government officers.

'Men such as Nkala do not have the support of the majority of Zimbabweans,' I said once I had regained my composure. 'The majority of citizens, including these officers, are good people who simply want to get on with their normal lives, if the politicians will let them.'

When I contacted head office the following morning, they were relieved that I had agreed to leave Bulawayo for a while for my own safety. I would take a two-week break after New Year to allow tempers to cool. Before the end of the day we were on the road, heading for the Midlands capital of Gweru, en route to Chivhu, having left Maruziva in charge of the paper, my secretary Patience Ncube in tears and the rest of the staff distraught. Monday 19 December 1988 effectively became my last day at the *Chronicle*.

On 31 December, I received an early thirty-eighth birthday present in the form of a story in the *Chronicle* under the headline 'Willowgate, first culprit nailed'.

Datelined Mutare, the story read: 'Jonathan Kadzura, the managing director of Rural Industrial Development (Pvt) Ltd, trading as Pamberi Marketing, who pleaded guilty to selling four Toyota Cressidas above the controlled maximum price, was fined Z\$9 500 here yesterday by Manicaland provincial magistrate Mr Philip Drazdik.'

Kadzura, an agro-economist who had become a flamboyant, loquacious and ostensibly prosperous businessman, had admitted selling three Toyota Cressidas for considerably more than the stipulated price of Z\$27 657. In one instance, Kadzura, said to be a nephew of political affairs minister Maurice Nyagumbo, sold a vehicle to a Mutare businessman of Indian origin for Z\$75 000, realising a profit of more than 250 per cent. Two other charges related to the purchase of Cressidas from Willowvale and their disposition to a Harare businessman for Z\$42 413 and to Lonrho Zimbabwe for Z\$65 000.

The controversial chief executive of Lonrho, Tiny Rowland, had cultivated strong relationships with Zanu-PF and PF-Zapu as far back as the liberation struggle, when he supported both parties financially. On visits to London, party officials were routinely accommodated free of charge at Lonrho's Metropolitan Hotel in Park Lane, overlooking Hyde Park.

In mitigation, Kadzura said his company had bought the cars for use by the field managers of projects in rural Manicaland, but had been forced to sell them due to cash-flow problems.

Any recently established trading company that allocated luxury sedans to its rural managers was bound to have serious cash-flow problems, I thought, and apparently magistrate Drazdik agreed.

'Why would the company buy the most luxurious cars for use in the rural areas? It is clear that the accused had some contact at Willowvale for him to have been able to obtain a whole fleet of luxurious cars,' he said in his judgment.

If the prosecution had done a thorough job, they would have informed the court that Kadzura's link at Willowvale was none other than Nyagumbo, whose nefarious dealings had been exposed by the *Chronicle*. When Drazdik asked Kadzura how he proposed to pay a substantial fine, the response was somewhat surprising.

'Can I have only five minutes, sir,' Kadzura asked, 'to get the money from the car – just five minutes?'

Outside the court, Kadzura boasted to enthralled journalists and bystanders that whatever fine the court imposed would be insignificant. He took a bulging briefcase from the trunk of his car and counted out Z$9 500 from the Z$60 000 in cash that he had packed 'just in case'. In addition to the fine, the court ordered Kadzura to refund Messrs Omar Enterprises of Mutare, Jaggers Wholesalers of Harare and Lonrho Zimbabwe a total of Z$75 000, the excess he had charged them collectively on vehicles worth Z$83 000.

My own annual salary at the time was Z$36 000, while that of a government minister was Z$24 000.

I was in Mutare when Kadzura was sentenced. We had never met, but as I entered the lobby of the Manica Hotel later that day, I encountered an immaculately dressed man of about my age. He stopped dead in his tracks, expensive briefcase clutched firmly in hand.

'Aren't you Nyarota?' he asked. Before I could respond, he continued: 'So this is the famous Nyarota! Well …'

By way of completing this utterance, he moved the left side of his jacket to reveal a handgun in a shoulder holster. Then he proceeded towards his car, a Toyota Cressida, parked in front of the hotel. I remained transfixed to the carpet. Mutare Central Police Station was located just across Third Street, less than a minute's walk from where I stood, but I decided in a split second that discretion was the better part of valour. Reporting to the police might not be the best way of handling this crisis. Whatever I said, it would essentially come down to Kadzura's word against mine, and he would probably have the police on his side, anyway. He was wealthy and the police were corruptible. His uncle was the fourth most powerful man in Zimbabwe, while I was arguably the most unpopular person in the country at the time. I picked up my keys from reception, went to my room, quickly packed my bag and checked out of the hotel, much to the astonishment of the front-desk staff.

A decade later, Kadzura and I would spend many amicable evenings together at my favourite watering hole, the Red Fox Hotel in Greendale, Harare. We debated the economic, social and political problems that were bringing our once proud and prosperous nation to its knees.

By then, Kadzura was a much sought-after and readily available economic analyst whose comments regularly graced the pages of the government's newspapers and who often appeared on the government-controlled ZBC-TV. Each time I sat down with Kadzura at the Red Fox or at the Mountview Hotel, which he owned in Mutare, I was reminded of his statement outside the Magistrate's Court.

'After all, who is not corrupt?' he had asked rhetorically as he counted out the cash to pay his fine.

During the second week of January 1989, I reported to head office as directed, intending to travel to Bulawayo afterwards. However, Rusike told me I could not go back immediately, as my life was still in danger. In any case, since I had been summoned to appear before the Sandura Commission, he said, it made sense for me to remain in Harare until I had testified. I pointed out that I could not prepare my testimony without reference to the relevant documents, which were in my office. My secretary, Patience Ncube, was instructed to pack the documents in a box and bring them to Harare herself. Meanwhile, I was installed in the presidential suite at the five-star Monomatapa Hotel, to prepare for my appearance before the commission. It was becoming increasingly apparent that I might not be returning to Bulawayo at all.

On Tuesday 26 January, the commission held its first hearing in the High Court on Harare's Samora Machel Avenue. The venue was opposite the Munhumutapa Building, which housed the office of the president and was the seat of government. Two days later, I took the witness stand before a packed court, agog with expectation. After I was sworn in, I was asked to relate details of the Willowgate investigation. I narrated the highlights, starting with Obert Mpofu's unexpected cheque and ending with the encounter between Maruziva and Nkala.

I told the commissioners that I believed the Zanu-PF company Zidco Holdings was the epicentre of the scandal and that we had hardly scratched the surface before the probe blew up in our faces. As fate would have it, Callistus Ndlovu had been appointed acting minister of information in January, while Witness Mangwende was on holiday, and I testified that Ndlovu had instructed the Zimbabwe Mass Media Trust to dismiss me from the *Chronicle* forthwith. Ndlovu vehemently denied this when he testified.

On 7 February, the commission grilled Don Ndlovu and Alvord Mpofu on the circumstances surrounding their acquisition of new trucks from Willowvale Motors with the assistance of their employer, Manilal Naran. Ndlovu reduced the packed courtroom to laughter when he explained how he had obtained a loan of more than Z$24 000 from Naran. He had intended to repay the loan from the proceeds of a poultry project that he and a friend had hoped to start, but which never took off because of a lack of finance. After taking delivery of the truck and realising he could not repay the loan, Ndlovu said, he had offered the vehicle to Naran in lieu of money, and this had been accepted.

While Ndlovu entertained both the commissioners and the public gallery with his creative testimony, controversial debate raged in parliament two blocks away after MP Byron Hove introduced a motion questioning unconfirmed reports that I had been removed from my position as editor of the *Chronicle*.

On 6 February I had been summoned to Dr Sadza's office. He told me it had been decided that, for my own safety, I was not to return to Bulawayo. I was being promoted and transferred to head office, where a new post had been created for me: group public relations executive of Zimbabwe Newspapers. It was a title that, as Shakespeare would have said, was full of sound and fury, but signified nothing. My new office was on the sixth floor of Herald House, where, exactly eleven years earlier, I had entered the world of journalism. Apparently, having been dissuaded from having me arrested, the aggrieved politicians were adamant that I should at least be fired. Beneath the sugar-coating on the pill, that was effectively what had happened, the pompous new title and greater remuneration notwithstanding.

I immediately visited Hove, one of the most outspoken and courageous post-independence members of parliament, and briefed him on the situation. He was incensed, and assured me he would raise the matter in parliament.

That night in my hotel suite, I was reduced to tears of frustration. Head office appeared to have finally succumbed to external pressure. Both Dr Sadza and Rusike had baulked from backing me. Instead, they had made me a sacrificial lamb on the altar of their own convenience, throwing the principles of press freedom, always publicly endorsed, out of the window. I considered the pending relocation of my family. I also thought about how this development would be received by the staff at the *Chronicle*. Enos Nkala and Callistus Ndlovu were bent on proving to the world that the sword was still mightier than the pen. I recalled Ndlovu's philosophy about the railway tracks that never converge. It appeared my own parallel tracks had finally met.

My promotion was a thinly disguised punishment for my role in Willowgate. Long before the Sandura Commission called its first witness, I became the victim of government retribution. The tiny office allocated to me was totally inconsistent with the grandeur of my new title. A position had been manufactured specifically to keep me out of active journalism and, in the eyes of the authorities, mischief. Ironically, my career as a journalist was dying in the exact location where it had begun at the now defunct cadet school.

Doing public relations for the government's largely kowtowing newspapers was a thankless task. A newspaper normally maintains its image through its content and its columns. Promoting newspapers that discredited themselves among the reading public on a daily basis was an impossible task. My bosses were aware of this, and they left me to my own devices. The very clear signal was that I was not wanted, and I seized the opportunity to plan a future of my own choosing. We sold our property in Bulawayo and paid a deposit on one in the Harare suburb of Highlands. For the next dozen years, our home would be at 16 Wingate Road. Fittingly, the easiest access to the house was via Ferris Road, named after Norman Ferris, editor of the *Herald* in the 1950s.

Realising that my future as a journalist was somewhat precarious in a country where government dominated the media scene, we invested Z$25 000 from the proceeds of our Bulawayo property sale in a business venture at Gwangwadza township, just outside Nyazura. This investment was to come to my rescue in future when I was faced with periods of unemployment.

For my role in exposing the Willowgate scandal, I won the Commonwealth Press Union's Terry Pierce-Goulding Memorial Award for excellence in journalism. In addition to a trophy, the prize allowed me to spend some time at the University of Western Ontario's School of Journalism in Canada.

When Justice Wilson Sandura finally threw the switch that caused Callistus Ndlovu's own philosophical railway tracks to meet, the result was dramatic, if not the most cataclysmic political occurrence in the eight years of Zimbabwe's independence.

Not only was Ndlovu summarily dropped from the gravy train, but as a direct consequence of the *Chronicle*'s name-and-shame exercise in 1988, the other major players in Willowgate – Enos Nkala, Maurice Nyagumbo, Fredrick Shava, Dzingai Mtumbuka and Jacob Mudenda – found themselves out in the cold as well, after gruelling and humiliating inquisition by the commission. Hundreds of Harare citizens witnessed the rare spectacle of the high and the mighty being held to account for their actions at long last.

On most days, the court was packed with spectators, some overflowing into the gallery above the austere room. When Nkala's long and anxiously awaited turn arrived, more than 200 people pitched up. His appearance had been announced in the *Herald* that morning. Editor Tommy Sithole could no longer pretend that Willowgate was nothing more than a figment of the imagination of the *Chronicle*'s editors. He swallowed his pride and proceeded to reap profits from the queues that formed every morning to buy his paper.

Outside, the police engaged in running battles with citizens who did not want to miss the unfolding spectacle of one-party Zimbabwe's ruling elite being subjected to public scrutiny and humiliation in front of the very people to whom they had presented themselves as untouchables, or, in the case of Nkala, a demigod.

On Thursday 13 April, police clad in riot gear and with fierce dogs on leashes rushed to the Bulawayo offices of the *Chronicle* to do battle with a 2 000-strong crowd that had converged on the premises to secure a copy of that day's newspaper, which carried details of the long-awaited Sandura Commission report.

Street vendors attempting to leave the premises on their bicycles, heavily laden with copies of the newspaper, were blocked. By the time Judge President Sandura presented the report to the president at State House, he had become a household name, while the reputation of five of Zimbabwe's most powerful men had been shredded.

Ndlovu was not the first minister to testify before the commission, but his appearance on 10 February was one of the most action-packed sessions. His main theme was that a number of names had been omitted from the list published by the *Chronicle*. He warned the commission that it was likely to 'unearth a lot of unpleasantries' if it investigated the whole motor industry.

However, he refused to name the lucky politicians whose names he claimed had been omitted from the *Chronicle* list. 'The list is much bigger than that,' he declared. 'Those who published it had to protect some people.'

The commission requested Ndlovu to furnish the missing names.

'I couldn't give you any names,' he said. 'I think the president's office has got those names and if you want them you can check there.'

Ndlovu suggested that while those whose names were missing from the list were not themselves holders of high office, they were people of 'sufficient influence'. Taking the commissioners by surprise, he then quickly passed a piece of paper to Sandura, commenting dourly, 'It's part of what you wanted me to do.'

There was a brief moment of pregnant silence. Neither Ndlovu nor the commissioners said anything about the note. My own assumption was that Ndlovu had scrawled a name or names on the piece of paper. His line of argument throughout was that the *Chronicle* had protected certain people, although even a cursory inspection of the published list revealed what was tantamount to a who's who of Zanu-PF's top echelons.

Analysis of the *Chronicle* list disclosed that all the leading Zanu-PF functionaries, with the notable exception of the president himself, had obtained a vehicle or two, or more, from either Willowvale Motor Industries or Leyland Motors or both. If the names of any culprits were missing from the list, as alleged by the minister, it could only be because they were never included on either the list provided by Willowvale staff or the one compiled by the police.

It was obvious that Ndlovu could not have been trying to implicate Mugabe, since he certainly did not qualify as being 'not a holder of high office', but the minister did seem to be implying that the president had received names that were not on our list, and had taken a deliberate decision to shield them.

Ndlovu could only have been referring to someone important or close enough to the president to warrant his protection. The judge president and his fellow commissioners had appeared stunned by whatever they read on the piece of paper, but they never called for testimony from anyone who had not been named by the *Chronicle*.

During the Willowgate investigation I had been accused of protecting one particular senior Zanu-PF official. The Zimpapers chairman, Dr Sadza, had asked me straight out if this was true. The person in question was the secretary of the Zanu-PF Women's League, First Lady Sally Mugabe.

Could it be that hers was the name scrawled on Ndlovu's piece of paper? Was it possible that Ndlovu and others genuinely believed that the *Chronicle* had protected Sally

Mugabe and that this was the true reason for their acrimony towards me? The implications were extremely serious, and the only inference that might be drawn if, indeed, Sally Mugabe's name was given to the commission by Ndlovu, would be that President Mugabe and the commission had conspired to stage-manage a serious cover-up.

Once the commissioners had recovered from the shock of Ndlovu's secret submission, the minister appeared emboldened by its effect and he returned to his pet subject.

'The stories published by the *Chronicle* are a shoddy piece of scandal conceived by tricksters and mobsters,' he declared. For good measure, he confronted the grumbling public gallery and, addressing the packed benches with an obvious reference to me, pronounced: 'You will probably pay his legal fees.'

The dignified ambience of the courtroom did little to moderate Ndlovu's legendary arrogance. In a show of rare mental dexterity, he swung back to the issue in hand and informed the commissioners that he did not wish to delve deeper into the subject of the *Chronicle*'s list of alleged wrongdoers. 'For very good reason, and I think anybody with a bit of common sense knows why,' he said with unconcealed sarcasm.

'Why?' asked lawyer Robert Stumbles, one of the commissioners, ignoring Ndlovu's reference to common sense.

'If you look at those names, it's politically obvious,' the minister responded, his voice rising aggressively. 'The political convenience to which this list was put is obvious to anyone who is aware of the politics of this place.

'We suspect the *Chronicle* deliberately left names off the list it printed, for political reasons. The *Chronicle* was involved in a campaign to discredit the Zanu-PF leadership in Matabeleland.'

Unable to endure this sustained insult to their collective intelligence any longer, the crowd let out a spontaneous and drawn-out 'aah' in protest.

Members of the public were obviously shocked that Ndlovu continued to suggest Willowgate had been a campaign by the *Chronicle* to discredit the Ndebele leadership of Zanu-PF. The number of Ndebele politicians on the list was far outnumbered by the Shona, who included the second and fourth most powerful men in the party: Simon Muzenda, vice-president and political affairs minister, and Maurice Nyagumbo, the party's secretary for administration. Even the name of the powerful army commander, Solomon Tapfumanei Mujuru, formerly known as Rex Nhongo, was on the list, and he was not Ndebele either. However, Mujuru had accounted for the vehicle that he obtained from Willowvale Motors.

It was a popular ploy among Zimbabwe's politicians to blame imaginary political adversaries or tribal opponents whenever they were caught with their pants down, but Ndlovu had obviously not reckoned with the unexpected public rebuke from the gallery. He turned to Sandura, as if appealing for protection from the irate spectators.

'I think you should tell these people to make less noise,' he said, exuding swelling arrogance.

After Sandura had restored order, Ndlovu continued. 'Everybody wanted to see my name on the list of people taking cars from Willowvale. I am glad to say they are going to fall flat on their stomachs. They will not succeed.'

When he appeared before the commission again a week later, Ndlovu changed tack, launching a personal attack on Sandura, whom he accused of treating him like a child.

'I don't like this line of questioning. I have been a university professor for a long time,' Ndlovu said to loud murmurs of sharp disapproval from the public benches when he couldn't answer a question at one point.

'You will know who you are talking to and how to ask questions,' he added, glaring at the bemused judges.

Completely unruffled, Sandura assured the former don that he was sufficiently empowered to deal with anyone who treated his commission with contempt.

'What has being a university professor got to do with the commission?' the learned judge asked the learned minister, apparently out of genuine curiosity.

'A lot, because that way you will know who you are talking to and how to ask questions,' Ndlovu said, evoking a loud burst of renewed laughter throughout the court. 'I am not going to be treated like a child and I will not answer questions like a child. This is what will make or break this interview.

'I am not on trial. If I am, I would rather get my lawyer. I will not answer questions that are irrelevant here.'

After Sandura pointed out firmly that the prerogative to determine what constituted relevant or irrelevant questions was his to guard jealously, Ndlovu mellowed somewhat.

'I am sorry if I have been in contempt of court,' he said. 'It is not my intention.'

Asked to explain his earlier allegation about the names published in the *Chronicle*, Ndlovu reiterated that the newspaper was bent on destroying Zanu-PF's Ndebele leaders.

'It is a fact that the *Chronicle* is being used as a political weapon,' he said. 'Every time I go out of the country, the *Chronicle* publishes something about me. Some people consider Nyarota an investigative journalist. He is a gutter journalist. Freedom of the press doesn't mean to insult. If that's it, then it can go to hell.'

Stumbles was obliged to warn Ndlovu not to assail the dignity of the court by consistently drawing on his reserve of foul language.

The first cabinet member called before the commission was Nathan Magunda Shamuyarira, minister of foreign affairs. He was also the only minister exonerated by Sandura in the end.

On 1 February, the commission had heard that a white farmer, Anthony Lendrum, had sold two trucks at inflated prices and insisted on payment being made in cash and partly by cheque.

Dimitri Markides, the buyer at Critall Hope Reliance, said he had negotiated to buy a Mazda B1600 from Lendrum for Z$60 000, more than twice the controlled price. Critall Hope was a subsidiary of Lonrho Zimbabwe.

'Lendrum asked me if the company could give him Z$21 000 in the form of a cheque and the balance in cash,' Markides told the commission. 'He said he wanted to protect himself. From what he did not say.'

Lendrum had also sold another vehicle, a smaller truck, at an inflated price. A witness testified that the farmer 'said he knew a minister, Shamuyarira, and was going to assist him'. It was this vehicle that appeared in the WMI register of allocations to or at the instigation of government ministers. On 14 December, the *Chronicle* had recorded that the entry for this vehicle included the legend: 'Lendrum TS/Shamuyarira', but it had been impossible to establish what had become of the vehicle in question.

Lendrum was a farm manager at Bar SL Ranch in the vicinity of Lake McIlwaine (renamed Lake Chivero), about thirty kilometres west of Harare, and he confirmed being a friend of the foreign affairs minister. They would 'have a chat and fish and chips together for lunch' when Shamuyarira was minister of information, post and telecommunications, the commission heard.

Lendrum said Shamuyarira had given him a letter of introduction to Zimoco when he needed assistance with the acquisition of two trucks. Zimoco, another subsidiary of Lonrho Zimbabwe, was the sole Mercedes-Benz franchise holder at the time. The company did not sell trucks.

According to Lendrum, the letter read in part, 'Could you please assist Mr Lendrum, whom I have known for many years, in getting a car.'

After the *Chronicle* broke the Willowgate story, said Lendrum, he met with Shamuyarira, who asked him to explain in writing exactly what had happened after he accepted the letter of recommendation.

Other beneficiaries of ministerial favour told the commission they had attended meetings with errant ministers to concoct evidence, but the meeting between Shamuyarira and Lendrum was deemed to have been entirely innocent. Neither man was asked what seemed to be an obvious question, namely why Zimoco would have required a letter of recommendation from a government minister before selling a luxury car to a well-heeled white farmer. Nor was Lendrum asked why, having started his quest for a vehicle in a showroom housing the world's most expensive luxury models, he had eventually settled for a Mazda B1300, just about the cheapest car on the Zimbabwean market.

At one point, Lendrum told the commission that he was looking to buy a Toyota Cressida. This was totally at variance with Shamuyarira's claim that the farmer was desperate for a truck to move his crop. In any case, if Lendrum told Shamuyarira that he wanted to buy a Cressida, the minister had addressed his letter of recommendation to the wrong dealer. The Cressida might have been the Japanese manufacturer's top model, but it was hardly in the same league as the German-made Mercedes-Benz.

Nevertheless, armed with the letter addressed to Zimoco, Lendrum had approached Dave Gibson, managing director of Willowvale Motors. He, in turn, referred the farmer to Elias Mabhena, who promptly made a telephone call, the commission heard.

'Mr Gibson,' Mabhena said, 'I have a Mr Lendrum here who is after cars. Could you assist him?'

Within a month, Lendrum had been allocated two trucks, yet, in its final report, the Sandura Commission expressed satisfaction that Shamuyarira had done nothing unlawful or improper.

Mabhena, the deputy secretary of industry and technology, as well as being chairman of WMI, admitted to the commission that not only had he known of the sale of the two vehicles to Lendrum, but had been approached by Shamuyarira to assist the farmer.

At this point in his vital testimony, the commission acceded to Mabhena's request that proceedings continue in camera, but not before he was asked to explain how Lendrum had come to buy two vehicles from Willowvale Motors.

'It was through the pleading of … the minister of foreign affairs, Comrade Nathan Shamuyarira,' Mabhena said. 'The minister telephoned and spoke to me. I told him that we had difficulties. The minister then made a plea after he had confirmed that the farmer was stuck with crops on his farms and really needed the vehicles.'

Mabhena said he could neither confirm nor deny remarks attributed to him by the *Chronicle* on 21 October, namely that a serious investigation into the Willowvale car racket 'might unearth certain unfortunate things'.

'I have no argument with the press,' Mabhena said. 'I am very unprotected. I'm a civil servant and I have my limitations. But I was under tremendous pressure from the editor of the *Chronicle* on the day of the interview. He telephoned every ten minutes.'

When Shamuyarira took the stand, he dismissed Mabhena's testimony out of hand. Not only was it false, it was also mischievous, according to the minister, who stated that he had never met Mabhena. In fact, Mabhena had told the commission only that he and Shamuyarira had spoken on the telephone.

To my mind, the commissioners were predisposed towards exonerating Shamuyarira from the moment he took the stand and announced that he had instituted legal proceedings against the *Chronicle* for linking his name to Lendrum in print. No one pointed out that it was rather presumptuous of the minister to take such steps before the commission had issued its findings. I believe that Shamuyarira's declaration that he was already suing the newspaper was seen as an indication of his innocence.

The Sandura Commission heard evidence from seventy-three witnesses during thirty sessions spread over eight weeks. Ten of the witnesses, including ministers, were recalled after fresh evidence surfaced that contradicted their initial testimony. Yet Mabhena was not recalled. Despite shocking proof of the extent to which government ministers were prepared to lie under oath in order to defend themselves, the commission appeared happy to accept at face value Shamuyarira's assertions that Mabhena had perjured himself.

Shamuyarira later won his defamation case against me and the *Chronicle* on a technicality, but I remain convinced that the evaluation of his evidence was a travesty of justice and that he was, indeed, guilty of at least an element of impropriety regarding the Lendrum vehicles. In my lay opinion, the commission did not probe deeply enough or ask all the pertinent questions that should have been put to the minister.

Shamuyarira said he gave Lendrum a handwritten letter on a plain sheet of paper and told him to go to Zimoco 'because John Mapondera who works there had told me at a social gathering that they were selling cars'.

Other testimony, of course, was that Lendrum had specified his need for a truck to move his crops. While it is true that I am sometimes guilty of expecting other people to possess the same above-average knowledge of the motor industry as I do, I still found it difficult to fathom that the erudite minister would refer the farmer to Mapondera at Zimoco when he was clearly anxious to purchase a truck. Certainly, Mercedes-Benz does manufacture trucks, but the salesmen at Zimoco never showed Lendrum one. They allegedly merely referred him to Willowvale.

While Shamuyarira wrote to Mapondera that Lendrum was 'looking for a car and can you please help him', he subsequently told the commission, 'My letter was about one truck and I don't know how he ended up getting two. My contact with him ended with the letter to Zimoco.'

Shamuyarira said that while the government scheme allowing politicians to access new vehicles directly from Willowvale Motors had been discussed by the cabinet in his absence, his understanding was that it had been introduced because authorised car dealers were giving preferential treatment to their friends, with most vehicles going to white Zimbabweans. The commissioners spared the minister from the embarrassment of pointing out that Lendrum was both a personal friend and a white Zimbabwean.

All in all, it seemed to me, the story of Lendrum and Shamuyarira's association was full of holes. The case of senior political affairs minister Maurice Nyagumbo, on the other hand, ended in tragedy.

The fourth highest-ranking Zanu-PF official and a senior minister in the president's office was inextricably linked to the spider's web that was Willowgate. By his own admission, Nyagumbo had helped more than thirty-six people secure new vehicles.

The courtroom was packed on the morning of his appearance. He was a soft-spoken, affable and popular minister and the author of a book, *With the People*, that he had written in prison to spell out his political vision for a future Zimbabwe. Nyagumbo was indeed a man of the people, who represented the poor constituency of Dzivarasekwa in parliament. The suburb, on Harare's western outskirts, had been conceived by the Salisbury city council during the Smith era as a housing scheme for low-income workers, mainly domestic servants.

It appeared that Nyagumbo's genuine affinity with the people had landed him in trouble with the law.

Sitting in the public gallery on the February morning when Nyagumbo took the stand were Zanu-PF's leading legal brains: maverick politician and former minister of justice and legal affairs Eddison Zvobgo and Byron Hove. Hove had been a London barrister before returning to Rhodesia during the negotiations that saw Muzorewa assume the mantle of power as interim prime minister. He was appointed joint minister of justice with a white counterpart, Hillary Squires, but, disenchanted with the half-hearted nature of the new political dispensation and retention of real political power in the hands of Smith's Rhodesian Front and the white minority, Hove had resigned in a huff and returned to London.

Elected to Zimbabwe's parliament in 1980, he became one of the most outspoken members in the house of assembly and, following Willowgate, had taken up the cudgels and put up a spirited fight on behalf of both me and press freedom. He tabled a motion in parliament to express 'concern and alarm at the progressive curtailment of freedom of the press and the right of the people of Zimbabwe to be informed'.

Describing me as a 'distinguished, fearless, patriotic and highly professional journalist', Hove said my removal from the *Chronicle* had been induced by pressure from ministers who were implicated in the scandal. He said my dismissal would have adverse and prejudicial implications on the good name of the government, the country, the freedom of the press and the people's right to be informed on matters touching on the integrity of their political leaders.

The firebrand Zvobgo was the minister of political affairs at that time, having been demoted by Mugabe from the ministry of justice, legal and parliamentary affairs. He would lead the fight for press freedom in 2000, when, as a backbencher, he was in the forefront of opposition to the draconian Access to Information and Protection of Privacy Bill that the voluble information minister, Jonathan Moyo, was pushing through parliament.

Nyagumbo told the Sandura Commission that he had assisted no fewer than three dozen people to obtain vehicles from Willowvale Motors, Leyland Motors and Duly's, Zimbabwe's largest car dealership. To the surprise and consternation of both the commission and the public, however, he categorically denied benefiting financially from those he had assisted.

'I don't think I deserve the aspersion you, Judge President, tend to cast on my name and character,' the minister said when Sandura asked if he had received any money. 'I want to raise the strongest objection to the way you have been asking questions to witnesses, questions such as whether those I have assisted, Mr Sam Levy, for instance, have given me anything for my assistance.'

Sandura attempted to interrupt this tirade: 'Mr Minister ...'

'Now, wait a minute,' Nyagumbo interjected, his political seniority getting the better of him. 'I regard this question as an insult to my character and my being. I have never been in jail for any dishonesty. I am now sixty-five and I have never been jailed for dishonesty.'

He was, of course, making the point that while he had indeed served jail time, it had been for his contribution to the liberation struggle, but his words evoked a loud roar of protest and laughter from the public gallery.

Sandura reminded Nyagumbo that the commission's job was to collect information, and that he was in no way suggesting that the minister was guilty of any wrongdoing.

'I am a minister of the government and my office is a public office. I am not a lawyer who can get payment for his services, so I did not ask for money,' a bristling Nyagumbo replied.

He then waxed lyrical about his profound respect for the Zanu-PF Leadership Code, introduced by the party to regulate the behaviour of its officials. The document, launched with much fanfare, had quickly fallen by the wayside as wanton acquisition and the capitalist predatory tendencies that the code sought to suppress reasserted themselves with a vengeance. Willowgate was ample testimony to the total failure of Zanu-PF's Leadership Code.

Nyagumbo denied ever writing a letter to the ministry of industry and technology or to any of its officials requesting assistance in securing vehicles.

Sandura suddenly showed Nyagumbo one such letter and asked if it had originated from his office.

'See, this is not my signature,' Nyagumbo promptly responded, but after closer scrutiny of the document, he had to amend his response. 'It is my letter,' he said hoarsely, adding as an afterthought, 'I assisted anyone who came into my office.'

Looking around the courtroom, Stumbles asked if anyone present could count on Nyagumbo for help if they approached him, to which he responded: 'I would do my best. I wish I had known better.'

Three days after his appearance, Nyagumbo was admitted to Parirenyatwa Hospital after sustaining injuries in an assault by persons unknown and in circumstances that remained a mystery until two months later, when, named by the *Chronicle* and shamed by the commission and the bureaucracy of which he was a part, he committed suicide.

Jonathan Kadzura, alleged to have benefited most from Nyagumbo's largesse, told the commission that he had obtained four Toyota Cressidas from Willowvale with the assistance of the minister, as well as trucks from Leyland Motors and Duly's.

'I asked the senior minister to help in the purchase of a truck,' Kadzura said. 'I received a telephone call from him, if I remember correctly, to say, "You may get a truck from Leyland." This was at about the same time I asked for the first two Cressidas in 1987.'

Kadzura denied being related to Nyagumbo, as was being widely suggested, but said he knew the minister through his father-in-law. He confirmed that Michael Nyabadza, another beneficiary of assistance from Nyagumbo who had used Kadzura's business address for his allocation, was, indeed, related to the minister. Nyabadza's father and Nyagumbo were first cousins, he said. The senior Nyabadza, a prominent businessman at a centre that bore his name twenty kilometres east of Rusape on the road to Nyanga, had been assassinated one night in 1977. He was known to have collaborated with Zanla guerrillas operating in the area and his death was widely suspected to be the work of the Selous Scouts.

On Wednesday 19 April, a day after the ninth anniversary of Zimbabwe's independence, to the achievement of which he had made tremendous personal contribution and sacrifice, Nyagumbo was readmitted to hospital, this time in a very serious condition. While the *Herald* of 21 April reported that the minister was in a stable condition, independent hospital sources painted a grimmer picture. He was in the intensive care unit and had remained unconscious throughout Thursday.

Announcing Nyagumbo's death the following day, the *Herald* pointed out that the police suspected no foul play. This phrase had become a euphemism in the press for suicide. The paper then disclosed for the first time that Nyagumbo had taken poison four days earlier, having resigned his ministerial post the week before.

After Robert Mugabe, Joshua Nkomo and Simon Muzenda, Maurice Nyagumbo was Number Four in the Zanu-PF hierarchy. Up to the signing of the unity agreement between PF-Zapu and Zanu-PF in 1987, he had been the third most senior party official as the secretary for administration.

Born in 1924, Nyagumbo attended St Faith's and St Augustine's mission schools. He joined the exodus of young Rhodesian blacks to South Africa at an early age and secured a job as a waiter at a Port Elizabeth hotel. He became a member of the Communist Party until it was banned in 1948, and was deported to Rhodesia in 1955 on the grounds that he was in contact with the Mau Mau rebels in Kenya. Back in Salisbury, he helped to launch the African National Youth League with Mugabe's cousin, James Chikerema. Nyagumbo had his first taste of political detention in 1959, and, on release, he joined Zapu. He became a founding member of Zanu in 1963, and was elected organising secretary.

Nyagumbo was again detained in 1964. Soon after being released in 1975, he was rearrested and charged with recruiting young men for guerrilla training outside the country. He was freed in 1979, just in time to attend the Lancaster House conference. Nyagumbo became Rhodesia's longest-serving political detainee, in and out of prison and detention camp over a twenty-year period. After his election to parliament in 1980, he was appointed minister of mines and energy resources, and subsequently became senior minister of political affairs in the president's office.

Notwithstanding his illustrious liberation struggle credentials, the Sandura Commission condemned Nyagumbo in strong terms for committing perjury about the acquisition and disposal of the many vehicles to which his name was linked. Speaking during the minister's burial at Heroes' Acre, Mugabe publicly acknowledged for the first time that Nyagumbo had committed suicide.

'We are left wondering why such a dour revolutionary character would have acted in the manner he did,' Mugabe lamented. 'Shocking and unbelievable as it is, he has taken his life and left us confused, bewildered and guessing. But once he had decided to go, there was no turning back. That was typical of his character.'

Nyagumbo's sudden death had a profound impact on me. The burial, on what became the saddest day of my journalistic career, cast a dark shadow. I watched the ceremony on television at home, unable to summon the courage to attend in person. Not once during the Willowgate investigation had I imagined that any of those involved would take their own lives. The funeral of Manicaland's most influential son was not an event to be taken lightly by anyone from that province. While nobody said so to me directly, I suspected people were accusing me behind my back of having caused the death of the good old man.

I tried to rationalise developments leading to Nyagumbo's suicide. The decision to take his own life was, no doubt, sparked by the report of the commission, but I reasoned that it was his innately good nature that had forced him down the path of suicide. Because his character was sound, he failed to weather the storm that engulfed him. As a government minister and senior party official he was used to political protection, and the commission had effectively removed his mantle of security.

'Although there is no direct evidence to show that Nyagumbo was given any payment for helping people to get vehicles, some of which were resold for fantastic profits, it is difficult to believe that he received no benefit at all,' the Sandura report stated. The commission particularly lashed Nyagumbo for falsely using the names of Mugabe and Zanu-PF to obtain vehicles from Willowvale Motors.

'The commission accepts the evidence of witnesses who said that the minister contacted Willowvale and stated that His Excellency the President had authorised allocation of motor vehicles for sale to the party. On the other hand, the minister's denials were quite unconvincing. In fact, generally speaking, he was an unimpressive witness. His evidence did not have a ring of truth. In the commercial sector it is well known that, in the present circumstances, no person would take the trouble to find a new motor vehicle for another person for nothing.'

On one occasion, Nyagumbo had asked Willowvale to allocate a luxury vehicle to Zanu-PF. Sam Levy, a businessman whose name had consistently been linked to allegations of corruption in Harare, purchased the vehicle for Z$29 821 and immediately resold it for Z$105 000, making a profit of more than 200 per cent.

'We found it incredible that a businessman like Levy would expect us to believe that he gave nothing to the minister in return for the assistance rendered to him in finding the two motor vehicles which he bought,' the commission said.

When Nyagumbo had approached the ministry of industry and technology for assistance in securing two Toyota Cressidas and a pick-up truck for Zanu-PF, he was turned down. The minister then approached WMI directly, saying allocation of the required vehicles had been authorised not only by the ministry, but by the president himself.

'It was on the basis of this information and assurance alleging authorisation by the highest authority in the land that in May 1988 Willowvale set aside three motor vehicles for purchase by Zanu-PF,' the report stated.

'However, as the witnesses subsequently discovered, neither the ministry of industry and technology nor His Excellency, the President had authorised allocation of the three motor vehicles.'

There is little doubt that the commission's report had shattered Nyagumbo's world.

His use of the president's name in facilitating his own nefarious activities would have rankled. To add to his discomfort, the minister of home affairs, Moven Mahachi, one of Nyagumbo's protégés from Manicaland, announced on Friday 10 March that people who had given false testimony to the Sandura Commission would soon be prosecuted. He told the white members of the Norton Farmers' Association that a number of dockets had already been compiled.

'President Mugabe has given us the directive that nobody is above the law and we will certainly proceed with prosecutions after the commission has completed its task,' Mahachi said. For Nyagumbo, both the venue and audience listening to this announcement must have been particularly humiliating.

Then there were the physical injuries that remained shrouded in secrecy until Nyagumbo's death. Unbeknown to the public at large, he had been involved in a hit-and-run accident in which the victim died. However, the minister was not prosecuted and the docket was allowed to gather dust at Harare Central Police Station. It was said that once the police were given the green light to prosecute previously untouchable politicians, they dusted off the docket and contacted Nyagumbo.

It has been suggested that Nyagumbo was forced to take poison, but I have never doubted that his was a genuine case of suicide caused by shame and remorse.

Predictably, the most sensational part of the Sandura hearings was the encounter between the commissioners and defence minister Enos Mzombi Nkala. It also became the turning point, after which the commission was able to pin clear cases of wrongdoing on some of the politicians.

When he first appeared on 4 March, Nkala argued that his actions in helping people to obtain new cars stemmed from his sense of responsibility.

'If I can get them I will help them,' he told the commission. Like Shamuyarira, he was quick to inform the commissioners that he planned to sue the *Chronicle*. At the time of writing, eighteen years later, he had still not done so and the three-year statute of limitations for a defamation suit had long since expired.

Throughout the Sandura hearings Nkala maintained that he saw nothing wrong with helping people obtain new vehicles.

'I would like to say that my actions were innocent, motivated by a sense of responsibility to help,' he said. 'I was not, and I am still not involved in any car racket – whatever car racket means – and if in your findings at the end of the day you do find a racket, I was not in any way in any racket.'

Contrary to his reputation and his hostile attitude, Nkala maintained a surprisingly impressive composure on the witness stand. He was a model of calm and dignity, gave his evidence lucidly and confidently, and displayed signs of slight agitation only when the public reacted audibly to some of his more outrageous statements and threatened to drown his testimony in protest.

Pulling political rank, he told the commission that since the inception of Zanu-PF in 1963 – he graciously refrained from mentioning that this happened in his own home – he had been regularly involved in raising funds for the party. Zanu-PF now controlled assets of more than Z$100 million as a result of some of his activities.

A Bulawayo trading company, the Treger Group, was the biggest donor to Zanu-PF, he said. His wife Thandiwe was employed by this company and she had told him at some point that the company was interested in buying her personal car, a Toyota Cressida. Though initially reluctant to sell the vehicle, said Nkala, he had eventually agreed to do so for Z$29 000. The managing director of Treger, Berwick Davis, also told the commission that his company had paid Z$29 000 to Thandiwe for her luxury vehicle. At the time, similar models were fetching more than Z$100 000 on the black market.

This transaction was to provide the commission with the break that had remained elusive throughout five weeks of testimony, much of it concocted by witnesses, including ministers, who lied under oath.

On Thursday 9 March, Mrs Nkala, a devout born-again Christian, took both the members of the commission and the packed public gallery by surprise when she turned the tables on her feared husband. She changed her story and admitted that the Nkalas had realised a whopping Z$90 000 from the sale of the Cressida, not the paltry Z$29 000 claimed by her husband.

In fact, it was her boss, Davis, who had sensationally upstaged the minister that morning when, after being recalled to the stand, a hushed courtroom heard him confess that Treger had paid Z$90 000 for the Nkala vehicle after all.

It was to be a day of soul-searching. Martin Simela, the non-constituent Bulawayo parliamentarian who had been at the forefront of castigating the *Chronicle* over its coverage of Willowgate, had also suffered an attack of conscience. Having previously testified about a car that he sold, he now told the commission that he wanted to come clean.

'I want to apologise to the nation for lying before the commission,' Simela said.

Davis admitted that he and Nkala had sat down to discuss a cover-up. The events were to provide a dramatic turnaround in the dying hours of the commission. The chairman made two quick decisions. He asked the president to extend the deadline to 31 March, then recalled the minister of defence to the witness stand.

But the wily Nkala smartly upstaged the commission. When he appeared the next day, he announced that he had tendered his resignation as a minister.

'Yesterday,' said Nkala, looking steadfastly at Sandura, 'when it was clear to me what was going to happen here, to show you the gravity with which I treat this matter, I went to the vice-president and submitted my resignation.'

As Nkala got to the word 'resignation', there was pandemonium in the courtroom, with thunderous applause erupting spontaneously from the public benches. It was both sensational and surreal. The people and their political leaders had quite clearly and inexorably drifted apart. The people had over the years endured abuse, humiliation and deprivation at the hands of their so-called liberators. Now it was payback time.

Nkala told the incredulous courtroom that he was also resigning from his position as Zanu-PF treasurer and from the party's central committee and supreme organ, the Soviet-style politburo. Zanu-PF's fifth most powerful functionary had fallen, been stripped of all power and reduced, in his own words, to 'a card-holder and loyal member of the party with no responsibilities'.

That night, I slept like a baby. I am sure I was not the only citizen of Zimbabwe who did so.

Strictly speaking, it was Davis, managing director of the Treger Group, who had finally caused the downfall of the mighty. When Thandiwe Nkala confirmed that the Cressida had been sold for Z$90 000 and that her husband had known this from the day of the transaction, it was clear that Nkala had lied under oath. Thandiwe said Z$29 000 was paid by cheque, while the balance was tendered in cash that had never been deposited in the bank, but was stashed in the house. She told the commission that had her bosses not informed her they were going to tell the truth, she would have stuck to the fictitious figure of Z$29 000.

Confronted with this revised account, Nkala admitted that he had held meetings with Treger executives to concoct evidence for the commission.

'I would like to say that, like a humble lamb, I was led to the slaughter by the performers,' he said. 'My interest and major motivation was to rescue my wife from a situation in which she had placed herself.'

When Stumbles asked whether he would not apologise to the commission for telling falsehoods, Nkala adamantly refused.

'I respect the commission,' he said, 'but I feel I will have to go without making apologies to anybody. I would not want to appear soft.'

Vice-President Muzenda had refused to accept Nkala's resignation in the absence of Mugabe at a conference in the Netherlands. The president was a regular foreign traveller before his movements were curtailed by smart sanctions slapped on him and members of his government by the European Union and the United States in protest against gross human rights abuses. On his return to Harare, Mugabe called a press conference and announced his acceptance of Nkala's resignation from government.

'When revolutionaries go wrong,' Mugabe said, 'they too must be punished, perhaps even more because they are the leaders. I hope the wrong they have done will be a lesson to them and to others and that they will work in future to follow the correct path of honesty and integrity and set an example to those who will still look to them for guidance, wherever they are.'

Turning to me, Mugabe said he was grateful that I had revealed the facts about Willowgate. I had, however, gone too far by lumping together all those who had acquired vehicles from Willowvale Motor Industries and making it appear as if they had all been involved in a scandal.

'That is that little degree of overzealousness that he suffers from,' the president pontificated.

He told the press conference he had been informed that although I was no longer involved in journalism, I had been promoted and was now earning a bigger salary.

'Can anyone complain about receiving more money?' he asked, smiling benevolently.

Mugabe certainly created the impression that he did not fully endorse the fight against corruption and only grudgingly accepted the Sandura Commission's findings. Subsequent events were to confirm that, essentially, Mugabe was on the side of the corrupt, as evidenced by the future of the five ministers who were forced to resign. For many years it remained a question of national debate whether the president of Zimbabwe was merely surrounded by corrupt cronies, or was himself corrupt.

Frederick Shava was the only minister to face prosecution for lying to the commission. He was convicted and sentenced to nine months behind bars for perjury. Mugabe immediately convened a meeting of the Zanu-PF politburo. A proposal to grant presidential pardon to all the ministers involved in Willowgate was tabled and instantly adopted. Mugabe called a press conference to announce the decision.

'Who among us has not lied?' he began. 'Yesterday, you were with your girlfriend and you told your wife you were with the president. Should you get nine months' jail for that?'

In the final analysis, the real victims of the Willowgate investigation were Maruziva, Nyagumbo and me, as the unrepentant ministers were pardoned. Shava and Mudenda were rehabilitated and brought back into the party fold. Nkala and Ndlovu pursued private interests, while Mutumbuka left the country for a fresh start in the United States with the World Bank.

My own tribulations were far from over. Nathan Shamuyarira stuck to his word and instituted legal proceedings against me in what became the celebrated case of *Shamuyarira v Zimbabwe Newspapers and Geoffrey Nyarota*.

Shamuyarira's name had appeared on both the police list and that drawn up by workers at WMI. In accessing this valuable information, I had given my sources the solemn undertaking that under no circumstances would I ever reveal their identities.

The protection of sources is one of the inviolate rules of ethical journalism. Casual revelation of confidential sources erodes the credibility of any journalist or newspaper and deters future informants from cooperating with investigative reporters. Had it not been for our assurances and the trust between the *Chronicle* and our various sources, we would never have been furnished with the information used to build the Willowgate story.

We had tried but failed to get Shamuyarira to explain the circumstances surrounding inclusion of his name on the list of suspects. While our patience was taxed to the limit by the hostility of some ministers and by the generally non-cooperative attitude of the rest, we were prepared to wait until we spoke to all whose names appeared on the list. But on 13 December, our meticulous and painstaking three-month investigation was thrown into total disarray when Nkala threatened Maruziva with our instant arrest.

There was no reason to think that his was an idle threat, and had Nkala carried it out, all our work on Willowgate would have been in vain. Under threat of detention without trial we had decided the best way forward was to publish immediately the information we had gathered and confirmed, albeit without the comment of some ministers, including Shamuyarira. Nothing was published about their involvement apart from the fact that the names of certain ministers were recorded alongside the allocation of certain vehicles to members of the public. Shamuyarira's name appeared with that of Lendrum, and this was never in dispute.

Simultaneously, we were careful to publish the rider that there was no suggestion that all the vehicles listed had been illegally obtained by the ministers named, or disposed of by them on the black market at exorbitant prices.

We thought this was adequate protection should any of the politicians take umbrage at not being granted an opportunity to put their side of the story.

In the ensuing defamation case, advocate Chris Andersen told the court that I stood by the article upon which the action was based. The legendary advocate Adrian de Bourbon, counsel for Shamuyarira, applied for an order compelling me to identify my sources of information. This I refused to do.

Retired Supreme Court Judge John Manyarara, who followed the case, later prepared a paper for the Media Institute of Southern Africa (MISA), in which he argued the case for protection of journalistic sources:

The right to freedom of information is clearly recognised in international and regional human rights standards, notably in Article 19 of the Universal Declaration of Human Rights, whose principles have been accepted by all member states of the United Nations; in Article 19(2) of the International Covenant on Civil and Political Rights; and in Article 9(1) of the African Charter on Human and People's Rights.

It is also set out in the constitutions of many countries, including Zimbabwe. The right to seek, receive and impart information necessarily implies a right not only to information that the government chooses to divulge or makes known through official sources, but also to information provided or obtained by non-governmental sources.

Obviously, an essential element in the effective exercise of this right is a free press, which can obtain and present to the public matters of public interest. Moreover, in a democratic society the press plays an essential role as public watchdog. If journalists are to perform this dual function effectively, they must be able to obtain information from sources who might not wish to be publicly identified. And people who have information about corruption, malpractice or wrongdoing which it is in the public interest to disclose must be able to do so without incurring criminal sanctions.

Accordingly, it is essential that there is a recognition of the right of journalists to preserve the anonymity of their sources of information unless in an exceptional case compelling reasons of public interest demonstrably require otherwise. In any particular case, the underlying presumption must be that such anonymity should be preserved; any decision to override that presumption should be made not by the executive branch of government, but on the basis of a reasoned assessment by an independent and impartial tribunal, which would normally be the courts, with the right of appeal to a higher judicial authority.

Moreover, in all cases journalists should be afforded full legal protection against criminal sanctions if they refuse on ethical grounds to disclose their sources.

Individuals who provide the press with information of public interest, or who otherwise bring such information into the public domain, if they are discovered or if they identify themselves, must likewise be given full legal protection, at all stages of the legal process, against criminal penalties for disclosing information. There should be no prosecution unless the disclosure of the information clearly endangers a legitimate national interest, and that risk is sufficient to outweigh the public interest.

In any case where legal action of any kind is brought against such an informant the court should give full weight to the defences of public interest and good faith. No person may be punished for disclosing information unless the disclosure causes actual serious harm, or a clear risk of such harm, to a legitimate national interest, which outweighs the public interest in knowing the information.

The very principles outlined by Manyarara were those applied by the court. It should be borne in mind that the protection of sources is essentially an ethical consideration, with legal standing only at the court's discretion. Factors in favour of compelling me to disclose my sources were that it would be prejudicial to Shamuyarira's case if they were not identified; I had solicited my information surreptitiously and the police source had shown me a confidential list of suspects in breach of the police code of conduct; the wrongs committed by both myself, as a journalist, and my police source were connected; above all, I had acted irresponsibly in publishing the list and thus had forfeited my claim for protection of my sources.

On the other hand, there were interests that militated against compelling me to disclose my sources. If they were not identified in court, the non-disclosure would in no way prejudice Shamuyarira as the plaintiff. Such failure to disclose would, however, effectively prejudice me, the defendant, because my refusal to identify the sources supporting my evidence would increase the burden on me to satisfactorily prove the truth of the allegations against the minister.

The informants were not motivated by any prospect of financial gain or other personal benefit, but by a wish to expose corruption in high places. It was justifiable in the circumstances that the police source should perceive his proper duty to be in that direction, and for me as a journalist to publish the information, because there was a real danger that the information might be suppressed by powerful politicians involved in the scandal.

The court noted in this regard defence minister Enos Nkala's open threat to silence Maruziva and me by detaining us. Moreover, the court noted, Vice-President Muzenda had publicly called on journalists to expose corruption wherever it existed and the president had urged the press to come forward with any evidence of corruption. The court rejected as unrealistic a suggestion by De Bourbon that the sources could be identified in camera, because such action would have exposed the police source to victimisation and disciplinary proceedings for breach of the police code of conduct.

The serious nature of the information given to me by the police source counter-balanced the illegal manner in which the information had been obtained.

Having balanced the factors in favour of enforcing disclosure against the interests favouring protection of my sources, the court ruled that public interest did not require me to disclose my sources. However, on the main issue of defamation, the court found in favour of Shamuyarira on a balance of probabilities, namely my word against that of the minister, that he had acted corruptly. The court entered judgment with costs against Zimbabwe Newspapers and myself.

Shamuyarira was thereby publicly vindicated. He had sought Z$15 000, but was awarded the much lower amount of Z$2 000 in damages. My sources remained anonymous, as I had promised they would. In their absence, however, I did not have corroborative evidence to back the allegation that the minister had acted corruptly. This landmark judgment delivered by the High Court in 1994 was a significant step in the legal recognition of the right of journalists not to disclose their sources.

Writing in Volume XXXVIII No. 1, March 2005, of the *Comparative and International Law Journal of Southern Africa*, Professor Sanette Nel of the department of criminal and procedural law at the University of South Africa examined the question of whether or not journalists have a legally protected right to refuse to disclose confidential sources and, if not, whether they should have such a right and the extent of such protection.

The learned professor had occasion to cite the case of *Shamuyarira v Zimbabwe Newspapers and Geoffrey Nyarota*. Her abstract was quite succinct:

> In the course of gathering news, journalists do, from time to time, rely on confidential sources. These sources claim that they will be subject to retribution for exposing matters of public importance to the media, unless their identity remains confidential. Journalists are frequently requested by the way of subpoena to reveal confidential sources and information they have obtained during news gathering.
>
> This creates a moral and ethical dilemma for journalists. Most journalists feel an obligation to protect their confidential sources even if threatened with jail. The media argues that confidential source protection ensures that the media is able to perform its role as a public watchdog uncovering wrongdoing, maladministration and corruption.

I still argue that our story did not accuse Shamuyarira of acting corruptly. We merely reported that in two lists compiled by management at Willowvale and the police, his name and that of Elias Mabhena were recorded against a certain vehicle allocation to Lendrum. Shamuyarira never denied trying to assist the farmer. Nowhere was it suggested that the minister of foreign affairs had in any way benefited from the allocation of this vehicle.

His protest was that the word 'scandal' had appeared in the headline over the story. As Mugabe had publicly and prejudicially declared when he accepted Nkala's resignation, in my 'overzealousness' I had lumped the names of all the ministers under that headline.

Convinced that there were sufficient grounds to challenge the assertion that Shamuyarira had been defamed, I suggested to Elias Rusike that we should take the matter further by way of appeal. He told me unequivocally that the company would not hear of it. Having settled the payment to the minister on behalf of both the company and myself, he was anxious to wash his hands of the case.

'If you wish to pursue this matter any further we cannot stop you,' he said, 'but you are on your own.'

I canvassed the opinion of Judith Todd, who was the most supportive of the Zimpapers board members. She advised that I should let sleeping dogs lie. With a huge lump in my throat I realised that I did not possess the private financial resources to engage lawyers to pursue the matter by way of a Supreme Court appeal. But I did not give up entirely.

Enlisting the assistance of my brother Arthur, a senior investigator with the Post and Telecommunications Corporation, I sought to track down Lendrum and get him to answer a few pertinent questions that I genuinely believed the commission should have put to him and Shamuyarira.

One would have been how Lendrum had formed the opinion that Shamuyarira was in a position to help him access a vehicle. I also wanted to ask Lendrum the name of the Zimoco employee who had referred him to Dave Gibson.

Why did Lendrum settle for a Mazda B1300 and a Mazda B1600, both of which were totally unsuitable for the task of transporting substantial harvests? How had he finally moved his crops after he sold the two trucks? Why did he demand to be paid partly in cash and partly by cheque when he disposed of the vehicles?

And why did he concede to the preparation, at the request of his benefactor, of a written statement that effectively exonerated the minister of any wrongdoing?

Since Lendrum and Shamuyarira were so close that they were in the habit of lunching together, was it not possible that he would go out of his way to protect the minister, given that the minister had gone out of *his* way in order to help Lendrum acquire the vehicles he sold for astronomic profit?

If these questions had been put to Lendrum and Shamuyarira by the commission, I contend, whatever their responses, the verdict on the culpability or otherwise of the minister might have been totally different and the minister might never have sued the *Chronicle*.

When Arthur and I eventually found our way to Bar SL Ranch, our hearts sank. Lendrum no longer lived on the farm, having resigned his position in the aftermath of the Sandura Commission. We surmised that he had left the country, adding fuel to our speculation that the farmer had, as a popular saying in Shona goes, been rescued from the jaws of a lion.

Further enquiry, however, revealed that our quarry was definitely still in Zimbabwe, though no one seemed to know where. Two months later, Arthur phoned me excitedly from Kariba, where he was on an official assignment.

'You friend lives in a houseboat on Lake Kariba,' said my brother, sounding deliberately mysterious.

'Which friend of mine lives on Lake Kariba?' I asked, genuinely puzzled.

'Anthony Lendrum, formerly of Bar SL Ranch,' said Arthur slowly, relishing every moment of his triumph.

We figured it all out. Realising that he had escaped through the eye of a needle, Lendrum obviously decided not to tempt fate by remaining where he might possibly be accessible to journalists or commissioners. What more convenient place to live than a houseboat on a lake, with no fixed address or telephone?

I did not have the financial resources to turn this new discovery to my legal advantage, but the mere knowledge that Lendrum was living in virtual asylum far away from regular lunches with government ministers was enough to assuage my injured professional dignity.

Meanwhile, my brother and I drank to the success of our fraternal investigative enterprise.

10

A-loota continua!

THE FIRST BLACK political reporter on the *Herald* was Tonic Sakaike. He flew to London to cover the Lancaster House conference for the newspaper, and soon after independence was promoted to political editor, becoming the first black journalist to hold that position as well.

With the general flight of white journalists from majority rule at the dawn of independence, Sakaike was appointed assistant editor, making him yet again the first black elevated to such a lofty position on the country's leading newspaper. Among those of us who regarded him as a trailblazer in the field of journalism in Zimbabwe, the expectation was that he would soon become editor of the *Herald*.

Unbeknown to us, however, the new political leadership associated Sakaike with the Muzorewa delegation and detested the fact that he had travelled from Harare to cover the conference in London. After Mugabe became prime minister, Sakaike accompanied him on his first state visit to Nigeria. There, President Shehu Shagari's government extended a grant of $5 million to be used to acquire the majority share-holding of the Argus Group of South Africa in the Rhodesian Printing and Publishing Company.

Clearly, the new government could not countenance control of Zimbabwe's biggest newspaper publishing company from apartheid South Africa. Far-reaching transform-ation took place in the media when the government embarked on a programme of 'restructuring and reorienting' in terms of the country's new political order. After the majority shareholding in RP&P was acquired, the Zimbabwe Mass Media Trust was set up in January 1981, ostensibly to act as a buffer between the government and the press to ensure that the media served the wide interests of Zimbabwe's citizens rather than those of the ruling elite.

After reporting on the political aspect of the Nigerian visit, Sakaike wrote a colour piece on Lagos, then the capital of the largest nation on the African continent. Being a first-time visitor from the Sunshine City, as proud residents called the neat and well-organised metropolis of Harare, Sakaike was dumbfounded by the abominable filth and traffic chaos in the West African country's capital.

Nigeria's newly appointed high commissioner to Zimbabwe was far from amused by the deprecatory and, in his mind, ungrateful tone of the article that appeared in the *Herald*. He duly lodged a complaint with the ministry of foreign affairs, which was transmitted to the ministry of information and, in due curse, filtered down to management at the publishing company, which was in the process of changing hands.

That complaint brought to an untimely end the illustrious career of the man who would have become the first black editor of the *Herald*.

Journalists who returned from exile to assume the top editorial posts at Zimbabwe Newspapers included Farayi Munyuki, who had worked on the *Daily Mail* in Zambia and became editor of the *Herald*, and Tommy Ganda Sithole, recently returned from Dar es Salaam, where he had been sports editor on the *Daily News*. He was appointed editor of the *Chronicle*. Sakaike resigned from the company and joined Reuters, the international news agency. He was appointed their correspondent in Harare, worked briefly in the London bureau and for a long time in the Kenyan capital, Nairobi, before retiring and returning to Harare as a media consultant.

Sakaike prided himself on a few philosophies that guided him as an individual, as a journalist and, ultimately, as a Zimbabwean. He regarded himself as a born nationalist and an absolute patriot. He practised his profession with missionary zeal and was passionately committed to informing his countrymen on all matters of interest and relevance, particularly in the area of politics, without fear or favour.

While he was intractable about protecting his professional sources, he defended his right to broadcast confidences shared over a drink at the Quill Club or any other part of Harare's hyperactive rumour mill.

'If someone says to me, "What I am telling you is highly confidential; don't ever repeat it to anyone," I will, of course, give that undertaking without blinking,' Sakaike would say as he poured a beer. 'But if people cannot keep their own secrets, why must they burden me with the obligation to do so for them?'

One of his pet subjects was the issue of patriotism, which had become a matter of much controversy since independence. Dr Eddison Zvobgo, one of Zimbabwe's most accomplished and outspoken politicians, had set the parameters for national fealty.

'My wife, Julia,' the fearless Harvard-trained lawyer would say over a double Scotch, his favourite drink, 'will never wear an item of clothing made out of material on which the portrait of a politician is printed.' This was a thinly veiled broadside on Mugabe, whose image appeared on the outfits worn by members of the Zanu-PF Women's League on ceremonial occasions, such as when they assembled at Harare International Airport to welcome the head of state home from his latest foreign trip. Because of Mugabe's uncanny penchant for travel in the early days of independence, members of the Women's League spent an awful amount of time each year on the airport tarmac, to the chagrin of some husbands.

Zvobgo was widely regarded as Mugabe's most likely successor, but it was common cause that he was not one of the Zanu-PF leader's favourite acolytes. Appointed minister of local government at independence, Zvobgo became minister of justice, legal and parliamentary affairs before he was shunted from one ministry to another until he died a broken man in 2003, without getting anywhere near State House, except as a guest at official functions.

Zvobgo incurred the wrath of many when he suggested that the best measure of a patriot was the number of mosquito bites sustained during the bush war. The *Sunday Mail* cartoonist Jack Garrs, or Jay Gee, crafted a hilarious but poignant masterpiece depicting Zvobgo, huge magnifying glass in hand, scrutinising the exposed back of a job interviewee for evidence of exposure to the pesky insects.

Sakaike's view of patriotism was closer to the dictionary definition. Anyone who loved and contributed to the development of his country was a patriot, especially if that contribution involved an element of risk.

'Ask not what your country can do for you,' former US president John F Kennedy said at his inauguration on 20 January 1961. 'Ask what you can do for your country.'

This profound sentiment was one that resonated with Sakaike. Patriotism, especially in the field of journalism, became a hot topic of discussion following the Willowgate disclosures by the *Chronicle*. Which was more patriotic journalism, the question was repeatedly asked: exposing corruption in the national interest or covering it up, ostensibly, also in the national interest?

The political establishment and their spirited defenders in the media, especially journalists occupying senior editorial positions at the government-owned newspapers and radio and television channels, did not mince their words. It was a definite lack of patriotism, bordering on treachery, for a journalist to investigate and expose corruption, thereby embarrassing the political leadership and tarnishing the image of Zimbabwe in the eyes of the international community. It was argued that, having become privy to such controversial information, a truly patriotic journalist would dutifully and quietly pass it on to the relevant authorities in the interest of national cohesion. The information would then travel along the correct channels until it reached the desk of the president, where His Excellency would prescribe the most appropriate solution to the problem.

A rival camp, including Sakaike and myself, argued that Deep Throat, the then secret source of *Washington Post* reporters Bob Woodward and Carl Bernstein, was being patriotic when he leaked vital information that brought about the downfall of US President Richard Nixon in the wake of the Watergate scandal in 1972. It was our view that the function of the journalist was to inform not the president secretly, but the public on matters of national interest, regardless of negative repercussions. Failure to expose the corruption of our national leaders was tantamount to aiding and abetting the culprits, we believed. Of course, this was an argument that easily prevailed, given the general consensus that the media has a watchdog role to play in a democratic society.

In Zimbabwe, those who preach ad nauseam about the need for patriotism are the very politicians who screw the country without batting an eyelid in the process of self-aggrandisement. The real patriots, the ordinary citizens who tighten their belts to the bone at the behest of the politicians responsible for their hardship, rarely, if ever, taste the milk and honey promised to them when they made sacrifices for the liberation of their country.

While espousing the dogma of African socialism, Mugabe and his fellow freedom fighters had inherited a solid capitalist economic infrastructure from Ian Smith's government. Despite the ravages of oppression and racial discrimination, Zimbabwe still had one of the best educational systems on the African continent, with the highest literacy rate and a rising life expectancy for the average citizen. While Zimbabweans celebrated the tremendous post-independence advances in education and healthcare, Zanu-PF's political hierarchy underwent subtle changes, mainly characterised by wholesale acquisition of material wealth. There was a belief within sections of the party leadership that they should be compensated for the danger, sacrifice, incarceration and deprivation they had endured during the course of the liberation struggle. They used their positions and influence to secure such compensation and accumulated much personal wealth in the process, including farms, transport companies, hotels, supermarkets and other businesses, usually registered in the names of proxies.

Corruption became one of post-independence Zimbabwe's biggest growth industries. Allegations were levelled against government ministers, civil servants, Zanu-PF officials and businessmen linked to the party. Occasionally the name of the president himself or those of his wives and their relatives were whispered in inauspicious contexts.

It would be impossible to determine the full extent of official graft. Government officials have long used fronts to conceal their links with private companies. Records at the registrar of companies in Harare have not been properly maintained and are often missing or out of date.

In 2004, Zanu-PF set up a committee chaired by party treasurer David Karimanzira to investigate alleged corruption at Zidco, the party's major trading company. Committee members included former finance minister Simba Makoni, former army commander Solomon Tapfumaneyi Mujuru and Obert Mpofu, the member of parliament who was the original Willowgate whistle-blower before he became a provincial governor.

Mujuru, who had emerged as a powerful politician after retiring from the army, became one of Zimbabwe's wealthiest citizens and led the pack in the 1990s in terms of acquiring vast and diverse business interests. With Mugabe's blessing and using capital allegedly earned from commission on the army's purchase of armoured cars imported from Brazil, Mujuru soon owned a hotel, farms, a chain of supermarkets and residential properties. At one point he owned virtually the entire town of Bindura, north of Harare, and home of Zimbabwe's largest nickel mine. By 2004 he was widely acknowledged as Zanu-PF's kingmaker. The appointment of his wife, Joyce, as Zimbabwe's first female vice-president, to the consternation of many both in and outside Zanu-PF, was ample testimony to the former soldier's growing political clout.

Mujuru's empire, however, paled by comparison with the behemoth created by Zanu-PF. Zidco was established as the party's major holding company in 1979 through a joint venture between M&S Syndicate, Zanu-PF's first business enterprise, and a UK-based firm, Unicorn Import and Export. Unicorn held 45 per cent of Zidco, while M&S controlled the rest. The London-based company was managed by Chandra Patel, whose nephew, Jayant Joshi, was Zidco's managing director.

One of the major recommendations made to Mugabe by Justice Wilson Sandura after Willowgate in 1989 was that Zidco's affairs should be thoroughly investigated. The president ignored this recommendation. Fifteen years later, the Karimanzira Committee was a belated response to Sandura's recommendation.

As soon as I started asking questions at Zidco in 1988, all hell literally broke loose at the *Chronicle* and we were never able to complete our investigation. The moment the Karimanzira Committee began to delve into the affairs of Zidco in 2004, the Joshi brothers, Jayant Chunilal and Manharlal Chunibal, fled Harare for the United Kingdom, effectively halting any further investigation. Speculation was rife that Zidco chairman Emmerson Mnangagwa had facilitated the flight of the Joshis, since any probe into Zidco's affairs would automatically demand scrutiny of his own affairs, as well as those of the brothers.

While there is little by way of conclusive evidence that Mugabe was directly involved in corruption, his name was twice linked to allegations of graft. During a US Senate hearing into the collapse of the Bank of Credit and Commerce International in 1992, a witness alleged that Mugabe and Joshua Nkomo had been given a bag full of cash and a subsequent payment of $500 000 by the BCCI branch in Park Lane, London, in return for preferential banking rights in Zimbabwe. In December 2000, the *Daily News* published allegations of bribery related to the contract for construction of Harare's new airport. The building of Mugabe's private mansion in the elite suburb of Borrowdale had allegedly been partly financed by Airport Harbour Technologies, the company that won the lucrative airport contract. AHT's Harare representative was Leo Mugabe, son of the president's sister, Sabina.

The Joshi brothers were among those alleged to have benefited from the AHT deal, but the major player and beneficiary in this web of corruption was alleged to be Mnangagwa, then the parliamentary speaker, whose name had featured in various other allegations of financial malfeasance.

Mnangagwa had served as Zanla's chief of intelligence during the liberation war. He became Zimbabwe's first minister of state security in 1980. As Zanu-PF's treasurer, he was in charge of both the party's finances and its burgeoning business empire. As chairman of both M&S and Zidco, he became a formidable force, working hand in hand with the Joshi brothers. At one point Mnangagwa, who for most of his political career was widely viewed as Mugabe's chosen successor, served as a director of fourteen companies that were wholly or partially owned by Zanu-PF. By the time the Joshi brothers fled the country, however, Mnangagwa had fallen out of favour, and before the end of 2004 he had been elbowed out of the running as a future president.

By the 1990s, Zidco boasted full or part ownership of twelve Zimbabwean companies and more than fifty properties. Mnangagwa indicated that Zanu-PF owned assets worth Z$486 million, and that companies owned by the party employed a workforce of 9 450 people. While Zidco focused on import and export, M&S managed companies involved in agriculture, property management and share ownership in selected Zimbabwean firms.

Zanu-PF companies thrived, in the main, on government contracts. Catercraft was a typical example. Based at Harare International, the company had an exclusive contract to provide in-flight catering services on all Air Zimbabwe flights and to the many international carriers flying into Harare and Victoria Falls at the time. They included British Airways, Air France and Sabena of Belgium. Lufthansa, the German airline, Portugal's TAP, Qantas of Australia, the Dutch airline KLM, as well as South African Airways and other African airlines, also flew into Harare. Not only was this a highly lucrative contract for Catercraft, it also generated valuable foreign currency in a hard-cash-strapped economy.

A company such as Jongwe Printers enjoyed a monopoly in a guaranteed local market, producing textbooks and other educational materials for Zimbabwe's expanding educational system. The company also printed *Hansard*, the official parliamentary record. Another golden goose, Zidlee Enterprises, imported and sold goods through duty-free outlets at the Harare and Victoria Falls airports and at Beit Bridge, the major border post between Zimbabwe and South Africa.

What irked ordinary citizens was the brazenness with which their leaders indulged in predatory self-enrichment at the expense of the so-called masses. While their followers wallowed in the suffocating squalor of impoverished suburbs such as Mbare, Makokoba and Sakubva, the politically connected and financially well-heeled carved mansions out of the hills north of Harare and parked fleets of luxury cars in their cavernous garages.

In many cases, the value of the real estate and fancy accessories bore no relation to the legitimate remuneration of the owners. Phillip Chiyangwa, one extremely wealthy tycoon, a flamboyant businessman and tempestuous politician with no pedigree in either real business or serious politics, was a typical example. He claimed to be related to Mugabe, and fully exploited the many opportunities offered by such a relationship. Rising literally from nowhere, he amassed such awesome wealth in so short a time that the Zanu-PF top brass became genuinely concerned about his ostentatious lifestyle at a time when most citizens were tightening their belts, unprompted by anyone, around their sparse frames.

When an online property magazine published details and pictures on its website of the palatial mansion that Chiyangwa had built, Harare was abuzz in mid-2004. Not given to modesty, Chiyangwa had taken a journalist on a tour of the opulent edifice, which was arguably the largest and most expensive residential property after State House.

Gifted with boundless energy, Chiyangwa spent half a day showing the reporter and photographer around his twenty-five reception rooms and eighteen bedrooms, all exquisitely fitted and furnished with items imported from the least likely corners of the globe. There were three heliports, perhaps in anticipation of relatives from State House dropping in for tea. The massive garage had room for seventeen vehicles. These included a BMW 745, a BMW X5 sport utility vehicle, an awesome Mercedes-Benz SL500 AMG V8 saloon, a Mercedes-Benz SLK sports car, a Porsche Cayenne and a stately Bentley Continental. The Cayenne, the world-renowned German manufacturer's first and highly successful venture into the burgeoning SUV market, had made its international debut only months before Chiyangwa's arrived in Harare. It was almost certainly the first one on the African continent.

Such extravagance had to be seen to be believed, no matter who was involved, but for a man who in his not-too-distant past had allegedly sold tomatoes by the roadside, it was truly remarkable. Public suspicion about the source of Chiyangwa's conspicuous wealth and inexplicable access to scarce foreign currency was vindicated when he mysteriously disappeared a few days before Christmas 2004. When he resurfaced, it was as the inmate of a dingy prison cell. Zanu-PF's self-styled paragon of virtue and patriotism had allegedly been spying on his country on behalf of unnamed foreign powers all along, according to a report in the *Herald*, the same newspaper that had previously canonised Chiyangwa.

I spat on the snow at Harvard University as I remembered a visit to Australia in 2002 that coincided with the screening of an Australian Broadcasting Corporation documentary on the *Daily News*, my newspaper. The programme featured an arrogant and virulently hostile Chiyangwa as he denounced what he described with disdain as my display of a total lack of patriotism in publishing a newspaper that criticised the revolutionary government of Zimbabwe. Finance minister Simba Makoni, always the epitome of eloquence and old-fashioned common sense, was also interviewed. He spoke of the need for government to put an immediate stop to widespread and bloody political violence. He said it was absolutely necessary to devalue the Zimbabwe dollar in the face of runaway inflation and a thriving black market in foreign currency.

Makoni was a good man. He had outstanding qualities as a politician, marred only by his fatal attraction for Mugabe. He came across in the documentary as someone who, as Callistus Ndlovu had put it during his post-Willowgate press conference, was whistling past the graveyard. I felt genuinely sorry for him. A few months later Mugabe fired him from the position of government minister for the second time, but not before Chiyangwa had launched a sizzling attack on the minister in parliament, which was quite shameful, considering that Chiyangwa was a political nonentity compared to Makoni.

While his alleged co-conspirators, who included Zimbabwe's presumably patriotic ambassador-designate to Mozambique, were hastily tried for espionage and dispatched to Chikurubi Maximum Security Prison, Chiyangwa was quietly released from remand prison. His case died an unnatural death. The *Herald*, which had suddenly taken to lambasting the mercurial politician during Chiyangwa's sojourn at Rhodesville police station, somersaulted to less controversial news. They refrained from asking any of the legitimate, relevant and interesting questions about the Chiyangwa affair that its readers were asking daily. Meanwhile, the profligate Chiyangwa became a born-again Christian, his quotations from the Bible constantly gracing the news columns of the *Herald*, even when they were completely out of context.

Whatever the source of the former vegetable hawker's untold wealth, Chiyangwa had consistently traded on Mugabe's name and their relationship. Yet, even in the face of allegations that he was a spy, the president apparently saw, heard and spoke no evil, and Chiyangwa escaped justice, as did many others of his ilk in the top echelons of Zanu-PF.

'A-*loota continua!*' screamed a placard held aloft by a university student during an anti-corruption demonstration in 1989.

A *luta continua* is Portuguese for 'the struggle continues'. The battle cry of freedom fighters in Mozambique – and still the ruling Frelimo party's slogan – was adopted by Zanla guerrillas who underwent military training in and operated from the former Portuguese colony during the liberation war. It quickly became a favourite mantra. At all-night *pungwes* addressed by guerrillas in the rural areas of Zimbabwe, political commissars repeatedly chanted, 'A *luta continua!*' to hearty responses of '*Continua!*' from the ecstatic villagers.

After independence, Zanu-PF officials continued to use the haunting slogan at party gatherings, and it found its way into the Shona lexicon. The cynical variation scribbled on the student's placard was entirely appropriate in view of the ruling elite's unmitigated dedication to self-enrichment less than a decade after vowing to improve the lot of the masses.

The embryonic nation of Zimbabwe remained in celebratory spirit for far too long. By the time reality dawned on the exultant populace, the country's revolutionary leaders had become steeped in the scourge of corruption, characterised by the looting of frequently scarce national resources and other generally predatory pursuits. Even as the rest of the nation celebrated independence, Mugabe's officials took their first steps into the realm of corruption by paying 'ghost' ex-guerrillas at assembly points in 1980.

The first time the public became aware that corruption had taken root with rather indecent haste was when businessman Samson Bernard Paweni was tried and convicted for inflating charges for the transportation of imported relief food supplies in the rural areas during the 1982–84 drought. Kumbirai Kangai, then minister of labour and social services, was linked by court testimony to this irregular disbursement of state funds, but while the case was tried in Harare, only the *Chronicle* in Bulawayo dared to publish the minister's name. The *Herald* effectively covered up Kangai's role, prompting the minister to confront me over what he obviously took to be a disrespectful indiscretion on my part. I stood my ground in the face of covert intimidation and the minister decided to let sleeping dogs lie.

The *Chronicle* had thus scored a victory and, as a result, when the next major case of corruption surfaced, it was exposed not in Harare, but in Bulawayo. Willowvale Motor Industries was the next port of call for Zanu-PF's ship of corruption. Thereafter, corruption became a free-for-all in the upper echelons of the ruling party. Land acquired with British funds for peasant resettlement was diverted to the ruling elite. Meanwhile, Zimbank channelled millions of dollars in unsecured loans to government ministers. The bank was owned by the state and a substantial amount of the money was allegedly never recovered. In 1997, the state paid more millions, this time in compensation for mostly bogus disabilities suffered by, in some cases, bogus war veterans.

The ship named graft was sailing at full steam.

'Corruption in Zimbabwe is now found at every level,' said Mike Auret, director of the Catholic Commission for Justice and Peace in Zimbabwe, 'from the lowest level of the civil service and private industry right up to the highest level. If we don't do something about it, it's going to be a very serious problem for Zimbabwe. If we get into the same state as Kenya or Nigeria, it's going to be a sad time.'

After recovering from the shock of the sordid details of the Paweni case and in an obvious bid to assuage public apprehension over escalating sleaze among both politicians and bureaucrats, Mugabe unveiled Zanu-PF's much-acclaimed Leadership Code on 10 August 1984. The code became the highlight of his party's second congress, held, rather incongruously, at the Borrowdale Horse Racing Course in Harare.

Government ministers and provincial governors, members of the judiciary and public service commissioners, as well as military, police and prison officers were subject to the wide-ranging terms of the code. Rather ambitiously, it also targeted all members of Zanu-PF's central committee, and the party's provincial, district and branch executives.

In a classic case of what Roman citizens of old would have termed *reductio ad absurdum*, or taking an otherwise sound argument or initiative to the limits of ludicrousness, thousands of lesser civil servants, parastatal and local authority officials were also covered by the code.

'It is,' the document's drafters postulated with rare simplicity, 'necessary, desirable and expedient to impose on leaders a strict code of behaviour to assure the advent of socialism.'

The set of ethics and moral guidelines sought to impose a minimum standard of behaviour and conduct on the ruling elite. One of the code's fundamental tenets required leaders to disclose their assets periodically. Not a single leader is on record as ever having done so.

'Political leaders will not make collusive arrangements with other people or secretly obtain consideration for themselves or other people or fail to disclose the full nature of the transaction to the party or to the government,' the code waxed lyrical.

'They will not decline to disclose their personal financial affairs to a properly constituted party or government body of officials investigating corruption.

'In no circumstances will relatives be used as fronts for business ventures. It will be the duty of a leader to defend the party and government at all costs against enemies; failure to do so will call for disciplinary action.'

The code was an ambitious package of Orwellian proportions, considering that, above all, Zanu-PF leaders were not allowed to own any businesses in the first place. They were required to declare their income, presumably including remuneration from sources other than the government, as well as all their assets and liabilities. The code conceded that by virtue of their positions, the politicians constituted a privileged class with access to diverse sources of public funds. As such, they could fall prey to temptation and pursue personal enrichment at the expense of service to the people.

Warming to the subject and getting somewhat carried away, Mugabe followed the unveiling of the code with an ultimatum to the gathered politicians: forgo wealth or quit masquerading as leaders.

'You cannot have it both ways', he held forth to thunderous applause and the shrill ululation of female congress delegates.

Time would prove that Mugabe himself was committed to having it both ways, consistently making sanctimonious anti-corruption pronouncements, yet harbouring corrupt elements within the top echelon of Zanu-PF. He protected them whenever they were exposed.

Any expectation that the ruling party's leaders would be above corruption and the accumulation of private wealth was based on a gross misunderstanding of political power. Power, indeed, corrupts and absolute power corrupts absolutely. Four years after the introduction of the Leadership Code, Willowgate would endorse this maxim. Predictably, the code that Zanu-PF's leaders professed to embrace in public while privately despising it soon fell by the wayside. The socialist leaders whose capitalist excesses and predatory tendencies the code sought to curtail jumped on the gravy train to embark on an all-out campaign of wholesale self-enrichment during the second decade of independence.

It was during this period that Zimbabwe's nouveau riche emerged, with Chiyangwa being the most conspicuous and ostentatious archetype, at least until the new First Lady moved into State House.

Mugabe's Ghanaian-born first wife, Sally, died in January 1992 after a long battle against kidney failure. While she clung to life through regular sessions on a dialysis machine, her husband took as mistress a typist in the presidential office. In due course, a baby girl was born of the adulterous affair. Those in the know were fully aware of the child's paternity, but, as if to leave no doubt, Grace Marufu's daughter was named Bona, after the president's beloved mother.

Grace and her husband, Stanley Goreraza, lived in Harare's suburb of Mufakose with their only child, a son. Long before Bona was born, Stanley's young and charming wife had started to behave in a manner that was at total variance with Shona custom. The young air force officer watched in growing consternation as Grace was driven home from work by presidential security men at odd hours. In 1987, the couple separated. Heartbroken, Stanley moved to Zengeza, a suburb of Harare's dormitory town of Chitungwiza.

Early one morning, Stanley, who had religiously abstained from alcohol throughout his adult life, knocked on the door of a close friend's apartment in the Glen Norah suburb of Harare.

'He arrived around 7 a.m.,' the friend later recalled. 'It was Saturday and my wife was up early to clean the house. She opened the door to admit a distraught Stanley. He said he had come to take me out for a drink.

'Stanley did not drink,' said the friend. 'But, even for the most dedicated drinker, the hour was too early. He left me with no option, though, and we became the first patrons that day in a shebeen across the road. I sensed that something was bothering my friend, but he did not divulge the nature of the problem. When he ordered two pints of beer, one for himself, I knew he was in serious trouble. From that day on, Stanley developed a drinking problem.'

Stanley quickly remarried, however, possibly in a bid to save his injured dignity. He was suddenly posted to the Zimbabwe embassy in far-off Beijing, where he remained for far longer than the normal four-year diplomatic posting.

'It was only many years later that I realised what had driven Stanley to drink,' said his friend.

In 1988, Grace had another baby.

The first public inkling that all was not well at State House came courtesy of a well-sourced article by Ray Choto in the April 1994 issue of *Horizon* magazine.

Choto's village was in the Chikomba district of the Midlands province. The Marufu family lived in the same district, which was also home to the then chief cabinet secretary, Dr Charles Utete, regarded as a de facto prime minister and thus the most powerful man in the country after Mugabe.

Solomon Mujuru was another son of Chikomba, as was the notorious Chenjerai 'Hitler' Hunzvi, the mercurial leader of the Zimbabwe National War Veterans' Association, who would lead the former guerrillas to revolt against Mugabe with devastating consequences in 1998 and to invade white-owned commercial farms with even more catastrophic results two years later. By the turn of the twentieth century, in fact, Chikomba had become a veritable epicentre of political power.

In 1994, Choto spoke to Grace's relatives, who confirmed that the president had paid a bride price to the Marufu family for their daughter. Neither Mugabe nor his officials challenged Choto's story, which was accompanied by pictures of the young Bona in school uniform. The child's striking resemblance to her paternal grandmother was unquestionable. The publisher of the *Financial Gazette*, Elias Rusike, editor Trevor Ncube and a reporter were arrested soon afterwards when the newspaper published a story suggesting that Judge Paddington Garwe had presided over a secret marriage ceremony between Mugabe and Marufu, and that one of the president's relatives, Enos Chikowore, the minister of energy, had been the best man.

In due course, however, Sally Mugabe died, and after her burial at Heroes' Acre, arrangements were made with unseemly haste for the nuptials of Mugabe, aged seventy, and Grace Marufu, his junior by four decades.

It was a wedding steeped in controversy, but accompanied by much pomp and ceremony. In attendance were South Africa's president Nelson Mandela and his own future bride Graça Machel, widow of former Mozambican president Samora Machel, whose successor, Joachim Chissano, was the best man. A host of other heads of state and dignitaries from southern Africa and beyond graced the occasion by their presence.

Archbishop Patrick Chakaipa, an old friend of the president, conducted the ceremony at Kutama Mission, where Mugabe had grown up. Chakaipa's decision to bless the marriage of a head of state who had committed adultery for years with a woman young enough to be his daughter did not endear him to Catholic worshippers in particular, or politically astute Zimbabweans in general.

What right-thinking citizens found thoroughly distasteful, if not downright immoral, was the fact that their president had been conducting an affair with Grace since 1987 and through Sally Mugabe's terminal illness.

Mugabe's long courtship of his secretary had been such a closely guarded secret that one journalist, who regularly accompanied the president on his many foreign trips, had a rude awakening on an official visit to Beijing. He had allegedly flirted with Grace during the flight to China and was shocked witless when, as the presidential party boarded the aircraft for the return flight to Harare, CIO boss Eddison Shirihuru waved him to the side and whispered a word of friendly advice in his ear. The bewildered journalist desisted from any further airborne flirtation.

With the arrival of Grace and the two children born of her illicit union, family life blossomed at State House and the president was instantly rejuvenated – regrettably, many critics said.

'I feel like a young old man,' pronounced Mugabe with uncharacteristic lack of decorum, much to the chagrin of observers, including leading musician Oliver Mtukudzi. He promptly composed a catchy lyrical warning to the elderly to accept reality when their days are numbered. As Mtukudzi struck the opening chords of 'Bvuma' during a concert at the Harare Conference Centre, a lighting technician turned a powerful beam of light on a portrait of the president that was hanging high up on one wall. The crowd went into a frenzy of ecstasy. The technician got into serious trouble.

In her brightly coloured designer outfits, huge flamboyant hats, fine jewellery and huge dark glasses, Grace cut the image of an African Imelda Marcos, with a wardrobe to match. Emulating the infamously profligate wife of former Philippines dictator Ferdinand Marcos, Zimbabwe's young First Lady became a regular visitor to the high-class shopping districts of London and Paris. At official functions and Zanu-PF rallies attended by the party's impoverished supporters, she was like a work of art at the president's side. Mugabe soon upgraded his own sartorial tastes.

Fashion turned out to be only one of the new Mrs Mugabe's extravagances. Comfortably ensconced in the palatial State House, she borrowed money from a housing scheme that had been established to help middle-income civil servants build their first homes. With Zanu-PF's mantra of 'Housing for all by the year 2000' long forgotten, there was a severe shortage of urban accommodation and a huge backlog. Grace was not a civil servant, neither was she desperate for a roof over her head. This did not stop the fund's administrators from granting her a loan, however. She used the money to erect a costly mansion. On completion she sold the imposing edifice to the Libyan government at the astronomical figure of Z$25 million. It was a fortune at a time when a million Zim-dollars amounted to real money, long before even beggars on the streets of Harare had a million worthless dollars in their pockets.

Like most urban-based Zimbabweans, Mugabe built a home in his village. Unlike the average citizen, however, what the president had built for Sally at Kutama was an imposing mansion. Grace would have nothing to do with this house and insisted on a rural abode of her own. The result was both bigger and better appointed than her predecessor's dwelling. Meanwhile, Chinese contractors were constructing yet another mansion of outrageous proportions and grandeur in Harare. This was ostensibly to serve as the president's retirement home, although, at the age of eighty, there was no indication that he was planning to leave office. On the contrary, a strong desire to stay in power at all costs became clearly discernible.

The *Daily News* reported that construction of the Harare estate was a spin-off of massive corruption surrounding the new Harare International Airport project. The centrepiece of the winning tender was the indigenous design that was inspired by the architecture of Great Zimbabwe. This had no doubt aroused the patriotism of members of the tender board. Consequently, while the tender submitted by Air Harbour Technologies (AHT) was not the lowest, the company's bid won the contract.

However, AHT's chief executive subsequently wrote to Mugabe complaining that he had been forced to pay millions of dollars in bribes to various government officials. In a long and lavishly detailed letter, Yani Hamani, son of a wealthy Saudi Arabian oil minister, offered his cooperation should the president wish to deal with the many corrupt officials allegedly involved. Surprisingly – or typically – Mugabe declined the offer.

Reporter Sandra Nyaira and I were arrested on the grounds that we had published a story defamatory of the president and a number of his ministers. At the time, the laws of Zimbabwe were very specific regarding defamation. Any aggrieved party had recourse to a libel suit and damages in whatever amount the plaintiff's lawyers deemed to be sufficient compensation for the tarnishing of a good name.

For a libel claim to succeed, however, the report complained of had to be patently false. We stood by the authenticity of our story, which was based on Hamani's letter to Mugabe, a copy of which we had in our possession. I had confirmed the contents during long telephone conversations with Hamani in the Middle East.

The storm eventually subsided, but the *Daily News* was now inexorably set on a collision course with Zanu-PF and the government.

When the First Lady's brother, Reward Marufu, became embroiled in corruption charges, the matter became a test of whether or not Mugabe was genuinely committed to uprooting corruption. Marufu and scores of Zanu-PF and government officials were involved in the shameless plunder of a fund set up by government in 1997 to compensate former guerrillas who had sustained injuries during the war of liberation.

As a fitting culmination to a series of bizarre events, the nature of which only

Zimbabwe's revolution could be relied upon to spawn, the most prominent veteran two decades after independence was an enterprising Polish-trained doctor, who had been in Warsaw for the entire duration of the liberation war.

Undaunted by this anomaly, Chenjerai Hunzvi returned to Zimbabwe after independence, accompanied by a lily-white Polish wife. Experiencing no marital bliss in Harare, Mrs Hunzvi abandoned her tempestuous husband and returned to Warsaw, citing abuse by the then obscure government-employed junior physician.

In 1997 Hunzvi emerged from the relative obscurity of his private surgery in Harare's high-density suburb of Budiriro, acquired the *nom de guerre* of Hitler and assumed leadership of the ZNWVA. Part of the mystery shrouding the affairs of war veterans, and a clear pointer to the extent of outright deception within the ranks of Zanu-PF was that, without any record of service as a guerrilla, Hunzvi not only acquired a war name at a time when most bona fide former combatants were reverting to their original names, but also assumed leadership of a powerful association of freedom fighters.

Thousands of gallant veterans appeared unperturbed by the dubious credentials of their new leader. Nor, apparently, did Hunzvi's tenuous connection with the liberation struggle concern Mugabe, patron of the veterans' association. The president would, in due course, be directly and publicly challenged by the new leader of war veterans with an arrogance never before witnessed in Zanu-PF. Hunzvi arm-twisted and threatened Mugabe with such dire consequences that the president capitulated to demands for a gratuity and a pension to compensate all veterans for their contribution and sacrifice during the war of independence. Perhaps the rank-and-file ex-guerrillas, now wallowing in abject poverty after having been marginalised by an increasingly corpulent and arrogant Zanu-PF leadership, saw in Hunzvi the skilled and dynamic advocacy that they lacked.

The prospect of monetary compensation for their services had certainly not featured as an inducement for military training, but in recognition of their remarkable personal sacrifice, returning guerrillas had received a once-off demobilisation payment and been accorded hero status. When they died, they were rewarded through burial in the various district and provincial heroes' acres. Those of a certain status were honoured through interment at the national Heroes' Shrine in Harare. None of the ex-combatants had ever been promised, nor made public, any expectation of financial reward sixteen years after achievement of majority rule.

Nonetheless, Hunzvi spearheaded a fierce campaign for compensation, Mugabe succumbed, and every war veteran was paid a pension of Z$50 000. The government also set up a War Victims' Compensation Fund (WVCF). There was no budget allocation for the disbursement, and government was forced to print the required money, triggering a soaring inflation.

The WVCF was set up for the benefit of those whose military service between 23 December 1972 and 29 February 1980 had resulted in physical disability, or what the boffins referred to as post-traumatic stress disorder. However, by this time corruption had so thoroughly permeated the whole hierarchy of Zimbabwe's ruling elite that disbursement revealed just how brazen the Zanu-PF leadership had become.

The amount paid to individuals was determined by the level of disability suffered. By the time labour minister Florence Chitauro suspended payments, 70 000 applicants had helped themselves to more than Z$450 million. In a case of naked fraud of gargantuan proportions, the WVCF was looted by men and women who cashed in on their liberation war credentials, whether real or imaginary, to plunder the meagre resources of a country that had been liberated while some of them were still babies in diapers.

This outrage would be underlined by Hunzvi's next campaign, three years later, when he led the wholesale invasion of land by 'war veterans', some of whom were patently too young to have been born when the ceasefire was signed in 1979.

For all his Polish medical training, Hunzvi seemed incapable of even the most basic arithmetic in calculating the age of some 'war veterans' or the disability level of others. Top government and ruling party officials, members of the defence force and the veterans' association were handsomely compensated for disabilities of up to an astounding 117 per cent. It was simply miraculous that such severely damaged individuals could hold down some of the most physically exacting jobs in the armed forces.

Ironically, Alexander Phiri, president of the National Council for the Disabled People of Zimbabwe, who was crippled and confined to a wheelchair, was officially rated only 20 per cent disabled in 1997.

Solo Shamu, a courageous fighter who had sustained serious injuries in battle and was also wheelchair-bound, received a total of Z$359 566, a paltry sum compared with the amounts awarded to pretenders.

One of the most bizarre payments was made to controversial Masvingo politician Shuvai Mahofa. Had she been endowed with the acumen and political astuteness of Great Britain's first woman premier, Mahofa might have become the Margaret Thatcher of Zimbabwe. However, to the embarrassment of First Lady Sally Mugabe, Mahofa's patron, and fellow politicians from Masvingo, especially vice-president Simon Muzenda, her political guardian, her career became mired in controversy amid allegations of corruption and indecorous behaviour. As a result, she never progressed beyond the periphery of influential politics.

Mahofa had been careful to avoid exposure to undue risk, injury or physical discomfort by remaining as far from military operational areas as possible during the war. But this did not prevent her from joining the queues lining up in 1997 to claim handouts for alleged battle scars. The sprightly if somewhat overweight Mahofa was judged to be 70 per cent physically disabled, but was paid compensation of only Z$29 300. No doubt her claim was seen as specious.

'If citizens such as Mrs Mahofa can be paid for disability caused by the war, I do not see why you should not claim compensation for loss of dentures and Cortina,' Ursula remarked acerbically.

'It was never my expectation that I would be compensated for our modest contribution to the war of liberation,' I responded forcefully enough to prompt a change of subject.

In normal circumstances, the public would expect a police chief to be 100 per cent physically fit. Yet Augustine Chihuri, the police commissioner, was assessed to be 90 per cent disabled. Hunzvi diagnosed 'dermatitis of both feet', possibly a legacy from Chihuri's traumatic sojourn in the wilderness of Cabo Delgado in Mozambique as a prisoner of Zanu-PF towards the end of the war.

Some of the medical jargon employed by the enterprising Hunzvi to describe injuries sustained by certain of Zimbabwe's gallant fighters caused even laymen to question his medical credentials.

For example, in medical terms, dermatitis is described as a non-specific irritation of the skin. The causative agent may be a bacterium, fungus, parasite or allergen. Contact dermatitis is an allergic reaction to a substance that comes in contact with the skin, such as soap, according to the experts. Atopic dermatitis, also known as eczema, is a chronic itching inflammation that tends to run in families susceptible to asthma and hay fever. Chihuri's apparent affliction, *stasis dermatitis*, or eczema of the legs, is caused by poor circulation. It is usually found in older persons suffering from vascular disorders.

Zimbabwe's top policeman was paid Z$138 645 for his 'war wounds'.

Cynics hinted disdainfully that with such an assortment of incapacitating, if somewhat unusual, ailments afflicting the top ranks of both Zanla and Zipra, it was no surprise that the liberation war had been concluded not on the battlefield, but around a conference table at Lancaster House.

The commander of the Air Force of Zimbabwe, Air Vice Marshall Perrence Shiri, was paid a modest Z$90 249 for 'poly-arthritis and mental stress disorder'.

There was understandable disquiet at the mere suggestion that Shiri, who had commanded the Korean-trained Five Brigade during the ferocious Gukurahundi blitz, might, after all, be mentally unhinged.

The commander of the Zimbabwe Defence Force, General Vitalis Zvinavashe, had been a gallant fighter under the *nom de guerre* Sheba Gava. According to Hunzvi, at the end of the war he was afflicted with 'skin allergy and chest injuries'. Joyce Mujuru, Zanla's leading female combatant, who was venerated for marksmanship that had allegedly brought down a Rhodesian Air Force helicopter in battle, qualified for compensation, according to Hunzvi, on account of poor eyesight and mental stress. Fortuitously, neither affliction prevented her from ascending to the lofty position of Zimbabwe's first woman vice-president in 2004.

As more details of this orgy of looting spewed out, the question on many lips was how an able-bodied and physically active human being, even an ex-combatant, could ever be assessed as being 100 per cent disabled. It was striking that few, if any, among the merchants of insatiable greed who rapidly depleted the WVCF coffers had ever displayed any visible sign of disability. There was genuine concern that a number of 'veterans', including the indomitable Hunzvi, had never ventured anywhere near the war front. But few dared voice concern publicly at the obviously flawed process, not even Mugabe himself. Why Mugabe allowed such daylight robbery to take place right under his nose has remained a mystery.

Most of the disability assessments were undertaken by Hunzvi at his Kuwadzana surgery. His own rating of 117 per cent was based on impaired hearing and 'sciatic pains of the thigh', resulting from shrapnel wounds allegedly inflicted by mortar bombs during a 1977 attack by Rhodesian forces on Zapu headquarters in Lusaka. Hunzvi collected a cool half-million dollars for his creativity, despite denials among PF-Zapu's top hierarchy that he had been anywhere near Zapu headquarters at the time of the said attack. How Hunzvi became so powerful within Zimbabwe's political establishment that not even Mugabe could challenge him is an enigma, but it is likely that he was empowered in exchange for the profitable assessments that he dispensed.

The president's brother-in-law, Reward Marufu, was rated 95 per cent disabled by Hunzvi. His afflictions were said to be ulcers and a scar on the left knee, for which the senior officer in the president's office – a euphemism for the notorious and much dreaded CIO – was paid Z\$822 668, equivalent at the time to a staggering \$70 000 (US).

While Marufu received what became the largest disbursement, ex-combatant Robin Shava, who had lost a leg during the war and was rated 100 per cent disabled, was paid only Z\$483 535. Shava, who was fitted with an artificial limb, was two years my junior at Goromonzi High School. He remained surprisingly cheerful and loyal to Zanu-PF despite the hardship that he endured after losing his job at the ZBC in somewhat murky circumstances. We occasionally met at the Quill Club before it was infiltrated by the CIO in the late 1990s, when Zanu-PF's growing unpopularity was becoming increasingly manifest.

We would discuss Zimbabwe's volatile political situation animatedly late into the evening, emboldened by bountiful supplies of Castle Lager. Shava reminded me of Boxer, the enormous carthorse in George Orwell's *Animal Farm* – steady of character, always ready to serve and defend, and forever committed to the cause. Zanu-PF clearly had no idea how to take care of its best.

The Godfrey Chidyausiku Commission, which was appointed by Mugabe to investigate the looting of the WVCF, recommended that Marufu and others who had defrauded the WVCF be charged. There was evidence that Marufu had obtained false official documents to back his claim that war injuries had prevented him from joining the army after independence in 1980. In fact, Marufu did join the army, but not until 1989. Chidyausiku found that Grace Mugabe's brother had submitted a false statement in order to get a higher rate of disability. This was a criminal offence, and the attorney-general's office immediately said Marufu would be prosecuted.

Such a step was bound to open a can of worms, however, since cabinet ministers and high-ranking government, army, police and CIO officials had all been implicated in this colossal fraud. Marufu was suddenly posted to Canada as a diplomat and, comfortably ensconced in Ottawa, escaped prosecution, thus effectively putting paid to the prospect of anyone else being brought to book.

Proceedings of the Chidyausiku Commission were suspended abruptly on 11 November 1997, when more than 250 ex-combatants turned rowdy in the courtroom, jumping and dancing on the bench behind which the dignified judges reposed. The interruption came while Hunzvi was struggling to explain how he had helped his father, aged seventy-seven, and other relatives to receive compensation.

In the end, none of the WVCF looters were prosecuted. Marufu had the audacity to seize Leopard Vlei Farm near Glendale, north of Harare, from a white commercial farmer in 2002. His sister, the First Lady, took possession of another farm in the same area. The Reward Marufu case was a prime example of how Mugabe paid mere lip service to the eradication of corruption in Zimbabwe.

Shepherd Mhongo, an internal auditor at the labour ministry who had blown the whistle on the WVCF scandal, was admitted to hospital after a suicide attempt. He said he had decided to end what had become a life of constant fear and harassment by some of those involved in the scam. Given that the official list of culprits included Vice-President Joshua Nkomo, cabinet ministers John Nkomo, Kumbirai Kangai and Joyce Mujuru, provincial governors Obert Mpofu, Herbert Mahlaba, Oppah Muchinguri, Mark Dube and Stephen Nkomo, a brother of the vice-president, Mhongo's fears were perfectly understandable. Those names could induce any weak-kneed civil servant to prescribe a rash solution to that kind of problem.

The looting of the WVCF was yet another symptom of how deeply entrenched corruption had become in the top echelons of government, the armed forces and the ruling party, but the episode was not entirely devoid of lighter moments.

Margaret Dongo, the member of parliament for Sunningdale from 1990 and for Harare South from 1995 to 2000, became one of the leading crusaders against corruption in Zimbabwe. But she was herself a beneficiary of the WVCF. Dongo defied attempts by Zanu-PF backbenchers to silence her in parliament when she tabled a motion calling on the auditor-general to investigate the pillaging of the fund.

'The whole thing is scandalous,' Dongo declared, to the dismay of fellow Zanu-PF lawmakers, 'because most of the people who received money did not deserve to get anything.'

Other MPs eventually supported her motion.

Dongo had crossed into Mozambique in 1975 at the age of fifteen to join the liberation struggle. She became a medical assistant with Zanla, but on return to Zimbabwe after independence, Dongo joined the CIO. She also served on Zanu-PF's central committee. In 1989 she quit the CIO to stand for parliament a year later. She was duly elected to represent the Harare constituency of Sunningdale.

Thereafter, she became increasingly critical of both government and Zanu-PF, especially on the subject of rampant corruption. She broke ranks with Zanu-PF when she championed in parliament the cause of the war veterans, contrasting their severe plight and abject poverty with the prosperity of the political leadership.

'I would have died for Mugabe,' Dongo declared, 'but once they got their farms, houses and limos, they forgot the people who put them there.'

Dongo had clearly overstepped the bounds. Zanu-PF's leadership ditched her in favour of Vivian Mwashita, a woman of equally impressive war credentials, in the 1995 parliamentary election. Relying on her obvious popular support, Dongo announced that she would stand as an independent candidate aligned to Zanu-PF, this time in the Harare South constituency, as a mark of loyalty to the party that had nurtured her politically. The party expelled her anyway.

At the height of the furore over the plunder of the WVCF, journalist Charles Rukuni wrote that the electoral contest between Dongo and Mwashita was 'really a battle of the disabled'.

'Flash back to the campaign, particularly the rerun after Dongo won the ruling that the elections should be conducted afresh because the first had been rigged, and if you are not totally baffled about what this is all about, worse is to come.

'Dongo has a 38 per cent disability rating, while Mwashita has a 94 per cent rating.'

The select readership of Rukuni's subscription-only *Insider* publication was indeed baffled. As far as they were aware, neither Dongo nor Mwashita was disabled, but the enterprising Hunzvi had diagnosed the clearly well-fed Mwashita's ailment as loss of appetite.

When Mwashita beat Dongo by a mere 1 097 votes, Dongo went to court to challenge the outcome of the Harare South poll. The court found that the number of ballot papers in the boxes exceeded the number of registered voters in the constituency by 1 025. Corruption had leached into the electoral process as well. The result was nullified and a triumphant Dongo returned to parliament.

One of the strangest revelations of the WVCF saga was the involvement of Edgar Tekere. The maverick politician was jailed for many years by the Smith regime, and on his release from detention in 1975, crossed the border into Mozambique with Mugabe to join the struggle.

When he finally returned to Zimbabwe, Tekere had no visible impairment, except, perhaps, the threat posed by his excessive intake of whisky. Inexplicably, during five years of exile with a guerrilla army, Tekere had acquired a fondness for whisky and fast cars. In due course, his high consumption of alcohol took its toll on both his personal judgement and his promising political career.

My first encounter with Tekere was soon after independence, when, as a journalist, I accompanied him and Chief Rekayi Tangwena on the chief's first visit back to his people at Nyafaru, in the Nyanga mountains.

Tangwena had shot to national prominence with a brave court challenge to efforts by the Smith regime to remove his people from their ancestral land on a white-owned commercial farm.

The Hanmer family, who had owned Gaerezi Ranch since the 1920s, claimed that the Tangwena, then numbering fewer than a hundred souls, had crossed the Kaerezi River from Mozambique around 1900. For many generations there had been free movement across a river that means little as an international boundary, to this day, to people who have lived in the area for generations.

The Tangwena had settled as far west as present-day Rusape in the eighteenth century, and there is a fair sprinkling of members of the clan's Simboti totem throughout the Makoni district.

By the 1960s, Tangwena clansmen who regarded Gaerezi Ranch as their ancestral home, where they grazed their cattle and buried their dead, numbered more than 500. To combat serious land erosion in the area, the Rhodesian department of internal affairs tried to persuade the Tangwena to move to the nearby Holdenby Tribal Trust Area. When the officials invoked the 1930 Land Apportionment Act to enforce the relocation, the spectre of a racial rather than a conservation issue was invoked.

Blacks were barred by this law from living in fertile areas reserved for whites, except as workers. The equally discriminatory Land Tenure Act replaced this legislation in 1970. While government was adamant that the Tangwena people had settled illegally on their former employer's land, the clansmen were convinced that the settler regime was trying to rob them of their ancestral grounds.

The government impounded their cattle, burned their huts and forcibly moved the people to Holdenby. By this act, the Tangwena people were turned into symbols of the white minority government's naked oppression. Rekayi Tangwena emerged as leader of the community and found sympathetic allies in Guy Clutton-Brock, a radical missionary, and Didymus Mutasa, a nationalist, who helped him mount a spirited fight against the Smith regime.

Subsequently, Rekayi slipped out of Rhodesia to guide Mugabe and Tekere across the Kaerezi River into Mozambique on their secret journey to join the liberation struggle. At independence in 1980, Tangwena was officially recognised as a chief and appointed to the senate. When he died in 1985, he was declared a national hero.

I first met Chief Tangwena, already a local celebrity, when he addressed students at the University of Rhodesia in 1972. The venue, a courtyard outside the dining hall at Manfred Hodson hall of residence, was instantly christened Tangwena Square.

When I drove the chief to an emotional reunion with his people in 1980, we linked up with Tekere at the Troutbeck Hotel in Nyanga before heading for Nyafaro, with Tekere at the wheel of his Jaguar XJ6. After Chief Tangwena had celebrated with the people he had abandoned five years before in pursuance of greater national goals, we stopped at the hotel again. As the hour grew late, my reporter's expense allowance became depleted and I had to dig deep into my own meagre resources to entertain Zanu-PF's secretary general, whose capacity for quaffing one whisky after another both astonished and concerned me.

Eventually we set off on the 300-kilometre journey to Harare. Driving a Zimpapers

Mazda 323, I soon lost sight of the tail lights of Tekere's Jaguar in the mist that customarily envelops the scenic Nyanga Mountains.

Tekere was Zimbabwe's first minister of labour and social services. However, his term of office was truncated by an event that not only shocked the country and the world, but also threatened to rend asunder the fragile political fabric that Mugabe had managed to weave through his policy of national reconciliation.

In August 1980, an elderly white farmer was killed on a farm near Harare. Tekere had led a group of seven armed bodyguards to the farm. He never denied his role in the murder, claiming that he was Mugabe's troubleshooter and that the farm attack had been aimed at foiling a *coup* in the making.

The trial of a high-ranking Zanu-PF official charged with killing a white farmer at a time when the party was preaching a new gospel of reconciliation was predictably sensational. To the surprise of observers and the shock of the white community, Tekere was acquitted after claiming immunity under the Indemnity and Compensation Act. Ian Smith's rebel regime had introduced this particular legislation during the war as a vehicle to exonerate government ministers or people acting on their behalf to suppress terrorism, and the firebrand Tekere cleverly turned his former enemy's law to his own advantage.

He was summarily dismissed from the cabinet, however, and the matter effectively signalled the beginning of the end of his career as a credible politician. In the atmosphere of relative freedom that followed the signing of the unity accord between Zanu-PF and PF-Zapu in December 1987, Tekere increasingly became a radical, if somewhat erratic, critic of both Mugabe and the party he had served as secretary general. As an MP, he mounted a single-handed and brave crusade against corruption. He publicly accused Mugabe of protecting the corrupt ministers and government officials who surrounded him. Tekere's venom went a notch higher. He charged Zanu-PF's leadership with behaving like vampires and chewing up the party's own code of ethics. He intimated that the president and several unidentified government ministers had secret foreign bank accounts.

'Democracy is in the intensive care unit,' Tekere declared to the delight of the urban populace, to whose ears such utterances were sweet music. He suggested that Zanu-PF should change its top leadership, which, in his opinion, had clearly failed to effectively lead the party, resulting in abandonment of the revolutionary principles formulated in the Zanla camps in Mozambique. Mugabe had become the protector of the corrupt and Zanu-PF had been hijacked by reactionary opportunists who had not even taken part in the struggle to liberate Zimbabwe, Tekere railed.

Called upon to substantiate his allegations before the party's central committee, he reportedly failed to do so. Tekere thus acquired the dubious distinction of being the first person to be expelled from a party that was notorious for protecting the corrupt, the errant and the wayward.

A month later, in April 1989 – shortly after the Sandura Commission released its report on Willowgate – Tekere formed his own party, the Zimbabwe Unity Movement (ZUM). Mugabe had challenged him to do so and go up against Zanu-PF in the next election. With characteristically witty turn of phrase, the president predicted that ZUM would 'zoom itself into doom'. Tekere's party, however, attracted an eager following in the black suburbs of Harare, Bulawayo, Gweru and Masvingo, and was especially popular in his home town, Mutare. Eleven years later, Manicaland was still a bedrock of support for Zanu-PF's opposition. Two rural areas in which the MDC performed particularly well in the 2000 parliamentary elections were Matabeleland and Manicaland.

In 1989, the University of Zimbabwe became the breeding ground for ZUM support amid widespread and often violent demonstrations. Under the leadership of Student Representative Council president Arthur Mutambara, students clamoured for an end to rampant corruption. As hundreds were rounded up and carted away in police trucks, the students vented their anger on vice chancellor Walter Kamba's Mercedes-Benz, a symbol of the elitist tendencies that they opposed.

Observers of Tekere's eloquent tribute in 1997 to the entrepreneurial acumen of business magnate Roger Boka at the official opening of the latter's multi-million-dollar tobacco auction floor on the outskirts of Harare must have been flabbergasted by press reports soon afterwards about Tekere's 90 per cent war disability and attendant payment from the WVCF. Having failed to beat the corrupt, the former crusader for clean administration had apparently joined them in the twilight of his political career.

Basildon Peta, a reporter on the *Financial Gazette*, was one of Zimbabwe's most undesirable journalists in the eyes of the ruling party and government. His name and mine appeared on a list of journalists targeted for assassination. Peta's 'crime' in 1994, for which he had not been forgiven a decade later, was publication of a list of commercial farms acquired by government for the resettlement of landless rural peasants. Instead, the farms had been allocated to well-heeled cabinet ministers, top-ranking army and police officers, and senior civil servants. In many instances, the new owners did not cultivate the land. Their greed underlined the ruling party's lackadaisical approach to the perennially burning issue of an equitable land redistribution programme in favour of the landless rural peasantry.

The Zanu-PF leadership had come to regard their corrupt dealings as justifiable compensation for their contribution to and sacrifices during the armed struggle. While Mugabe did nothing to punish the culprits, he had no qualms about persecuting journalists who exposed them. In the post-Willowgate climate, it was as if Nyagumbo's suicide and the fallout from the Sandura Commission had spurred a vengeful political establishment in Harare to unprecedented levels of sleaze.

The chief executive of Zimbabwe Newspapers, Elias Rusike, had resigned from the company soon after my relocation to Harare. He and two other entrepreneurs, Fanuel Muhwati and Eric Kahari, acquired Modus Publications, publishers of the *Financial Gazette*, an independent weekly newspaper. Owned jointly by editor Clive Wilson and publisher Clive Murphy, the newspaper was well established as an upmarket business publication with an exclusively white target readership.

Rusike and his partners wanted to transform it into a more general publication that also covered social and political news and appealed to a broader Zimbabwean audience. They recruited Trevor Ncube, a lecturer in economic history at the University of Zimbabwe, to understudy Wilson as the next editor. On the eve of his departure, however, Wilson advised Rusike that Ncube was not ready to take over. He had no previous experience in journalism and had not been at the *Financial Gazette* long enough. In a state of panic, Rusike called me.

Since effectively dumping me as editor of the *Chronicle*, he had published a book, *The Media of Zimbabwe*, in which he professed to be a staunch Zanu-PF supporter, and confessed that he had been forced by political considerations to remove me from Bulawayo. But, troubled by his conscience and unable to accept government interference in the way he ran Zimpapers, he wrote, he had quit.

Rusike invited me for a drink at the Country Club in Highlands and offered me the job of executive editor of the *Financial Gazette*. As if in anticipation of my predictable concerns, he assured me that, as executive editor, I would have full editorial autonomy. He would concentrate on the business side. He was more aware than anyone that outside interference could undermine a publication's credibility and viability, he said, and was not about to repeat the mistakes he had been forced to commit at Zimbabwe Newspapers.

I pointed out that I had never edited a financial newspaper. Rusike had done his homework and seemed to have all the answers. He laid out the plan to transform the newspaper into a more general interest publication, while not neglecting the established business readership, and emphasised that my task would be to strike the required balance and attract new readers from among the black elite.

As my deputy, Ncube would ensure that the business and financial content remained of the highest standard. Modus would pay me a highly competitive salary, and my 'perks' would include a vehicle of my choice, as well as two air tickets to a foreign destination for Ursula and me every year.

We toasted the deal and, after a meeting with Dr Sadza, the chairman of the board, I resigned from Zimbabwe Newspapers. Both Dr Sadza and the new chief executive, the youthful Davis Midzi, seemed relieved that I was leaving. Management laid on a lavish party where I bade friends and colleagues farewell after twelve years, interrupted only by a year at Linquenda House and State House.

I departed from Zimbabwe Newspapers with my ultimate ambition unfulfilled. Becoming the editor of the largest daily newspaper in the country was only one promotion away, but Rusike had not needed to push too hard for my acceptance of his offer. Any editorial position was infinitely better than being group public relations executive for Zimbabwe Newspapers. I could only hope that Rusike would keep his word about editorial freedom.

I took over the editorship of the *Financial Gazette* on 1 January 1990, my fortieth birthday. Sales of the paper soon began to escalate. We moved publication from Friday to Thursday, and long queues of readers formed each week outside our offices on Simon Mazorodze Way and at the main post office on Julius Nyerere Way in the city centre. The paper usually sold out well before noon. In one year, circulation nearly doubled, to 19 000 copies a week. We published articles that the *Herald* and the *Sunday Mail* did not dare touch. We investigated corruption. We published daring editorial comments. We printed cartoons that were witty and made poignant comment on topical issues. We tested the limits of press freedom.

While the readers were ecstatic, the politicians were up in arms. Columnist Bill Saidi waxed lyrical, pounding away at Zanu-PF every week. At a time when there was no viable opposition party, the *Financial Gazette*, Zimbabwe's only independent newspaper, virtually assumed that role.

In 1990, schoolteachers staged a demonstration over several days for better remuneration, gathering in their thousands every morning in Africa Unity Square, directly opposite Herald House. The police occasionally used teargas to disperse them, and the pungent gas wafted across the street and through the open windows of the third-floor *Herald* newsroom. While the reporters coughed and sneezed, they never wrote a word about the strike. The minister of education, Victoria Chitepo, had issued a directive that the industrial action was not to be publicised.

The story was finally published when the *Financial Gazette* hit the streets, but by then the demonstration was several days old. More than ever, I realised there was a dire need for a good independent daily newspaper.

'Can't Saidi write on any topic other than Zanu-PF?' Rusike asked one Thursday morning. 'We have friends in Zanu-PF and they tell me they sometimes think we don't seem to know what's good for us.'

If the *Financial Gazette* had any friends in Zanu-PF, Rusike had certainly never confided in me about them, and I said so. My editing philosophy was motivated by public interest and the pursuit of fairness and justice, but I realised soon enough that my publisher invoked the spectre of our unnamed friends in the ruling party whenever some scathing criticism of Zanu-PF appeared in the paper, such as an uncomplimentary cartoon featuring foreign minister Nathan Shamuyarira, one of Rusike's friends in Zanu-PF.

During his brief stint as a university lecturer, Ncube had had a close relationship with a colleague in the political science department, Professor Jonathan Moyo. Moyo had contributed the odd column to the *Financial Gazette*, and, impressed by his style, eloquence and choice of topics – the one-party state was his favourite – I asked Ncube to find out if Moyo would consider writing a regular column under his name.

Moyo agreed, and thus embarked on the tortuous road that saw him achieve both fame and notoriety. A decade later he routinely attacked independent newspapers, including the *Financial Gazette*, and journalists for their alleged lack of patriotism, this from his office as Zimbabwe's minister of information. By then he had been transformed from Mugabe's most ardent critic to his greatest defender and most gifted and wily spin doctor.

Back in 1991, sales of the *Financial Gazette* continued to soar. Rusike asked me to draw up a blueprint for a daily newspaper. Amid preparations a few weeks later for the purchase of a new printing press in Sweden, I presented him with my proposals before Ursula and I left on our first visit to the Nordic countries.

On the day of our departure for Stockholm, agents for the Solna printing press we were buying were at Modus House for discussions with Rusike. The purchase was to be funded through a loan from Zimbank, in which government was the major shareholder. Zimbabwe faced a serious shortage of foreign currency at the time, and allocations for the import of capital equipment and spare parts had to be approved through the Reserve Bank. This was a hurdle that Rusike would somehow have to clear. Printing presses were certainly not on the national list of priorities, especially those destined to print newspapers that relentlessly poured scorn on the government's policies and actions.

When I shook hands with the Solna representatives at Modus, they promised to contact me in Stockholm and to take me to their factory to inspect the press. Up to the date of our departure from Sweden for Copenhagen, I had not heard from them. Since in my experience Swedes were not prone to going back on their word, I assumed that on their return from Africa they had been preoccupied with preparing to ship the new press to Harare.

Ursula and I had such a marvellous time in Copenhagen that I soon forgot about the lost opportunity. Then we proceeded to Oslo, starting point for the highlight of our trip, a daylight train journey to Bergen on the west coast of Norway. We felt as if we were travelling through paradise. As the train sped across the snow-capped Norwegian Alps, I made early mental plans for the *Daily Gazette*, the paper we were soon to launch.

With the credibility of the *Financial Gazette*, my own professional reputation, the support of a fine team of journalists, a supportive management and a printing press of our own, only an act of preposterous stupidity could possibly prevent the paper's success, I mused. There was, of course, the prospect of a ban by an intolerant government, but even that sounded unthinkable.

But there was a bombshell waiting when I arrived home. The timing of this particular communication, when I was feeling on top of the world, was particularly cruel. I tore open the letter from Rusike. I had been fired from the *Financial Gazette*. There had to be a mistake, I told myself, but when I went to see him, Rusike was hostile and impatient. His decision was final, he said. The staff was not happy with my editorship.

This was news to me.

Rusike said I should pack my things and vacate the editor's office immediately. I knew at once that he was lying about complaints from the staff. If he had a valid reason to dismiss me, we would have discussed the matter first and there would have been a warning issued, perhaps two. There would have been no need for him to be so curt. My deputy, Trevor Ncube, was not helpful, being far too busy preparing to take over editorship of the paper. Other members of staff either phoned or sent messages of support.

In due course, I figured out what might have happened.

The new printing press was duly delivered and installed, and the new daily was launched with Mike Hamilton, a commercial farmer, as editor. I knew him by name as a constant writer of letters to the *Financial Gazette*. I found it strange that Rusike should appoint a rank outsider rather than the eminently qualified Bill Saidi, who was already on board. While I had fleeting memories of Fred Cleary's unenviable task of pushing sales of the *National Observer* in the black townships, Rusike was no doubt mindful of Saidi's relentless condemnation of Zanu-PF.

The *Daily Gazette* was the first newspaper launched after Zimbabwe's independence, but its debut in 1992 coincided with a severe economic slump. The reading public did not have much disposable income. Advertisers slashed their budgets, as they always do when profitability is threatened, and confined their adverts to traditional government-owned newspapers, which had established high circulations. Advertisers are inevitably influenced by circulation figures.

At its peak, the *Daily Gazette* sold 55 000 copies, quite impressive for a new publication, but no comparison, for advertisers, against the *Herald*'s 160 000.

When he appointed Hamilton to edit a largely black paper, Rusike more than likely hoped to attract a white-controlled advertising market. Even though Zimbabwe had been independent for a dozen years, 80 per cent of the economy remained in white hands. But the advertisers didn't take the bait and the newspaper ceased publication in 1994.

Meanwhile, the long queues of readers who had lined up to buy a copy of the *Financial Gazette* also melted away. Ten years later, after we launched the *Daily News*, large bundles of the distinctive pink of the *Financial Gazette* occasionally lay on the pavement, unsold, from one edition to another.

After my departure, I sued Rusike. He eventually paid me a hefty out-of-court settlement for wrongful dismissal, but this was not before I had endured trauma, humiliation and deprivation. Zimbabwe's labour laws dictate that any worker suing an employer for wrongful dismissal automatically forfeits the claim if alternative employment is secured. Had I taken another job while the legal battle played out, I would have had to sacrifice any prospect of success. The family business at Nyazura came to our rescue. It was not very profitable, but we tightened our belts and survived.

I found myself in an invidious situation. I had now been fired from both a government-owned newspaper and the only viable independent newspaper around. There were no further opportunities for me to edit any existing publication in Zimbabwe. I had previously been appointed to the board of the Nordic-SADC Journalism Centre, an advanced training institution operating throughout the southern African region from the Mozambican capital, Maputo.

Funded by Sweden, Denmark, Norway and Finland, the centre offered specialised training for practising journalists throughout the Southern African Development Community. In 1994, I was asked to join the centre full time as a project manager. I relocated to Mozambique for my first period of self-imposed exile. I travelled frequently to Tanzania, Malawi, Zambia, Namibia, South Africa, Botswana and Swaziland to set up training programmes and teach the art of investigative reporting, media law and journalistic ethics, drawing heavily on my own experience. Our programmes were popular and in great demand.

My contract was for a period of three years. As I criss-crossed the region, I exploited the opportunity to study the operations of newly launched newspapers. I regularly communicated with Fred M'membe at the *Post* in Lusaka, visited Methaetsile Leepile's *Mmegi* in Gaborone, Gwen Lister's *Namibian* in Windhoek and *Savannah* in Maputo. The *Post* was the paper that appealed to me most – robust, daring and investigative. I also liked the quality of the *Mail & Guardian* in Johannesburg, but was not enthusiastic about its limited appeal and circulation. Trevor Ncube, my former deputy at the *Financial Gazette*, subsequently also parted ways with Rusike, joining forces with Clive Murphy and Clive Wilson to launch the *Zimbabwe Independent* and the *Sunday Standard*. He eventually took over the papers and in due course became the publisher of the *Mail & Guardian* as well.

While based in Maputo, I visited the Nordic countries on fund-raising trips, all the time mulling over my own future plans.

I returned to Harare at the end of 1996, more convinced than ever that the time was right for an independent daily newspaper. I had already formulated elaborate plans for such a publication and had even acquired a few pieces of essential equipment, including computers, printers and a photocopier. My old friend Farayi Munyuki, former editor of the *Herald*, with whom I worked in Maputo, donated a Nikon camera, complete with accessories, to the proposed newspaper.

'This may come in handy,' he said as he handed it over.

I was filled with optimism that my venture would receive backing from patriotic Zimbabweans, especially from the emergent black business community. I was convinced that large numbers of citizens must be fed up with Zanu-PF's corruption and arrogance, the shocking decline in the performance of the economy and of our once revolutionary government, as well as by the mediocre and partisan performance of the major news-papers. They would surely welcome a newspaper that campaigned vigorously against abuse of power, corruption and the country's economic malaise.

Many, even within the ranks of Zanu-PF, were not happy with the prevailing state of affairs, especially since the government's own media empire seemed to favour only some, and not all, among the party leadership.

I had secured a tentative commitment of funding from at least one donor.

Donor funds had been used to wrest Zimbabwe Newspapers from South African interests, I reasoned. Zanu-PF's Jongwe Printers had been built on donor funds. Donors had supported the purchase of new transmitters for the ZBC. Dr Ibbo Mandaza's *Southern African Political and Economic Monthly* had been launched on donor funds. Many post-independence print and broadcast journalism training programmes had been supported by foreign donors. Donors were active in the media sector throughout southern Africa. The journalism centre for which I worked in Maputo was fully donor-funded.

In Zimbabwe, donors were also active in other spheres – the ongoing HIV/AIDS campaign, education, rural electrification, the sinking of boreholes and training of parliamentarians, to mention but a few noble initiatives.

There should be nothing wrong with foreign donors supporting just one more Zimbabwean media initiative. But when we finally embarked on the initiative to launch the *Daily News*, there was no recourse to donor funding.

A luta continua!

11

Writing against the grain

I N THE PUBLISHING WORLD, conventional wisdom has it that when a new publication is launched, anything that can go wrong, will.

The birth of the *Daily News* in March 1999 was no exception. It was an occasion marked by a host of hiccups – logistical, financial, technical and even political – usually associated with the creation of a newspaper by a cash-strapped publishing company under the watchful eye of an authoritarian regime, especially on the African continent.

Journalists in Zambia had experienced similar problems when they launched the *Post*. Its timely arrival precipitated the downfall of President Kenneth Kaunda in 1991 after twenty-seven years in office, but he put up a vicious fight before going down. At the president's instigation, Fred M'membe, publisher and editor of the *Post*, and a number of his journalists were arrested several times on largely spurious grounds. By the time Kaunda succumbed to the irreversible force of political change, M'membe and his staff faced more than 100 defamation claims, most of them intended merely to harass or intimidate.

Paradoxically, once Kaunda's successor Frederick Chiluba assumed office, M'membe was sporadically imprisoned. I was in Lusaka in September 2001 when he invited me to a dinner at which his former tormentor, Kaunda, was the guest of honour. Asked to say grace, Kaunda, a devout Christian, prayed to God to take care of M'membe, to guide him in his endeavours and, no doubt, to keep Chiluba on his toes.

In Malawi, the *Nation* and a host of other new independent newspapers had combined their efforts in 1994 to dislodge the ruthless dictator, Hastings Kamuzu Banda, after thirty years in office. Banda's regime was particularly brutal on journalists, many of whom were arrested, while foreign correspondents were expelled. Until the emergence of a vibrant independent press in 1993, Malawians had for decades been forced to read only two newspapers, the *Daily Times* and *Malawi News*, a Sunday paper, both published by the president's own company, Press Holdings.

When I arrived in Malawi's commercial capital, Blantyre, in May 1994, twenty-one daily and weekly newspapers were scrambling for the attention of readers on the dusty pavements of the poverty-stricken city. Smelling blood as age exposed the Life President's vulnerability, the newspapers became bolder and more ferocious until, throwing all caution and ethics to the wind, they exposed the corrupt and occasionally defamed the innocent. Over the next two years I returned to Malawi three times to organise much needed training programmes for journalists and to help set up a self-regulating media council.

While executives of Associated Newspapers of Zimbabwe (ANZ), publishers of the *Daily News*, were genuinely apprehensive about the challenges ahead, they had not expected the level of political fallout that ensued. Against all odds, the *Daily News* did become highly successful as Zimbabwe's only independent daily, until its forced closure by the government in 2003. While we had anticipated that the launch of the paper would possibly spark friction with authorities long pampered by an acquiescent government-owned daily press, we had not reckoned on the series of traumatic events that would bring our newspaper to its knees as it rode on a wave of popularity and success.

Wilfred Mbanga and I co-founded the *Daily News*, named after the *African Daily News*, the most significant independent newspaper to carry the flag of revolution in the 1960s. The editor of that newspaper was Nathan Shamuyarira, who became the first minister of information after independence. Ian Smith's agenda when he came to power had been to stifle nationalism and anything that supported its cause. He viewed the *African Daily News* as a serious threat. The paper was banned in 1964, the same year that Joshua Nkomo, Ndabaningi Sithole, Robert Mugabe and the rest of the nationalist leaders were detained.

Mbanga became ANZ's first chief executive, while I was the founding editor in chief of the *Daily News*. The staff included many journalists from the *Financial Gazette*, the very people who had complained about my management style, if Elias Rusike was to be believed. Mbanga and I vowed to avoid some of the obvious pitfalls that had precipitated the demise of Rusike's *Daily Gazette*.

At independence, the Inter-African News Agency, Iana, which had served Rhodesia for years, became the Zimbabwe Inter-African News Agency, or Ziana, government-owned under Dr Davison Sadza's Zimbabwe Mass Media Trust. Despite claims to the contrary, Ziana was not a new agency created after independence. Mbanga was appointed the first editor of the reconstituted Ziana. When the government-owned Community Newspaper Group (CNG) was formed, he became chief executive, holding this position until he and I purchased the joint shareholding of a shelf company, which we registered in July 1998. This company, Motley Trading (Pvt) Ltd, became the forerunner of ANZ, a joint venture with foreign shareholders.

CNG had established a string of rural community newspapers before purchasing the long-established *Times of Gweru*, which became its flagship. The government's rural newspapers were not particularly successful, sustained for the most part by regular injections of donor funding.

A newly established British consortium, African Media Investments (AMI), was ANZ's foreign partner through its special-purpose vehicle, AMI Zimbabwe (AMIZ). Eventually AMIZ became the majority shareholder, with 60 per cent of shares, after we failed to attract the requisite level of local investment in ANZ. Mbanga and I held nominal shares in the company, with more substantial options being warehoused for allocation to us once the company was up and running. Forty per cent of the shares were reserved for future local investors, including us.

AMIZ was a subsidiary of AMI, a rather ambitious venture created by a conglomerate of newspaper companies in the United Kingdom to facilitate high-quality media products throughout anglophone Africa. The concept envisaged the creation of an innovative venture by British investors in the potentially profitable African media industry. Spearheaded by the publishers of independent British regional newspapers, this venture would deploy capital, modern technology and expertise to enable usually cash-strapped African media organisations or initiatives to consolidate or take root and hopefully prosper, while serving a rapidly growing market.

The idea was no doubt inspired by the successful investment in South Africa and elsewhere on the African continent of the biggest Irish media concern, Independent Newspapers PLC. Headed by press baron Tony O'Reilly, better known as a major shareholder in the US multinational HJ Heinz & Co., of which he was chairman in 1998, the company also owned newspapers in Australia, New Zealand, South Africa and the UK, where it published the *Independent* and the *Independent on Sunday*.

After taking over majority shareholding in the Argus Group of South Africa, former owners of the Rhodesian Printing & Publishing Co., Independent Newspapers became the largest newspaper publisher in South Africa, with fourteen titles to its credit. These included the *Star* and *Pretoria News* in Gauteng; the *Cape Times* and the *Argus* in Cape Town; the *Mercury*, *Daily News* and *Tribune* in Durban; as well as the *Sunday Independent*, and thirteen community newspapers in Cape Town.

The group had captured 58 per cent of the English-language market, and its titles accounted for 48 per cent of the total advertising spend in South African commercial newspapers.

Mbanga and I were told in confidence that Independent Newspapers would be one of the prime movers in AMIZ and therefore a major shareholder in ANZ, but that O'Reilly was reluctant for his involvement to become public knowledge.

His caution was understandable, given that HJ Heinz was one of the major new investors in Zimbabwe after independence. It acquired Olivine Industries in 1982, producing vegetable oil, toilet soap, candles, canned foods and margarine. In 1992 it established Chegutu Canners in the small town of Chegutu, 100 kilometres west of Harare, to produce the famous Heinz baked beans and ketchup.

Unfortunately, after a few anxious weeks on our part, Independent Newspapers pulled out of the venture. O'Reilly was said to have a good rapport with Mugabe, so, had the deal been concluded, we probably would not have encountered the financial and political tribulations that beset ANZ from the start.

With adequate capital investment, an independent editorial policy and sound management, it was envisaged that the British investors would rake in millions, while undercapitalised local investors would benefit from the rare opportunity of a joint venture with foreign partners who had access to capital and the latest technology.

Initial emphasis would be on the SADC region, which at the time had a combined population of 350 million people. The pilot project would be launched in Zimbabwe, which had a long-established tradition of fine newspapers, exceptionally high literacy levels and an economy that was robust enough to provide a sound advertising base for any professionally run independent publication. The plan was to launch similar projects in Swaziland, Zambia and Botswana in turn at a later stage.

The meeting to launch AMI was held in London on 24 February 1998. Chaired by Derek Smail and held at the offices of the Newspaper Society, it was attended by twelve representatives, mostly the chairmen or chief executives of regional publishing companies throughout the United Kingdom.

Smail, who became the first executive chairman of AMIZ, was the chairman and managing director of the Tweeddale Press Group, an independent publishing company based in Berwick-upon-Tweed in the Scottish Borders, which had been in his family for eight generations. In 1997, Smail had formed Commonwealth Publishing Ltd, publishers of *New Zealand News UK* and *South Africa Times*, two weekly newspapers for expatriates from the two countries living in Britain. Smail had been a president of the Scottish Newspaper Publishers Association and a council member of both the Newspaper Society and the Commonwealth Press Union (CPU). I received my first journalism award, the Terry Pierce-Goulding Memorial Award for excellence, from the London-based CPU in 1989 in recognition of the Willowgate exposé.

Michael Stent, a South African–born journalist with twenty-two years of experience in the field, had been the assistant editor of the *Rand Daily Mail*, South Africa's leading daily newspaper, until its closure in 1985. He moved to London in 1986 and joined the team that launched the *Independent*, becoming the paper's night editor, and later, managing editor of the *Independent on Sunday* at its launch.

Stent, who by then was a freelance journalist, attended the AMIZ meeting as the key project promoter. Also in attendance were three Zimbabweans, Wilfred Mbanga, Clive Murphy and Clive Wilson. The Two Clives, as they were commonly known in Harare's newspaper publishing circles, were respectively the publisher and managing director of Zimind Publishing and Standard Press Ltd, publishers of the *Zimbabwe Independent* and the *Zimbabwe Standard*.

Mbanga had met Stent at a CPU conference in Cape Town early in 1998. Over a drink one evening, Stent told the Zimbabwean about the advanced plans to launch AMIZ in the UK. Mbanga was interested. He said he could put together a consortium of Zimbabwean media entrepreneurs. A few weeks later he arrived in London, accompanied by Wilson and Murphy, to attend the February meeting.

Wilson and Murphy had previously owned the *Financial Gazette*, which they'd sold to a consortium headed by my former boss at Zimbabwe Newspapers, Elias Rusike. The two Clives then established Zimind Publishing in partnership with my former deputy at the *Financial Gazette*, Trevor Ncube.

Apparently there was no synergy between the Zimbabwean group and their British counterparts, and Mbanga returned to Harare with a mission to rebuild a partnership. He came to see me at Landmark Publishing, where, having secured a funding grant from the Open Society Institute, I was advancing my own plans for the launch of a weekly newspaper as a prelude to a daily.

My passion for an independent newspaper went back to 1992, when Tonic Sakaike and I had registered our first publishing company, Publishing Ventures (Pvt) Ltd. Morgan Tsvangirai, then secretary general of the Zimbabwe Congress of Trade Unions (ZCTU), High Court judge Eshmael Chatikobo, political activist Judith Todd, Bulawayo businessman John Gomiwa, academic Rene Lowenstein, entrepreneur Nhlanhla Masuku, Sakaike and I each invested Z$2 000 in the project, while wealthy business magnate Roger Boka donated the same amount. But we fell far short of the capital investment required to launch a newspaper, and in due course some of the investors withdrew.

From time to time, Mbanga liaised with us from his office at CNG, where he had acquired considerable expertise in raising funds from foreign donors for the government's rural newspapers. Our combined effort failed to yield fruit, however. Potential donors required us to raise a certain percentage of the necessary capital from our own resources and we simply could not do so. Disillusioned, I left Harare to work in Maputo, and Sakaike was invited by Tsvangirai to help him launch *The Worker*, official publication of the ZCTU.

A few weeks after Mbanga returned from his abortive London trip in 1998, I was introduced to Stent and Smail, and the ANZ project took off. Responding to my personal invitation, Todd, who over the years had become a close friend, became not only the first Zimbabwean prepared to invest money in the new company, but also a founding director of ANZ.

Judith Todd was born in 1943. In January 1972, she and her father, former Rhodesian prime minister Sir Garfield Todd, were arrested by the Smith regime under the notorious Law and Order (Maintenance) Act. Seven months later, she was allowed to leave Rhodesia to go into exile in the United Kingdom. She was banned from returning.

After the Lancaster House conference, Lord Soames, the transitional governor, lifted such restrictions and Todd came back home, arriving a few days before the triumphant return of Mugabe's entourage from Maputo in February 1980.

Until 1988 she was director of the Zimbabwe Project Trust, a non-governmental organisation dedicated to the advancement of the war veterans.

The Todds were among the non-institutional shareholders of Zimbabwe Newspapers. In 1991, Judith was elected to the company's board, only to be removed in 1993 by Dr Sadza, the government-appointed chairman. By that time I was a shareholder of Zimpapers, courtesy of a generous donation of shares by Sir Garfield. When minority shareholders tried to get me onto the board, Dr Sadza saw red and blocked the move. For good measure, he used his veto as representative of the majority shareholder to dislodge Judith as well, since she had spearheaded the move to get me appointed.

Long regarded by the Smith regime as a thorn in the flesh of the Rhodesian government, the Todds were treated with disdain by the Mugabe regime. In 2001, Tobaiwa Mudede, Zimbabwe's registrar general, refused to renew Judith's passport. He claimed that, since her parents were born in New Zealand, that should be her country of citizenship. Zimbabwe Lawyers for Human Rights took this to the High Court as a test case, and in 2002 the court ruled that Todd was a citizen of Zimbabwe by birth. The court ordered the registrar general to recognise her citizenship and issue a passport, but Mudede adamantly refused to comply. Todd was forced to leave Zimbabwe and settle in Cape Town.

In 1999, our former colleague, Morgan Tsvangirai, became the first president of the Movement for Democratic Change, a new opposition party that posed the most critical political challenge ever encountered by Zanu-PF.

While Tsvangirai and I had collaborated at Publishing Ventures, the emergence of the MDC soon after the *Daily News* was launched was an act of sheer coincidence and not the political strategy alleged by Zanu-PF. However, both events were undeniably inspired by popular disenchantment with deteriorating social, economic and political conditions, and it is entirely likely that civil society organisations, including the ZCTU, took advantage of a new voice in the media to hasten the advent of what would be the first viable political opposition since PF-Zapu's demise in 1987.

My first meeting with Stent and Smail was in May 1998, in the tranquil ambience of the well-appointed and beautiful courtyard garden at Harare's Bronte Hotel. This literally became ANZ's original office, where we drank countless cups of coffee, as well as beer, while working late into the night to plan the proposed company and its newspapers.

I found our British counterparts to be affable and dedicated professional news-papermen, committed, ambitious and confident that they would raise the required foreign capital. I was satisfied that they had no association whatsoever with the British government, as was occasionally and falsely alleged by Zanu-PF and government officials, especially Shamuyarira and Jonathan Moyo, minister of information after 2000.

If Smail and O'Reilly ever envisaged investment in the media of Zimbabwe and South Africa as part of some sinister recolonisation plot, Smail kept such intentions close to his chest. I was very much on the alert to ensure, if they did have any such grandiose plans, that they did not use ANZ as the vehicle to accomplish their mission. I certainly had not forgotten my traumatic and dehumanising ordeal at the hands of Ian Smith's agents.

To ensure that we received reasonable support from local investors, Mbanga and I approached a number of prospects. I pinned my hope largely on Strive Masiyiwa, whom I knew well, having met him when he resigned from the Post and Telecommunications Corporation to start his first enterprise, Retrofit, an engineering company. After an arduous struggle, he had scored a major victory over government by obtaining an operating licence to establish Econet Wireless, Zimbabwe's first and largest cellphone company. Masiyiwa quickly became a living legend and, subsequently, a wealthy, if somewhat controversial, entrepreneur. He was based in Johannesburg after fleeing government persecution in Harare. I also approached Nigel Chanakira of the newly launched Kingdom Bank, which would also go on to be extremely successful. Also forced to live outside his country of birth, Chanakira had settled in Cape Town.

In desperation and much against my better judgement, I even approached the capricious Phillip Chiyangwa. He owned numerous companies, including a shoe factory in Bulawayo and a large foundry in Harare. Fortunately, I made no headway with him. His lifestyle later became altogether too controversial and ostentatious and his political outlook too partisan on the side of the ruling elite for any newspaper to regard him as a valuable asset.

While we struggled to raise capital, the prospect of salvation emerged from a highly unlikely quarter. Finance director Lovejoy Charidza informed us he had been approached by a potential investor with an offer of a Z$20-million investment in return for a sizeable chunk of ANZ. Like the prospect of a hungry beggar picking up a wad of banknotes on the street, this sounded too good to be true. Our proverbial knight in shining armour was one Daniel K Shumba, a retired colonel and emergent businessman, who told Charidza that he had made a fortune in Zambia. As the custodian of the *Daily News*'s political welfare, I was concerned about Shumba's military background, and conducted a clandestine check. To my utter consternation, I found that he had even stronger connections with Zanu-PF than with the security establishment. Many years later, Shumba became the party's provincial chairman in Masvingo.

On Friday 16 April, two weeks after the launch of the *Daily News* and at a point when ANZ was in desperate need of capital, Much Masunda, Smail, Charidza and I held a marathon meeting at which Masunda and I expressed our reservations in the strongest terms possible about the proposed sale of ANZ shares to Shumba. His offer was duly rejected.

On 5 May, I met with Masiyiwa and Econet chairman Professor Norman Nyazema at the mobile telephone company's impressive new head office in the Msasa industrial area. Nyazema had been my junior by two years at Goromonzi High School, and we had met again at university.

Masiyiwa's response was typical of the general attitude we came up against. While he fully endorsed our plan in principle, he was still consolidating Econet after a gruelling legal battle to secure the operating licence. Vice-president Joshua Nkomo, already an ailing old man, had to come to Masiyiwa's aid before he was finally granted the licence. To the astonishment of many, Nkomo had broken ranks with his cabinet colleagues, even exchanging harsh words with information minister Joyce Mujuru, in taking a calculated political risk to back the young entrepreneur.

Masiyiwa told me that if Mbanga and I could secure the funds to cover operating expenditure in the meantime, he would review his position and possibly invest at a later stage. Most of our targeted investors were wary of sinking money into a newspaper that was likely to take the political establishment head on at a time when government displayed growing hostility towards the independent press.

We had officially launched our private placement initiative at the Monomatapa

Hotel on 25 September 1998, when ANZ, described by Mbanga as a new and dynamic newspaper publishing company, was introduced to potential investors. We offered them 40 per cent of the shares in exchange for Z$50 million. Our goal was to raise a total of Z$127 million for capital expenditure on equipment, vehicles and property, as well as initial working capital. AMIZ was to raise 60 per cent of the capital offshore.

Mbanga pointed out to prospective local investors that the market dominance of Zimbabwe Newspapers was vulnerable to any dynamic and properly run private sector competition. Then he made a statement that was characteristic of our general naivety at the time:

'The state,' he said confidently, 'is considered unlikely to take public action to inhibit the development of ANZ because of government's declared intention to encourage foreign direct investment, its commitment to international agreements on foreign investment and its adherence to the free trade rules of SADC.'

Inherent in Mbanga's words was the clear message that ANZ was not a British-backed initiative seeking to destroy the Mugabe regime. The statement was totally devoid of the confrontational intentions assumed by many who walked the corridors of power.

Two years and four months later, saboteurs did the unthinkable. Under cover of darkness they planted four powerful bombs on the refurbished Goss Urbanite printing press at our new factory along James Martin Drive in the Lochinvar industrial area. The machinery was reduced to a pile of scrap metal and rubble, never to print another issue of the *Daily News*.

Despite Mbanga's persuasive presentation, we failed to attract sufficient investor attention. By 14 December, we had raised only Z$6.3 million of the Z$53.8 million we needed. The board put our lack of success down to the prevailing economic climate, in which the money market offered far superior returns to investors, and at lower risk. Investing in an independent daily newspaper in Zimbabwe at the time was considered particularly perilous. Some potential investors told us candidly that they would never put money into so hazardous a sector as Zimbabwe's independent press, or that they were worried about the future of the country as a whole and had no confidence in the way the economy was being managed.

As if investors were not already skittish enough, the arrest and severe torture of two leading journalists contributed to the derailment of our investment campaign. Mark Chavunduka, editor of the *Zimbabwe Standard*, a Sunday newspaper, and Ray Choto, a reporter, were arrested by the army and severely tortured. It was Choto who had exposed Mugabe's secret payment of a dowry for his second wife, Grace. Now he put together what the *Standard* said was a well-sourced article, alleging an abortive *coup d'état* by disgruntled army officers. The military refused to release the two men, even in the face of an international outcry. The interest previously expressed by many of our putative backers simply evaporated, while those committed enough to invest reduced their level of exposure.

Bad publicity was another significant factor. On the grounds of adverse media reports about ANZ, our attempt to secure office space in Bulawayo was turned down by the insurance company that owned the building in Tenth Avenue.

Surprisingly, existing independent newspapers, the *Financial Gazette* and the *Zimbabwe Independent*, were at the forefront of the onslaught on ANZ. On 30 October 1998, the *Independent* carried a front-page article headlined 'ANZ placement hits snag'. Some ANZ board members were of the opinion that the half-truths and conjecture in this article were the major factors that dissuaded prospective investors from supporting our private placement.

At its first board meeting in August, ANZ adopted a resolution to 'remain cool in the face of provocation from various quarters, including government and rival newspaper publishing companies, and forge ahead, instead, with preparations for the launch of the company's publications'.

Chairman Much Masunda told the board that in a conversation with Trevor Ncube, editor in chief of the *Independent*, the latter had complained bitterly about ANZ poaching and depleting his staff. The board's response was that it was common practice the world over for new publications to lure journalists and other staff away from existing titles. After all, Ncube himself had all but crippled the *Financial Gazette* when he poached editorial staff to launch the *Independent*.

As chief executive, Mbanga spearheaded ANZ's campaign to raise local capital. He worked hand in hand with chairman Masunda, a respected lawyer, and despite the many setbacks, both men remained effervescent and contagiously optimistic.

As editor in chief, my own task was no less daunting. I concentrated on the editorial aspects of the project, making elaborate plans to launch not just a daily, but a string of weekly provincial newspapers as well. Recruiting top journalists for such an array of publications was a challenge of near insurmountable proportions. But Zimbabwe's leading journalists, tired of working in the sanitised environment of Zimbabwe Newspapers and earning the paltry salaries offered by the existing independent news-papers, flocked to ANZ, drawn by the promise of genuine press freedom and generous salary packages.

We did not even have to advertise, our problem eventually being who to keep out. Rival companies complained bitterly that ANZ was destabilising the market by upsetting existing salary structures. My own philosophy was that journalists should receive remuneration packages commensurate with their challenging task, their contribution to the welfare of society and the attendant risks of the profession. Ethically, it made no sense that journalists should routinely hobnob with the rich, the powerful and the famous, while perpetually remaining on the receiving end of their generosity and charity. It was necessary to create a new breed of journalist, bold, confident and ready, if the need arose, to dip into their own pockets to buy a round of drinks for the business executives, sports administrators and politicians their work required them to socialise with. Our editorial staff had to be independent in every sense if they were to earn the respect of their news sources and the public.

We became the first newspaper publishing company in Zimbabwe to go public with an editorial charter. We promised that our reports would be fair, balanced and accurate. Diversity of opinion on editorial pages would be valued and encouraged. Errors of fact would be speedily and prominently corrected. The privacy of individuals would be fully respected, except in instances of demonstrable public interest. Fact and opinion would be clearly separated and identified. Reports of a sensitive nature would be handled with great care to ensure that the rights of free speech and a free press did not diminish any other basic human rights, nor directly incite feelings of contempt, hatred or aggression in one section of the population against another.

Great care would be taken with reports that might be deemed to encourage crime or violence. Full cognisance would be taken of the fact that media products were accessed by people of all ages, including children.

Our charter promised vigilance in ensuring that reports on events that might be deemed by a reasonable person to be of a lewd or salacious nature were sensitively handled and used only if they could be shown to be in the public interest.

Wherever practicable, ANZ would appoint an ombudsman to represent the interests of readers, another groundbreaking innovation for the press in Zimbabwe.

ANZ pledged itself to independence from any political, commercial or sectional obligations or commitments. It would not represent the interests of any one section of the population at the expense of another. In its employment practices and reporting, the company would strive to ensure an absence of discrimination on the basis of race, gender, religion, ethnic group, sexual orientation or any other physical attribute.

In due course, the *Daily News* would incur the wrath of government when it started to cover the activities of the Gay and Lesbian Association of Zimbabwe and to carry their advertisements. An anonymous document, malicious by Zimbabwean standards, soon circulated, claiming that I was homosexual. The allegation was dismissed with the contempt that the few who read it thought it deserved. Ursula laughed her head off, having developed a thick skin over time.

'In the *Daily News* we are hoping to create a general interest newspaper, a newspaper for all readers,' I assured guests at a promotion breakfast. 'Our guiding principle will be that of public interest. That will be the paramount consideration in all our editorial endeavours. We will also strive to become a democratic watchdog.'

The cornerstone of our strategy was to publish a tabloid newspaper, our main rival, the *Herald*, being a broadsheet. As editor of the *Chronicle*, I had presided over the transformation of the Bulawayo paper from broadsheet to tabloid, with a very positive effect on circulation. The smaller size of the tabloid endeared the *Daily News* to commuters, who could not easily handle or fold a broadsheet newspaper while squashed in minibuses, which were the most common form of urban transport.

For a publication pledging to campaign for freedom and democracy in a country where both were increasingly under threat, it seemed propitious that our physical address was on the corner of two streets named in honour of the two leading foreign protagonists of the struggle for Zimbabwe's independence. Trustee House stood at the intersection of Samora Machel Avenue and Julius Nyerere Way, named after the presidents of Mozambique and Tanzania respectively. Both had played decisive roles in supporting the liberation war and providing rear bases, training facilities and logistical requirements.

What worried me, though, was the biblical symbolism inherent in the juxtaposition of Trustee House, a ten-storey structure and one of Harare's older buildings, and the magnificently opulent Karigamombe Centre. Built by the National Railways of Zimbabwe Pension Fund in the 1980s, our neighbouring twenty-one-storey edifice became a symbol of growth and development in newly independent Zimbabwe. The then transport minister, the outrageously flamboyant Herbert Ushewokunze, named the building Karigamombe – he who defeats the bull. It was Mugabe's nickname. A charging bull had been the symbol of Nkomo's PF-Zapu.

Karigamombe and the newspaper operating on the lower floors of Trustee House were to engage in a David and Goliath duel and, unlike the biblical story, Goliath would win the bloody combat in Harare in September 2003, when the *Daily News* was banned.

Despite the poor response to our investment drive, we forged ahead with our programme to launch six newspapers in three phases. Stage One involved three weekly regional newspapers: the *Express* in Chitungwiza, the *Dispatch* in Bulawayo and the *Mercury* in Gweru. Stage Two entailed two more regional weeklies – the *Tribune* in Masvingo and the *Eastern Star* in Mutare. The launch of the *Daily News*, originally scheduled for February but pushed back to March 1999, would be the grand finale.

The *Express*, launched on 11 September 1998, became our pilot project. We appointed Zambian-trained journalist Desmond Kumbuka as editor. Before the year was out, we had another four weekly titles on the streets, in keeping with our strategy of covering every region of Zimbabwe through a local newspaper before we launched the national daily. ANZ's other pioneer editors were Lawrence Chikuwira of the *Dispatch*, Innocent Kurwa, who launched the *Mercury*, and Farayi Makotsi at the *Eastern Star*. Vimbai Makamure, ANZ's first female editor, was appointed at the *Tribune*.

The *Eastern Star* encapsulated all the enterprise, determination and sheer creativity that lay behind the creation of ANZ. Deputy editor in chief Davison Maruziva and I drove to the eastern border city of Mutare, arriving early on a Monday morning. We checked into a hotel that had recently been acquired by my old foe Jonathan Kadzura, who, ten years before, had stood in front of the Manica Hotel and shown me the weapon concealed under his jacket. From Kadzura's Mountview Hotel, Maruziva and I proceeded to our empty office premises and unloaded computers from the car.

By the end of the day, we had furnished the offices, addressed a skeleton staff and settled down to produce a newspaper from scratch. It was a virtually impossible task, but by mid-morning on Wednesday we had sufficient material for a twenty-four-page inaugural issue of the *Eastern Star* on disk. We had worked non-stop for fifty hours to produce the first issue. The security guard went off duty on Monday evening. When he returned the next morning, he found us still glued to our computers. The same thing happened on Wednesday morning, and in the absence of any sign that we had left the building at all, he could not help remarking: 'I can't wait to see what kind of paper you are producing, sir. I have done guard duty at the *Manica Post*. This is not the way they produce their paper.'

The *Manica Post*, where I had cut my teeth as an editor, had been publishing for more than a century, so it was to be hoped that their production was rather more orthodox than our own, but I wasn't sure if the guard was paying us a compliment or warning us. We returned to the hotel to pick up our bags and settle our bill without once having set foot in our rooms.

'We were wondering why you checked into the hotel in the first place,' the duty manager remarked as she handed over the receipts.

In my Australian-built Ford Fairmont, I believe I broke the record for driving from Mutare to Harare, and that without having slept a wink for two nights. We rushed the disks to the originators, who processed the plates in time for that night's deadline.

We printed 20 000 copies of the first issue of the *Eastern Star*, and were back in Mutare on Thursday evening to officially launch the paper. It sold out completely the following morning, making this the most successful launch of the five weekly newspapers we introduced.

Once the *Eastern Star* hit the streets, we focused our attention on the *Daily News*.

In recruiting staff for the editorial, advertising, distribution and management departments, we had mostly targeted the *Zimbabwe Independent*, *Sunday Standard*, *Financial Gazette* and the *Mirror*. Their journalists were of a high calibre, but publications owned by Zimbabwe Newspapers, the *Herald* and the *Sunday Mail*, were not spared our predatory poaching campaign, and neither was Ziana.

We were thus able to assemble the finest editorial brains in Zimbabwe under one roof and to build a newspaper team that far surpassed any existing group in terms of qualifications and sheer experience. Since we had depleted the human resources of our rivals and left them with slim pickings from which to fill the resultant gaps in their establishments, our bitterest foes initially were aggrieved newspaper editors rather than government ministers. Long before we hit the streets, existing newspapers, both independent and government-controlled, launched a relentless and vicious attack on the *Daily News*.

In a bid to scare journalists against signing up, rival publications predicted the imminent collapse of the new paper even before the first issue hit the streets. Because of our foreign links, government newspapers portrayed us as reactionary and neo-colonial tools of Western imperialist interests. They said we were bent on subverting Zimbabwe's cultural values and facilitating the return of Zimbabwe to its former colonisers. Our failure to raise reasonable amounts of local capital would see ANZ collapse in no time, they said.

A rare coincidence at a newsstand
on Monday 29 January 2001

Scene at the *Daily News* printing factory
after the bomb explosion

Daily News deputy editor Davison Maruziva,
left, and assistant editor Bill Saidi
inspect a section of the printing press
after the bomb explosion

While ANZ chief executive Much Masunda,
second from left, briefs journalists at the
bombing scene, government journalist
Reuben Barwe confers with an
unidentified man at right

No arrests three months after
bombing of Daily News press

Staff Reporter

EXACTLY three months last Saturday after the $100 million printing press of *The Daily News* was bombed, police have not yet arrested any suspects despite an undertaking by the government that it would move swiftly to bring the culprits to book.

The printing press was reduced to a wreckage on 28 January following a series of verbal threats by Jonathan Moyo, the Minister of State for Information and Publicity in the President's Office, and Chenjerai Hunzvi, the chairman of the Zimbabwe National Liberation War Veterans' Association.

Police spokesman, Assistant Commissioner Wayne Vudzijena, refused to comment on the matter on Friday.

Police experts who waded through the mangled remains of the printing press said as many as four highly explosive devices were laid on the press to cause maximum damage.

Since then The *Daily News* has been printed by commercial printers.

The bomb blast came barely a few hours after Moyo threatened to silence the newspaper, alleging that it posed a security risk to the nation.

After the bombing, Moyo was

POLICE forensic ballistics expert Superintendent Charles Haley, right, and assistants look for bomb evidence in the destroyed printing press of *The Daily News* on 28 January. The police at that time promised to swiftly bring to book the culprits – Reuter

newspaper would be burnt wherever war veterans came across them. Within 48 hours of Moyo and Hunzvi's threat, the printing press went up in smoke.

the police to increase their efforts in the investigations. Time will never heal the wounds of the bombing incident. Therefore, even if it drags on for years, people will always want to

Daily News headline three months
after bombing of the press

Ursula with sons Tafirenyika Julian and Itayi Jethro
and daughter Rufaro Thelma in Harare
while the author lived in Mozambique in 1995

Away from the *Daily News*, the author with Ursula
and daughter-in-law Isabel Bvumbi on the occasion
of her wedding to their son, Tafirenyika, in 2001

The author and Ursula,
after Tafirenyika's graduation at
the University of Zimbabwe

As *Daily News* editor, the author receives the
MISA Press Freedom Award from retired Zimbabwe judge
John Manyarara, in Mbabane, Swaziland, in 2001

Author's collection of
international media awards

ANZ co-founder Wilf Mbanga, left, and
the author leave the Magistrate's Court in Harare
after being granted bail on 9 November 2001

The author and *Daily News* reporter Lloyd Mudiwa, left, leave the
Harare Magistrate's Court on 22 July 2002. They were the first journalists
to be prosecuted under the Access to Information and Protection of Privacy Act

Respected politician Dr Simba Makoni was briefly chief executive
of Zimbabwe Newspapers. Here he enters parliament as
minister of finance in November 2001 to present the annual Budget

At Harvard University, Nieman fellows celebrate in 2004. From left: the author,
Bryan Munroe (USA), In-Yong Rhee (South Korea), Russell Mills (Canada), Shyaka Kanuma (Rwanda),
Andrew J Martin (USA), Frank Langfitt (USA), Mark Travis (USA) and Kevin Cullen (USA)

President Mugabe's second wife,
First Lady Grace Mugabe

Zimbabwe's first speaker of parliament, the
controversial Didymus Mutasa, mounted a campaign
against the *Daily News* in the town of Rusape

Powerful politician Emmerson Mnangagwa, for long
regarded as President Mugabe's chosen successor,
became the first ever person to sue the *Daily News*

Perrence Shiri, commander of the
Air Force of Zimbabwe, and former commander
of the infamous Five Brigade

© Tsvangirayi Mukwazhi

Wanton destruction during government's
Operation Murambatsvina in Harare in 2005

Former *Daily News* photographer
Urginia Mauluka displays an
award presented for her work
with the Refugee Council
in London in 2005

Author's grandchildren, Geoffrey and Chiedza

We soldiered on, unfazed but determined to ensure that the newspaper would not be found guilty as charged on any count.

Scare tactics had no effect on those wanting to be a part of this brave new venture. The average journalist found the conditions and remuneration offered by ANZ and the editorial freedom promised by the *Daily News* too tempting to spurn. A continuous stream of applicants visited our new offices on the mezzanine, first and second floors of Trustee House in Samora Machel Avenue. We offered an unfettered professional atmosphere, the challenge of being part of a unique newspaper and salaries way above the norm. Zimbabwe's top journalists were soon tendering their resignation from the *Herald* and other newspapers.

In 1998 we had wooed Lovejoy Charidza, finance director of Zimbabwe Newspapers, and Agnes Gomwe, advertising director at the *Financial Gazette*, thereby creating the nucleus of a management team that would attract the best brains in the business. Maruziva, my former deputy at the *Chronicle*, who had been shunted to the *Herald* after Willowgate, became the first deputy editor of the *Daily News*. Other big names followed: Barnabas Tondlana (news editor); Jahoor Omar (sports editor); David Linsell (business editor); John Mauluka (chief photographer); Tarcey Munaku (political editor); William Bango (training editor); Bill Saidi (assistant editor); and Thandi Kapambwe (women's editor).

With Lawrence Chikuwira, former editor of the *Chronicle*, Fanwell Sibanda, Basildon Peta, Eunice Mafundikwa, Leonissa Munjoma, Reyhana Masters-Smith, Todd Hogwe, Julius Zava, Tambayi Nyika, Sandra Nyaira, Ngoni Chanakira, Nevanji Madanhire, Desmond Kumbuka and the Nyakunu brothers, Tendai and Nyasha, our newsroom became a who's who of Zimbabwe's journalism in 1999.

Many of our staffers were household names. Saidi, Zimbabwe's oldest practising journalist at the time, had worked in Zambia for many years. His no-holds-barred style of writing had incurred the wrath of Kaunda, who was sometimes described as a benevolent despot. On a number of occasions the Zambian president had publicly rebuked Saidi, who returned to Harare in 1980. When I was editor of the *Chronicle* in Bulawayo, he edited our sister publication, the *Sunday News*. His tenure was short-lived, however, as the government-owned paper was too critical of the political establishment.

On my return from Maputo in 1997, I found Saidi languishing at Andy Moyse's *Horizon* magazine, which was in its death throes. Saidi was among the first journalists in Harare with whom I discussed my plans to launch a newspaper, and I assured him there would be a place for him. Thereafter, he became a regular caller at Landmark Publishing to check, sometimes too frequently, what progress I was making. When plans for the launch of the *Daily News* took off in earnest, Saidi was the first journalist I appointed. Other ANZ executives were apprehensive about a man who had already reached retirement age. I persuaded them that Saidi was an asset. He was a fine writer, especially of features, columns and editorial comments, and we made him assistant editor. My enthusiasm for the man's abilities was not generally shared by younger members of staff, and, sensing their resentment, Saidi sometimes grumbled, but he soldiered on like the old workhorse he was.

In advance of the launch, we contracted a leading market research organisation, Q-Mulative Research, to conduct a nationwide survey to determine the level of support for a new daily newspaper in Zimbabwe and to find out what the target readership would expect.

'Ninety-four per cent of the readers are waiting for a new daily,' Mercy Mkushi, managing director of Q-Mulative Research, announced at the breakfast that we hosted for advertising executives and prospective clients. 'That represents not only a window of opportunity, but I think a whole door and a wall of opportunity.'

'Judging from the way people are talking about the existing newspapers on the streets, they are ready for a new daily as an alternative to existing publications,' said Monica Mutume, a media director with advertising agency Linsell, Saatchi & Saatchi, on a *Daily News* promotional video.

Never Mhlanga, managing director of National Discount House, put the whole issue in a nutshell on the same video: 'We need a credible newspaper that will give us balanced views.'

The last word went to Jill Day, managing director of Ariel Associates: 'I think this is the most wonderful news since newspapers came into being in this country.'

We felt both reassured and delighted.

Following a series of successful trial runs on the recently installed printing press, coupled with a well-orchestrated promotion campaign, the paper was scheduled to hit the streets on Wednesday 31 March 1999. The newsroom was fully operational for six weeks before this date, putting together a dummy issue every night. Each working day started with the morning editorial conference. The news editor presented a realistic assignment diary for the day, while the business, sports and features editors came up with their own story ideas. During the afternoon conference, the editors selected the top stories of the day, after which the subeditors designed the pages, crafted headlines, and illustrated the stories with appropriate pictures or graphics.

The stories were captivating, the photographs by John Mauluka and Tsvangirayi Mukwazhi colourful, the pages boldly and attractively laid out and the general impact captivating. We designed the *Daily News* as a reader-friendly newspaper, and loaded the news columns, sports and business sections, foreign and entertainment pages with well-written and interesting articles. For me, the most important sections after the front page were the leader/opinion page and the letters page. The latter became so popular that within a short time we occasionally had to devote two pages to letters from readers. This became one of our strongest selling points. Editors at Zimbabwe Newspapers had systematically reduced their letters' pages to glorified lost-and-found columns. Contentious letters addressing the burning political, economic and social issues of the day were routinely spiked.

I remember finance minister Bernard Chidzero asking a meeting of Zimbabwe

Newspapers editors what happened to the bulk of letters submitted for publication. He said he had been amazed on a visit to Highfields by the number of relatives and friends who complained that their letters to the editor of the *Herald* on matters of national importance were never published.

During the six-week trial period, the dummy issues were not sent to the printers, of course. Stories that had a long shelf life were saved for the launch issue, but the dummy runs provided excellent practice and training for the editorial, advertising and production staff. They acquired essential experience in working to daily deadlines, especially those among them who had previously worked on weekly newspapers. Working on a weekly is an entirely different experience than working on a daily. All of us also acquired vital experience on the QuarkXPress electronic publishing system that had been installed.

As launch day approached, we became more confident. We learned from our mistakes and, above all, we built a gigantic stockpile of stories, mostly features, for inclusion in the forty-eight-page launch issue and the next few editions after that.

The final days of preparation were dogged by serious problems relating to structural weaknesses on the floor underneath the printing press at the factory. Engineers worked feverishly around the clock to solve the problem. The second-hand press was supplied by Cross Graphics, an AMIZ shareholder, and had been dismantled, refurbished and packed in containers in the UK before being shipped to Harare. The press was then quietly installed in a secluded part of the Lochinvar industrial area, away from the prying eyes of inquisitive CIO agents.

On the big night, to our utter mortification, the press failed to run – this in front of scores of dignitaries, staff and other guests holding glasses of champagne to toast the historic moment. Engineers, sweat pouring from their brows, tried frantically to get the equipment up and running. In the early hours of the morning, they admitted defeat and the senior executives finally trooped out of the factory in frustration and anger. The invited guests, not wanting to witness our growing embarrassment, had already departed surreptitiously, one by one.

By the time the new tabloid eventually reached the streets of Harare late on April Fool's Day, we were both bewildered and sapped of energy. Our immediate suspicion was that we had been sabotaged, and, looking back, I believe this was indeed the case. Thousands of readers speculated that we were Harare's latest fly-by-night con artists. Dozens of new advertisers or their agents, painstakingly canvassed over months with promises of a truly independent newspaper and high-quality full-colour reproduction, telephoned or arrived at Trustee House in person to cancel their bookings and contracts. Our credibility and viability were instantly imperilled.

Any celebration that day would have been confined to the upper floors of Linquenda House, headquarters of the ministry of information and publicity, and Herald House. The *Herald*, the government's once profitable flagship that had become staid and boring, with a fast diminishing pagination and even more rapid decline in circulation, stood to be the major victim of any *Daily News* success, and on that fateful first day, *Herald* staff were jubilant.

Conceiving and producing a better paper than the *Herald* was not particularly difficult.

'The success of the *Daily News* and other independent newspapers in Zimbabwe is directly attributed to the decline and unpopularity of government newspapers,' opined Elias Rusike at the *Financial Gazette*. 'Zimbabweans were being fed a daily news diet of lies and propaganda by government newspapers and the Zimbabwe Broadcasting Corporation. The government uses the two publicly owned companies to promote the president and Zanu-PF to the exclusion of the opposition parties.'

As former chief executive of Zimbabwe Newspapers and confidant of erstwhile information minister Nathan Shamuyarira, Rusike was eminently qualified to express such sentiments.

'The appointment of Bornwell Chakaodza as editor in chief of the *Herald* was the worst decision ever made. Here was a man who was director of information, the government's chief spokesman and chief government censor, who was made editor in chief of a national, not even government or party, newspaper. The result has been disastrous.

'The independent newspapers are perceived as fair, objective and balanced, accommodating the views of government and the ruling party. Their non-racial approach to reporting has earned the independent media support in both readership and advertising from both black and white readers.'

Newspaper readers, long disenchanted with the *Herald*'s sycophantic editorial policy and sanitised news content that verged on obsequious propaganda, had long christened it *Pravda*, after the Communist Party's mouthpiece in Moscow. The *Herald* routinely covered up rampant corruption, fuel, food and other shortages, unchecked lawlessness and general abuse of power by an administration that had become increasingly unpopular with a once adoring electorate.

The unflinching support and unquestioning loyalty of the state's media empire to Zanu-PF ensured that Mugabe and the ruling party remained dominant and unchallenged in the political arena. While a multiparty democracy on paper, Zimbabwe had been a de facto one-party state for years. Apart from two daily and four weekly newspapers, the government's empire included radio and the sole television channel, both operated by a moribund ZBC. In its heyday in the 1980s, the *Herald* had printed and sold 165 000 copies a day. A year after the launch of the *Daily News*, that figure had plummeted to a mere 50 000. During the same period, circulation of the *Daily News* grew to more than 100 000 copies a day.

The editors at Zimpapers were shaken out of their customary lethargy by the sudden emergence of the *Daily News* and the prospect of serious competition and a challenge to the monopoly they had long cherished. By the time the *Daily News* appeared, government spokesmen had become hysterical in their denunciation of it, but condemnation of any newspaper by representatives of a discredited government is excellent publicity.

On 26 April, three weeks after the *Daily News* was launched, Mugabe appointed a commission of inquiry into Zimbabwe's constitution. It was chaired by Judge President Godfrey Chidyausiku, with Bishop Jonathan Siyachitema of the Anglican Church, former University of Zimbabwe vice chancellor Professor Walter Kamba and former National Railways of Zimbabwe public relations manager Grace Lupepe as vice chairpersons. The appointment of so many deputies was indicative of one of Mugabe's most notable weaknesses: indecision, the same flaw that had lumbered Zimbabwe with two vice-presidents since the unity agreement was signed.

The 396-member commission comprised all members of parliament and 241 other people, including opposition politicians, activists and ruling party hangers-on. Also included were business leaders, trade unionists, farmers, lawyers, journalists and civil society representatives.

Public hearings were to be held on the existing constitution, and the commission was to submit a report to the president before the end of the year. Their findings would form the basis of a new constitution. Once the proposed constitution was drafted, the government launched a vigorous campaign for acceptance, spearheaded by Jonathan Moyo. He had returned to Zimbabwe after years of exile in the Kenyan capital of Nairobi, where he worked for the Ford Foundation, and in South Africa, where he was a researcher at the University of the Witswatersrand in Johannesburg.

This was the same Moyo who had shot to prominence in 1990 as a columnist on the *Financial Gazette*. Not only was he a prolific writer, he was also a hard-hitting critic of Mugabe and all things Zanu-PF. An American-trained political scientist, Moyo waged a spirited and virtually single-handed campaign against Mugabe's pet project, the one-party state. His regular column in the *Financial Gazette* became the paper's most popular feature.

Moyo had left Zimbabwe for Nairobi suddenly, amid rumours that he had crossed unspecified swords with justice minister Emmerson Mnangagwa and been forced to flee, though Moyo himself later denied this.

In 1999, he resurfaced in Harare as mysteriously as he had disappeared. He surprised all who knew him by immediately aligning himself with Zanu-PF and government. Operating from the upper floors of Harare's five-star Sheraton Hotel, he became the official advocate for acceptance of the proposed new constitution. His campaign was vehemently opposed by the MDC, constitutional lawyer Lovemore Madhuku's National Constitutional Assembly (NCA), the ZCTU and a host of civil society groups.

The proposed constitutional amendments would have limited future presidents to two terms. However, the legislation would not be retroactive, meaning that Mugabe could stand in two more elections. In addition, government and military officials would have been rendered immune from prosecution for any illegal acts committed while in office. The government would also have been given the power to confiscate white-owned commercial farms for redistribution to blacks without payment of any compensation.

A national referendum on the far-reaching proposals was held on 12 and 13 February 2000. Turnout was low at 20 per cent, mostly urban, but when registrar general Tobaiwa Mudede announced the results, Mugabe, Moyo and the government had lost. In reality, many voters could not be bothered with the intricate details of the proposed changes. They were simply fed up with their president and his party and seized the opportunity to drive their point home.

When Mugabe appeared on television to declare that he would 'abide by the will of the people', he looked distinctly unhappy. The vote not only took Zanu-PF by surprise, but was also a major embarrassment with parliamentary elections due in June. The first defeat at the polls for Mugabe and Zanu-PF in two decades of unchallenged political supremacy triggered a series of events that very nearly cost the ruling party its coveted and entrenched position of power.

To start with, the success of its campaign against the new constitution fuelled the MDC's popularity. For the *Daily News*, the outcome of the referendum signalled the start of a period of re-energised growth.

Four months earlier, while the constitutional commission canvassed public opinion, the newspaper had conducted a rudimentary opinion poll of its own. Readers were asked to respond to questions on the desirability of the proposed constitution. The most popular question was which candidate respondents would vote for if a presidential election were to be held immediately.

While the response was dismal, with only 254 questionnaires filled in and submitted, the statistical result was stunning. Opposition leader Morgan Tsvangirai polled by far the largest number of votes among *Daily News* readers as the next president. Limited and unscientific though it was, if our poll accurately reflected public sentiment, Mugabe was clearly in trouble. In fact, his rejection was so overwhelming that we got cold feet and refrained from publishing details of the poll on the grounds that they were really not empirical enough to be reliable. I placed the questionnaires in a file and locked them in a drawer.

Three months later, at the height of the referendum campaign in January, the *Daily News* was experiencing financial hardship. The paper had never recovered from its disastrous launch, despite an injection of funds from the Gaborone-based Southern African Media Development Fund (Samdef). Our inauspicious debut had done little to persuade potential investors that their money would be safe. ANZ was therefore experiencing serious cash-flow problems. In November and December we had been unable to pay the staff on time, and they had resorted to industrial action. Our business plan had projected sales in excess of 100 000 a day before the end of the first year, but in reality, circulation was hovering around 30 000. As a result, our pages were not exactly loaded with advertising, the mainstay of any commercially viable newspaper publishing operation. The salaries of senior staff were habitually late, and only our tenacity and faith in the project kept us going.

One evening, I pulled out the referendum file and took it to our next news conference. We decided to ask the department of statistics at the University of Zimbabwe for a professional assessment of the results. Their analysis had the makings of a fascinating story, and we published it a few weeks before voters went to the polls.

That issue of the newspaper sold out within hours, while correspondence on the outcome of our poll dominated the letters page right up to the referendum.

The *Herald* was livid, dismissing the poll as thoroughly unprofessional. We insisted that it was representative of political sentiment in the country and boldly predicted that the majority would vote against the draft constitution. When this prophecy came to pass in February, the *Daily News* was given a new lease of life, its credibility instantly endorsed.

Within a fortnight, circulation jumped to 50 000. By the beginning of April it reached 70 000, with continued growth threatened only by a serious shortage of newsprint. We managed to acquire a huge consignment from South Africa, and by the beginning of May, our sales figures had rocketed to 90 000. In June, we broke through the psychological barrier of 100 000 copies, before setting a record that stood throughout the four short years until the newspaper was banned.

Our moment of glory was on 28 June, when we published the results of the controversial, violence-wracked parliamentary election. We gambled on a mammoth print run – 127 500 copies. The issue sold out.

Far from confirming that Zanu-PF was invincible, as had been the case in four previous parliamentary polls, the 2000 election rocked the ruling party. Despite having mounted a campaign of vicious violence against the MDC, the independent press, the judiciary and white farmers, whose land was invaded and seized in a bloody operation mounted by war veterans and Zanu-PF activists, Mugabe's party came closer to losing power than at any other time during his two decades in office.

Zanu-PF scraped through with a majority in only 62 of the 120 contested constituencies. This was just five seats more than the 57 won by Tsvangirai's MDC. The Reverend Ndabaningi Sithole's Zanu, which drew its support from among the Ndau people of south-east Zimbabwe, was the only other party of the sixteen that fought the election to win a seat. Independent candidates totalled eighty-eight. But the ruling party was still assured of a clear majority in the 150-seat legislature, thanks to a constitutional provision that allowed the president to appoint thirty members of parliament.

The MDC challenged the results, accusing Zanu-PF of securing victory by means of manipulating the poll and resorting to violence. Tsvangirai claimed that up to 20 per cent of would-be voters had been turned away from polling stations, mostly because they were not on the electoral roll.

'The intense coercion, intimidation and violence some of our people experienced shines through in the results,' he said.

While the MDC failed to win enough seats to dislodge Zanu-PF, the party's gains would allow it to block any attempt by the ruling party to amend the constitution. An estimated 2.8 million ballots were cast, the highest turnout since independence. Of these, a total of 1.2 million were in favour of Zanu-PF, while the MDC drew 1.17 million votes, its strongest showing being in Harare, in the Matabeleland constituencies to the west and in the eastern province of Manicaland.

Remarkably, voters throughout Matabeleland chose the MDC over the newly launched Zapu, which sought to revive Joshua Nkomo's PF-Zapu. Surprisingly, since memories of the Gukurahundi atrocities were still fresh in many minds, the new Zapu received only a handful of votes. One inference to be drawn from this could be that the people of Matabeleland were not overly enthusiastic about the ethnic-based political agenda propagated by some of their more radical and younger elite.

At least ten of the ruling party's heavies lost seats that had been considered safe. Dumiso Dabengwa, the home affairs minister once feared as Zipra's security supremo, was trounced by 20 380 votes to 3 644 by a previously unknown MDC candidate in Bulawayo. In the Midlands, justice minister Emmerson Mnangagwa, whose name was sporadically linked to allegations of corruption and who was widely perceived to be Mugabe's anointed successor, suffered humiliating defeat in the town of Kwekwe.

His rival, the MDC's Blessing Chebundo, made international history as the first – and possibly last – candidate to win an election while in hiding. He had been assaulted and driven underground by Mnangagwa's supporters.

The election result also gave the *Daily News* a major boost. The paper had consistently campaigned for political change, and although Zanu-PF remained in power, its supremacy had been significantly diminished. The politically tense election campaign had seen a phenomenal 325 per cent growth in our sales, from a modest 30 000 to 127 500 copies, with practically every issue selling out.

In 1993, a group of independent media practitioners met in the Namibian capital of Windhoek to set up the Media Institute of Southern Africa. Founder members included Gwen Lister (editor of the *Namibian*), Govin Reddy from South Africa, Tanzanian journalist Ndimara Tegembagwe, who later became a politician, Fernando Lima of Mozambique, Mario Paiva of Angola, Fred M'membe, founder of the highly successful Zambian newspaper, the *Post*, Makani Kabweza (editor of *Moto* in Zimbabwe), Methaetsile Leepile from Botswana, and me.

MISA's Windhoek Declaration set out a number of recommendations by African journalists for promoting an independent and pluralistic press and supporting freedom of expression and access to information. Internationally, the declaration's impact was such that the United Nations decided to celebrate its release as World Press Freedom Day in future.

Leepile narrowly pipped me to the post as MISA's first chief executive, but when the organisation set up Samdef as its regional media support fund, he retired in order to head up the financial arm.

In August 1999, when cash-flow problems struck the *Daily News* in earnest, ANZ's chief executive, Much Masunda, flew to Botswana to negotiate funding from Samdef. We had consciously refrained from seeking donor funding, as we feared this could compromise the newspaper's credibility.

The fledgling newspaper publishing company had experienced a series of overwhelming changes at executive management level in its first few months. Just two weeks after the launch of the *Daily News*, Masunda stepped down as chairman to assume the new position of chief executive officer. Wilf Mbanga, previously managing director, was relegated to the position of deputy CEO. He resigned soon afterwards.

From July to October 1999, the board was headed by financier Nkosana Donald Moyo, who represented two shareholders, Batanai Capital Finance and NDM Investments. When he resigned, he was replaced by Stuart Mattinson, representing the foreign investors. After the 2000 elections, Moyo was appointed to Mugabe's cabinet as one of the so-called technocrats, but it wasn't long before he quit this position and went to live abroad.

Masunda travelled to Gaborone to seek funding after a period of agitation among staff, a number of tempestuous meetings between management and staff, and several strikes in protest against late payment of salaries. Samdef sent consultants to Harare to undertake a due diligence study and, satisfied that ANZ possessed potential for growth and viability, the fund deposited $200 000 (US) into the company's bank account in November.

Of course there were strings attached. Samdef nominated Edwin Manikai, a lawyer and senior partner at Dube, Manikai and Hwacha, one of the more successful of Harare's many emergent legal firms, to the ANZ board. The fund also expressed concern that the board had too many executive directors, and raised questions about the performance of some members of the executive. As a result, finance director Lovejoy Charidza and advertising and marketing director Agnes Gomwe were asked to leave the company.

Their departure, and that of Mbanga just a couple of months earlier, upset me deeply. They had done much to shape ANZ, but Mbanga's failure to attract local investment had not gone down well with the majority shareholder, AMIZ. In addition, sales of the regional newspapers had fallen far short of the figures projected by Mbanga on the basis of his experience with CNG. A decision had been taken to phase out the weekly publications and consolidate our effort and resources to save the *Daily News*.

Nevertheless, it was sad to see Mbanga go. I had argued with Stent over the decision, concerned that the sudden departure of ANZ's founding managing director so soon after the launch of the *Daily News* could send the wrong signal into the market. But there was also a personal sense of loss. Mbanga and I had set out together, less than a year before, on the journey that would turn our shared dream into reality.

He set himself up as a public relations consultant and later went to live in the Netherlands. In 2004 he launched a weekly newspaper, *The Zimbabwean*, based in the United Kingdom and aimed at the growing number of politically disgruntled Zimbabweans now living in the diaspora. Copies were also printed in Johannesburg and flown to Harare every week.

Much Masunda and I first met at the University of Rhodesia in 1971. He was equally at home on the tennis and squash courts as on the golf course. By 1998, Masunda played tennis or squash with a mixed bag of distinguished partners, including business executives and diplomats. Cabinet ministers Nathan Shamuyarira (foreign affairs) and Simba Makoni (finance and economic development) were his regular partners.

Masunda had the uncanny ability of reeling off the names of ministers, diplomats and the chief executives of many of Harare's larger corporations. In the case of the Zimbabweans, he would throw in details of their families and academic background without batting an eyelid. In matters pertaining to corporate affairs, sport and politics he became an invaluable asset to the *Daily News*. He possessed the proverbial memory of an elephant. To the newsroom staff, his office became an easily accessible and enthusiastic reference library.

At the time of his appointment at ANZ, Masunda was chairman of the executive council of the Institute of Directors of Zimbabwe. He was also chairman of seven companies and a director on numerous others. He had helped to establish and later run the Commercial Arbitration Centre, which sought to resolve legal disputes amicably without the attendant glare of unwanted and often unwarranted publicity that court cases usually generate.

Masunda's greatest asset was his useful connections in the corporate world. On Wednesday 12 May 1999, he held a meeting with Hillary M Duckworth, CEO of TZI, the holding company for Mutare Board & Paper Mills, Zimbabwe's largest supplier of newsprint. They discussed terms for settling a long-outstanding debt and securing future supplies of newsprint in order for ANZ to remain in business.

A month later, when ANZ was in even deeper financial difficulty, Masunda met Duckworth again, this time to stave off a threat by Mutare Board & Paper to cancel our supply of newsprint. ANZ's credit facility was frozen and the company was required to pay cash in advance for future deliveries. This often saw Charidza waiting for Kennedy Midzi, the distribution manager, to hand over the day's cash collections in the afternoon. Charidza would then dash to the bank just before closing time to deposit the required amount in the Mutare Board & Paper account. Once the deposit was confirmed by phone, a consignment of newsprint would be loaded in Mutare and trucked 260 kilometres to Harare.

Occasionally, the truck left the eastern border town after 6 p.m, which meant that it was well past midnight by the time the reels of newsprint had been unloaded and put in place on the printing press. Copies of the newspaper had to reach Mutare, Bulawayo, Masvingo and other centres by road before 6 a.m. in order to meet the morning rush. Sometimes, this just wasn't possible and the newspaper would go on sale as late as noon. Fortuitously, we were rescued on many such an occasion by a hard-hitting front page that ensured sales despite the late delivery.

I was initially apprehensive as to whether Masunda, a man so closely linked to the political establishment, could pilot a publishing company whose flagship was controversial and viewed by the same paranoid politicians as the voice of the opposition. His close relationship with my old nemesis, Shamuyarira, who had remained Zanu-PF's influential information and publicity secretary after retiring from active politics, was of particular concern, but Masunda was phlegmatic about their association.

'The trouble with many company directors in this country is that they race to see ministers only when things go wrong,' he would say. 'That is obviously a time of conflict, and they retreat, hurt, saying that either the minister won't see me or he can't see my point of view.'

Masunda honed to a fine art his dual role as chief executive of a fiercely independent newspaper and a friend of politicians who hated his newspaper with a passion. He often related the story of Makoni telephoning to invite him to play squash.

'I've had a rotten day and I need some exercise,' he quoted Makoni as saying. 'Please come by and pick me up.'

In due course, Masunda stopped his car in front of Munhumutapa Building, the main government office building. An overbearing policeman immediately approached, gesticulating frantically, as bored policemen are wont to, for Masunda to move on.

'Go inside and tell the minister of finance that you have moved his lift two blocks up,' Masunda politely advised the young policeman. The officer soon returned and, gasping for breath, effusively saluted Masunda, while pleading with him not to move an inch. Shortly afterwards, Dr Leonard Tsumba, the governor of the Reserve Bank, and his deputy Sam Malaba emerged from the building.

As Masunda greeted and chatted with them like old friends, the minister and an aide arrived on the scene.

'The aide couldn't believe that the chief executive of ANZ, publishers of the *Daily News*, had come to give the minister a lift so that they could play a game of squash,' Masunda said. 'You may well hold opposing political views, but that doesn't mean you can't talk to each other, or that you can't be friends.'

I often reminded him that it was Zanu-PF and the government that desperately needed to hear his words of wisdom. Not to be outdone, I once recounted details of my own encounter on a tennis court, when the then minister of political affairs, Maurice Nyagumbo, had beaten me five games to one at the Holiday Inn in Bulawayo in 1988. Masunda's large frame shook with laughter.

It was a highly developed sense of humour that kept the two of us going when the going got tough at the *Daily News*, which was virtually every day. For me, Masunda became an irreplaceable pillar of support, his involvement in and intimate knowledge of Zimbabwe's corporate world a source of comfort for a company viewed with suspicion and hostility by many.

'People tell us we've made an invaluable contribution to the political landscape of our country, and that makes everything worthwhile,' he said of his role at ANZ. 'They also ask if we have bullet-proof vests or a coterie of bodyguards!'

After a series of run-ins with Zanu-PF and government over stories deemed to be provocative, inflammatory or downright unpatriotic, a front-page report, which confirmed that the *Daily News* was irrevocably set on a course of confrontation with government, appeared on 28 November 2000. Under the headline, 'President linked to airport deal', the story was the ultimate stirring of the proverbial hornet's nest. It alleged that Mugabe had benefited from the payment of unauthorised commissions during construction of Harare's new international airport. As the project neared completion, a serious rift had emerged between Air Harbour Technologies, the Cyprus-based main contractor, the company's local representatives and a number of government officials.

The project was rife with allegations of major cronyism involving Mugabe's controversial nephew Leo and Hani, the equally controversial son of a powerful former Saudi oil minister, Sheikh Ahmed Yamani. In a departure from regular tales of corruption in Harare, this one included a senior Palestinian diplomat. Mugabe was presented with the names of senior government officials who had allegedly taken substantial bribes. The president took no action. While Mugabe himself was publicly linked to this allegation of corruption, he decided, after the customary fulmination of his officials against the *Daily News*, to let sleeping dogs lie.

Hani Yamani, the owner of AHT, listed Mugabe and Mnangagwa among top officials whom he claimed to have paid a total of $3 million (US) to ensure that his company won the Z$5 billion tender to design and build the new airport.

Yamani claimed that he had made substantial payments to Leo Mugabe and to two former transport ministers, Simon Khaya Moyo and Enos Chikowore. Moyo, a Joshua Nkomo protégé, was appointed Zimbabwe's high commissioner in Pretoria soon afterwards, while Chikowore relieved himself of the misery of destitution by committing suicide in April 2005. Yamani claimed he had paid a smaller amount to then finance minister Herbert Murerwa, one of Mugabe's favourite ministers, who had served as high commissioner in London.

Yamani also claimed that his representatives in Zimbabwe, Heena Joshi, Jayant's daughter, and Tony Kates, had paid $10 000 (US) to the dean of the diplomatic corps in Harare, Ali Halimeh, ambassador of the Palestinian Liberation Organisation (PLO), and had also paid a number of junior-ranking government officials. The name of my former colleague and editor of the *Herald*, Tommy Sithole, appeared on the list of alleged recipients.

'Ambassador Halimeh has been demanding much more money from me over the past two years, over and above the large sums that he has been receiving. This is extremely sad for me because I genuinely like him and I will continue to care for him and his family in his serious illness,' Yamani claimed.

When approached for comment, the PLO ambassador responded: 'I know Yamani. He is a friend of mine. I know the gentleman very well, but I know nothing about the payment.'

If we went ahead and published the story, he had a way of dealing with people, warned Halimeh, throwing diplomatic caution to the wind.

Heena Joshi denied ever paying the named people anything. 'I resigned from the company after I realised that Hani Yamani was conducting himself outside the boundaries of ethical business practice,' she said coolly.

Leo Mugabe said: 'I have nothing to do with AHT. All I did was introduce one of the company's representatives to influential people in the country and that was six years ago. This is an old story. The problem is that you don't like President Mugabe and end up painting us with the same brush. I am a capable businessman who has a right to receive commissions, but on this one I did not get anything.'

But the full details of the alleged payments were contained in a letter Yamani had written to President Mugabe in 1999. He complained that he'd lost $3 million (US) – or Z$165 million – through paying bribes to Zimbabweans. Zanu-PF's trading company, Zidco, was named as the official agent for AHT. Yamani stated that his company had also paid a total of $20 000 (US) through Zidco for construction of the president's residence in his traditional village. AHT had allegedly paid the Yugoslav contractors.

Yamani said a total of $1.2 million (US) had been paid directly to Zidco through the personal bank account of Jayant Chunilal Joshi, on the instructions of Mnangagwa, Jayant and his brother, Manharlal Chunibal Joshi. Yamani had allegedly channelled a total of $50 000 (US) to Zanu-PF through the same bank account.

The Joshi brothers, who were the key players in Zidco, along with Mnangagwa, maintained strong personal links with the Mugabes. Heena Joshi was a close friend of the First Lady, and served on the board of Grace's charitable organisation, the Children's Rehabilitation Trust.

In his letter to Mugabe, dated 15 July, Yamani alleged that a 'dirty conspiracy' had been hatched to destroy his relationship with Mugabe and his family in order to hide certain financial transactions. Describing the president as a father, Yamani listed the officials to whom illicit payments had allegedly been made.

'It is crucial for me that you know all the facts, and that my reputation with you and your family is restored,' Yamani pleaded. 'You are more able than I am to determine the good sheep from the bad ones in your flock and I have no choice but to come to you in the present circumstances for help and protection.'

The most intriguing part of the letter dealt with Mnangagwa's alleged role in laundering funds through Zidco for Mugabe's residence and payments to Ambassador Halimeh 'to cover his living and medical expenses'.

'Normally, we would take Heena to court for mismanagement and fraud and we can stop her this way, but this is impossible in our present case as it would hurt Zimbabwe and your family. Most important to me is my relationship with you and the First Lady, which is worth more to me than money and fame. I respect you and I am honoured by your trust in me. I am a victim of plotters who derive all their power from you, but who deal for their personal ambitious agenda,' Yamani wrote.

He said he had last met with Mugabe in July 1998 and with the First Lady in September of the same year in Paris. Attempts to travel to Zimbabwe and accompany the president on a tour of the new airport had been blocked by Heena Joshi, he claimed.

Responding to these detailed allegations, presidential spokesperson George Charamba said Mugabe would instruct the attorney-general to press charges against the *Daily News* for branding him corrupt.

Mnangagwa denied taking any bribes. 'The allegations are unfounded,' he said. 'I have already instructed my lawyer to institute litigation against the newspaper.'

The lawyer in question was Edwin Manikai, who had served on the ANZ board. For four months, no more was heard of the threats to sue the newspaper, but we were determined to defend ourselves against any litigation, and we said as much, repeatedly. After all, we had a copy of Yamani's incriminating letter in our possession.

The nightly appearance on television of government officials frothing at the mouth in panic-stricken condemnation of the *Daily News* merely seemed to whet the public's appetite for the newspaper.

With the motto 'Telling it like it is' boldly emblazoned under its masthead, the *Daily News* refused to acknowledge the existence of any sacred cow on Zimbabwe's political landscape. A combination of daring and thoroughly investigated exposés, coupled with hard-hitting editorial comment, in-depth articles and adroit cartoons that parodied the many shortcomings or excesses of an increasingly unpopular and beleaguered regime, quickly endeared the paper to readers.

This, of course, was far more than Zanu-PF's politicians could stomach. In their eyes, the paper's reporters were clearly writing against the grain. The *Daily News* had created a public platform for the MDC and its allies, the ZCTU and various civil society organisations.

By then the ruling party had launched a vicious campaign to destroy both the newspaper and every vestige of political opposition.

12

The sword is mightier

T HE NEW GOVERNMENT'S true intentions in setting up the Zimbabwe Mass Media Trust in 1980 and acquiring a controlling share in Zimbabwe Newspapers were spelled out by the trust's first chairman, Robert Mandebvu.

He was Zanu-PF's official representative in Libya during the war of liberation and served a brief stint at the ZMMT before being sent out on a diplomatic posting. On paper, the trust professed to act as a buffer between the government and the media empire that it now controlled, but at a press conference soon after his appointment, Mandebvu's message was mildly menacing.

'We will not interfere with the right of the press to report the truth,' he said, 'but journalists will also need to remember that they are citizens of the country and should be wary of issues that may discredit or embarrass the government. The press will not be controlled by the public.'

Though he carefully refrained from adding 'but by the government', that was clearly the message he wanted to convey.

Whatever level of control Mandebvu might have envisaged, it would have paled into insignificance against the wave of media repression that engulfed Zimbabwe two decades later, when Professor Jonathan Moyo, formerly Mugabe's harshest critic, became his most ardent defender and spin doctor while serving as minister of information and publicity.

From 2000 to 2004, journalists working for the independent media were relentlessly harassed and harangued, tortured and threatened with death, wantonly arrested or run out of town. War veterans and Zanu-PF activists banned the distribution of non-government newspapers in rural areas and small urban centres; a printing press was destroyed by a bomb; editorial offices were targeted for attack.

After Zanu-PF's close shave with defeat at the parliamentary polls in 2000, the state-sponsored campaign of violence spiralled. The motto of the *Daily News*, 'Telling it like it is', did nothing to endear the paper to the country's rulers, but notwithstanding concerted efforts to repress and silence all critics, political opposition mounted.

Rampant corruption, a decline in the standard of living, a breakdown in the rule of law, political violence, widespread abuse of basic human rights and shortages of essential commodities all conspired to undermine the public standing and image of the ruling party and government. And all the while, the MDC was gaining support as the most viable political opposition party since the demise of PF-Zapu in 1987, when it merged with Zanu-PF in what had effectively become a one-party state.

In January 2002, Reporters sans Frontières, the international non-governmental organisation that fights for press freedom and routinely highlights and denounces the violation of human rights all over the world, submitted a damning report on the Zimbabwe government's persecution of the independent media to the UN Commission for Human Rights.

Mugabe was cited as one of thirty-nine 'predators' of press freedom in the world, while Zimbabwe was included among African states that had done the most to stifle independent media operations during 2001. Both local and foreign journalists had been targeted for victimisation by government with total impunity, and, due to ongoing threats and arrests, the independent press found it increasingly difficult to act as an efficient public informer. A total of twenty local journalists had been arrested, while three foreign correspondents had been expelled from the country.

'Throughout 2001, the president and his government uttered shocking comments against the press,' the report stated. In September, Moyo had announced: 'In the interest of law and order, competent authorities will crack down on some well-known individuals in order to curb the law of the jungle they are trying to create in the country through the media.'

At the end of June, the European Union's ministers of foreign affairs called on Zimbabwean authorities to uphold the rule of law, freedom of the press and the independence of the judiciary. A few days earlier, the American government had accused Zimbabwean authorities of forbidding the press to report on what was really going on in the country.

There can be no doubt that the success of the *Daily News*, by far the most sought-after daily newspaper in Zimbabwe by the end of 2000, caused the government to tighten the screws. Ably assisted by the capricious Moyo, Mugabe lambasted, threatened and intimidated journalists throughout 2001 and 2002. Particularly vulnerable were reporters who tried to tell the truth about the invasion of commercial farms by ruling party militants.

Zanu-PF accused us of supporting the MDC. My attitude was that whereas the *Herald* denied all parties except Zanu-PF a platform, we provided one for all political organisations, including the opposition movement. If the MDC came to power, the *Daily News* would treat it at arm's length and call it to account as a matter of course. Regrettably, we never had the opportunity to prove our point, but we would certainly not have given a new government the easy ride that the media had offered Zanu-PF for many years after independence in the interest of nation-building.

'We thought we were being patriotic,' one journalist lamented bitterly, 'but they just took it for granted and put their hands deeper in the till. Our forbearance earned us nothing. When we did at last begin to criticise, they were furious – and it was too late.'

The first major sign that matters were getting totally out of hand was in April 2000, when I received a letter from a previously unknown group calling itself 'Revival of African Conscience'. The writer accused the *Daily News* of 'lack of respect for our dear

President' and of 'creating dissatisfaction' in the government. I was told to 'stop publishing negatively' about the invasion of white-owned farms.

The letter concluded: 'If you fail to abide by our command, please prepare yourself a highway in the skies before we descend violently on you and your imperial organisation. Think twice – don't betray your motherland.'

The Revival of African Conscience was never to be heard of again, suggesting that it was probably a one-man outfit. There was something of a familiar ring to the intimidating turn of phrase.

Then an anonymous phone call warned us that a bomb had been planted in Trustee House, where the newspaper had its offices, and would go off at any time. We all scrambled out of the building and stood at a safe distance across the street to watch in fearful anticipation. The cellphone number that the warning call had been made to was one of several listed on the front page of the *Daily News*. We accessed the phone's memory to retrieve and dial the number from which the hoax call had been made.

'Zanu-PF headquarters, good day,' a cheery voice answered.

A few days later, there was a real explosion. Over the Easter weekend, a hand grenade was lobbed through the plate glass window of a curio shop on the ground floor of Trustee House. Because of the public holiday, the shop owner, Hope Dauti, and his staff were away, so there were no injuries. However, the damage was severe, extending to my office, which was situated directly above the shop and was almost certainly the target of the attack. This was the first indication that Zanu-PF had imported the political violence that had wracked the rural areas for months, to downtown Harare.

Obert Zilwa, a photographer with Associated Press, did what comes naturally to all professional purveyors of news. He was the first person to arrive at the scene of the blast. When the police made their appearance, they promptly arrested and charged him in terms of the draconian Law and Order (Maintenance) Act for launching the attack.

Created by the former Rhodesian government, this pernicious piece of legislation carried a maximum sentence of life imprisonment, and placed the onus on the accused to prove innocence rather than on the state to show guilt. After holding him for two days, the police suddenly dropped the charges against Zilwa. He was rushed to the airport and placed on the next flight to Johannesburg.

The threatening letter I had received, the hoax bomb call and the hand grenade explosion were unsettling and explicit signs that someone, or some organisation, was determined to destabilise or even destroy the *Daily News*. Before long, we received confirmation that the dreaded Central Intelligence Organisation and a high-ranking official who was related to Mugabe were responsible for the terror campaign. Our information came from a most unlikely source – a paid assassin with a bad case of conscience and cold feet.

My second son, Itayi, protests that I am too friendly in the company of strangers. I am one of those people who will strike up a conversation with someone while waiting in a bank queue. All attempts to explain to Itayi that a genteel demeanour – including the salutation of total strangers while enquiring about the health of their family – is a cultural requisite among the Shona, failed to spare me from his frequent castigation.

Until the day when this effusive traditional etiquette literally saved my life.

About a month after the parliamentary poll in June 2000, I stepped into one of the two ancient elevators that laboriously ferried workers and visitors between the ten floors of Trustee House. As the doors slid shut, I pressed the 'open' button for a late arrival, an athletically built man about ten years my junior.

In the dimly lit interior, I noticed two things about the man. First, while my companion's attire was the last word in sartorial elegance, he appeared ill at ease. One of Harare's many rising and increasingly powerful indigenous business executives, late for an appointment to sign another multi-million-dollar deal, I surmised. As fate would have it, the top floors of the building served as the headquarters of Zimbabwe Defence Industries (ZDI), which manufactured munitions and other military equipment for the army and for export, while constantly fielding allegations of corruption. ZDI chief executive, retired Colonel Tshinga Dube, and most of the military top brass were highly respected patrons of casinos from Nyanga to Victoria Falls, where they won and lost millions of dollars without batting an eyelid.

The second thing that caught my attention was that the man with me in the elevator did not press any of the floor buttons.

'Just in time,' I said to break the silence as we began moving upwards at an agonisingly sluggish pace. 'So, how is the family?'

His response was not what I expected.

'You must be Mr Nyarota, the editor?'

'How did you know?' I asked, feigning surprise. I was accustomed to strangers recognising me, since my photograph occasionally graced the pages of various news-papers when I was being mercilessly lambasted by government officials or whoever was editor of the *Herald* on a given day. Between 1999 and 2002, the newspaper had no fewer than four editorial chiefs: the long-serving Tommy Sithole, Bornwell Chakaodza, Thomas Bvuma and Pikirayi Deketeke. Each, in turn, perpetuated the hostility towards me. As the man who had ruined their newspaper's reputation and circulation, I was probably regarded as the reason for the high turnover of editors.

My face had also become familiar to the public through fairly regular appearances on ZTV, when I was routinely interrogated by one or other overzealous news anchor. Supa Mandiwanzira's merciless grilling had generated much public sympathy for me, not at all the effect he had been hoping for. My son Tafi videotaped one of Mandiwanzira's sessions with me. It provided popular entertainment for visitors to our home.

Before my fellow elevator passenger could explain how he came to know my name, we reached the second floor and I exited, leaving him to proceed to whatever upper floor he was destined. Two days later, the same man visited my office. Our security manager had long since introduced certain rudimentary safety measures, one of them being that under no circumstances was any stranger to be allowed into my office without a prior appointment.

The man from the elevator had indeed arrived unannounced, insisting that it was imperative he be allowed to see me. My personal assistant, Annie Musodza, was equally insistent that he could not do so, and quizzed him intensely about his purpose.

It might have been his warning that my life was in serious danger and that his intervention was required to avert impending calamity, but something in the man's demeanour eventually convinced Annie that he should not be dismissed out of hand.

When Annie entered my office to suggest that I should speak to the man outside, deputy editor Davison Maruziva and assistant editor Bill Saidi were still in my office at the tail end of the morning news conference. We decided that they should stay and, as an added precaution, Annie posted a security guard outside the door.

In the seventeen months of its existence, the *Daily News* had defied both the odds and vigorous and hostile opposition from the ruling party and government to become Zimbabwe's largest and most popular newspaper. Its reputation had grown in proportion to the decline in popularity of Mugabe and Zanu-PF.

But the party had vowed that it would not go down without a spirited fight. After the February referendum, supporters and officials of the increasingly popular MDC and the wealthy white farmers, who still owned the lion's share of Zimbabwe's fertile commercial farming estates, became the victims of a campaign of violence orchestrated by Zanu-PF. Also targeted were the *Daily News* and, to a lesser extent, the *Financial Gazette*, the *Zimbabwe Independent* and the *Zimbabwe Standard*. These four publications represented a vibrant and ever more vocal independent press, while the *Daily Mirror* and its Sunday edition remained distant cousins, positioned strategically and metaphorically on the political fence.

As the three most senior editorial executives at the *Daily News*, Maruziva, Saidi and I were no strangers to the adversity of African journalism. But despite working for many years in the turbulent environment of Zimbabwe's post-independence press, none of us was prepared for the saga that was about to unfold in my office.

While hundreds of opposition activists were being murdered or maimed, the CIO had hatched a plot to kill me. The immaculately dressed man with whom I had come face to face in the elevator forty-eight hours before, and who was now seated across my desk, was Bernard Masara, the hired assassin.

He told us everything.

His handler was Innocent Mugabe, son of the president's politician sister Sabina, and a high-ranking CIO officer. Masara had been ordered to 'liquidate' me in order to silence the *Daily News*, which had become a 'formidable opponent of the government'. He and four men he had recruited had spent the previous fortnight conducting surveillance on Trustee House and on my movements. Attempts to gain access to me in my office had been foiled by his failure to give a plausible reason over the phone for wanting to see me, so he had deliberately staged our meeting in the elevator in order to positively identify his intended target.

But, he told us, he came away from that brief encounter with a change of heart.

'It was just the two of us in the lift,' Masara said, addressing Maruziva and Saidi, 'and he greeted me. He asked me about my family. I decided there and then that I was not going ahead with the assignment. I decided I was not going to let him be killed. My conscience worried me. I realised he was different from the man that had been described to me.'

Afterwards, he said, he had been gripped by a determination to see me. He persuaded security guards to take him to Annie, to whom he first confessed the gruesome nature of his task. When he gave her his identity card and offered to leave it with her as a sign of his new good intentions, she thought it best that we should talk.

Masara exposed the full details of the plot, including the identity of the senior CIO officers directly involved. To prove the authenticity of his story, he produced his national identity card and revealed the names of the four people who had helped him keep Trustee House under observation. He also disclosed that the CIO had an informer in our editorial department, and named him. We decided it would be imprudent to confront the journalist in question, but when we published the Masara story, reference was made to the CIO's infiltration of our newsroom. The reporter identified by Masara resigned soon afterwards.

From my office, Masara telephoned his CIO handler. While we listened incredulously, he discussed on a speakerphone details of the assassination plot with Innocent Mugabe. He made several subsequent calls to the CIO, each time identifying himself just by his first name and on each occasion being immediately recognised. In one conversation, Masara confirmed that his fee for killing me would be Z$100 000, about $2 000 (US). I listened awestruck as my would-be assassin and the CIO's deputy director, whose uncle was the president of Zimbabwe, haggled over the bounty on my head.

Masara divulged that four or five other people were also earmarked for assassination. Their designated killers were former liberation war guerrillas who were now based at the provincial headquarters of the ruling party in the capital city. One had been posing as a cigarette vendor outside Trustee House.

'There are a number of people they want eliminated or injured – 100 per cent disability,' Masara said. 'They said that our first target was the *Daily News* because the paper has become a machinery of the opposition.'

We convinced Masara that in the circumstances, the only guarantee of his safety and my own security was to publish details of the plot. The CIO would become suspicious if I remained alive beyond his deadline. Having made arrangements for Masara to remain in a safe house, his story and picture appeared on the front page of the *Daily News* on Tuesday 1 August 2000.

Both Innocent Mugabe and another senior CIO officer, Robert Manungo, were identified in the report by both name and rank. Neither ever challenged our story.

Mugabe subsequently died, reportedly after a long illness. By then, 'long illness' had become a euphemism for HIV/AIDS among Zimbabweans, who, for the most part, pretended that the pandemic did not exist.

A fortnight after we'd published the confessions of a would-be assassin, there was an ominous knock on my bedroom window half an hour after midnight. My security guard stood in the darkness outside. There were some policemen at the gate, he said. They had demanded entry or they would force their way in. I immediately phoned Masunda to inform him of this new development. He, in turn, called Lawrence Chibwe, our enterprising and unassuming lawyer, while I advised the guard to confirm that the visitors were, indeed, policemen, and to open the gate if they were.

There was a wrought-iron screen around the veranda. As I proceeded to the enclosure, a police vehicle came up the driveway. Two officers in plain clothes approached the house and, once they had identified themselves, I unlocked the outer gate. As I shook their hands in greeting, my nostrils were assailed by the powerful stench of liquor.

They introduced themselves as Detective Chief Superintendent Boysen Mathema and Chief Inspector Henry Dowa of the Law and Order Section. They said I was under arrest, and that they were taking me to Harare Central. My enquiry about the reason for this nocturnal intrusion on my privacy drew a blank. I would be informed at the station when charged, Mathema said abruptly. He was extremely hostile.

Over the following year, Dowa, accompanied by an Inspector Matira, would become a regular caller at my office. In 2002 he was named by several victims as having directed their torture, including prolonged beatings on the soles of their feet and electric shocks that caused convulsions. The allegations were backed by medical evidence. Human rights groups urged the UN to arrest Dowa, who by then was in Kosovo with a UN contingent, and charge him with torture. The UN declined, citing a lack of funds, and sent him back to Zimbabwe.

Back on the veranda, I had a sneaking suspicion why the police had come for me. The *Daily News* had stirred a royal hornet's nest by reporting that police vehicles had been used to ferry goods stolen from invaded commercial farms north of Harare. The fact that the police had failed to maintain law and order during the farm invasions had been repeatedly reported, both in Zimbabwe and abroad.

But that the law enforcers had themselves become the thieves or accomplices to larceny was a new and totally disconcerting dimension. As part of the ongoing saga surrounding the farm invasions by war veterans and Zanu-PF-sponsored thugs, the *Daily News* had reported police complicity in the ransacking and looting of several properties, followed by the removal in police vehicles of goods stolen from the farmhouses.

The headline, 'Police vehicles used in farm looting', was explicit, and the story identified official vehicles as being used in 'well-orchestrated acts of lawlessness'. Between March and August, ruling party militants had invaded more than 1 700 white-owned commercial farms. Our report followed a week of violence in the Chinhoyi maize and tobacco district, seventy miles north-west of Harare, where at least thirty homesteads were looted and white families evacuated from about 100 farms.

That night, I sensed that in their drunken stupor, the policemen on my veranda were hell-bent on avenging the newspaper's humiliation of the ZRP and were relishing every sliver of the power that they wielded. There was nothing for it but to get into their vehicle and drive to the police station. As we turned from Rhodesville Avenue into Samora Machel Avenue, heading west into the city, I saw the headlights of Ursula's car following at a respectful distance.

Assistant editor Bill Saidi, news editor John Gambanga and reporter Sam Munyavi, who had written the story, were arrested in the morning and joined me at Harare Central. The entire day was devoted to interrogating and fingerprinting us. In the evening, we were led to the holding cells in the basement. My three colleagues were released later that night, while I was locked in a cell.

It was at this point that I learned, first-hand, exactly how precarious Mugabe's hold on power had become. From the moment I was handed over to the junior officers on duty, they were effusive in their display of what I was convinced was genuine support and friendship.

'You must sue these people,' said one, 'don't let them get away with it. You have not committed any offence and they know it. They simply want to harass you.'

This was my first night in a cell since January 1977, my first incarceration in an independent Zimbabwe. In the prison at Rusape, we had found comfort in constantly reminding ourselves that Zanu would deliver us from injustice and humiliation. Twenty-three years later, my 'saviour' had become my jailer.

'If a black government detains you on political grounds,' the saying goes, 'they throw the keys away.'

After relieving me of my jacket, shoes, belt and tie, one of the duty officers led me to a little room away from the reception area.

'You cannot spend the night with the criminals and the drunkards, Mr Nyarota,' he said. 'Please sit on this bench. I will be back.'

He returned within minutes and handed me two blankets, not spotlessly clean, but nowhere near the ghastly state of the shared blankets in the cells.

Mugabe had the support of the drunken geriatrics that came to arrest me, but it appeared the *Daily News* had on its side the younger officers who would serve the Zimbabwe of the future. I fell asleep on that comforting note.

The following morning I met my colleagues at the High Court on Rotten Row, where we were charged under a now defunct law that prohibited the publishing of rumours or false reports likely to cause alarm by discrediting the police or military. Under the sweeping Law and Order (Maintenance) Act, such charges carried a penalty of up to seven years in prison. The court ordered our immediate release.

A week later, Basildon Peta, a former *Daily News* investigative reporter who had become a correspondent for the British *Independent*, revealed that he was on a 'blacklist' of wanted journalists, along with Iden Wetherell, editor of the *Zimbabwe Independent*, Mark Chavunduka, editor of the *Standard*, and me. On 24 August, two UN special rapporteurs, Asma Jahangir, who was responsible for looking into arbitrary executions, and Abid Hussain, who monitored freedom of expression all over the world, expressed concern for our lives.

One evening at dusk I drove my Ford Fairmont up the alleyway from the parking lot at the back of Trustee House on my way home. Regrettably, my car had turned out to be easily identifiable. Duly's, the Ford franchise-holder in Zimbabwe, had imported only six of that model from Australia and only two, one of which was mine, were a dark shade of green.

Heading east, I stopped before turning left into First Street. On checking for oncoming traffic from the right, I saw the headlights of a parked Mazda 323 suddenly switch on. As I headed north and indicated my intention to turn right into Samora Machel Avenue, I noticed in my rear-view mirror that the Mazda was behind me, and following suit. Acting intuitively, I indicated a left turn and quickly switched lanes. So did the Mazda.

This confirmed my suspicion that I was being followed. Less than 100 metres down the street I turned left again, and pulled into a parking bay in front of Trustee House. The other driver did the same, leaving an empty parking space between our vehicles. In sheer panic I pressed continuously on my horn, attracting the attention of the security guard in front of the building. On recognising the Fairmont, he rushed to my assistance.

Pointing to the Mazda, I told him I was being followed and quickly explained. As the guard cautiously approached the car, with me a safe distance behind, the driver yelled: 'Who does he think he is?'

Then he thrust the car into reverse and took off, tyres squealing, down the now mercifully empty Samora Machel Avenue. The UN, it seemed, had good reason for concern over the safety of Zimbabwean journalists.

By the end of January 2001, no one was left with any doubt that the *Daily News* was top of the government's hit list. On Friday 26 January, information minister Jonathan Moyo appeared on the prime-time evening television news and told a stunned nation: 'The *Daily News* has become a threat to national security and must be silenced once and for all.'

Events in the distant and war-ridden Democratic Republic of Congo (DRC) had sparked a chain of events that almost brought the newspaper to its knees and certainly put paid to any prospect of further success. Since 1997, the government of Zimbabwe had deployed 11 000 soldiers in the DRC, an ill-advised and economically ruinous decision that ordinary citizens neither understood nor supported. There was no common boundary between the two countries, and sending Zimbabwean troops to shore up the DRC government's forces in a no-win war against rebels backed by Uganda and Rwanda was seriously eroding Harare's dwindling and precious foreign currency reserves.

Mugabe's decision to intervene in the DRC was hardly altruistic. It soon became common knowledge that his political and military cronies were reaping rich rewards from the illicit diamond trade, while selected businesses were cashing in on lucrative government contracts and tenders. A transport company owned by the ZDF commander, General Vitalis Zvinavashe, ferried military supplies to the DRC. A UN report singled out Zvinavashe and Mugabe's heir apparent, parliamentary speaker Emmerson Mnangagwa, among many on the African continent who were growing rich on the DRC's natural resources.

Meanwhile, Zimbabweans endured untold hardship and ongoing commodity shortages, as foreign currency was diverted to fund a distant war that produced a heavy casualty toll. Long lines of motor vehicles formed at petrol stations that had run out of fuel. Many frustrated motorists abandoned their cars on the service station forecourts or on the street. Supermarket shelves, once well stocked, were bare for weeks on end as essential items such as maize meal, bread, sugar, rice and cooking oil disappeared.

Zimbabweans blamed the war in the DRC for all their economic woes. When news of DRC strongman Laurent Kabila's assassination – initially denied while his body was secretly spirited out of the DRC capital Kinshasa to Harare – finally hit the streets of the Zimbabwean capital, public reaction was predictable.

True to its motto, the *Daily News* told the story like it was. On 23 January, political editor Tarcey Munaku put together a story quoting ordinary residents who were openly celebrating the demise of their president's erstwhile ally.

Before the day was over, more than 500 war veterans and Zanu-PF supporters marched down Samora Machel Avenue from the party's headquarters. Led by Chenjerai 'Hitler' Hunzvi, they demonstrated in front of Trustee House.

The *Daily News* staff peeped nervously from behind heavy curtains as the youthful and zestful 'war veterans' sang, danced and chanted slogans in denunciation of the newspaper. The protesters broke windows and – more ominously – made a huge bonfire of copies of the *Daily News*. They recognised reporter Julius Zava on the street, forced him to the ground and assaulted him. Zava freed himself and fled. He died a few months later.

Minister of youth Border Gezi, widely accused of orchestrating violence in Mashonaland and elsewhere, brazenly shouted in parliament, '*Vana Tarcey, mava kuda kufa manje!*', Shona for, 'Tarcey, now you seek to die.'

The notorious Border Gezi National Youth Training Centre, where Zanu-PF's dreaded youth militias, the Green Bombers, were trained, was named after this determined purveyor of violence. He died in a horrific road accident less than four months after shouting this profanity at Munaku. Munaku died of natural causes in 2004.

Around 1.30 a.m. on Sunday 28 January, the nocturnal peace of Harare's western suburbs was shattered by a massive explosion. Armed saboteurs had overpowered security guards at the factory housing the *Daily News* printing press and, under cover of darkness, attached powerful limpet mines along the length of the Goss Urbanite press.

Ballistic experts said the explosives were of a type that could be found only in the

Zimbabwe National Army's stores. When the incendiary devices exploded, the heavy printing press and the entire roof of the huge building flew into the air before crashing down in a smoking pile of scrap metal and twisted roofing material.

Two days after Moyo's TV appearance, the *Daily News* had indeed been silenced, but not for long.

To the total astonishment of anxious readers and the obvious chagrin of those behind the attack, the newspaper was back on the streets, a little late but none the worse for wear, the very next day. A number of commercial printers had rushed to our rescue.

The defiant and somewhat illogical front-page banner headline was: '*Daily News* press destroyed'.

One factory guard had managed to record the registration number of the vehicle in which the bombers had sped into the dark night. I took the details to the Central Vehicle Registry to try to identify the car's owner. After listening to my report, the officers on duty slowly punched the details into a computer. Up popped not only the name of the person in whose name the vehicle was registered, but, presumably, details such as a residential address.

The officers stared at the computer screen, then at each other, without uttering a word. Then, like programmed robots, they both turned to me. 'We cannot help you on this case,' one of them announced with what sounded like finality. The case effectively died on that sombre note.

The bombers left something else at the scene of the explosion – a handwritten note. Identifying themselves as the Authentic MDC, they claimed responsibility for the destruction, and accused the *Daily News* of siding with the 'racist white minority' in the opposition MDC. The Authentic MDC had never been heard of before and, like the Revival of African Conscience before it, was never heard of again.

Retaliation was swift. Angry youths attacked vendors selling the *Herald* in the politically volatile town of Chitungwiza and threatened to attack anyone who brought copies of the government mouthpiece into the area. People believed to be MDC supporters assaulted a *Herald* truck driver and made a bonfire of 4 000 copies of the newspaper. Copies of the *Herald* were also destroyed in Harare and Karoi, a Zanu-PF stronghold 150 kilometres north of the capital.

Police failure to investigate the explosion fuelled growing suspicion that government agents had been behind this dastardly attack. Luckson Chipare, the regional director of the Media Institute of Southern Africa, wrote to Mugabe in protest, copying the letter to Moyo and home affairs minister John Nkomo.

'MISA takes a very dim view of the reported threats against the *Daily News* by your minister of information and publicity, Professor Jonathan Moyo, and Dr Chenjerai 'Hitler' Hunzvi, the leader of a faction of war veterans and a member of parliament. The minister and the MP must be held accountable for their threats as they have now materialised,' he said. Chipare also deplored the confiscation of newspapers by political activists, pointing out that 'these cowardly acts violate the right to freedom of expression and opinion'. Typically, Mugabe ignored MISA's protests, as well as those of other international organisations.

On Saturday 14 April, *Daily News* reporter Sandra Nyaira travelled to Mount Darwin, about 200 kilometres north of Harare, to attend a social function hosted by Saviour Kasukuwere, an MP and rising star in Harare's increasingly shady business world. Widely regarded as one of the most successful beneficiaries of Zanu-PF largesse, Kasukuwere, a former CIO operative, owed his wealth to Mugabe's patronage.

Since 2000, the president had strengthened his position through the strategic disbursement of the many resources of patronage at his disposal – farms, jobs, contracts, foreign diplomatic postings, scholarships, computers for village schools (some of which had no electricity) and food handouts to hungry villagers, so long as their Zanu-PF membership cards were visibly displayed. If a politician strayed from the party line or generally fell out of favour, Mugabe would strike immediately; repossessing a farm or farms, cancelling a lucrative government contract or recalling a diplomat. Fear of loss of material wealth kept politicians and government officials under tight control, and their political ambitions remained inaudacious.

Among the guests at Kasukuwere's party was Jonathan Moyo, who confronted Nyaira with a warning that individual journalists were to be targeted for unspecified action.

'You ain't seen nothing yet,' the American-trained academic told Nyaira in obvious reference to the campaign of arrest and harassment that the government had unleashed on independent journalists.

Ironically, Moyo himself would taste Mugabe's viciousness when he fell out with Zanu-PF in 2004, but, back then, we shrugged off his threat as an occupational hazard.

It wasn't long, however, before Moyo made good on his warning. Sandra Nyaira, Julius Zava and I were charged with criminal defamation of Mugabe. The charge arose from our five-month-old story about alleged bribery in the awarding of tenders for the new Harare airport. A month after our arrests, the police said the docket had been sent to the attorney-general. We never heard another word about the case, and nothing came of my five other arrests, sometimes along with members of my staff, while I was editor of the *Daily News*.

On 9 May, I was again arrested and charged with criminal defamation under the Law and Order (Maintenance) Act. We had reported that the MP for Mutasa, the MDC's Evelyn Masaiti, and three relatives of victims of the June 2000 election violence had sued Mugabe in the United States.

I was taken to Harare Central moments after the arrival of a five-person delegation from the US-based World Press Freedom Committee. The executive director, Marilyn J Greene of the US, European representative Ronald Koven of France, David Dadge of the International Press Institute in Austria, and South Africans Joe Mdhlela of the Media Workers' Association and Raymond Louw, editor of *Southern Africa Report*, were in Zimbabwe on an official mission.

They had held a meeting with Moyo in his office that morning, and, on hearing about my arrest, had rushed to Harare Central. They followed me into the charge office, but were asked to leave. The police insisted the visitors had no legitimate business there.

While the Zimbabwe government denied the fact, the US-based lawyers who had filed the Z$20-billion lawsuit confirmed that Masaiti, Elliot Pfebve, Maria Stevens and Adella Chiminya had indeed sued Mugabe, as reported.

Chiminya's husband Tichaona, who was the MDC leader's campaign manager, had died in a petrol bomb attack on his vehicle that also killed MDC activist Talent Mabika. Pfebve's brother Matthew was murdered in Bindura just before the election, while Stevens's husband David, a commercial farmer, was shot dead by war veterans at Murehwa. Masaiti sued Mugabe for what she described as his failure to run the country in a democratic manner. US judge Victor Marrero had passed a default judgment in the civil suit in New York's Manhattan District Court, with Stevens, Pfebve and Chiminya in attendance.

On World Press Freedom Day, 3 May, Mugabe's name was on a list of ten world leaders accused by the New York–based Committee to Protect Journalists (CPJ) of gross abuse against the media. At the top of the list were Iran's Ayatollah Ali Khamenei, President Jiang Zemin of China and Liberia's President Charles Taylor. Referring to Zimbabwe, the CPJ said: 'Robert Mugabe's government has launched an all-out war against independent media, using weapons that range from lawsuits to physical violence.' In September, the *Daily News* serialised *Animal Farm*, George Orwell's classic fable about encroaching tyranny. The symbolic message of the book, which for a long time had been a prescribed English literature text in Zimbabwe's high schools, was lost on no one. For months the newspaper's letter columns were flooded with correspondence about the uncanny resemblance between the political contradictions of Zimbabwe and the political absurdity depicted by Orwell.

To drive the point home, *Daily News* cartoonist Watson Mukutirwa crafted a caricature of the farm's autocratic pig, Napoleon, sporting spectacles that looked remarkably like those worn by Mugabe. The cartoon accompanied each instalment for the two months of the serialisation.

In retaliation, the government stepped up the tempo of harassment.

On 8 November, fifteen months after Wilf Mbanga had left ANZ, he and I were charged with fraud. Mbanga came from a family of policemen. His father was a detective sub-inspector with the British South Africa Police, while two of his brothers were senior officers in the Zimbabwe Republic Police. This was the first time he had been arrested.

A radio station in Botswana had called the night before to arrange an early morning interview, so I had set my alarm clock for 6 a.m. But it was not the shrill ring of the alarm that aroused me, it was the loud clanging of the metal security gate on our veranda. It was the police, again. Ursula cunningly delayed our departure by pleading with the officers that I be allowed to have my breakfast, since I was a diabetic and had to take my medication first thing in the morning, with a full meal. Meanwhile, I phoned

Masunda to advise him of my arrest and Mbanga to warn him that he would be next. When the police arrived, he was waiting.

Because my landline phone was bugged, I had asked the radio station in Gaborone to call me on my cellphone. The call came through just as the police were locking me in the back of their Brazilian-built Santana truck. So it was that the foreign radio station's bemused early morning listeners, including a growing number of Zimbabwean economic and political refugees living in Botswana, were the first to learn of my latest ordeal. By the time the police got wind of what was happening in the back of the truck, the interview was over.

Our trials and tribulations at the *Daily News* were not without moments of humour. Mbanga and I were interrogated at CID headquarters and formally charged, but for most of the day, the police left us to our own devices in a side room. Astonishingly, our cellphones were not confiscated, so Mbanga and I had a field day communicating with family, relatives, friends and the press, both local and international – until our phone batteries went flat. We could have saved them by switching off the phones, but that would have defeated the purpose of carrying a mobile phone in the first place, especially on such a day.

We spent the night in a vermin-infested and foul-smelling cell at Rhodesville police station. It did not quite match the appalling conditions in Cell Number 4 at Rusape, but the paradox of incarceration on spurious grounds by our former colonisers, and now by our erstwhile liberators, was too vivid to pass unnoticed. Mbanga and I had the honour of being showered with praise and respect from an unlikely quarter. Once they realised who we were, the dozen or so common assault, shoplifting, robbery and drug-dealing suspects in whose cheerful company we passed the night sacrificed their own meagre bedding so that we would be more comfortable on the cement floor.

Reading the graffiti on the walls, I noticed that bank executive Nigel Chanakira had once spent time in the same cell. He had bequeathed to future occupants an unprintable message high up on one wall. I wondered how he had reached the top of the wall, but concluded that angry men have a way of doing things. Chanakira was no doubt angry that he had been targeted on suspicion of association with the political opposition. Eventually he was forced to leave Zimbabwe altogether and set up home in Cape Town, becoming one of dozens of banking executives who had fled from Gideon Gono's purge after the former Jewel Bank chief executive and official keeper of the First Family's purse was appointed governor of the Reserve Bank.

After an early breakfast inside the wire enclosure in front of the cells under the watchful eye of Ursula and Mbanga's wife, Trish, we were transported to the High Court, formally charged and granted bail.

The charges centred on accusations that we had supplied 'false information to a lawful authority' when we registered ANZ. The truth, as the *Daily News* reported that morning, was entirely different.

The state alleged that sometime in July 1998, purporting to be the two subscribing shareholders of Motley Investments, Mbanga and I had sought to register ANZ with the Zimbabwe Investment Centre (ZIC), saying we had formed a partnership with a British-owned company, Africa Media Investments (Zimbabwe).

The correct name of the company we owned was Motley Trading, but a typist at PricewaterhouseCoopers, the firm of chartered accountants and management consultants that had handled the paperwork on our behalf, had erred in documents submitted to the ZIC.

Our advocate, Eric Matinenga, furnished the court with a letter in which Price-waterhouseCoopers accepted blame for the clerical error and deplored as 'deserving of censure' the circumstances in which we had been arrested without warrants at dawn, interrogated for hours and detained overnight.

'Someone here does not know the basics of company law,' Matinenga argued. 'For a police officer of average intelligence to fail to see that there was no offence in that is inexcusable. There is nothing on the facts that points to the accused persons having committed an offence. This ... is an abuse of process, meant to harass the two and it was done in bad faith.'

The charges were dismissed. Chibwe, efficient as always, said the order for our arrest had come from 'very senior police authorities and political heavyweights'.

The CPJ issued a hard-hitting statement condemning the arrests. 'This is only the latest instance of what CPJ believes is an orchestrated campaign against the independent paper, which began early this year with the bombing of its printing presses and has gained intensity as next year's presidential elections approach,' said the international organisation.

The way our arrest was covered by the various media underlined the extent of polarisation between the privately owned press and the government-controlled media, particularly the *Daily News* and its archrival, the *Herald*.

ZIC had accused ANZ of violating investment laws and exchange control regulations following claims by Diamond Insurance – a minority shareholder in ANZ and an associate of Africa Resources Limited, owned by emergent business mogul Mutumwa Mawere – that it had unearthed possible fraudulent misrepresentation in the publishing company's registration. Mawere was closely linked to Zanu-PF, especially Emmerson Mnangagwa, and had built an extensive business empire virtually overnight. Apart from the insurance company, his interests included Shabanie and Mashava Mine, Turnall Holdings, First Banking Corporation, smaller mining concerns and large commercial farms.

The *Herald* had a field day, relying solely on information fed to its reporters by Mawere and on a letter from ZIC to ANZ, advising erroneously that, due to irregularities, ANZ's investment licence was being cancelled.

Comment from ANZ was conspicuously absent in the *Herald* article. It was only when the *Daily News* published a strong rebuttal by Masunda that the public was given the other side of the story.

Under the front-page headline, 'Daily News in trouble' and the sub-headlines 'Investment certificate cancelled' and 'Criminal violations cited', the Herald's report was clearly calculated to deliver a lethal blow. 'This means that the basis on which the company was established has been removed and the company should cease to exist,' the paper opined optimistically, going on to claim that we had failed to comply with investment laws and exchange control regulations, and citing the non-existent Motley Investments as the reason behind the cancellation.

'We have now established that in truth and fact, no such company was registered with the Registrar of Companies. Accordingly, had the centre been aware that Motley Investments was not a registered company, the certificate would not have been issued,' our rivals crowed.

On 7 November, under the headline 'Herald lies again' on the front page of the Daily News, Masunda countered the lies and gross misrepresentations. He pointed out that ZIC had not cancelled ANZ's certificate, but that the certificate itself – valid for two years – had in fact expired.

'If ZIC now wishes to cancel an expired certificate it is their prerogative,' Masunda, a master of caustic sarcasm, pointed out.

'In any event, the High Court has given a ruling on this issue in favour of ANZ. It is most extraordinary for an acting director of the ZIC to seek to reverse a High Court decision. He needs to be careful that he is not held in contempt of court.'

In the same article, Masunda accused Mawere of being at the forefront of a campaign to discredit the Daily News.

'Never before in the history of corporate affairs has so much energy been expended by one minority shareholder to cause the downfall of a company in which it is an investor,' he pointed out sardonically.

Notwithstanding Masunda's lucid logic, the Herald ignored the information provided and continued its campaign against ANZ. They refused to allow the facts to stand in the way of their salacious story.

'The investment laws were clearly violated and we are not protected as a country,' the Herald quoted Mawere as having stated.

The Independent published the following observation by Masunda: 'It has really got to a point where the aggrieved parties will have no option but to take action against police officers in their individual capacities, because there is no way in which it can be argued they were acting in their official capacity or public interest.'

This phase of the campaign against the Daily News took place at a time when our journalists were routinely denied access to government sources, forcing us periodically to publish important stories without official comment, only to be chastised by the minister of information for doing so. To add insult to injury, Mugabe, Mnangagwa and Moyo routinely filed specious but tedious defamation suits against independent newspapers.

Ironically, the most prolific sources of news reports in the Daily News were found among those who walked the corridors of power daily.

In April 2002, Moyo threatened me with arrest unless I retracted a story that criticised the manner in which the recent presidential election had been handled, while calling for a fresh poll.

Moyo described as patently false our report on a meeting at which parliamentarians from the African, Caribbean and Pacific (ACP) countries, as well as the European Union, had adopted a resolution calling for a rerun of the election under international supervision.

Unless the story was retracted, Moyo told me in writing, I would face prosecution under the newly passed Access to Information and Protection of Privacy Act (AIPPA), which prohibited the publication of false news. Conviction under this law invited a two-year prison sentence.

'I would rather go to jail, if it pleases the honourable minister,' I responded in a statement published in the *Daily News*, 'than be forced by him to publicly correct a story that is 100 per cent correct.'

The resolution, adopted at a meeting in Cape Town, had been widely reported internationally. However, the *Herald*, no doubt acting on instructions from the ministry, as had become common practice, claimed the ACP countries strongly supported Mugabe's re-election as a legitimate expression of voter opinion.

The forum of parliamentarians later confirmed that the *Daily News* report was, in fact, accurate. Moyo neither withdrew his threat nor apologised, but by that point his credibility had been utterly shredded in any event.

Mugabe had signed the controversial and draconian AIPPA into law just four days after being sworn in for yet another term of office. It had been passed by parliament in January after a tempestuous passage and opposition even from Zanu-PF backbenchers, but the president had held off on signing the bill due to enormous pressure from the international community.

AIPPA required all local journalists to apply for accreditation annually through a government-appointed Media and Information Commission (MIC). Newspaper publishing companies, radio stations, news agencies and even NGOs were required to register with the commission in order to operate, and restrictions were placed on media access to government information.

Two weeks later, on 16 April, I was arrested and charged with fabricating a story about Mugabe's election victory being due to vote rigging. The *Daily News* had accused the registrar general, Tobaiwa Mudede, of manipulating the results. He denied doing so, despite issuing an amended ballot count that cut Mugabe's majority by 4 000. The figure was not significant enough to alter the outcome of the election, but it did confirm that the original result had been tampered with.

Diligent as always, our attorney Lawrence Chibwe outperformed himself on this occasion. I was arrested, charged and released in record time – three hours. Police did not indicate when I would be brought to court and I never heard from them again on a matter that carried a potential two-year jail term.

The *Daily News* staffer who endured the most harrowing experience was Urginia Mauluka. She had followed in the footsteps of her illustrious grandfather, John Mauluka, chief photographer and founding father of our photographic department. He taught Urginia to shoot and process pictures from early childhood, so that by the time she turned twenty, she was a chip off the proverbial old block and a valued member of our staff.

A relative informed Urginia about the very first invasion of a white-owned farm by peasants, supported by war veterans. Smelling a scoop, she informed news editor William Bango, who assigned the young mother of one and reporter Collin Chiwanza to visit the farm in the Wedza district. Mduduzi Mathuthu, a cadet reporter in our Bulawayo bureau who was in Harare for training, accompanied them. Trust Mpofu drove the *Daily News* vehicle.

On arrival, they found the farm deserted, except for two men who were packing some goods and loading them onto a bicycle. They were reluctant to talk to the journalists.

The farm compound had been reduced to piles of ash and rubble.

'There was total destruction and I shot many pictures,' Mauluka said. 'We noticed there were a number of soldiers around. We approached one of them. He was somehow cooperative. He came across as one who did not support the destruction of the farm compound.'

A ZBC crew had also arrived and started filming the scene of destruction. A police Land Rover drove up shortly afterwards, disgorging several-plain clothes policemen. Another police vehicle, a truck, had stopped at the gate.

Feeling uneasy and sensing growing tension, the *Daily News* crew decided to leave. They piled into their vehicle, and as Mpofu engaged gear, the police truck started moving towards them from the gate. It stopped in front of their vehicle, blocking the narrow road.

'While the lorry was marked as a police vehicle,' Mauluka said, 'the occupants were quite clearly not policemen. They were obviously war veterans. A man who said he was the leader of the group introduced himself as Comrade Chigwedere. They confronted us and asked what our business on the farm was.

'One of the war veterans approached me. Without a word, he slapped me hard on the cheek. Then he slapped me again. It was very painful, and that side of my face felt numb. He said he knew we were journalists from the *Daily News*. Chigwedere said we were misguided to side with the white capitalists and colonialists who had stolen land from out forefathers. It sounded weird that anyone should suggest I was on the side of the whites.'

The war veterans, all twenty of them, then set upon the *Daily News* team, assaulting them viciously and making wild accusations. Then they separated the group and began interrogating them individually. Mauluka was grilled by a group of six men. 'I realised that one of them was, in fact, Superintendent Wayne Bvudzijena,' she said. Bvudzijena was the official police spokesman.

'As I was being questioned, I heard Mduduzi cry. They were beating him with a bicycle chain.'

One of her assailants had flipped through the pages of a copy of the *Daily News* that was in the car. A story in the paper appeared to have upset him terribly, and he started to beat Mauluka again.

'I felt as if my head was exploding,' she said. 'I had Z$2 000 in cash on me in the new Z$500 bank notes that had been introduced only that morning. The man removed the money from my bag, saying: "This is money for our drinks." I never saw that money again.'

She saw another group assaulting Mpofu, the driver, kicking and stomping on him as he lay sprawled on the ground.

'The soldier whom we'd met on arrival suddenly arrived on the scene,' Mauluka said. 'He ordered the war veterans to stop assaulting us and cocked his gun to make his point. The assaults stopped. Chiwanza took advantage of this lull and fled in the direction of the main gate before disappearing into the bush.'

He sought refuge on a neighbouring farm. The soldier ordered the rest of the *Daily News* crew back into their car. As they departed, a *Herald* team arrived.

'The reporter, Rex Mphisa, spoke to us,' Mauluka continued. 'He seemed to sympathise, but he proceeded to write a scandalous story that appeared in the *Herald* the following morning. For me, reading that story was a more painful experience than the assault I had endured on the farm.

'As I lay on my bed at home, recovering from the savage assault, I vowed that I would not be intimidated; that I would continue to take as many pictures as possible to expose the injustices meted out by the government on innocent people like me.'

Mauluka's determination and resilience were to prove short-lived, however.

The MDC had made elaborate plans to commemorate Soweto Youth Day, the anniversary of the 1976 student uprising in the sprawling township south of Johannesburg. The uprising was a milestone in the long-drawn and bitter struggle of the majority black population of South Africa to dismantle the apartheid rule of the Afrikaner-dominated National Party.

The commemoration in Harare was scheduled to take place in Africa Unity Square on 16 June, but in one of post-independence Zimbabwe's ideological ironies, the police had cordoned off the square to prevent any such activity.

Undeterred, MDC supporters marched west to a venue on Mbuya Nehanda Street, where food was being prepared for them. Mauluka and reporter Guthrie Munyuki were driven to Mbuya Nehanda by Shadreck Mukwecheni.

'Suddenly, the riot police confronted us,' Mauluka said, narrating the ordeal of the *Daily News* crew. 'They were beating people up savagely. People were crying and screaming. Some people were attacked as they lay on the ground. I saw the police removing pots of food and loading them onto their vehicles. As we approached the scene, they signalled us to stop.

'Mukwecheni attempted to execute a quick U-turn. A policeman cocked his rifle and we stopped. A police lorry had come up behind us and blocked any escape. Suddenly, we were surrounded. Then the party started. As we emerged from the vehicle, I was the first to be attacked. I saw Mukwecheni fall to the ground. They kicked and trampled upon him. They knew we were from the *Daily News*, although they did not ask us to identify ourselves.

'They were beating everybody up. There was much violence. A woman ran away, leaving her baby behind. The baby cried and cried and nobody cared. A pregnant woman who happened to be walking past was assaulted. They beat her up as she pleaded for mercy. One young woman was menstruating. She told the police about her condition as they beat her up. They beat her up for telling them and she cried out in pain. It was so sorrowful that for a moment I forgot about my own ordeal.'

Mauluka had then been singled out by a policeman who accused her of taking his picture, which of course she had not.

'By this time, pain had given me strength and courage. I told the policeman off, denying that I had taken his picture. He beat me up and, snatching my bag, he pulled out my digital camera. He removed the memory chip and broke it. He beat me with a baton stick. He removed a heavy camera lens from the bag and hurled it at me, catching me on my arm.'

Among the victims of this savage attack was Munyaradzi Gwisai, the member of parliament for Highfields. A radical and controversial opposition politician, Gwisai was a member of the International Socialist Organisation, and said he had joined the MDC because it was formed out of the struggles of Zimbabwe's workers. He was unpopular with Zanu-PF because he preached socialism at a time when Mugabe and his geriatric cohorts had abandoned their Marxist-Leninist pretensions in favour of capitalism. In due course, his radical stance saw him also fall foul of the MDC, whose membership included dyed-in-the-wool capitalists, white farmers and industrialists.

Gwisai had become openly critical of what he said were the wrong strategies and tactics employed by MDC leaders to confront the Mugabe regime. He argued that the MDC was dancing to the tune of the employers and had become too close to the West, to the governments of Great Britain and the United States, and to the International Monetary Fund and World Bank. These were the very same people who had worked with Mugabe to introduce the Economic Structural Adjustment Programme in 1990, which, he argued, had undermined the welfare of workers. Even the MDC found Gwisai ideologically too hot to handle and expelled him in 2002.

On the day of the commemoration, Gwisai was singled out for particularly vicious punishment by the police.

Daily News reporter Guthrie Munyuki was a hefty fellow, by far our biggest member of staff. The police set on him with a vengeance. They accused him of growing fat on money received from Zimbabwe's enemies. They said he was a sell-out and beat him up for it.

Meanwhile, a continued search of Mauluka's handbag yielded a priceless jewel – the business card of Sophie Honey, the British High Commission's press officer.

'Armed with this indisputable evidence of my role as a sell-out, they set on me again,' she said.

The fact that Honey's business card rubbed shoulders with the cards of a government minister and a Zanu-PF official in Urginia's handbag did nothing by way of mitigation in her favour.

She and Mukwecheni were ordered into the *Daily News* vehicle. A police officer took the wheel, while another two officers sat in the back with Urginia wedged between them as the vehicle set off in the direction of Harare Central. Guthrie travelled on the open back of a police Puma truck.

'Along the way a minibus nearly collided with our vehicle after the driver cut in front of us,' Urginia said. 'Slamming the brakes on, our driver jumped out and hauled the hapless minibus driver out of his seat by the collar and beat him up in full view of his passengers and bemused onlookers. He then ordered him to follow us to the police station in his vehicle.'

The driver and his passengers spent the night in the stinking cells of Harare Central, together with MDC supporters, the *Daily News* staff and a host of other people who had no idea whatsoever why they had been arrested. There was a total breakdown in law and order in Zimbabwe by this time. Far from protecting law-abiding citizens, the police had themselves become agents for the abuse and humiliation of innocent people.

The group of seventy arrested that day included one solitary white figure, Tony Spicer, a freelance journalist for some of the British papers. I was not amused when a journalist phoned me from London that night to ask exclusively about Tony's welfare. I felt obliged to remind him that three *Daily News* staffers, apart from dozens of MDC supporters, were also behind bars.

Because Urginia was badly hurt and swollen, I was furious that the British press appeared interested only in the welfare of the white correspondent. If Mugabe had eavesdropped on my phone conversations that night, he would have felt somewhat vindicated in unleashing a racist, anti-white campaign.

'There was a man who was very badly injured,' Mauluka said afterwards. 'The women joined forces and cried, pleading with the police to release him or at least take him to hospital. He was in a terribly bad condition, groaning all the time and breathing heavily. Eventually they removed him. I never found out what became of him. Gwisai was also in a bad way.'

Whether through divine providence or routine carelessness, the police did not search their prisoners. Munyuki had his cellphone in his pocket when they locked him up and had sufficient presence of mind to switch it off. Later that night, he contacted the *Daily News* newsroom, and from deep inside Harare Central Police Station he dictated to reporter Lloyd Mudiwa the details of the ordeal, which were splashed on the front page of the morning newspaper, much to the dismay of police headquarters.

The cellphone was snatched away at the earliest opportunity. After almost forty-eight hours in holding cells, the prisoners were eventually taken to court and charged under the notorious Public Order and Security Act (POSA), which was every bit as wide-ranging and draconian as Ian Smith's Law and Order (Maintenance) Act. They were all released, and at their next court appearance two days later, the magistrate dismissed all charges. He said the case was a total waste of time, money and resources.

A short while later, Urginia came to see me. She was leaving for London, she said. I was sad to lose such a young and talented photographer, but I was glad she was escaping from the insanity that had engulfed our country.

My greatest frustration as editor in chief of the *Daily News* was my total inability to offer any form of protection to staff covering dangerous assignments on a routine basis, at a time when ruling party and government agents targeted them for violent retribution. Bidding farewell to Mauluka was painful, but I was relieved that she and her child would be out of harm's way. When we met in South Kensington, London, in June 2005, there was little in her cheerful demeanour to suggest she had endured a soul-searing experience in her own country.

Mauluka had become one of the millions of talented young Zimbabwean professionals eking out an existence in far-flung corners of the diaspora, while a candidate long overdue for admission to an old-age home presided over the disintegration of their once prosperous homeland.

From the outset, it was obvious that while AIPPA was couched in general terms to suppress Zimbabwe's vibrant privately owned press, its specific target was the *Daily News*. The paper had grown into the largest selling daily in little over one year of existence. It posed an ominous political threat to a ruling party and government whose popularity and entrenched position were clearly on the decline. ANZ, in turn, challenged the commercial viability of the government's newspaper publishing conglomerate. Zimbabwe Newspapers had failed to rise to the challenge or devise an efficient strategy to counter the growing success of the newcomer.

Under the new media legislation, masterminded with singular determination by Moyo, no company could run a newspaper, radio or television station unless registered by the MIC, whose members were hand-picked by the minister. Journalists were not allowed to practise unless accredited by the same commission, which was chaired by Dr Tafataona Mahoso, an eccentric academic and zealous Zanu-PF apologist. He had previously headed the Harare Polytechnic's mass communications division. Zimbabwe's media industry generally credits Mahoso with the rapid post-independence decline in the standard of professional journalism in the country.

Determined to lead by example, he regularly penned lengthy diatribes against the privately owned press and Western nations. The *Sunday Mail* obliged by publishing the articles, usually without editing them. Not many readers possessed either the stamina or the determination to digest Mahoso's eloquent epics from beginning to end. It was perhaps no coincidence that the circulation of the paper nose-dived while Mahoso waxed lyrical on topics that were of little interest, even to fellow academics.

One of the more ominous provisions of AIPPA was that publication of a falsehood, no matter how unintentional, became a criminal offence. Senior *Daily News* reporter Lloyd Mudiwa and I acquired the dubious distinction of becoming the first Zimbabwean journalists prosecuted under AIPPA for publishing an alleged falsehood. A visit on 22 April 2002 to the MDC's headquarters in Harvest House by a bereaved villager from Magunje, 200 kilometres north of Harare, heralded this dark episode in my career.

Enos Tadyanemhandu and his wife, Brandina, had first visited the *Daily News* in December 2000, during a period of escalating political violence. They told our reporters that their twenty-year-old son, Tichaona, an MDC youth activist, had gone missing in the politically volatile Magunje area of the remote Hurungwe district. His body had been found six months later in the mortuary at Harare Central Hospital.

The MDC and ZimRights, a human rights organisation, each gave the couple Z$15 000 to help them bury Tichaona. Throughout 2000, newspapers carried regular reports of the violent political bloodletting that had been triggered by the referendum in February, continued to rage during the run-up to the June elections and spiralled thereafter.

The two political parties fuelled the political polarisation of the media. Zanu-PF supporters expected and usually obtained sympathetic coverage from the *Herald*, complete with comment on the latest act of violence and condemnation of the MDC by the police.

MDC supporters, on the other hand, were generally assured of a sympathetic ear from the *Daily News*, not least because our reporters were themselves victims of constant violence perpetrated by Zanu-PF militants and agents of the state.

In the run-up to the parliamentary elections in 2000, one Zanu-PF decision in particular exacerbated media polarisation and endorsed the perception that the *Daily News* was partisan towards the MDC. The party's information department imposed a ban on any Zanu-PF election advertising being placed in independent newspapers. At the same time, the *Herald* and ZBC were instructed not to carry MDC adverts.

The opposition was left with no option but to divert the bulk of the party's advertisements to the *Daily News*, the only daily newspaper that would accept them. As a result, the paper was soon replete with full-page MDC adverts. In the eyes of those who lacked the capacity, and sometimes the will, to make the important distinction between editorial content and paid advertising space, no further evidence was required to confirm that the *Daily News* was truly an MDC mouthpiece.

If our news coverage seemed to favour the MDC, it was for similar reasons. Government-owned papers churned out Zanu-PF propaganda, leaving the independent media – of which we were the only daily – to record what was really happening.

One of the biggest obstacles to fair reporting was that our journalists received no cooperation at all from the police, who simply ignored their enquiries. Official spokesman Wayne Bvudzijena had declared virtual war on the independent press, and on the *Daily News* in particular. He spurned my efforts to cultivate a professional working relationship between the country's largest newspaper and the ZRP. He normally refused point blank to respond to any of the paper's enquiries. The ministry of information, and Moyo in particular, repeatedly castigated the paper for resorting to the unethical practice of publishing one-sided reports.

We were caught between the proverbial rock and a hard place. Unable to obtain the necessary confirmation from the police and other official sources, we had proceeded, towards the end of 2000, to publish details of the six-month-old search for Tichaona Tadyanemhandu. Since the deceased MDC activist's sobbing parents were the source of the information about his grisly murder, the paper appeared to be on solid ground. If new evidence subsequently emerged that contradicted the story, we could resort to the time-honoured remedy of publishing a retraction and tendering appropriate apologies to all concerned. The ethics of professional journalism clearly anticipate the commission of error no matter how diligently editorial staff try to avoid them.

In the aftermath of the parliamentary elections in June, many Zimbabweans had expected the security situation to revert to normal, leaving them once more to enjoy the peace that had been ruptured by Zanu-PF's various and vicious perpetrators of violence. Ordinary citizens prayed that the six months of intra-party intimidation and violence, the bloody farm invasions, and the attendant hostile and racist rhetoric of the election campaign would be consigned to the annals of the country's political history, ushering in a new era of peace, rule of law and national development. From the second half of 2000, those hopes had been largely shattered, and sixteen months after first turning to the *Daily News* on the subject of his son's murder, an ashen-faced, visibly distraught middle-aged man from Magunje sat across the desk from reporter Lloyd Mudiwa.

Between gut-wrenching sobs, Tadyanemhandu related a bizarre and gruesome tale of wanton political violence and personal bereavement. Zanu-PF militants had visited his homestead in the aftermath of the presidential election. Not only had they assaulted his wife Brandina, aged fifty-three, but in an orgy of bloodletting they had ruthlessly decapitated her in the presence of the couple's two teenage daughters.

Generally speaking, when a man tells you that his wife has been murdered, especially in such a macabre manner, you don't ask him to wait while you check with the police if he is telling the truth. Nevertheless, Mudiwa telephoned both Bvudzijena's office and the police at Magunje. Such calls remained part of the reporter's routine, if only to cover themselves and the newspaper by stating in their stories that the police had refused to comment. All that Mudiwa's calls evoked was the stock response: the police were not allowed to speak to the press.

Sending Mudiwa to Magunje to seek independent corroboration of Tadyanem-handu's story would have been foolhardy in the prevailing climate, since he could not rely on the protection of the highly politicised rural police. Because *Daily News* journalists were routinely and publicly denounced as being enemies of the state, I had admonished them not to take unnecessary risks in their quest for news in violence-prone districts.

Many of the rural policemen, some of them former Zanla fighters, professed unswerving support for Zanu-PF, and for Mugabe personally. They were openly hostile to journalists from the privately owned press.

Having exhausted all possible avenues of official confirmation, Mudiwa thus sat down to write the front-page lead for the next issue. The source of the story, the dead woman's husband, appeared solid enough. In any case, at the time, stories of murder and mayhem were disseminated regularly by the *Herald*, the *Daily News*, radio and television without police confirmation.

Over its brief lifespan, the *Daily News* was blessed with much success and glory, but its moment of excruciating shame was on the morning of Tuesday 23 April 2002. Mudiwa's story appeared under the heading, 'Young girls see their mother's head cut off', and read in part:

> Two young girls, aged ten and 17, watched in horror as their mother was murdered brutally by having her head chopped off at the neck. Brandina Tadyanemhandu, 53, was butchered inside her hut in Magunje on Sunday by about 20 youths, who were suspected to be Zanu-PF supporters.
>
> The reason for the grisly murder was the accusation by the youths that the deceased woman was a supporter of the opposition Movement for Democratic Change (MDC). Tadyanemhandu will be buried today at Magororo village in Magunje, Hurungwe East. She was the mother of MDC youth activist Tichaona Tadyanemhandu, 20, who went missing in Hurungwe in June 2000. His body was found six months later in the mortuary at Harare Central Hospital. Brandina Tadyanemhandu's attackers, who were allegedly led by a war veteran known as Comrade Chifamba, also burnt the family's main house, destroying property worth thousands of dollars.
>
> 'When I saw my wife's remains, the head and the body were cleanly separated,' Tadyanemhandu said. 'I had to push them back together.'
>
> He said when he reported the murder to the police at Magunje, they had asked him to apprehend and bring the suspects to the police station.

I had been duty editor the previous night and had personally touched up the article. When the story hit the streets, the full might of the government machinery – the media, the ministry of information and the police – descended on the *Daily News* like the proverbial ton of bricks. The reaction was as swift and vicious as that of a giant spider that spins its web and sits patiently at the centre for days, waiting for the first insect to stray into the snare.

Daily News readers were still digesting the macabre details of the Magunje murder when the *Herald* dropped a bombshell. Our story was a pack of lies, the paper declared unequivocally. I wondered how the *Herald* could speak with such authority on the basis of a police denial.

The government's flagship had a field day. In fact, the *Herald* reported, distressed by the unfolding disaster, I had absconded from the *Daily News*. Of course this was absolute nonsense, calculated to embarrass me and undermine my credibility.

Fortunately, I had a fail-safe alibi for the day on which I was alleged to have fled the *Daily News*.

'I was in the office on Friday and we can produce a number of cheques that I signed on the day,' I responded in a statement in the *Daily News*. 'I also attended the Tanzanian National Day celebrations at the residence of the high commissioner, Mr Alexander Muganda. He can testify to this. So can Dr Ibbo Mandaza, the publisher of the *Mirror*, Mr Elias Rusike, the publisher of the *Financial Gazette*, and the ambassadors of the Netherlands, Norway, India, Libya, Iran and Israel, among other people with whom I had a chat.'

But my foolproof defence merely fuelled the anger of the *Herald* editors. Not about to let me slip through their fingers, they intensified their campaign of malicious personal attack. Each of the many international journalism awards presented to me over the years had been won on the basis of false articles, the paper's dumbfounded readers were informed. Fortunately, the *Herald*'s reputation as a credible source of information had long since plummeted inexorably. Notwithstanding this, I briefed our lawyers to initiate legal action for defamation against Moyo and the youthful *Herald* editor, Pikirayi Deketeke, after the paper quoted the minister as stating categorically that I had won awards for excellence in journalism through false claims.

Separately, the *Herald* claimed that Brandina had never existed at all, and that the story about her murder exposed both the MDC and the *Daily News* as liars.

Whether by coincidence or design, this drama unfolded as I was preparing to travel to Manila, in the Philippines, where I was to receive the Guillermo Cano Press Freedom Prize from Unesco. I was also scheduled to visit Belgium, where the World Association of Newspapers would present me with the 2002 Golden Pen of Freedom. Amid the vilification, public humiliation and rumours that my arrest was imminent, I wondered if the Tadyanemhandu storm was part of a well-orchestrated strategy to discredit me on the eve of my twin moments of professional glory.

These and my many other achievements as a journalist were obviously an embarrassment to an embattled government fighting to destroy the press at a time when its own international reputation lay in ruins. Both the European Union and the US had imposed smart sanctions to prevent senior members of government from travelling abroad.

Subsequent events and developments lent weight to my growing suspicion that Tadyanemhandu was part of an elaborate CIO sting operation. The MDC spokesman, Learnmore Jongwe, issued a statement on 29 April stating that when the party reported to the police that Tadyanemhandu had concocted the story about his wife's brutal murder in order to extort money, the police had bluntly refused to arrest him.

'It is somewhat puzzling,' Jongwe said, 'that the police, who denied the murder story that very day, would decline to question the person responsible.

'We suspect the report was stage-managed to undermine the party's integrity as a reliable source of information.'

Jongwe pointed out that of more than 100 reports of MDC members who had been murdered by suspected Zanu-PF militants, this was the first one that had turned out to be false. Jongwe's own life was to end tragically a short while later. He was arrested and charged with manslaughter after he had stabbed his wife repeatedly with a sharp knife. Prison officials claimed the young and popular politician then committed suicide by taking an overdose of tablets. How he had laid his hands on the fatal prescription while he was a closely guarded prisoner, they never explained.

It was quite clear that Tadyanemhandu should have been arrested and charged under the Miscellaneous Offences Act for making a false report. Alternatively, he could have been charged with fraudulently obtaining money from the MDC. The intricate web of falsehoods spun by Tadyanemhandu sounded too sophisticated to be the exclusive creation of a grieving peasant farmer. It turned out that he had, indeed, lost his wife, but she had succumbed to an AIDS-related disease.

Tadyanemhandu had produced a post-mortem report to bolster his claim that Brandina's head had been severed with a sharp instrument. In retrospect, the report may have been forged. He had refused to part with it when he told his tale to Mudiwa, promising to return the next day with a copy.

By the time Tadyanemhandu returned, the *Herald* had shredded his story to pieces, leaving the *Daily News* with no option but to recant and publicly apologise to Zanu-PF. The retraction, prominently displayed on the front page, appeared to enrage Tadyanemhandu, and he challenged the police to exhume his wife's remains for examination. The *Herald* responded by alleging that his protests were stage-managed by me. Undeterred by our own objections, the *Herald* went off on another tangent. Mudiwa had travelled to Magunje and apologised to the police for publishing a false story, the paper claimed.

In fact, it was another *Daily News* reporter, Collin Chiwanza, who had risked a trip to Magunje. His assignment was to follow up on the original story by talking to people about Brandina's burial and find out whether the police had, indeed, received a report on the murder. Chiwanza denied tendering any form of apology to the police.

'I simply enquired about the alleged murder,' Chiwanza said. 'I never apologised, because there was no reason for me to do so.'

The atmosphere was too fraught with life-threatening situations for us to pursue conclusively the full circumstances of Chiwanza's alleged apology, and the worst was yet to come.

Tadyanemhandu suddenly turned hostile. Initially a fully cooperative source, he became first antagonistic and then elusive once we confronted him with information that his wife had, in fact, died of AIDS in the Seke district, about fifty kilometres south of Harare. He no longer kept appointments, and soon disappeared from our radar screen altogether. Pedzisai Ruhanya, the reporter who was assigned to investigate Tadyanemhandu, became frustrated. He was taken on a wild goose chase through the streets of Mbare and Chitungwiza before being tipped off that Tadyanemhandu was living in a CIO safe house in the suburb of Marlborough, nowhere near the dusty streets of Mbare and Chitungwiza.

By then, there was little doubt that the *Daily News* had fallen prey to an elaborate CIO ruse.

I was in Manila when Mudiwa and Chiwanza were arrested. They were soon joined in their cell at Harare Central by foreign correspondent Andrew Meldrum, who had filed the Magunje story to the *Guardian* in London. He became the first foreign journalist to be prosecuted under AIPPA. Charges against Chiwanza, who had not been involved in the original story at all, were dropped.

Fully expecting to be arrested on my return from abroad, I attended a hearing of Mudiwa's case at Rotten Row Magistrate's Court. I wasn't arrested or formally charged, but I was called to the dock and put to my defence, thus joining Mudiwa as the first Zimbabwean journalists against whom AIPPA was invoked.

Instead of fighting the case in the lower court, Lawrence Chibwe decided to challenge the constitutionality of the section of AIPPA under which we were being charged. He argued that what became known as the 'false news offence' constituted a violation of Sections 18 and 20 of Zimbabwe's constitution, which guaranteed freedom of expression and protection under the law.

The state neither opposed Chibwe's claim nor filed any arguments when called upon by the court to do so. On the day the matter was set down for hearing, the state filed notice that it would not oppose Chibwe's argument on unconstitutionality.

On 7 May 2003, the Supreme Court passed a landmark judgment against AIPPA, and declared Section 80 of the Act, which made it an offence for journalists to 'abuse journalistic privilege by writing falsehoods', unconstitutional. The ruling by a full bench, headed by then Chief Justice Godfrey Chidyausiku, soon to be appointed minister of justice, effectively absolved Mudiwa and me of any culpability.

The Zimbabwe chapter of MISA hailed the ruling as 'a victory for freedom of expression and for the rights of the journalists of Zimbabwe'. I sent a congratulatory e-mail to Chibwe from Harvard University in the United States, where I was living in exile at the time. That night, Ursula, our son Itayi and daughter Rufaro joined me in celebrating this victory over the evil machinations of Jonathan Moyo.

At the time of my sudden departure from the *Daily News* at the end of 2002, the ongoing investigation of Tadyanemhandu had receded to the sidelines as more dramatic events, which threatened the very existence of the *Daily News* and my own safety, unfolded.

Not long after my departure, ANZ company secretary and legal adviser Gugulethu Moyo became the victim of official brutality when she visited a police station to rescue a *Daily News* photographer from the jaws of the police crocodile.

Her nightmare began when she was assaulted with batons by policemen as she made enquiries about the journalist who had been arrested while covering a national workers' strike. Then, in a departure from what had become routine, Moyo was viciously attacked by the civilian wife of the Zimbabwe Defence Force commander.

'The police said they did not have our photographer, Philimon Bulawayo,' Moyo said, 'but I saw him in the cells. An army Range Rover pulled up. A woman came in, talking on a cellphone. My own cellphone rang and I answered. The woman shouted: "Who is that woman on the phone?"

'I said I worked for Associated Newspapers of Zimbabwe, and she went wild. She shouted at me: "So what if you are a lawyer? Your paper wants to encourage anarchy in this country. You want to represent our enemies."

'Then she twisted my arm and slapped me in the face,' Moyo recalled.

'I am Jocelyn Chiwenga, the wife of the army commander,' the woman told Moyo. 'Your paper says there is no rule of law in Zimbabwe. Well, I will show you the rule of law.'

Chiwenga's business at the police station was never established, but for some reason she told Moyo that she was very rich and had lots of cars.

'She said she was powerful and would kill me,' Moyo said. 'She said she would shoot me. She kept hitting me. Policemen folded their arms and watched.'

After beating and interrogating Moyo while accusing her of working for the British government, the police took her to Harare Central, where they locked her up for two nights. They denied her access to legal or medical help.

As Moyo clambered onto a police truck with about thirty other prisoners, Mrs Chiwenga shouted to the police: 'That woman is trouble, beat her!'

Eventually, Moyo was released without any charges being brought. Normally cool as a cucumber, her ordeal at the hands of Chiwenga and the police left her traumatised.

Journalists became demoralised. If a lawyer they normally relied on to rescue them from police brutality could herself be brutalised by the spouse of the army commander with total impunity in the presence of the police, their own lot was certainly not a happy one.

13

Dreams shattered

W HEN THE *DAILY NEWS* staff encountered seemingly insurmountable problems, like not getting paid on time, a colleague being arrested and assaulted by the police, or being roundly denounced by Jonathan Moyo on national television as unpatriotic or as enemies of the state, I tried to console them with a happier scenario, as one would a child after a bad dream.

'One day, many years from now,' I would start, 'we will all sit on a sun-drenched beach on the beautiful island of Mauritius and cast our collective mind back to this day. I know there will be consensus then that our sacrifice was well worth the while.'

Mauritius, a former French colony in the Indian Ocean, is one of southern Africa's most popular tourist destinations. In the late 1990s, the island that had shed its low-income, agriculture-based economy in favour of growing industrial, financial and tourist sectors also became popular among Zimbabwe's increasingly enterprising women traders.

Every Saturday they loaded the weekly Air Zimbabwe flight from Harare to Port Louis with huge bags of crocheted goods, wood and soapstone carvings, as well as other handmade artefacts that found a ready market on the island. Having sold their wares, the women then thronged the well-stocked shopping arcades in Port Louis in search of cheap clothing and electronic goods to sell in Harare. In this way, they supplemented the meagre earnings of those husbands who were lucky enough to still have a job, met the increasingly high cost of sending their children to school or bought costly basic commodities to feed their families.

The women would spend a week at a time in Mauritius, occasionally returning to Harare without having sold as much as they hoped, only to try again as soon as possible.

Accounts of such informal trade missions also filtered out of Johannesburg and Durban in South Africa, prosperous Botswana's capital city, Gaborone, and the Namibian capital of Windhoek. Musician Oliver Mtukudzi composed a song lamenting the plight of Zimbabwe's womenfolk, forced by the deteriorating economic situation in their own country to venture so far from home. It was not uncommon to hear Shona being spoken by groups of women on the streets of foreign cities. The political leadership in their own country seemed oblivious to the desperate measures the mothers of the nation were forced to take.

Mugabe's government had reduced a once prosperous country to the status of a mendicant, its roadsides dotted with soapstone carvers and hawkers selling bait-worms to anglers, its women transformed into nomadic peddlers. Zimbabweans, once arrogant and contemptuous of the lower living standards in Zambia, Malawi and Mozambique, swallowed their pride and embarked on missions of survival to those very countries.

The traders from Harare were rarely found exploring the coral reefs and golden beaches for which Mauritius is famous, but in my island idyll, the hard-working *Daily News* staff would naturally visit under more propitious circumstances.

Sometimes, I simply tried to boost morale by reminding my colleagues that the growing circulation of their newspaper was tangible proof that the majority of Zimbabweans stood solidly behind us. While *Daily News* staff could go about their business unmolested in Harare's First Street Mall, Mugabe and Moyo, for all their power, risked jeers and verbal abuse should they venture to the same mall without heavily armed bodyguards.

The staff had heard such platitudes often enough, but they nevertheless listened to the latest version politely and soldiered on, no matter what the challenge or obstacle. Their fighting spirit flagged but never failed, even when the printing press jammed at the start of the nightly run. The ANZ employees were truly indomitable, driven by a rare combination of optimism about the future of their country and a profound faith in their paper and its mission of change.

After the *Washington Post*'s Watergate exposures, journalists Bob Woodward and Carl Bernstein won the coveted Pulitzer Prize and became celebrities, recognised and fêted both at home and abroad. An entire generation of journalists was inspired by their courage and aspired to emulate their performance. Willowgate, the *Chronicle*'s investigation into government corruption in 1988, was one of many exposés that would pay homage to Woodward and Bernstein by having 'gate' tagged onto a name to create an international catchphrase.

But in the Third World, achievement of journalistic excellence remains elusive, its pursuit often fraught with personal danger. Woodward and Bernstein were never denounced on television or roughed up in police cells for causing Richard Nixon's downfall. As a rule, dictators and corrupt politicians don't take kindly to the media sniffing out their personal peccadilloes and financial follies.

Critics often accused me of being too idealistic in expecting that a newspaper such as the *Chronicle* or *Daily News* could force transparency and accountability on so powerful and corruption-ridden an administration as Mugabe's. I lost count of how many times I was reminded that it was folly to believe in the mission rather than the business of journalism. But in my view, if the success of a publication such as the *Daily News* were to be measured only in terms of the bottom line, with total disregard for its influence on public opinion, journalism would be an exercise in futility.

It was my genuine conviction that newspapers such as the *Daily News*, the *Post* in Zambia and the *Nation* in Malawi laboured under the weight of greater social obligation and responsibility than their much bigger, more sophisticated and more celebrated counterparts, such as the *New York Times* and the *Daily Telegraph* in London.

In truth, however, the *Daily News* was doomed to perish from the moment of its creation. The odds were stacked too heavily against it for the paper to survive in its original form and concept. The mere fact that it sold briskly for four years in those areas of Zimbabwe where the politicians grudgingly allowed the newspaper to circulate was not so much a tribute to the enterprise and resilience of its distribution personnel as it was an act of timely divine intervention.

When Zanu-PF militants made a bonfire of copies of the *Daily News* in front of our offices in Harare, when the printing press was reduced to a heap of smouldering debris, common sense suggested that we were approaching the end of the brief but glorious existence of a newspaper that had defied the odds for too long. In the small towns and rural areas, the stronghold and new lifeblood of Zanu-PF, marauding party-sponsored youth militias and liberation war veterans imposed an illegal but effective ban on the newspaper.

While party activists disrupted distribution of the *Daily News*, bureaucrats in Harare devised more effective means of sabotaging the paper's editorial operations. Not only were journalists denied access to official sources of information, they were also subjected to harassment, including routine arrest.

But while neither death threats nor bombs forced the *Daily News* off the streets, two events did have a direct bearing on the newspaper's eventual demise: the introduction of harsh new laws governing the media in early 2002, and the appointment in the same year of Sam Sipepa Nkomo as executive chairman of ANZ.

In light of the company's continued cash-flow problems, I had visited business tycoon Strive Masiyiwa in Johannesburg. The chairman and founder of Econet Wireless had settled there after fleeing persecution and possible arrest in Zimbabwe. I had originally approached Masiyiwa, a British-trained telecommunications engineer turned entrepreneur, as a potential investor in the *Daily News* back in 1998. He was fighting other battles at the time, and declined. Four years later, the newspaper's impressive circulation figures and evidence of its growing political influence prompted Masiyiwa to take a second look. By then, Econet was firmly established and had spread its operations to South Africa, Nigeria, Botswana, Kenya and further afield. After negotiating favourable terms with ANZ's foreign shareholder, AMIZ, partly through my intervention, Masiyiwa came aboard with a Z$100-million rescue package. The Independent Media Group (IMG), in which he and Kingdom Bank founder Nigel Chanakira were the majority shareholders, became the largest stakeholder in ANZ with 60 per cent of the shares.

Masiyiwa was a leading light in black empowerment circles and a founding member of the Indigenous Business Development Corporation, set up amid great fanfare and with the Zimbabwe government's blessing to promote emergent black entrepreneurs by facilitating access to financing by banks.

Masiyiwa, originally a technician with the Post and Telecommunications Corporation, however, committed a cardinal sin when he established Econet without inviting anyone from the political establishment to join his venture. In retaliation, the government denied an operating licence to Econet, a company that was destined to become Zimbabwe's first and most successful operator in a growing sector of the economy. Information minister Joyce Mujuru favoured the government's own carrier, Net-One, while Telecel, which had its roots in the Democratic Republic of Congo and was fronted in Zimbabwe by politician and business tycoon James Makamba, counted various political figures among its shareholders, including the ubiquitous Leo Mugabe.

With a tenacity and resilience that turned him into a living legend, Masiyiwa fought and eventually won a protracted legal wrangle when the High Court granted him a licence and Econet secured a lion's share of the lucrative cellphone industry. However, it is doubtful that Masiyiwa would have scored this major victory against the Mugabe government had he not secured the backing of an unlikely ally, Vice-President Joshua Nkomo. Until Nkomo's death in 1998, the rationale behind the ailing old man's intervention remained shrouded in mystery. When I approached Masiyiwa to bail out the *Daily News*, I was concerned about the future of the paper, not the origins of his company.

'I am not a newspaper man,' he told me, as he agreed to become ANZ's white knight. 'I will leave management of the company to you, the experts.'

I could not ask for more. With fresh capital investment and a daily newspaper that was already riding a wave of editorial success, ANZ had a new lease on life.

However, to the astonishment of staff and readers, as well as Zimbabwe's media fraternity at large, Masiyiwa appointed Sam Sipepa Nkomo, a rank outsider with a murky past, to replace Much Masunda as chief executive of ANZ. Nkomo was to serve in the re-designated capacity of executive chairman, a position that concentrated too much power in the hands of a man who had only just entered the media industry. This move was to have catastrophic consequences on the company's future welfare. Nkomo's management style was both imperious and imperial, which was not surprising for one who was appointed to manage what he essentially did not understand. By the end of 2002, our once robust paper was headed for the graveyard. In due course, Jonathan Moyo would deliver the *coup de grâce*.

Before he was appointed to head the newspaper company, the *Daily News* had caused Nkomo's downfall a little more than two years earlier, when it investigated and published serious allegations of fraud against him.

At the time, he was the little-known principal officer of the Mining Industry Pension Fund (MIPF). Nkomo's nineteen-year-old tenure was summarily terminated when he became an early target of the newspaper's voracious appetite for investigative journalism. Documents linking Nkomo to massive fraud and corruption in the awarding of a tender for construction of Angwa City, an MIPF-owned high-rise building in downtown Harare, found their way to the *Daily News*. Following an intensive probe over several weeks, we broke the sensational story on 9 December 1999. Nkomo immediately resigned, and was charged with fraud and corruption totalling Z\$4.5 million, a staggering amount before the currency plummeted and became virtually worthless.

Nkomo was the alleged beneficiary in forty-five cases of fraud linked to the Z\$564-million construction project.

SBT Juul Africa, owned by Harare businessman Trevor Carelse Juul, had recommended a leading British company, Taylor Woodrow Construction, as the main contractor. Carelse Juul was a former chairman of the Zimbabwe Football Association (ZIFA). His term of office was prematurely terminated when his entire executive was forced to resign amid allegations of misappropriation of funds. More significantly, Carelse-Juul was Nkomo's bosom buddy. A man of mixed blood, he was linked to the prominent Khumalo family of Matabeleland. The Nkomos were another prominent Ndebele family in Matabeleland, although they were not, strictly speaking, direct descendants of the royalty among the Ndebeles who had trekked all the way from the present-day KwaZulu-Natal with King Mzilikazi.

In a letter signed by Nkomo and addressed directly to Carelse Juul in June 1997, MIPF appointed SBT Juul Africa to manage the Angwa City project. It was alleged that when he awarded the contract to Juul, Nkomo knowingly bypassed the normal tender procedures because he stood to benefit from illicit payments by his friend.

With the contract safely under his belt, Carelse Juul recommended the main contractors, who, in turn, entered into a joint venture with MIPF to form a new company, Taymin Zimbabwe. MIPF thus effectively became a significant shareholder in the official contractor for its own project.

'MIPF bought 26 per cent shareholding in the new company worth Z$780 000,' the charge sheet read in part. 'Taylor Woodrow Construction were to own 49 per cent and the balance of 25 per cent was issued to Makoni Cooper International (MCI), a company owned by Trevor Carelse Juul.'

When MIPF authorised Nkomo to acquire the shareholding, he allegedly issued a cheque for Z$3 million, which was deposited into MCI's account. Of this amount, Z$750 000 was used to purchase MCI's shareholding in Taymin, while Z$250 000 was paid to a company called Sipepa Enterprises, leaving a balance of Z$2 million. Sipepa was Nkomo's middle name.

Nkomo was charged separately with misleading MIPF to enter this partnership without disclosing his personal interest in the deal.

'Through the fraudulent activities of the accused,' read the charge sheet, 'MIPF suffered an actual prejudice of Z$3 million.' Cheques issued in these transactions, as well as a summary of company accounts, were to be presented as evidence.

We had in our possession documents revealing that more than Z$1 million had been paid to Sipepa Enterprises through various advances by MCI, trading as Concept Office Furniture. The sole owner of Concept was Carelse Juul's own wife. Reporter Julius Zava and I visited Carelse Juul in his swanky offices in the city centre. He explained that Sipepa Enterprises was a joint venture between his wife, Anita, and Nkomo's spouse, Nomagqweta. Any payments made to that company by Concept Office Furniture were part of a capital injection in Sipepa Enterprises by Anita Carelse Juul.

Concept had made several payments, including electricity and telephone bills, to

Sipepa's creditors. It had also covered salaries and wages, rentals, purchase of materials and general running expenses.

'If my wife and Nkomo's wife do business together, are they breaking the law?' Carelse Juul asked with what sounded like sincerity.

However, state prosecutors insisted that, far from being normal business transactions, the payments were, in fact, bribes paid by Trevor Carelse Juul to induce Sam Sipepa Nkomo to favour SBT Juul Africa for the lucrative Angwa City contract.

It was also alleged that there had been substantial cost overruns on projects previously contracted by MIPF to SBT Juul Africa. Nkomo had totally ignored this unsatisfactory previous performance and appointed Carelse Juul gatekeeper of the huge Angwa City contract.

'They were not happy with our work,' Carelse Juul admitted to us. 'We have learned from our mistakes.'

Despite assurances that his company would not repeat its previous errors of judgement, an astronomical Z$184-million overrun had occurred on the originally projected cost of Angwa City.

A thick file containing comprehensive documentation of alleged backhand payments to Nkomo formed the basis of the *Daily News* investigation into the MIPF scandal. Apart from the settlement by companies associated with Carelse Juul of telephone and electricity bills for Nomagqweta Nkomo's clothing factory in Southerton, two payments of Z$400 000 each were made by Concept Office Furniture to udc, a finance company of which Nkomo was a director and to which he owed a total of Z$1 million.

In February 1999, MCI had paid £1 867 on behalf of Taymin into Nkomo's Diner's Club account in London. Six months later, Taylor Woodrow Construction paid $5 644 (US) to Southwestern Adventist University in Texas, in the United States of America, where Nkomo's son was a student. Nkomo was an elder of the Seventh Day Adventist Church.

In November, Taymin paid £1 342 to the Royal Garden Hotel in London on Nkomo's behalf. It appeared that Nkomo was living like royalty, and the paper trail was long.

Nkomo refused to talk to the *Daily News* throughout our investigation, but when we broke the story, neither he nor Carelse Juul challenged us.

Zava and I had subjected Carelse Juul to a gruelling interview in his plush office suite in the new Southampton Building on Second Street. Confronted with the allegations, he became as slippery as an eel, but the information and documents in our possession were too overwhelming. Carelse Juul pleaded for time to respond to the allegations, saying he had to travel to Johannesburg on urgent business. He said he would be back within a week and would then respond to all our questions and clear both his own name and that of Nkomo. He did return to Harare briefly, but carefully avoided another blistering confrontation with the *Daily News*. Then he left town, never to set foot in Harare again, to the best of my knowledge.

While Carelse Juul had at least agreed to see us, albeit grudgingly, Nkomo turned evasion into a fine art. He played hide-and-seek with Zava and me for weeks. Each time one of us telephoned his office, his secretary, Charity Mbuse, routinely swore her boss was out of the office.

When Nkomo joined ANZ in 2002, she came too, and I endured the embarrassment of having her office right next to mine. Also imported from MIPF was Nkomo's former legal adviser there, Gugulethu Moyo, who became ANZ's company secretary. Mordecai Mahlangu, the MIPF's lawyer, was appointed ANZ's legal representative by Nkomo, replacing Lawrence Chibwe, who had kept us out of trouble for so long.

After repeatedly failing to reach Nomagqweta Nkomo on the phone during our investigation, I decided one morning to visit Sipepa Enterprises, her clothing factory in Southerton. While working on investigative assignments, journalists sometimes resort to such unscheduled visits in the hope of ambushing people who refuse to make themselves available for interviews. The average company executive or government official will happily accommodate a journalist seeking to write a complimentary story about them or their work, but when the story seeks to expose wrongdoing or failure, they will try every trick in the book to be unreachable.

I was accompanied by photographer Tsvangirayi Mukwazhi, who was to win an award for his work on the *Daily News*, and driver Shame Mukamba.

While I had not exactly expected a friendly reception, I was totally unprepared for the scene that awaited us. Wielding a broom-handle, the managing director of Sipepa Enterprises emerged from her office as soon as our presence was announced and charged without warning. I raced the young photographer between the rows of brand new sewing machines towards the exit, to the suppressed amusement of the motley gathering of seamstresses. Tsvangirayi missed a golden opportunity to win his first award – a picture of his incipiently pot-bellied editor in chief in full flight, with an angry (and armed!) woman executive in hot pursuit.

Hell hath no fury like an ostensibly successful entrepreneur confronted with damning evidence of alleged fraud.

On another occasion, arriving late for a diplomatic function at the Sheraton Hotel, I had a fleeting encounter with a man who was on the point of departure. He was of diminutive stature, appeared to be in his early sixties and was elegantly dressed. I did not know him, but there was instant recognition in his eyes as he pumped my hand like that of a long-lost friend.

'May God bless you – and the *Daily News*,' he said, as he dashed out.

Standing in a far corner, I espied ANZ chief executive Much Masunda engaged in a spirited discussion with some young executive, stylishly dressed in the exaggerated custom of the new tsars of Harare's corporate world. Any executive not personally known to Masunda was not worth knowing, or was yet to make his mark. Masunda was held in high esteem in the corporate world, where he sat on the board of more than a dozen entities. As ANZ chief executive, he was not beyond relying on his personal relationship with the chief executive of another company when our newspaper's advertising volume was running low and 'extorting' a booking, or, when payment for advertising was long overdue, extracting instant payment from the debtor. When a payment by ANZ was in arrears, Masunda would happily use his contacts to plead with a creditor for more time.

'Who is he?' I asked Masunda, after I had described the man I had just encountered.

'Holy mackerel!' he exclaimed before he burst into laughter. 'You have just been granted the rare opportunity of meeting your quarry of the past few weeks and what do you do? Literally, let him slip through your fingers.

'That, Mr Editor in Chief, was none other than Mr Samuel Sipepa Nkomo.'

After two preliminary court appearances, the prosecution surprised all concerned, Zava and I, especially, when it withdrew the charges against Nkomo before he had entered a plea, pending further investigation by the police. In Zimbabwe, withdrawal of charges before plea is not synonymous with acquittal. This procedure is usually followed when the prosecution feels the need for further investigation in order to build a stronger case, or when a vital witness cannot be brought to testify. The charges are generally re-filed once the prosecution is satisfied that it has a more solid case or has subpoenaed the elusive witness.

In the Nkomo case, however, a substantial and detailed dossier simply faded away. The accused went underground for a couple of years, and, when he resurfaced, it was at the helm of the most unlikely company, ANZ.

Arriving at Trustee House on April Fool's Day in 2002, Nkomo had effectively forced the *Daily News* off the streets by the first week of December, following a massive strike by staff over a salary dispute. On 31 December, the ZBC gleefully announced that I had been summarily dismissed as editor, a story that was jubilantly confirmed by the *Herald* the following morning. On 12 September 2003, the *Daily News* was banned after Nkomo refused 'on a matter of principle' to register the paper with the Media and Information Committee in terms of AIPPA.

Where the government of Zimbabwe had tried and failed to destroy the *Daily News* since its first issue hit the streets in 1999, Sam Sipepa Nkomo succeeded in less than eighteen months of his appointment.

When the newspaper was banned, Trevor Ncube, publisher of the *Zimbabwe Independent* and the *Zimbabwe Standard*, issued a statement pointing out that the chief executives of all Zimbabwe's independent newspapers had agreed in 2002 to act in concert and register their publications.

In a simultaneous but separate initiative, independent journalists had met under the auspices of the Zimbabwe Editors' Forum (of which I was chairman), the Independent Journalists' Association of Zimbabwe (IJAZ), the Zimbabwe Union of Journalists (ZUJ) and the Media Institute of Southern Africa (MISA). During a heated debate at the Monomatapa Hotel, one group, supported by voluble lawyer and political activist Brian Kagoro, argued for non-compliance with AIPPA and agitated for defiance. This group included representatives of non-governmental organisations, some of which published periodicals and were therefore affected by AIPPA. Some members of IJAZ also lobbied for non-registration of journalists, but, in general, the mainstream fraternity felt it was inappropriate for people like Kagoro to advocate a plan of action whose consequences would be felt most keenly by those for whom journalism was a primary rather than a secondary profession.

On behalf of the editors, I explained that while we all deplored government's draconian media legislation, we had decided that registration would be the only practical solution. By refusing to comply, the independent newspapers and their editorial staff would be playing right into the hands of Jonathan Moyo and the government. Their publications would simply be banned and the journalists barred from working in Zimbabwe.

'If we register, we will continue to fight AIPPA and other injustices through the medium of our newspapers,' I argued. 'The path of non-registration will take us to daily protests in Africa Unity Square, but with no newspapers to back our campaign. We will be at the mercy of the *Herald*.'

A vote was taken and the majority of journalists voted for accreditation in principle, though it would be up to each individual to decide what to do.

It was thus not surprising that when the *Daily News* was silenced over non-registration, Ncube was perplexed.

'I cannot say I understand the reasons for the decision not to register the *Daily News*,' his statement said, 'but I am convinced it was most unfortunate. The *Daily News* has basically given the government a "legitimate reason" to shut the paper down. The decision not to register when it was obvious that the government hated the *Daily News* with a passion and wanted to close down the newspaper was tactless and played right into the hands of Moyo and Mahoso.'

In retrospect, it appeared that the position that I, as editor in chief of the *Daily News*, had publicly articulated in favour of registration was at variance with the opinion of ANZ's executive chairman. Nkomo and I were thus clearly at loggerheads on a crucial issue that would affect the future of not only the *Daily News*, but that of the independent press as a whole in Zimbabwe.

With the banning of the *Daily News*, the hands of time were effectively turned back four years to the era of Zimbabwe Newspapers' publishing monopoly and the unmitigated propaganda of the *Herald*. Whether newspapers such as the *Zimbabwe Independent*, the *Financial Gazette* and the *Zimbabwe Standard*, which registered with MIC while their journalists were officially accredited, were unprincipled or patriotic for doing so, became the burning question of the day.

From the very moment of its launch, the *Daily News* sailed perilously close to destruction by the Mugabe government. The newspaper's most determined foes and detractors walked the corridors of power at Munhumutapa Building, the seat of government, or at Zanu-PF headquarters.

They accused the *Daily News* of being the neocolonial running dog of capitalists and imperialists bent on re-colonising Zimbabwe from their power bases in London and

Washington. More charitably, they denounced the paper as the shameless mouthpiece of the MDC, while Morgan Tsvangirai was derided as an unprincipled and semi-literate puppet of the same unrepentant Western colonialists.

I have never ceased to be amazed by the capacity of Zimbabwe's ruling clique to dismiss any sign or evidence of ingenuity or enterprise on the part of the country's highly literate, creative and ingenuous black population as being either the work or the influence of white commercial farmers or latter-day imperialists lusting after our beautiful country and its abundant resources. Zimbabwe's white farmers and South Africa's Afrikaner community were both accused of influencing the black electorate to vote against Mugabe's constitutional reforms in February 2000. During the struggle for independence, Ian Smith had blamed the communist regimes of China and Eastern Europe for inciting Rhodesia's blacks to rise up against his racist government. As his popularity waned, Mugabe accused the capitalist leaders of the West, George Bush of the United States and Tony Blair of the United Kingdom, of turning his own people against him.

In each instance, the assumption was that Zimbabwe's black population was incapable of independent thought. A black man had to be told by a white man when he was starving, it seemed. The same brush was used to tar any politician who expressed an opinion or position contrary to that of the Zanu-PF leadership, any newspaper editor who exposed their corruption or wrote a spirited editorial in castigation of the ruling clique's many shortcomings.

Any entrepreneur who dared to launch a successful venture without doling out shares to politicians or offering kickbacks in return for bureaucratic shortcuts or state contracts invited similar disdain. Strive Masiyiwa was living testimony to this phenomenon. In the blurred vision of Zanu-PF's circle of geriatric politicians, behind every black success story stood, without fail, a white man or woman, unless, of course, achievement was perceived as the fruit of clandestine association with ruling party bigwigs.

Zimbabwe's politicians occupied a heaven on earth, which they shamefully turned into a living hell for ordinary citizens, and woe betide any newspaper that tried to tinker with that status quo. In the process, dubious heroes were created through the misplaced patriotism of sycophantic media. They nurtured Border Gezi, who, having risen from the status of an absolute nonentity, quickly attained notoriety as the force behind the brutal Zanu-PF Youth Brigade. He died in a traffic accident after government mechanics had fitted the wrong wheels on his official Mercedes-Benz – the victim of his government's failure to maintain the luxury vehicles which it disbursed to appease its top politicians and bureaucrats. His remains were interred at the national Heroes' Acre.

Chenjerai 'Hitler' Hunzvi, the mercurial Polish-trained medical doctor who became chairman of the veterans' association without having fought in any war, succumbed to HIV/AIDS just when the nation had reached the end of its tether in relation to his total disregard for the rule of law. He had spearheaded the bloody farm invasions that triggered a downturn in the output of Zimbabwe's once productive agricultural sector, a backbone of the country's export-driven economy. Hunzvi's surgery in the suburb of Budiriro was converted into a torture chamber where opponents of Zanu-PF endured unspeakable horrors. He, too, lies buried at Heroes' Acre.

The government media deified Leo Mugabe, the president's favourite nephew, whose companies were guaranteed to win the most lucrative tenders. They hero-worshipped Philip Chiyangwa, the flamboyant businessman whose shameful profligacy was tempered only after a month spent in a smelly cell at Rhodesville police station, following his arrest in December 2004 as an alleged spy. Hailing from the same Zvimba district as Mugabe, he laid claim for years to being one of the president's privileged relatives.

The most sensational media creation was Gideon Gono, said to be a close relative of First Lady Grace Mugabe, who came from the same district of Chikomba in Mashonaland East. His surprise appointment as governor of the Reserve Bank of Zimbabwe was hailed by the government media as the definitive answer to the country's deep-seated economic woes. Gono, who displayed a passionate love for publicity, was promptly dubbed 'Hurricane', as he dashed from the front page of one newspaper to another. One of the not-so-well-concealed secrets of Mugabe's power was his total control of a vast array of resources of patronage – jobs, farms, contracts and a host of other favours that he shrewdly dispensed in return for unflinching support and unquestioning loyalty. Occasionally, these resources were exploited without his knowledge or approval by some of his more cunning underlings.

The government's propaganda machine, meanwhile, strove to create traitors out of citizens who were, perhaps, the real heroes of the post-independence revolution – hard-working and enterprising entrepreneurs such as Nigel Chanakira, founder of Kingdom Bank, Strive Masiyiwa, and the controversial Mutumwa Mawere of African Resources Limited, once an adoring admirer of Mugabe, his benefactor before he was alienated and went to live in exile in Johannesburg. These were some of the entrepreneurs we had initially approached as potential investors in the Daily News.

In the eyes of the Zanu-PF establishment, the newspaper was always hell-bent on disrupting the political status quo. The surprise announcement on state radio on Monday 30 December 2002 that I had been sacked as editor in chief thus came as no great surprise to me. It was the culmination of a series of dramatic events designed to shut the newspaper down or dislodge me from the helm, or both. The fact that ZBC radio, which was not even on speaking terms with ANZ executives, was the medium used to make the announcement and the speed with which ZBC laid its grubby hands on this particular scoop, were indicative of the extent of external complicity in the unfolding drama at the publishing company's headquarters on the twentieth floor of the Karigamombe building.

It was alleged that Nkomo had, in fact, personally informed Moyo that I was on my way out at last, and that it was Moyo himself who had telephoned his cohorts at Pocket's Hill with the news. When I questioned him on this matter while writing this book, he responded rudely and denied it, but the fact is, the ZBC was never first with any news and existed on an unmitigated diet of official propaganda.

Nevertheless, on the morning of 30 December, while I held in my hands a letter advising me that I had been suspended without pay pending the ministry of labour's approval of an application for my discharge from the *Daily News*, ZBC, our newspaper's implacable enemy, announced that I had actually been fired. The *Daily News* and the *Herald* confirmed the story the next day, both quoting Nkomo as the source.

While not entirely surprised by these developments, I was shocked by the extent of the duplicity and treachery on the part of my comrades-in-arms only two months after a $3.6 (US) million state-of-the-art printing press had been imported and installed in total defiance of the greatest of odds. I had travelled halfway around the world to canvass funds from donors to purchase the Swedish-manufactured Solna D300 printing press. It had become apparent to Masunda and me, as top ANZ executives, that the company's shareholders were not keen, assuming they even had the money, to spend such an astronomical figure on a new press that would probably go up in smoke, just like its predecessor.

By a strange coincidence, my departure from the *Financial Gazette* in 1991 had come just as Elias Rusike's Modus Publications was in the process of importing a Solna from Sweden.

Perhaps I would have been less prepared for dismissal had a story about my impending departure not appeared in the *Tribune*, a Zanu-PF-aligned newspaper owned by Mutumwa Mawere, whose Diamond Insurance Company held shares in ANZ, earlier in December. Mawere had close links with politicians in the upper echelons of Zanu-PF, notably Emmerson Mnangagwa. I should have smelled a rat when Nkomo refused to repudiate the *Tribune* claim. It was left to Masiyiwa to issue an official denial from Johannesburg on 21 December, and even then Nkomo refused to release the statement in Harare as executive chairman. Masiyiwa was forced to re-channel his statement directly to me for release.

Notwithstanding Masiyiwa's assurance of support, however, I was indeed dismissed just nine days later. My offence – siding with striking workers – was allegedly committed on 24 December, exactly two weeks after the *Tribune* reported that I was about to be fired, but the stage had been set since 2000 for the series of dramatic and often comical events that culminated in my departure and, ultimately, the shutting down of the *Daily News*.

What had prompted Masiyiwa to appoint Nkomo as chairman and, a short while later, to elevate him to the position of executive chairman of ANZ has remained one of the Zimbabwean media's most closely guarded secrets. It was no secret, however, that as principal officer and chief executive of MIPF, Nkomo sat on a huge pile of miners' pension money at a time when the new owners of the *Daily News* – Masiyiwa, Chanakira and Nicholas Vingirai of Intermarket Holdings – were in the process of building their own highly successful business enterprises and thus scouting for investment capital.

Nkomo had told me that he was a half-brother of former vice-president Joshua Mqabuko Nkomo. However, people close to the Nkomo family told me that Joshua, Sam and John Landa Nkomo, who as minister of home affairs was responsible for the police at the time of Sam Sipepa Nkomo's arrest and prosecution, were cousins.

While Econet launched its mobile phone network in July 1992, it took a five-year battle through the courts and the surprise intervention of Joshua Nkomo, who was virtually bedridden by the end of the period, for the company to obtain an operating licence. Masiyiwa's victory was a major concession on the part of Zanu-PF. No explanation was ever offered as to why the 'Old Man', as Nkomo was affectionately known to loyal supporters of his former party, PF-Zapu, had gone to Masiyiwa's rescue.

There was open speculation later as to whether Sam Sipepa Nkomo's appointment as chairman of ANZ by Masiyiwa had been sheer coincidence, or whether it had been payback for the elder Nkomo's support for Econet's licence application. The ANZ executive chairman certainly seemed to lead a charmed life. When the fraud charges against him were withdrawn in 2000 pending further investigation, the man in charge of the police was none other than John Landa Nkomo, his other politically influential kinsman.

News of Nkomo's appointment at ANZ was met with foreboding by the *Daily News* staff. It did not help that neither Masunda nor I could explain to journalists or anyone in the corporate, diplomatic or government circles how the situation had come about. We were in total darkness ourselves. I decided to play it by ear.

While fully understanding the concerns of shareholders, Masunda and I had fully embraced the challenge of keeping the *Daily News* afloat. Our own futures were on the line, along with the jobs of more than 300 workers, many of whom I had personally persuaded to leave the security of their previous employment.

But Nkomo's appointment saw the affable and energetic Masunda retired as chief executive, the positions of chairman and chief executive merged, with Nkomo becoming executive chairman.

Within eight months, the *Daily News* was forced off the streets for a week. Nkomo had reneged on an undertaking given to staff in July 2002 that their salaries would be increased in January 2003. When management failed to confirm the promised windfall, and efforts to negotiate with Nkomo reached deadlock in early December, the staff went on strike and, for the first time in its brief existence, publication of the *Daily News* was suspended. In the midst of this crisis, Nkomo nonchalantly departed for the Christmas break.

On the morning of 24 December, I telephoned Masiyiwa in Johannesburg to point out that unless the standoff with staff was resolved urgently, the paper faced a real prospect of collapse. Masiyiwa was unequivocal. I was the most senior executive on hand, he said, and I should find a solution. Then he made a startling statement.

'Be assured, however, that any collapse of the *Daily News* is, to me, good riddance,' he said. 'I am not making any money out of the paper.'

In an attempt to pacify the majority shareholder, I reminded him that with the acquisition of a new printing press and new vehicles for the editorial and circulation departments, all donor-funded, he stood to benefit from the company's anticipated recovery. Then I asked him why, if he felt so frustrated by the newspaper's poor financial returns, he did not disinvest.

'I think you misunderstand me,' he said. 'It's not that I want to make money from the *Daily News*.'

From his inimical tone I sensed that it was futile to pursue this particular dialogue any further. At least I had secured from him the authority to resolve the immediate problem. As editor in chief, my primary responsibility was to ensure that the newspaper appeared on the streets every morning. By failing to publish, ANZ was in breach of a contractual obligation to both readers and advertisers, especially those who had paid for subscriptions in advance or signed and paid for long-term advertising contracts.

Before his departure, Nkomo had instructed the company's bankers to withhold the December salaries of striking staff. Under pressure during the busiest period of the commercial year, the bank had evidently decided it would be simpler to pay no salaries at all rather than conduct the apparently mammoth task of separating strikers from those who had remained at their posts. This came to my attention only when my own bank manager called to say that my December salary had not been transferred and that there were insufficient funds in my account to cover cheques that I had issued.

In the last edition before the strike started, we had apologised for the disruption in publication and assured readers and advertisers that the newspaper would be back on the streets on Tuesday 31 December. Nkomo had gone on holiday without making any arrangements to ensure that promise would be kept.

The crisis was particularly painful for me. Having endured so much agony, deprivation and humiliation over four and half years while building the *Daily News*, I was now expected to stand aside and watch as the whole enterprise imploded, thanks to the machinations of a man with what appeared to be a personal agenda. It was inconceivable that, having toiled so hard with Masunda's backing to raise a staggering amount of donor funding for the purchase of a new Solna D300 printing press, just commissioned two months earlier, I should fold my hands while our sweat and tears went down the drain.

The intention had always been for the *Daily News* to take up the cudgels on behalf of the beleaguered people of Zimbabwe and fight the dictatorship of the Mugabe regime or any subsequent government. We were never supposed to go to war against the courageous men and women who had made personal sacrifices and took immense risks to create and develop the newspaper. I would not fire the first shot of that battle.

With trepidation, I hastily convened a staff meeting in the newsroom. The situation was tense, if not hostile. Like the chief executive, the employees were mostly devout Christians, but, unlike their absent boss, they faced the grim prospect of Christmas without money in their pocket. The shops had long since been cleared of essential commodities, which meant empty fridges and no presents for the loved ones of ANZ staff. Many had cancelled plans to visit their families in the rural areas, as urban Zimbabweans customarily do over the festive season.

In an effort to break the deadlock and ensure that the newspaper would appear on 31 December, as promised, I made an offer to the staff. It was not possible for their salaries to be processed, but I would make a personal effort to source the money to pay them an advance in the meanwhile, so that they could spend Christmas with their families. Once the dispute had been resolved, their December salaries would be used to cover the advances.

There was instant jubilation and not a single dissenting voice when I explained that, in return, they would all have to solemnly promise to be at work on 30 December to produce the *Daily News*.

I had no idea where I was to find the money, but with the staff's full assurance in hand, I bolted out of the newsroom to my office and made frantic telephone calls. I struck gold on my third attempt. A well-wisher agreed to provide me with Z$9 million to pay the staff. He would hold me personally responsible for the return of the money in the New Year. The entire arrangement was subject to one condition: his identity was not to be revealed.

Not long afterwards, my personal assistant Annie Musodza and I met our benefactor in a banking hall. By prior arrangement with the bank, I had parked my vehicle in the basement, and under several pairs of watchful eyes, boxes of crisp banknotes were loaded into the vehicle. Then, escorted by security guards, we drove the short distance to the basement parking of ANZ's headquarters.

It was well after 4 p.m. when the first payment was made and almost midnight when the last employee still on the premises signed for his pay packet. Word got around to those who had already left by the time payments started, and some of them arrived early on Christmas Day to collect their money. I was among the many *Daily News* employees who travelled to their holiday destination late on that day.

On Sunday 29 December, Masiyiwa telephoned to inform me that Nkomo had filed a report outlining the events on Christmas Eve and a decision had been made to relieve me of my position.

I protested that such drastic action could not be taken on the basis of a telephone conversation or without granting me an opportunity to present my side of the story. Masiyiwa said he was personally handling the case and wanted me to travel to Johannesburg, possibly to discuss my severance package. Meanwhile, when I returned to Harare, I was to talk to Norman Nyazema, chairman of IMG, to make the necessary travel arrangements. Masiyiwa pleaded with me not to go public on this matter until we had reached a settlement.

I telephoned Annie to warn her that trouble was brewing. Our thoughts immediately turned to the Z$4 million in cash that remained unpaid to staff in my office. On Christmas Eve, the accounts department had given me the global figure for ANZ's payroll and we had ended up with almost half the cash left over because some staff members and all the executives had already gone when we made up the pay packets. Now, although it was a Sunday, Annie immediately drove to the office to retrieve the remaining cash.

She was shocked on arrival at the office to find the door to my office wide open and a locksmith working on the door between her office and mine.

'Standing beside the locksmith was ANZ's finance director, Brian Mutsau. The locksmith sensed that something was wrong and he quietly disappeared,' Annie later said.

An embarrassed-looking Mutsau also left, giving Annie the chance to check on the boxes of money behind my desk. As she secured the last box, operations director Innocent Kurwa, the founding editor of the *Mercury* in Gweru, walked in and took a seat in the corner, for all the world as if he were there to guard Annie. Company secretary Gugulethu Moyo arrived as well. Apparently, I was the only ANZ executive who was not in the office that afternoon. Moyo demanded that Annie hand over our office keys, though they were now of no value, once the locks had been changed.

The next morning, I arrived at the office early. We had a long day ahead, preparing a paper for publication after a strike and the Christmas break. None of the early pages had been prepared in advance, as was normal practice, and much required to be done if we were to meet our deadline.

Annie was standing at her office door and did not seem to be her usual, cheerful self. Too hectic a holiday, I surmised. But I was wrong. Almost in tears, she recounted details of her encounter with the three ANZ executives the day before, adding miserably: 'I understand Mr Nkomo ordered all the locks changed and I don't have a key to get into my office. I think there is serious trouble.'

She had been unable to contact me earlier, because my cellphone battery had run down. I found Nkomo in his office with Norman Nyazema. Nkomo informed me that I was to step down immediately as editor in chief. I told him that I had already spoken to Masiyiwa and that my next step was to travel to Johannesburg.

'In any event, surely it is not necessary to lock me out of my office? It's not as if I have defrauded the company. My personal assistant is standing in the passage outside her office right now. It's not very dignified,' I pointed out.

I looked at Nyazema. Nyazema looked at Nkomo. Nkomo reached into a drawer and handed over the new keys. I went out and gave them to Annie, and we immediately checked on the money situation. It appeared untouched. Mercifully, the locksmiths had been blissfully ignorant that they were working within pocketing distance of a cool Z$4 million, and, bear in mind, this was long before Zimbabwe was reduced to a nation of penniless millionaires.

I returned to Nkomo's office and was handed a brief, unsigned letter confirming my suspension, and stating that the reasons for this action would form part of the application for my dismissal to be submitted to the labour ministry.

This was at complete variance with the discussion I had had with Masiyiwa less than twenty-four hours before, and I said so. Nyazema agreed, adding that his presence was at Masiyiwa's request in order to assure me that a satisfactory deal would be worked out. He and I were to travel to Johannesburg two days later for that very purpose.

I thanked Nyazema and requested time to digest the content of Nkomo's letter in my own office. Having briefed Annie and my deputy, Davison Maruziva, of my imminent departure, I composed a letter of resignation, which I addressed and e-mailed to Masiyiwa and copied to Nkomo.

A short while later, Nkomo walked into my office, holding a copy of the letter. Procedurally, he said, I was wrong to address my letter to Masiyiwa and not to him. I reminded him that Masiyiwa had emphatically said he was personally handling all matters pertaining to my position. Nkomo and I were still arguing about the best way of resigning or being fired when my phone rang. It was Tommy Sithole, former editor of the *Herald*. We rarely communicated, and I was mystified that he should call me at this particular juncture. He asked me to confirm that I had been fired from the *Daily News* as ZBC radio had just reported.

I was dumbfounded. It was simply not possible.

I challenged Nkomo with the information Sithole had just imparted. He vehemently denied knowing anything about the broadcast, but by the next day, ZBC, the *Herald* and the *Daily News* were all citing him as their source of information. Looking flustered, Nkomo stood up and left my office. That was the last I ever saw of him.

The executive chairman went straight to Maruziva's office and offered him the post of editor in chief. Maruziva tendered his own immediate resignation on a matter of principle, he said.

He and I had been forced out of the *Chronicle* in 1989 and had teamed up again in 1998 to prepare for the launch of the *Daily News*. Maruziva was one of Zimbabwe's finest journalists, a knowledgeable, experienced and hard-working professional and a glutton for punishment, who toiled daily from early morning until late at night. He was fully groomed to take over from me. Now we were leaving the *Daily News* together. My heart sank.

As agreed in my Christmas Eve pact with the staff, the *Daily News* was back on the streets on Tuesday 31 December.

Its front-page banner headline was, 'Nyarota fired'.

Nkomo had temporarily taken charge in the newsroom. The *Daily News* and the government-owned media, now virtual comrades-in-arms, rallied to communicate Nkomo's side of the story, with no effort to present mine. Inspectors Makedenge and Mlutshwa of the Law and Order Section visited the office moments after my departure. When Annie phoned to tell me, I decided to go into hiding. After I left, Makedenge visited my home on four occasions, three of them after midnight. During the day he phoned incessantly.

Without the protection of the *Daily News*, I was now extremely vulnerable.

While I drove back to Harare, Ursula purchased an air ticket to Johannesburg. I bid a few friends and relatives farewell and took the next flight out of Harare. I hoped to see Masiyiwa in Johannesburg, as previously agreed, but he adamantly refused to meet me. Meanwhile, I put a call through to Inspector Makedenge in Harare and said I was returning his many calls.

'Yes, can you please come in to see us,' he said, a hint of menace in his voice. I asked him why. He said I would be told on arrival.

'I will call you to say when I am coming,' I said, and cut off the call. I still have his number and will certainly call him on my return to Harare, if his number has not changed.

Within weeks I was winging my way across the Atlantic to the United States, where Bob Giles, curator of the Nieman Foundation for Journalism at Harvard University, had offered me a fellowship. Ursula, Itayi, Rufaro and I arrived in Boston mid-morning on 31 January 2003. Having recovered from the shock of the coldest winter in New England for twenty-three years, that night, for the first time in many months, I slept soundly.

Nine months later, the *Daily News* finally succumbed to the machinations of its determined foes.

Three other high-profile independent newspapers – the *Financial Gazette*, the *Independent* and the *Standard* – were in circulation in Zimbabwe long before the advent of the *Daily News* and were just as critical of the Mugabe regime. All three registered with the MIC and continued to publish and hold the banner of press freedom high. Simultaneously, they challenged AIPPA's constitutionality in the Supreme Court.

ANZ also challenged AIPPA, but refused to register in the meanwhile. When the *Daily News* finally sought registration, four days after the Supreme Court had dismissed ANZ's petition, the MIC rejected the application, thus effectively banning further publication of the paper.

'I believe that all this could have been avoided had Nkomo agreed to join Rusike and myself in our decision to register our newspapers and then launch a constitutional challenge against this Act,' Trevor Ncube said in his statement.

Elias Rusike, my former boss at the *Financial Gazette*, had said as far back as June 2002 that this would be their course of action. In the same article, published three days before the original registration deadline of 16 June 2002, Nkomo was quoted as saying: 'We will go ahead and register but there are some objectionable sections in the Act that we feel need to be looked at.'

Any decision not to register must therefore have been taken after expiry of the extended deadline on 31 December, my first day away from the *Daily News*.

Nkomo had entered the fray at a time when the *Daily News* and the other privately owned newspapers were locked in mortal conflict with the government over press free-dom. Moyo's draconian AIPPA had just made its stormy passage through parliament.

The major target of the law was always going to be the *Daily News*. Since its launch in 1999, the paper had seriously challenged the monopoly of the government's own newspapers. More ominously, it had undermined the entrenched political position of Mugabe's ruling party. Zanu-PF had lost a referendum and very nearly a general election in 2000. The *Daily News* had incurred the government's wrath by providing Zimbabwe's traditionally voiceless political opposition with a platform from which to address daily an electorate grown weary of corruption, tyranny and ruthlessness. The paper had further angered the political establishment by condemning the many shortcomings of Mugabe's necessary but violent, ill-conceived and controversial land reform programme, and launching a relentless campaign against the rampant corruption in his government.

The ruling party's militant youths and the war veterans, alongside government agents such as the CIO and the Law and Order Section of the police, had, in turn, retaliated viciously in an attempt to destabilise or suppress privately owned newspapers in general, and the *Daily News* in particular.

Given that I headed Zanu-PF's list of undesirable journalists, with six arrests and two death threats to my credit, not to mention three bomb attacks on *Daily News* premises, it would be folly to assume that my dismissal on so-called administrative grounds on the eve of the deadline for the registration of journalists and newspapers under the abhorrent AIPPA was sheer coincidence, although Nkomo spiritedly argued along those lines.

In my view, the dismissal was the culmination of a well-planned and perfectly executed sting operation, taking into consideration the spurious nature of the allegations levelled against me and the fact that I was never given an opportunity to challenge them and defend myself. Above all, these were the actions of a man who had a major grievance against me after I exposed his shocking campaign of predatory self-enrichment at MIPF, confirmed in court documents before Mugabe's government allowed him to go scot-free.

Francis Mdlongwa, who succeeded me as editor in chief of the *Daily News*, left seven months after his appointment and one week after the paper was banned. His departure had nothing to do with the closure of a paper that he was trying to steer out of the doldrums into which it had been steered by Nkomo.

'It had become clear to me that either Nkomo or I had to go,' Mdlongwa said when I contacted him at Rhodes University in South Africa, where he became director of the Sol Plaatje Institute.

Nkomo had told the *Financial Gazette* that former *Daily News* news editor John Gambanga had been his personal choice for editor. He said Mdlongwa had, in fact, been appointed by Masiyiwa. Mdlongwa disputed this, pointing out that his appointment had been made by the board of directors, which included Nkomo.

After my departure, Nkomo abolished the powerful post of editor in chief and leapfrogged Gambanga over senior editors to become editor, serving at the executive chairman's pleasure.

It was a mark of the confusion then reigning at the paper that when Mdlongwa arrived two months later, not only was the post of editor in chief reinstated, but

Gambanga was relegated to the meaningless and previously non-existent position of editor at large.

In one fell swoop, the *Daily News* had a new editor in chief, a new editor, a new deputy editor and a new news editor, clearly a recipe for disaster, as none of these new appointees, apart from Mdlongwa, who had worked on the *Herald* two decades earlier, had any experience on a daily newspaper.

Mdlongwa had sought absolute clarity on his position and authority in relation to Nkomo, given what he called the unhappy circumstances of my own departure. He had moved quickly to recover those functions that Nkomo had wrested from me towards the end of 2002.

The editor in chief became solely responsible once more for all editorial operations, including the hiring, dismissal, promotion and supervision of staff. Nkomo had hijacked that responsibility a month before my dismissal.

At the same time, he had made me answerable to him rather than to the board, as had always been the case. When I resisted these manoeuvres, Nkomo informed Masiyiwa that I was defying his authority. Strangely, Masiyiwa sided with him.

Yet Mdlongwa had stood his ground on the same issues, with Masiyiwa's tacit support. His contract was unequivocal. Mdlongwa was answerable only to the board.

'When Gambanga and others lost their positions and a new team was appointed, the decision was taken unanimously by the board, sitting in Johannesburg. Nkomo was present and he did not utter a single word of opposition,' Mdlongwa recalled.

'Evidently Nkomo was unhappy with these changes, but he only raised this, almost as a joke, on the plane as we flew back to Harare. He said he thought Gambanga could have been spared the axe. In his view, Gambanga was a good man, whatever that meant.'

This, Mdlongwa said, had precipitated his first clash with Nkomo.

'Eventually I had to call an emergency meeting with Nkomo and all editors to make it clear that his way of doing things was unacceptable to me as group editor in chief and ran counter to the mandate that I was given by the board.

'Nkomo's defence was that as the "father-figure" of the company, he felt he needed to be "consulted, not in the normal manner, but for wisdom coming from my advanced age and experience, over issues such as the appointment or dismissal of journalists".

'I kept Masiyiwa, who had become board chairman, up to speed on these and many other troubling issues. Strive promised to talk to Nkomo and get him to stop meddling in editorial matters, but I am not sure if he did, because Nkomo's behaviour didn't change. If anything, it appeared to get worse.

'Eventually, I told Strive that I wanted to leave because I could not fulfil my mandate. Strive insisted that I stay on and that he would talk to Nkomo. The situation deteriorated until, on returning from a trip to Europe, I found that Nkomo had sent a memo to editors suggesting that they needed to hold separate meetings with him on "non-editorial" issues.'

Mdlongwa challenged Nkomo to elaborate on what he meant by this.

'He did not explain, merely blaming his "poor English" for what he claimed was just his way of letting the editors know that his door was always open for any discussion,' Mdlongwa said.

'I told Masiyiwa I was leaving because of the latest affront and sent him my letter of resignation, which I copied to Nkomo. This happened just as the crisis was developing about registration.

'I stalled my resignation for a little while and took on the role of being the group spokesman as I explained the police raid and closure of the newspaper to a stunned world. But as the situation dragged on, I eventually left with a heavy heart, fully aware that some people might wrongly interpret my departure as that of a captain deserting a sinking ship.

'It was clear to me that either Nkomo or I had to go, and I felt that Strive was not reining in a rampant Nkomo. I said so, among many other things, in my letter of resignation.'

A week after my own sudden departure from the *Daily News*, Judith Todd, both a shareholder and board member, sent an anguished letter to IMG chairman Norman Nyazema.

'Some years ago,' she wrote, 'I had the misfortune to be on the board of Zimpapers when editor Geoff Nyarota was fired without the knowledge or consent of the board. This year I have been reliving that nightmare.

'But now, not only do we have the usual, serious responsibility of a newspaper board to fellow directors, editors and all other company employees, we have the very existence of an all-important and very fragile newspaper, the *Daily News*, to protect. I am therefore asking you to institute urgent action not only in restoring the possibility of justice for Nyarota, Maruziva and others but also to save the *Daily News*. I fear it almost certainly will suffer an ignominious demise unless action is taken to restore in the eyes of the public here and abroad the integrity of the paper, the company, the board and the shareholders.

'I remarked to some of our colleagues after last Friday's meeting that the two phrases we hear so much – "the ruling party" and "the majority shareholders" – have a distinctly similar ring and a totally identical purpose – simply to shut out any dissenting views, such as the ones I tried to express at our board meeting last Friday. It is a grave injustice to all concerned for a board (or a newspaper, or a court etc.) to be allowed to hear only one side of a dispute. Board members are also, alas, culpable, as we should not have allowed this travesty of justice and this undermining of our moral and statutory obligations.

'I do not understand how Sam Nkomo has been able to accrue and wield such power, such destructive power as it turns out, without the knowledge let alone consent of the board. In fact, since the formation of IMG there have been some inexplicable events in its subsequent dealings to do with ANZ, like the present role of Sam. One was the appointment of Mats Kunaka, hot from Zimpapers. As he said himself, his appointment there had been effected by Chen Chimutengwende, which shows that the ruling party must have had great faith in his ability to meet their requirements.'

Chimutengwende was appointed minister of information in 1995. Jonathan Moyo succeeded him in 2000. Kunaka was appointed as IMG's first chief executive officer in 2001. His tenure was so remarkably short that it cast aspersions on the judgement of those who had appointed him.

'It was also well known before Kunaka joined us,' Todd continued, 'that his tenure had not been beneficial for the finances of Zimpapers. I hope that Mr P Timba remembers how dubious I was about that appointment.'

Patterson Timba of Renaissance Financial Holdings was IMG's financial and investment consultant.

'Then came the appointment of Sam Nkomo in the extraordinary circumstances that it was already public knowledge amongst our readers that he was being scrutinised by the *Daily News* regarding possible fraud at the MIPF. I have nothing personal against either of these two gentlemen. I like them both very much, particularly Sam, whom I first had the delight of meeting many years ago. But in terms of their attachments to us, one could be forgiven in thinking that IMG has been used as a vehicle by someone whose intentions towards the *Daily News* are not good.

'That false headline "Nyarota fired" in the *Daily News* with which our year began has been widely interpreted, rightly or wrongly, as being simply a greetings telegram to Jonathan Moyo with which shareholders, board members and some staff are associated. We have all been put in the most invidious situation and I only hope it is still possible to clear the reputation of ANZ.

'It goes without saying that in contemporary Zimbabwe people like Strive, Geoff and yourself are seen as heroes and people get very heart-sore when they feel let down.

'The *Daily News* is one of the few lifelines to sanity we have left. I do not want to be complicit in allowing it to be destroyed. I have a strong feeling that you may be able to rescue the situation. I certainly hope so.'

Nyazema was a man of few words.

'Thanks,' he said in a prompt response to Todd's letter. 'I hear you loud and clear. I have had a word with Strive, Nigel and Sam. I can assure you that the *Daily News* will survive. An amicable parting of ways will be sought with Geoff so that he continues to play an important role. I really do not understand why Davison resigned. He was offered the acting position, which he turned down. I shall keep you posted.'

By April 2006, a total of forty months after Nyazema's misleadingly optimistic and conciliatory communication, no amicable parting of ways had been achieved and I had not received a cent of my terminal benefits, let alone any settlement. Nor had the outstanding issue of my shareholding in ANZ been resolved, although Masiyiwa had personally assured me in March that the issue was being resolved.

On 10 February 2005, an intriguing article appeared in the *Financial Gazette*, which Rusike had sold to the new Reserve Bank governor, Gideon Gono, before retiring comfortably to his farm at Goromonzi. He had earlier sought to fulfil his latent political ambition by standing for parliament in 1995. Mugabe had personally dashed those dreams by recalling Zimbabwe's high commissioner to London, Herbert Murerwa, to stand in Rusike's Goromonzi constituency, before appointing him minister of finance.

The *Financial Gazette* reported: 'Strive Masiyiwa, one of Zimbabwe's *nouveau riche*, and his partners have written off debts owed to them by the publishers of the *Daily News*, to ensure the group relaunches on a clean slate.' The newspaper quoted observers, unidentified as usual, as suggesting that Masiyiwa might be selling a dummy to the government to facilitate the registration of the *Daily News*, pointing out that the Supreme Court was soon expected to deliver judgment on the fate of the paper. Zimbabwean reporters are notorious for using unidentified analysts to express views and opinions that are often entirely those of the journalists themselves.

Masiyiwa informed the *Financial Gazette* that he had finalised plans to transfer ownership of the *Daily News* to a trust that would include both employees and management as beneficiaries.

'The trust … received the shares as a free gift with a cash endowment to meet the future financial needs of the business,' Masiyiwa said. 'This effectively turns the majority control of the paper over to a trust, which will make it easier for the newspaper group to access donor funding when it resumes operations.'

Masiyiwa was quoted as saying that the board of trustees was made up of prominent Zimbabweans and South Africans who had been chosen for their integrity and professional track record.

'They will each serve a single five-year term and will be replaced by someone selected by the remaining trustees. This will make the trust self-perpetuating and will have no recourse to its founders.'

One almost expected Masiyiwa to add, 'And every Zimbabwean will live happily ever after.'

When the Supreme Court delivered its long-awaited judgment a month later, just before the 31 March 2002 general election, it did not rule that the newspaper should be allowed to relaunch. Instead, it gave the MIC sixty days to reconsider and make a final decision on the ANZ petition. The final outcome was that the MIC denied the *Daily News* a publishing licence.

Meanwhile, Zanu-PF swept the board by winning seventy-eight parliamentary seats. The MDC's tally dropped significantly, to forty-one, though the party gave notice that it would challenge the result in another sixteen constituencies on the grounds of alleged vote-rigging by Zanu-PF. Because Mugabe had thirty seats that he could fill with handpicked appointees, Zanu-PF technically secured the magical two-thirds majority in the 150-seat parliament. For the first time in Zimbabwe's history, the ruling party could amend the constitution at will.

While the absence of the feisty *Daily News* was painfully obvious during the 2005 election campaign, the prospect of democratic change after the election became as distant a pipe dream for the citizens of Zimbabwe as the beaches of Mauritius were for the journalists who had made the paper great.

While some of them walked the streets of Harare in a state of near destitution, others worked at menial jobs, unrelated to the profession they loved, in London and elsewhere in the diaspora. The brand new Solna D300 gathered dust while lawyers made a killing arguing over the constitutionality of AIPPA.

By some rare coincidence, Jonathan Moyo and Sam Nkomo, the two men who had contributed most to the demise of the *Daily News*, both hailed from Sipepa in the Tsholotsho district of Matabeleland North. Two years after the collapse of the *Daily News*, Nkomo, who was still chief executive of the now defunct paper, revealed his secret political ambitions by attempting to secure nomination as the MDC candidate for Tsholotsho in the March 2005 general elections. He did not make it beyond the primaries. MDC supporters nominated a different candidate. Nkomo had another go when he stood for the MDC in elections for the reconstituted senate in November 2005. Having been forced to resign from ANZ in order to enter politics, he suffered a humiliating defeat in Tsholotsho, and promptly returned to ANZ to demand his job back.

Meanwhile, Moyo had resigned from Zanu-PF following the so-called Tsholotsho Conspiracy, which had threatened to tear the ruling party asunder in December 2004. Mugabe had accused Moyo of masterminding a revolt in what he must have seen as an unforgivable display of treachery. Undaunted, Moyo stood as an independent candidate in Tsholotsho and beat the MDC by a narrow margin. Taken together, the votes cast for Zanu-PF and the MDC were greater than those secured by Mugabe's former spin doctor, but Moyo nevertheless became the only independent member of parliament, thus ending his five-year marriage of convenience with Mugabe.

During his term as outspoken, impetuous and impish minister of information, he had become the public face of a ruling party that was clearly in intensive care. He had also spearheaded the government campaign to gag the press, the highlight of his term as minister of information being the enactment of the draconian AIPPA.

At a personal level, my only tangible reward or consolation for the hardship, deprivation and humiliation that marked the four and a half years that I was ANZ editor in chief was the collection of major media awards that I received from international and Zimbabwean organisations.

In 2002, I was honoured to receive Unesco's Guillermo Cano World Press Freedom Award at a ceremony in Manila attended by the president of the Philippines, Gloria Arroyo. The prize carried a purse of $25 000 (US), and was instituted in 1987 to honour an individual, organisation or institution that has made an outstanding contribution to the defence and promotion of press freedom anywhere in the world, especially if some risk is involved. The award was named in memory of Guillermo Cano y Isaza, a Colombian journalist who was assassinated in December 1986 in front of his newspaper's offices in Bogotá, on the orders of Medellín drug lord Pablo Escobar.

Cano's fate exemplifies the price paid by members of the media the world over. Journalists are imprisoned and maltreated on account of their profession every day. In many instances, those who persecute journalists do so with total impunity. It is alarming that they go unpunished.

I won the award for courage and persistence in denouncing corruption and criminal activities among government officials in Zimbabwe, despite death threats and two bomb attacks on the *Daily News*.

In 2002 as well, I received the Golden Pen Award of Freedom from the Paris-based World Association of Newspapers. A year earlier, I was presented with three international awards: by the *Economist* in London, the Committee to Protect Journalists in New York and the International Center for Journalists in Washington, DC. Among the distinguished guests at the New York ceremony was civil rights activist Jesse Jackson. A picture of him congratulating me graced the front page of the *Daily News* at the time.

The National Association of Black Journalists in the US honoured me with their Percy Qoboza Foreign Journalist Award in 1989 for my work on the *Chronicle*, and again in 2003 for my work on the *Daily News*. The latter presentation, a colourful affair in Dallas, Texas, was attended by more than a thousand top black journalists, with the future US secretary of state, Condoleezza Rice, as guest of honour.

In Africa, MISA presented me with their Press Freedom Award at a ceremony attended by southern Africa's leading journalists in Mbabane, Swaziland. On home ground, I was the runner-up in 1989 for the Communicator of the Year Award from the Zimbabwe Institute of Public Relations. The winner was the First Lady, Sally Mugabe. However, one of the judges later revealed to me that I had actually been adjudged the winner, but the institute lacked the courage to publicly acknowledge my role in exposing Willowgate and to name the First Lady as a runner-up. Eleven years later, in 2000, I finally did win the award, which by then was sponsored by the British American Tobacco Company.

Ursula accepted the honour on my behalf, as I was travelling abroad.

14

The revolution
that lost its head

A s THEY REEL from the ravages of economic meltdown, there are Zimbabweans who swear that Robert Mugabe has mismanaged their country and that he has been a tyrant and a profiteer since 18 April 1980. To some considerable extent, this extreme view is no doubt tinged with the wisdom of hindsight. I have difficulty, even now, convincing some foreigners, black Americans in particular, that the glorious picture they continue to paint of Mugabe as a revolutionary and gifted African visionary is no longer supported by facts on the ground.

I must confess that on my travels abroad in the early days of independence, I basked in the reflected glory of Mugabe's then ostensibly illustrious name. Soon afterwards, his government introduced what appeared to be far-reaching social reforms in the health and education spheres. Zanu-PF had inherited a well-established but mostly urban-based infrastructure, which Mugabe's government extended for the benefit of rural Zimbabweans, the majority of the population. The government also made great achievements in reversing the racially discriminatory policies and practices of the colonial past.

New schools and clinics were built. The training of teachers became a priority. Additional teachers and doctors were imported in large numbers. Average literacy rose to an astounding 82 per cent of the adult population, while the public health system was second to none on the African continent.

'Health/Education/Housing For All By The Year 2000' became the oft-chanted slogans of Zanu-PF politicians. When I travelled abroad, even as Matabeleland reeled under the Gukurahundi massacres, people regarded Mugabe as a charismatic and visionary leader, pointing to his unprecedented policy of reconciliation and the social and economic development then unparalleled in post-colonial Africa.

Having guided Zimbabwe to nationhood in 1980, Mugabe could easily have defied the Third World stereotype of independence followed by grinding poverty, unbridled corruption and gross abuse of power. He had the benefit of learning from the mistakes of many countries that had gone that way before. Remarkably, however, in little more than two decades, Mugabe reduced a prosperous nation, once the breadbasket of southern Africa, to a basket case, mired in violence and lawlessness and shunned by the global community.

Many of the thousands who had thronged his rallies at independence came to openly despise him. The foreign capitals where Mugabe was wined and dined by the world's most powerful leaders closed their portals to him as the result of his government's human rights abuses, while the international community shunned him as a ruthless dictator. In September 2005, Zimbabwe narrowly escaped expulsion from the International Monetary Fund by making a surprisingly substantial payment against its massive and long-standing debt.

In self-defence, Mugabe blamed the Western world's condemnation of Zimbabwe in the new millennium on incipient racism, triggered by his campaign to dispossess white commercial farmers of land that ought long ago to have been transferred to black ownership.

But Zanu-PF had quietly discarded the utopian slogans about free education, health and housing many years before 2000. Education had become largely unaffordable, with facilities stretched to breaking point. The University of Zimbabwe was a shadow of its former glory, and starving lecturers departed in droves for greener pastures in other lands. The health system had all but collapsed at a time when up to 500 people a day were succumbing to the scourge of HIV/AIDS. Even those who could still pay for them were unable to get life-saving drugs due to severe shortages, while Zimbabwe's highly trained doctors and nurses emigrated *en masse*.

Every municipal authority had on its books a growing housing backlog that it failed dismally to address, resulting in the erection of wooden shacks and other ramshackle structures that turned already overcrowded high-density suburbs into major health and fire hazards. Meanwhile, government officials, including the First Lady, Grace Mugabe, hijacked funds from a government scheme designed to alleviate the housing shortage.

By 2003, inflation had reached an unprecedented high of more than 640 per cent, while unemployment stood at more than 70 per cent. By February 2006, month-on-month inflation had spiralled to a record 800 per cent. Zimbabweans encountered perennial shortages, with supermarket shelves bare of essential commodities such as maize meal, bread, cooking oil and rice. Long queues for petroleum products became a permanent facet of urban existence.

Mugabe and his government did not seem unduly perturbed that the majority of Zimbabweans lived under conditions that pushed them beyond all limits of endurance. While growing discontent over the failing economy posed a threat to Mugabe's authority, the image of Zimbabwe as a model of economic development, democracy and multi-racial coexistence disintegrated. Being identified as a Zimbabwean ceased to be a source of pride. In the United Kingdom, Zimbabweans posed as South Africans or Malawians. Some were discovered by hostile immigration authorities and deported, not back to Zimbabwe, but to their countries of false origin.

The tone of curiosity about Zimbabwe had changed completely. The questions now were: 'What went wrong?' or 'How could the people of Zimbabwe allow this to happen?'

The answers were far from simple.

Almost four years before independence, Mugabe had shared his vision of a future Zimbabwe with the media during the abortive Geneva conference: 'One cannot get rid of all the trappings of free enterprise. After all, even Russia and China have their *petit bourgeoisie*. What I am saying is that we are socialist and we shall draw on the socialist systems of Mozambique and Tanzania.'

Fifteen years later, as a member of President Canaan Banana's delegation, I visited one of the African states that Mugabe considered a model of socialism. Banana officially opened the 1981 Dar es Salaam trade fair. Notwithstanding Julius Nyerere's honourable intentions, the Tanzanian exhibition was shamefully amateurish by comparison with Bulawayo's annual international trade fair. Nyerere did not merely preach socialism, as Mugabe would do for many years before finally abandoning doctrinaire Marxist-Leninism altogether. Albeit with limited success, the Tanzanian leader had implemented *Ujamaa*, his own brand of socialism. Like a true disciple, he led a frugal existence, devoid of the more conspicuous trappings of capitalist indulgence. After that visit to Tanzania, I began to have serious reservations about Mugabe's vision for my own country.

Also on the junket was Dr Witness Mangwende, Zimbabwe's minister of foreign affairs. He had been my senior at the University of Rhodesia, and we spent our free evenings in Dar es Salaam reminiscing about our student days over a drink – a Scotch for him and a Tusker beer for me – in a bar at the Kilimanjaro Hotel, where we were staying.

At the time, Tanzania was experiencing serious economic setbacks, totally alien to many members of the Zimbabwean delegation, including me. Despite the fact that Ian Smith's Rhodesia had been buffeted by international economic sanctions for fifteen years, we had no previous experience of the parlous economic conditions in which countries such as Tanzania, Mozambique and Zambia, all of which had achieved independence before Zimbabwe, wallowed. After eighteen years of *Ujamaa*, Tanzania was a depressing lesson in hardship. That visit opened my journalistic eyes to the wretched conditions that an otherwise sound economy can be reduced to if not properly managed.

Overlooking the harbour across Kivukoni Street and situated near the city centre, parliament and government buildings, the eight-story Kilimanjaro Hotel was the pride of Dar es Salaam. There was a serious shortage of many basic commodities in the city, and during our stay, cigarettes were particularly hard to come by.

A hotel guest could purchase a packet through the expedience of paying an exorbitant cover charge to enter the dimly lit in-house nightclub. Such commercial exploitation of guests was, in my opinion, wholly inconsistent with the socialist principles regularly preached by Mwalimu Nyerere, as the president was affectionately known. The hotel managers were so steeped in capitalist exploitation that I wondered if any of them ever attended Nyerere's rallies.

Having paid their way into the nightclub, many guests did that which came naturally – settled down to have at least one drink, customarily under the watchful eyes of a bevy of ebony beauties poised strategically and expectantly under the subdued but colourful and mesmerising lighting. They alternated between sipping slowly and elegantly from glasses of Konyagi, a popular Tanzanian gin, and gracefully rearranging their beautiful legs for the benefit of newcomers.

Mangwende and I, both heavy smokers, found seats away from the pulsating *rhumba* music and shared our memories of campus life in colonial Rhodesia. If we remarked on the deplorable conditions of Dar es Salaam at all, it was by way of extolling the many virtues of Harare. Not only had Tanzania been at the forefront of support for Zimbabwe's armed struggle by allowing Zanla to set up offices and training camps in the country, but Nyerere was Mugabe's personal hero. As custodian of Zimbabwe's international relations, Mangwende could hardly speak ill of a host country during a visit, however strong the temptation.

Nyerere had visited Zimbabwe in December 1980, the second foreign head of state to do so. The first was Mozambique's Samora Machel, who had arrived in August. The Tanzanian president was honoured by having Kingsway, the main thoroughfare from Harare to the airport and the satellite city of Chitungwiza, renamed after him during his visit. As Nyerere's motorcade wailed its high-speed passage through downtown Harare, I was in a dentist's chair at the Kingsway Shopping Centre, or KwaAmato as it was more popularly known. The dentist was struggling to remove the stump that had remained embedded in my lower jaw after the rest of the tooth had broken off, courtesy of my unforgettable encounter with Spur and Mhike three years before.

Travel outside Zimbabwe with President Banana, and later with Mugabe, broadened my perspective and alerted me to some of the excesses in which our government indulged after *uhuru*. I first went to the United States in September 1983 as editor of the *Chronicle* to cover Mugabe's first official visit. He was given a standing ovation when he addressed the United Nations General Assembly, and was a big hit with the black communities of Detroit and Atlanta, where he attended a memorial service in honour of slain civil rights leader Martin Luther King, whose widow Coretta was in attendance.

In New York, Mugabe's huge delegation stayed at the Waldorf-Astoria, then said to be the most expensive hotel on earth. Members of our group, some normally resident in Harare's crowded low-income suburbs, spent two glorious days living in the lap of luxury. The management of the hotel, where the guest list routinely included the rich, famous and powerful, would unquestionably have frowned upon the gastronomic arrangements made by some of those accompanying Zimbabwe's head of state. Far from sampling the culinary delights created by the hotel's world-renowned chefs, those of us on limited expense accounts sneaked Big Macs from underneath the nearest golden arches into our rooms for supper. Not once did we venture into the well-appointed hotel restaurants. In fact, it would be eighteen years before Ursula and I dined at those tables, while attending a ritzy gala when I received a media award.

The dinner hosted by the Committee to Protect Journalists was a far cry indeed from the loaf of sliced bread and tin of sardines from the nearest convenience store that I had smuggled into my plush room in 1983. I believe the cheapest nightly rate at the time was around $200 (US), while Mugabe's suite reportedly cost twice as much, the equivalent of a reasonable monthly salary in Zimbabwe. It occurred to me even then that my government had embarked on a reckless spending spree with limited foreign currency reserves.

Why Mugabe required such a large delegation and why an official group from a poor and newly independent state had to stay at the Waldorf, boggled my mind. Such spendthrift practices set a pattern of unbridled expenditure that was the cause of successive budget deficits of devastating magnitude.

On the next leg of the trip, Mugabe met with Prime Minister Pierre Trudeau in Ottawa. Afterwards, the Canadian premier escorted his guest down to street level, and as we jostled for seats in a fleet of limousines, Trudeau strolled down the pavement and was swallowed by the pedestrian throng, barely a bodyguard in sight. If Mugabe noted this absence of pomp and ceremony, he learned nothing from it. His own security arrangements became more elaborate by the year, his official convoy decidedly grotesque.

In times of hardship, resilient Zimbabweans find spiritual fortitude in a wry sense of humour, inculcated over generations. The presidential motorcade became the butt of much uncharitable mirth. A *Daily News* cartoon once depicted an incredibly long convoy, complete with troop carriers, an ambulance and a fire tender. The Public Order and Security Act, enacted not long afterwards, rendered it a punishable offence to ridicule the president. One motorist, tired of waiting in a queue along Samora Machel Avenue for fuel that never came, gestured towards Mugabe's motorcade as it sped westwards, sirens wailing menacingly, towards the Sheraton Hotel. Another motorist burst out laughing at the fellow's joke. Moments later, an open truck approached at speed from the direction of the hotel and screeched to a halt beside the wretched motorist's vehicle. Two soldiers jumped down and meted out ruthless instant physical punishment to the hapless man. He was fortunate that they did not bundle him away.

At a well-attended rally in Toronto, with Mugabe exuding his customary eloquence and verbose turn of phrase, a black woman at the back of the hall seized any opportune moment to shout one word at the top of her voice: 'Murderer!' Her embarrassing interventions were brought to an abrupt end when two burly police officers led her away. All these years later, I apologise for the fact that this juicy titbit never found its way into the *Chronicle*.

In the wake of the historic fall of the Berlin Wall, that symbolic divide between capitalist West and communist East during the Cold War, I visited Germany as executive editor of the *Financial Gazette*. The Frederick Ebert Stiftung, a non-profit foundation committed to the concepts and basic values of social democracy and the labour movement, invited twelve political and civic leaders to the reunified country for a fortnight in October 1990.

The delegation included Chief Justice Enoch Dumbutshena, agriculture minister Dennis Norman, Zimbabwe Congress of Trade Unions secretary general Morgan

Tsvangirai and retired journalist Lawrence Vambe. Also in the group were human rights and political activist Judith Todd and University of Zimbabwe political science lecturer Jonathan Moyo, then a fiery columnist on the *Financial Gazette*.

This was my first close contact with my columnist, and we spent evenings nursing huge glasses of beer and discussing the vexing and deteriorating political situation in Zimbabwe. Our visit coincided with the Oktoberfest, a two-week festival held each year in Munich and celebrated by up to six million people. During the festival, Germans consume large quantities of *märzen*, a classic beer characterised by a medium body and broad range of colour. We joined in the festivities with reckless abandon. A huge picture of Moyo and me sailing down the Rhine on a boat was to grace a wall in my office at the *Daily News* a decade later, as a reminder to me and visitors of the good old days.

Ten years later, Moyo took Zimbabwe by surprise when he threw caution and his former revolutionary zeal to the wind and jumped onto the Zanu-PF bandwagon. At a time when the party was virtually grinding to a halt, he campaigned for the election that Zanu-PF almost lost to a one-year-old political upstart, the MDC. The campaign gave Moyo a springboard to launch his own tempestuous political career. Mugabe appointed the garrulous intellectual as minister of information, replacing the affable but ineffectual Chenhamo Chakezha Chimutengwende, who lost his parliamentary seat.

Moyo had no known Zanu-PF credentials, apart from his tenuous connection to the party's founding president, Ndabaningi Sithole, and allegations (which he haughtily denied) that he had absconded from a Zanla training camp at Mgagao in Tanzania. He did not have a political constituency either, but Mugabe invoked his right to nominate a specific number of MPs. This single appointment was to influence political developments in Zimbabwe over the next four years to a greater extent than any other since independence. Moyo single-handedly unleashed the forces of repression on the independent press, especially the *Daily News*, a growing voice of influence and authority on the political landscape after just one year.

It has weighed heavily on my conscience that I was probably personally responsible for inadvertently launching Jonathan Moyo's political career. At a time when Mugabe's image was on the wane, the American-trained professor turned out to be not only an adroit political strategist and a passionate if unrepentant adversary of the free press, often in pursuance of personal causes, but also as skilled a purveyor of propaganda as was Josef Goebbels during Adolf Hitler's Nazi reign of terror. Like Goebbels, Moyo was equipped with rare oratory skills and an uncanny ability to slant arguments to his view. He placed his neck on the block on behalf of a beleaguered Mugabe at a time when most of the president's trusted cronies and long-standing acolytes were receding to the sidelines as political uncertainty enveloped Zimbabwe.

When I became executive editor of the *Financial Gazette* in 1990, my deputy, Trevor Ncube, recommended that we commission a regular column from Moyo, an unknown but apparently indefatigable political science professor at the University of Zimbabwe.

He had been a sporadic contributor to the *Financial Gazette* on political issues, and, never one to be daunted by the prospect of running against current wisdom, Moyo rose to the challenge with both courage and passion. His hard-hitting and controversial writings contributed to the newspaper's popularity and he became an instant hit, much to publisher Elias Rusike's consternation. He complained that Moyo's column and the writings of Bill Saidi, another regular contributor, did little to endear the publication to its friends in government.

Rusike had the galling habit of disclosing the existence of the *Financial Gazette*'s so-called friends in the upper echelons of government and Zanu-PF only when they objected to articles that were not particularly complimentary. Because of our independent editorial line, investigative stamina and hard-hitting columns that attracted thousands of new black readers to a paper that had originally targeted a white readership, Rusike's list of 'friends in the corridors of power' inevitably lengthened by the week.

My own position was simple. I routinely advised Rusike, a self-proclaimed Zanu-PF activist who paradoxically became the publisher of an independent newspaper, to cultivate the habit of referring to the editor any politicians or bureaucrats who were aggrieved by the *Financial Gazette*'s content. I also suggested that he might find a thick skin quite handy.

Since there was usually no factual basis for their complaints, no angry politicians ever approached the editor directly. But as the political establishment's indignation intensified, Moyo's reputation grew. Every week he launched a scathing attack on Mugabe in particular, casting aspersions on his credentials as a socialist leader, on Zanu-PF and on the government, denouncing the corruption, human rights abuses and economic mismanagement that had lowered the standard of living in Zimbabwe to less than pre-independence levels. At a time when it was sacrilege to openly challenge the ruling elite, Moyo campaigned against Mugabe's pet subject, the one-party state, which the *Financial Gazette* fervently opposed until it was cast into the dustbin of Zimbabwe's tempestuous political history.

On our visit to Berlin in 1990 I was struck by the large number of Trabant cars on the streets. Hordes of men and women liberated from Erich Honecker's bastion of communism, which Mugabe was bent on emulating in capitalist Zimbabwe, drove their Trabants back and forth across the fallen Berlin Wall each day.

The ubiquitous Trabant symbolised the real polarisation between East and West. Before the wall came down, many East German citizens were killed while trying to drive a Trabant through Checkpoint Charlie to the Western sector of Berlin. The tiny car became an icon of freedom from communist dictatorship. More than three million Trabants had been built before production was phased out after reunification.

Despite public pretensions of socialist equality, the *nomenklatura*, the leadership of the German Democratic Republic, as East Germany was officially called, never lowered themselves to travel within the Spartan confines of the Trabant. The six-cylinder Sachsenring luxury sedan was built in limited numbers for the convenience and comfort of the ruling elite. Had prophetic George Orwell not stated in *Animal Farm* that while all animals are deemed equal, some are more equal than others?

Despite having a two-stroke, two-cylinder engine, the Trabant was a sturdy little car. During our two-day stay in Berlin I saw numerous Trabants, television set or refrigerator strapped to the roof, spewing black smoke as they negotiated their way home after a fruitful expedition to the capitalist shopping malls that had opened their doors to East Germans for the first time since the Second World War. I was reminded of Zambians in 1980, just after Zimbabwe had gained independence, thronging the streets of Harare, the women balancing huge cartons of shopping on their heads. In 2004, I visited Lusaka from the United States, where I was living in exile, and saw hordes of Zimbabwean women, similar cartons balanced precariously on their heads, rushing to catch a bus back to Harare.

From Berlin, we travelled to Potsdam, where I experienced instant culture shock. Not even in Harare had I seen such abject poverty. A middle-aged man parked his Trabant station wagon at an open-air market, where a number of traders were selling their wares on makeshift stalls or the trunks of their cars. The newly arrived man appeared forlorn and tired as he opened the tailgate of his vehicle. He had brought a total of four cabbages to market. The scowl on that man's face as a group of blacks subjected him to what must have appeared unwarranted scrutiny became indelibly etched in my memory.

Even residents of Zimbabwe's poor working-class townships, such as Harare's Mbare and Bulawayo's Makokoba, had a happier countenance and more cheerful disposition. I wondered, therefore, what our African leaders such as Nyerere, Mugabe and Machel found so laudable in Honecker's East Germany and Nicolae Ceauçescu's Romania. During their numerous visits to the capitals of Eastern Europe, they were no doubt whisked in air-conditioned limousines from the airport to luxurious guesthouses reserved for visiting dignitaries, far removed from reality.

Any leader who deliberately wished to reduce the status of his people to the squalor and deprivation that I observed in Potsdam had no right to remain in office longer than was absolutely necessary, I secretly declared. Paradoxically, it was the dream of such leaders to cling to power for life. It was no surprise that an angry mob brought Ceauçescu's dictatorship to an untimely and bloody end while his trusted soldiers and policemen conveniently looked the other way.

One of Zimbabwe's most committed adherents to socialism was Charles Chikerema, editor of the *Sunday Mail* and later of the *Herald*. Long after the Zanu-PF leadership, including Mugabe, had abandoned socialist rhetoric, Chikerema churned out lengthy articles espousing the positive attributes of Marxist-Leninism and praising the old captains of communism such as Honecker, Ceauçescu and Cuba's Fidel Castro. While the majority of the Zanu-PF leadership had embraced capitalism and the wanton and predatory acquisition of wealth, Chikerema, who had studied in Cuba, maintained a frugal existence of self-denial.

Undaunted, Comrade Charles, as he was fondly called by Zanu-PF cadres, fought a losing battle as he tried to transform the newspaper into an authoritative and doctrinaire socialist publication. Throughout his virtual one-man campaign to transform Zimbabwe into a rigid socialist state, Chikerema watched uncomprehendingly as the once popular newspaper's circulation nose-dived. Subscribers cancelled orders and loyal readers deserted by the score.

Amazingly unperturbed, the powers that be rewarded Chikerema with a promotion to editor of the Zimpapers flagship, the *Herald*. Even in the most auspicious circumstances, putting a newspaper on the streets every morning can exact a toll on its editor. Chikerema was imbued with a singular determination to turn twelve million people to his point of view. But, faced with the impossible task of transforming Zimbabwe through relentless propaganda into a working socialist state long after the concept had become an anachronism, he died a frustrated man in 1997.

By then it must have finally dawned on him that his compatriots were light-years away from wholeheartedly embracing the socialist doctrine that he preached daily. Even the leadership of the political party whose original manifesto he continued to advocate had long since abandoned the socialist cause.

After a decade in power, the politicians had become preoccupied with the brazen accumulation of wealth in the fashion of the capitalist moguls of the West whom they publicly scorned at party rallies that drew ever-smaller crowds. They had thrown themselves into the hedonistic pursuit of pleasure perfected by Hollywood stars whose immodest lifestyles were depicted nightly in soap operas that were soon banned from TV screens in Zimbabwe. By the turn of the twentieth century, Zanu-PF's leaders boasted ownership of preposterously huge mansions and luxury limousines. After the violent seizure of most of the country's vast commercial farms from whites who were accused of possessing multiple properties, Mugabe's ministers themselves boasted ownership of huge and multiple farming estates.

The battle cry of 'one man one farm' had been cast to the wind in true Orwellian fashion.

The degeneration of the Republic of Zimbabwe into a state of near collapse never lacked elements of peripheral melodrama. As Zanu-PF's circle of friends in the international community diminished, the December 12 Movement of Harlem in New York shot to prominence in Harare.

Much to the amusement of Zimbabweans, the head of the movement acquired an avant-garde name, Comrade Coltrane Chimurenga, to reinforce his revolutionary credentials. Comrade Chimurenga and one Sister Violet Plummer undertook an annual pilgrimage from Harlem to Harare, their visits timed to coincide with Zimbabwe's independence celebrations on 18 April.

The delegation from Harlem was flown across the Atlantic and accommodated in the five-star Sheraton Hotel at taxpayers' expense. After being fêted, entertained and flown to exotic tourist attractions like the Victoria Falls, they were paraded at the independence day festivities.

They inevitably granted so-called exclusive interviews to the *Herald*, the *Sunday Mail*, and the Zimbabwe Broadcasting Corporation's radio and television channels, in which they extolled the virtues of the ruling party and the allegedly profound wisdom of its leaders. They told Zimbabwe's long-suffering taxpayers what a good job their president was doing for the nation and urged them to support Zanu-PF unflinchingly.

Soon after the land invasions in 2000, Comrade Chimurenga was quoted by the government media as having unreservedly endorsed the 'Third Chimurenga', or Third Revolution, which had as its centrepiece the violent occupation of white-owned farms.

In New York, Mugabe relied on the December 12 Movement to organise an occasional demonstration, even at short notice – rent-a-crowd events, as Bill Saidi aptly summed up their timely interventions – in support of Zimbabwe's president and government.

By 2002, the movement had become the laughing stock of all perceptive Zimbabweans, who by then constituted the majority of the electorate, especially in urban constituencies. Comrade Chimurenga and his retinue were denounced as Zanu-PF's paid praise-singers, prepared to sacrifice their dignity in exchange for a free annual holiday in sunny Africa.

There was never a time, after independence, that Mugabe was not in conflict with some or other form of opposition. It started with Joshua Nkomo's PF-Zapu and included Ndabaningi Sithole, Abel Muzorewa, Enoch Dumbutshena, Margaret Dongo and, finally, Morgan Tsvangirai on the purely political front. But he also set his sights on the press, the commercial farmers, the judiciary, the teachers and all Zimbabweans living in the diaspora. By the end of 2000, any Zimbabwean of whatever colour, tribe or religion who did not openly identify with Zanu-PF had become an enemy. Mugabe literally saw a foe in every crevice. The revolution was consuming its own children.

The plight of the post-independence schoolteacher is particularly instructive of how Mugabe's revolution lost direction. Despite their role in the vanguard of the liberation war, characterised by selfless dedication and unrewarded sacrifice, members of the teaching fraternity, particularly those in rural districts, received a raw deal once political power was consolidated in the hands of the former guerrilla fighters. By the 2000 parliamentary elections, Zanu-PF regarded the rural teacher as an enemy, and said so publicly.

During the colonial era, the teaching profession attracted the elite of the black population. Throughout the war, teachers were part and parcel of the struggle. Without their material and logistical support, thousands of guerrillas, deployed in most cases with nothing but their AK47 rifles, could never have survived.

Time was when the Rhodesian schoolteacher was regarded with a respect that bordered on veneration. The teacher was the pillar of the community, a shining example of achievement, integrity and personal advancement, a role model for the young, especially in the rural areas. But by 1997, when Mugabe's government decided to pay former freedom fighters Z$50 000 each in compensation for their sacrifice, teachers had become marginalised and impoverished 'enemies of the state'. The former elite in colonial Rhodesia had become objects of official and public ridicule, unable to afford even the most basic requirements of life.

My widowed sister-in-law, Irene Kahwa, a teacher of twenty-eight years' standing in Bulawayo, earned a net salary of Z$3.5 million a month, worth less than $70 (US) on the black market. This was barely enough to fill her car's tank with petrol if she resorted to the extortionate but resourceful underground suppliers.

Mugabe was a teacher once. His legendary didactic prowess, even while in detention for a decade, his leadership qualities and, above all, his humility among people less accomplished than himself, initially inspired many to join a profession in which they prospered. Later, however, he would bear most of the blame for bringing his former profession into disrepute and close to total ruin.

By 2000, Zimbabwe's teachers and university lecturers were among the lowest paid in southern Africa. A constantly changing string of education ministers did little to improve conditions.

The once elevated social status of the teacher took a nose-dive. He or she was treated with disdain. While some teachers led a life of misery, their charges were in many cases the offspring of Zimbabwe's well-heeled *nouveau riche*. After walking a long distance or taking an overcrowded minibus to school, the teacher stood, in some cases, in front of a class that included the children of company executives, government ministers and diplomats. Some of the youngsters were chauffeur-driven to school in the latest models from Mercedes-Benz, BMW or Lexus.

Boys attending private schools such as Hartmann House, St George's College and St John's in Harare wallowed in the lap of luxury, while their tutors eked out a living on a pittance. How monumentally heartbreaking a challenge for any teacher to establish authority and inspire confidence in pupils under such lopsided conditions.

Because of growing discontent, teachers increasingly expressed political dissent, resorting to sporadic strike action in their quest for better working conditions. During demonstrations at Africa Unity Square in the centre of Harare, the police took particular delight in teargassing a class of people they had always regarded as arrogant and contemptuous of their own contribution to society. When the authorities openly declared war on teachers, they were sucked into the vortex of opposition politics. When Tsvangirai launched the MDC in 1999, the party's ranks were swelled by disgruntled teachers. In rural areas, they formed the backbone of the opposition movement until sustained attacks by agents of the ruling party broke them.

The growing influence of politics in many sectors contributed to the decline in the standard and welfare of the teaching profession. Prospects of promotion were limited for those deemed by the ruling party to be politically incorrect. To compound the many problems, the government slashed education budgets and diverted funds to the ministry of defence after embarking on expensive foreign military adventures in Mozambique and the Democratic Republic of Congo.

If teachers had faced similar tribulation during the war of liberation, it is doubtful that the armed struggle would have succeeded.

After only fifteen months as a teacher before independence, I had saved enough for the deposit on a Cortina GT. After 1980, the prospect of owning a car became a pipe dream for most teachers. They stoically accepted life as permanent pedestrians as their lot in independent Zimbabwe.

Apart from the miserable plight of the people, which seemed to escalate with each celebration of independence, other factors contributed to the derailment of Zanu-PF's revolution – corruption, abuse of power, economic mismanagement, and a breakdown in law and order, to mention the most glaring. If not for the high security wall separating the Cuban ambassador's residence in Harare from that of former rebel leader Ian Smith, the latter might have been tempted occasionally to remind his neighbour, with a smirk on his face, 'Well, it's not as if I did not warn people about the dangers of black majority rule, but nobody would listen to me.'

The Cuban ambassador might very well have responded, 'At least Comrade Mugabe never declares, "Not in a thousand years."'

To those who closely monitored the ruling elite's long trail of alleged corruption, the escape to London of three men who had managed Zanu-PF's sprawling business empire for decades was a shocking anticlimax.

They fled in April 2004, a few days after Zanu-PF finally established an internal committee to investigate long-standing allegations of widespread corruption within its upper echelons. The investigation would have focused on men who, while managing the party's affairs, had gradually become untouchable.

Two of them, Jayant and Manharlal Joshi, had a long history of association with Zanu-PF. Before independence they lived in Mozambique, where they first established links with the party. Afterwards, Mugabe invited the Joshi brothers to manage Zidco Holdings, through which Zanu-PF controlled its business interests.

While they settled in Harare, the Joshis, with rare foresight, clung tightly to their British passports. The *Daily News* revealed in 2000 that, despite their elevated status within the ruling party, the brothers were not Zimbabwean citizens. Any other mortal would have incurred the wrath of Everisto Magwadi at the department of immigration. The Joshis, however, were in a league of their own.

Emmerson Mnangagwa, the powerful parliamentary speaker, was both their guardian and their link to the party leadership. It was rumoured that he had personally escorted the fleeing Zidco directors to the airport. He promptly denied this and, as usual, threatened to sue the paper that published the story. The fearsome politician had been minister of state security before serving as minister of justice for twelve years. More significantly, during the two decades that he acted as the ruling party's finance secretary, he was chairman of Zidco and sat on the board of fourteen companies owned by Zanu-PF. Despite his public image as a ruthless and allegedly corrupt politician, Mnangagwa had been widely touted as Mugabe's chosen successor. The president's attachment to a politician whose name was routinely linked to allegations of corruption was the cause of much speculation about Mugabe's own moral rectitude.

While Mnangagwa and the Joshi brothers had repeatedly been fingered for alleged corruption, the former guerrilla leader's aura of power ensured that they all became sacred cows, even when well-investigated and documented examples of graft were exposed by the press, as occasionally happened. In 2004, Mnangagwa was linked in court to illegal gold trading. Surprisingly, the press was barred from publishing his name. In 2002, a UN report named him in regard to exploitation of diamonds and other resources in the DRC. I questioned him on the allegations and published his half-hearted denials in the *Daily News*. Two years earlier, we had published claims of his involvement in crooked tenders for construction of the new airport. His attempt to sue fizzled out like a damp squib.

When the Joshi brothers ditched a lifestyle of consummate luxury in Harare and fled abroad on 1 April 2004, there was widespread expectation that the end was near at last for Mnangagwa. The brothers, along with fellow Zidco director Dipak Pandya, left soon after Zanu-PF set up the corruption probe headed by party finance secretary David Karimanzira, and which included former finance minister Simba Makoni and former army supremo Solomon Mujuru, a known opponent of Mnangagwa. Following the departure of the Joshis, the probe came to nothing. Mugabe's legendary lack of commitment to eradicating corruption was exposed once more.

The committee had a mandate to probe kickbacks, mismanagement and security breaches, as well as the shareholding structures and benefits accruing to the party from the operation of its many companies. Should any irregularities have been detected, Mnangagwa would have been held to account. Deep-rooted graft within Zanu-PF could be traced back to 1988, when the *Chronicle* disclosed vice in high places. Since then, Mugabe had been accused of condoning endemic corruption, while protecting crooked cronies and hastening to reprimand those seeking to expose or prosecute cases of fraud and bribery.

The Sandura Commission's findings confirmed the *Chronicle*'s accusations against the president's lieutenants, yet Davison Maruziva and I were relieved of our positions on the paper. After submitting his report to Mugabe, the chairman of the commission, Justice Wilson Sandura, climbed no higher within the judiciary. He was regarded by many as the obvious choice for chief justice after rogue war veteran Joseph Chinotimba visited the incumbent, Anthony Gubbay, in his chambers and forced him into premature retirement. Sandura was by far the most experienced of the black judges who were eligible to step into Gubbay's shoes, but Judge Godfrey Chidyausiku was appointed instead. His Zanu-PF credentials were strong, and he could be relied upon not only to hand down politically correct judgments, but also to facilitate the appointment of malleable judges through the Judicial Services Commission.

Sandura's report in 1989 had recommended a thorough investigation of Zidco's affairs. It took fifteen years for Zanu-PF to finally heed his call, but no sooner had the committee been set up than the primary suspects were allowed to leave the country. Mugabe never commented or demanded that the Joshi brothers be brought back to Zimbabwe, though this could doubtless have been arranged.

As for Chinotimba, the bearded war veteran who had spearheaded the violent campaign against farmers and intimidated the country's most senior judge into resigning, his remains will more than likely be interred at the national Heroes' Shrine.

Construction of this memorial on Harare's western outskirts is widely believed to have been funded by the North Korean government. Carved out of the granite hills opposite the National Sports Stadium, the burial ground was set aside for Zimbabweans deemed by Zanu-PF to have been heroes of the liberation struggle. However, two decades after independence, all available space had been used to bury scores of Zanu-PF cadres, including some whose status as heroes surprised even their own families. The accomplishments of some were so obscure that members of the party's politburo squabbled for hours before bestowing the final honour on them. They then assigned to the party's praise-singers at the *Herald* the task of putting together contrived obituaries to convince the public, sometimes in vain, that the deceased was, indeed, someone of heroic exploit. In such cases the turnout at the burial would be embarrassingly low, even after residents of Mbare, Highfields and Chitungwiza had been forced by Zanu-PF youths to board buses bound for Heroes' Acre.

Meanwhile, indisputable heroes such as Zipra commander Lookout Masuku were spitefully denied burial there. Many Zimbabweans vowed that their remains would be transferred to the shrine at an appropriate time.

Zanu-PF's corporate octopus had spread its predatory tentacles to the DRC in the late 1990s, when First Bank, a Zanu-PF-linked institution, opened its doors there. Until his escape to London with the Joshi brothers, Zidco director Dipak Pandya had been the bank's all-powerful non-executive chairman. A UN report published in 2002 cited Mnangagwa and then Zimbabwe Defence Force commander Vitalis Zvinavashe as key players in the plunder of Congolese resources, mostly diamonds. Heena Joshi reportedly worked for Oryx Natural Resources, which had had a stake in Congo-Kinshasa's Gecamines since 2000. Zimbabwean government and military officials were linked to the company.

Many of the allegations that would have been probed by the Karimanzira Committee had already been thoroughly investigated and well documented, but Karimanzira, Makoni and Mujuru never exposed the sharks swimming in Zanu-PF's ocean of corruption. To the dismay of the public, what passed for Mugabe's crackdown on corruption netted only political small fry – finance minister Chris Kuruneri, businessman and politician James Makamba, Mashonaland West Zanu-PF chairman Phillip Chiyangwa and business mogul Mutumwa Mawere, Mnangagwa's ally. Some observers believed that Mawere had been relentlessly pursued by a party scared of confronting Mnangagwa. Kuruneri and Makamba were respectively detained without bail for more than a year and seven months, causing a public outcry. There was speculation that the two men were subjected to extrajudicial punishment for reasons not remotely connected with their alleged externalisation of foreign currency.

On Sunday 29 February 2004, the *Zimbabwe Mirror* published an article by Tendai Dumbutshena, a leading Zimbabwean journalist, who was based in Johannesburg. At independence, he had been the editor of the *Zimbabwe Times*, but his career in mainstream journalism had come to an abrupt end in 1981 after three months as a political reporter on the *Herald*. Editor Farayi Munyuki had allegedly objected to Dumbutshena's use of the word 'alleged' in regard to a statement made by Mugabe, on the grounds that it implied the prime minister had lied. Dumbutshena was banned from further coverage of Mugabe, starting with the cancellation of a trip to Europe with the prime minister.

'That's how I lost my appetite for the media,' Dumbutshena explained.

He was the son of Zimbabwe's first indigenous chief justice, the illustrious and highly respected Enoch Dumbutshena, a man with a profound commitment to the rule of law and a fearless campaigner for an independent judiciary.

After distinguished service on the bench, the judge retired at the age of seventy, but was denied certain benefits to which he was entitled by virtue of his position. Close associates said the younger Dumbutshena never forgave Mugabe for humiliating his father and became one of his harshest critics.

While the *Mirror* article bristled with unbridled anger, it also raised pertinent questions about Mugabe's growing abuse of executive power and gross interference in the judiciary. Tendai Dumbutshena was a close friend and confidant of Makamba. His article, which appeared under the headline, 'A hatred gone too far', is worth quoting at some length:

> Since independence in 1980, there have been many cases of prominent people charged with corruption. The case of James Makamba who has the dubious distinction of being the first victim of the Presidential Powers (Temporary Measures) (Amendment of Criminal Procedure and Evidence Act) Regulations of 2004, boggles the mind. Here is a man who is a bona fide luminary of the so-called black indigenous business class; whose many companies employ hundreds of Zimbabweans. A former legislator for Zanu-PF, he is a current member of that party's central committee. He has served the party both as Mashonaland Central provincial secretary and chairman. He is on first-name terms with the high and mighty of this land.
>
> All these accolades and achievements do not, of course, place Makamba above the law. On the contrary, his position of leadership places an onerous obligation on him not only to obey the law but also to be its custodian. So why was it necessary to treat him like a dangerous and violent criminal or the leader of a rebel army? Armed policemen descended on his house and office causing pain and anguish to his family and employees.
>
> His farm in Mazowe was occupied by rifle-wielding policemen. It was deemed necessary to use the public broadcaster to announce to the nation that he was a

wanted man. Yet those in charge of Zimbabwe's law enforcement agencies know where Makamba works and lives. They also have his mobile telephone number.

The heavy-handedness in [*sic*] which his arrest was executed is unprecedented. Equally unprecedented is the manner in which the head of state, President Robert Mugabe, got involved. Before the man was even formally charged in a court of law, the president publicly tried and convicted him. All indications are that presidential powers were used to deny Makamba due process. It is to stretch the bounds of credulity to believe that Makamba's arrest and the promulgation of the statutory instrument were coincidental.

Over the years it has been common knowledge in ruling party circles that the president loathes Makamba for reasons that only he knows. Recent events have confirmed this. On the eve of his 80th birthday, the president gave an interview on what was supposed to be a happy occasion. This did not stop him from launching a vitriolic attack against Makamba, calling him an underling of the late Tiny Rowland.

For the benefit of young readers, Rowland was the CEO and founder of the London-based Lonrho multinational conglomerate. Until recently, Lonrho had vast interests, employing thousands in Zimbabwe. After independence the controversial tycoon soon assumed the mantle of benefactor to elements of Zimbabwe's ruling elite. They were eager recipients of Lonrho largesse.

Accommodation at the London Metropole was on the house, with extras also covered. In times of illness, real or imagined, the favoured were attended to in London by Rowland's personal physician. The Lonrho office in Harare issued many first or business class tickets to London and other destinations. Money was pushed in brown envelopes, with British pounds sterling the currency of choice. The Lonrho New Year's Eve dinner was the social event of the year in Harare. If you were anybody, you had to be there to confirm your high standing in society. Some of the recipients of these goodies still sit in cabinet and the much-vaunted politburo, spouting anti-imperialist mantras.

It came as no surprise that Nathan Shamuyarira remonstrated with Lonrho PLC when Rowland was ousted in a boardroom *coup d'état*. An indignant Shamuyarira, a leading party ideologue and politburo bigwig, said Rowland's ouster threatened to end warm relations between Lonrho and the Zimbabwe government.

Makamba is not a violent man. He has no previous convictions. All this is known to the people who head the police, CIO and defence forces. As stated above, many of these people can justifiably be considered friends. Police Commissioner Augustine Chihuri has a warm personal relationship with Makamba. It is, therefore, impossible to believe that the crude paramilitary operation to arrest Makamba was his brainchild. He was simply obeying orders. Those orders were given to the public broadcaster to tell the multitudes that Makamba's whereabouts had to be divulged as he constituted a moral danger to national security.

It may well be the case that in the 1980s, when Mugabe was strongly pushing for a one-party Marxist-Leninist state in Zimbabwe, the presence in Zanu-PF of capitalist-roaders like Makamba made his blood boil. Not only did his ilk pose a danger to the socialist revolution, their financial independence put them beyond his control. Hence the animus. But can it be rationalised today? The Marxist-Leninist one-party project was abandoned long ago. The party is now home to a motley collection of self-seekers. A crude form of capitalist accumulation is now the dominant ethos.

These buccaneers do not, however, pose a threat to the supreme rule of the *chef de grande*. There is no ideological purity to preserve as party leaders create individual islands of prosperity in a sea of squalor. It cannot be true, as suggested by some self-proclaimed analysts, that Makamba is being victimized for political reasons. To be brutally honest, politically Makamba is inconsequential. Like many in Zanu-PF and government with lofty titles, he is expendable fodder. He poses no threat to anyone. The idea that President Mugabe sees Makamba as some political threat is patently ludicrous.

If Makamba has committed crimes, he must face the music. The rule of law must, however, prevail. The presumption of innocence must apply. Undue pressure on the judiciary by an all-powerful head of state to convict must cease. This is personal hatred gone too far. It must stop forthwith.

These were harsh words, especially in the Zanu-PF-aligned *Zimbabwe Mirror*. But Harare's hyperactive rumour mill offered answers to Dumbutshena's questions even before he posed them. Makamba's ordeal had nothing to do with any perception by Mugabe that he was a political threat, or with any alleged breach of law through externalising foreign currency, said 'usually reliable' sources. The law would have been allowed to take its course, if that were the case.

The real cause of the businessman's arrest – or so it was unequivocally rumoured and stated on the Internet – was a love affair between Makamba and the youthful and vivacious First Lady, Grace Mugabe. People in the corridors of power said the relationship was common knowledge at the highest level of Zanu-PF and government. A clandestine meeting between the alleged lovers in Johannesburg had attracted the attention of Mugabe's omnipresent CIO. People close to Mugabe were said to be quietly dismayed by both the embarrassing affair and Makamba's controversial and merciless arrest. For Makamba, it was the beginning of the end of his vast empire.

Because of the scathing nature of the attack on Mugabe, the *Zimbabwe Mirror* editor and publisher, Dr Ibbo Mandaza, sought to play it safe by adroitly distancing himself from Dumbutshena's damning article.

'The views presented in this article,' he declared in an addendum, 'are entirely the author's and do not in any way represent those of the editor and publisher of this newspaper.'

In normal circumstances, no editor can legitimately dissociate him- or herself from any article in his or her publication. Journalism carries with it serious legal responsibilities, and, quite simply, publishers and editors cannot have their proverbial cake and eat it, as Mandaza was clearly trying to do. As this chapter was being written, the weekly *Zimbabwe Independent* reported that Mandaza's publishing empire had effectively been taken over by the CIO, along with the *Financial Gazette*. In due course, Mandaza endured the indignation of being pushed out of his own enterprise by the gentlemen in dark glasses, who brought his controversial career as a newspaper publisher to a premature end. The takeover of the *Financial Gazette* remained a printed rumour.

Dumbutshena's article was illuminating, not only for what it revealed about Makamba's legal predicament, but also for what it exposed about the duplicity and hypocrisy inherent in Zanu-PF's ignominious revolution.

Dumbutshena was one of four prominent and informed Zimbabweans whose opinion I canvassed in trying to determine how the post-independence revolution had been derailed or hijacked. The others were Morgan Tsvangirai, Jonathan Moyo and Mutumwa Mawere, who had rapidly built a business empire through alleged Zanu-PF patronage and lost everything when he fell from favour. Mawere, whose rise was as meteoric as his downfall was catastrophic, always denied that he had traded on his political affiliations.

In 1980, Mugabe said:

> The change is not in me. I am not the one who has undergone a metamorphosis. The transformation really is taking place in the minds of those who once upon a time regarded me as an extremist, a murderer, a psychopathic killer ... they are the people who have had to adjust to the change. I have remained my constant self. What I was, I still am.

He said this in response to a question by British journalist David Martin about the widespread perception that the man who became prime minister in 1980 was very unlike the guerrilla leader who had waged a ruthless campaign against the white regime of rebel leader Ian Smith. According to some observers, Mugabe's self-assessment could just as easily be applied in response to suggestions that he had undergone a radical transformation at some point during his first twenty-five years in power.

It was in search of clarity on the latter presumption that I prepared and distributed a brief questionnaire to twenty dedicated Mugabe-watchers who could be relied upon not only to hold strong opinions, but also to express them on record. The anonymous or non-attributable views of so-called experts and analysts have become the bane of journalism in Zimbabwe and other southern African states. Astute media observers have learned that the alleged but unnamed experts are, more often than not, the journalists themselves. For the sake of credibility, therefore, it was vital to link any assessment of Mugabe's governance to specific individuals.

Of the twenty people approached, six responded and only four were finally taken into account. They were asked:

- On the assumption that during his term of office Mr Mugabe underwent dramatic transformation as a politician and a leader, what is your own analysis of this change?

- When, in your opinion, should he have retired?
- Do you share the oft-expressed view that Mr Mugabe was an honest leader, who found himself surrounded by corrupt politicians?

The respondents unanimously endorsed the substance of Mugabe's statement on change as being equally relevant and candid in 2005 as it was in 1980. 'What I was, I still am,' he had said, and that had continued to be the case.

However, while Mugabe intended to convey that he had always been and remained a good leader, the wisdom of hindsight caused his critics to conclude that he had been and still was both incompetent and a dictator.

Mutumwa Mawere was the first to rise to the challenge, responding within twelve hours of receiving his set of questions.

'I am not sure that Mugabe ever changed ideologically from who he was during the liberation struggle,' he said. 'There was limited transformation, if any, on the critical defining qualities of Mugabe as a politician and leader.

'I am not sure whether he and his colleagues will agree that Zimbabwe's failure as a state is attributable to them. They are more likely to say the world has failed Zimbabwe. I am also not sure whether anyone can claim that Mugabe was ever competent as a leader. What may be nearer the truth is that the inherited economy was robust enough to accommodate any experiment that he came up with.'

Jonathan Moyo, the president's dedicated spin doctor for four years, was more dismissive of suggestions that Mugabe had undergone any transformation as a politician or national leader.

'My own view, first from a distance and then from a somewhat closer encounter, is that Mugabe simply moved from bad to worse,' he said. 'He has always been a ruler, never a leader, and his rulership has progressively deteriorated.'

Asked in a follow-up question what he had hoped to achieve by joining Zanu-PF and government in 2000 if it was already his opinion that Mugabe was moving 'from bad to worse', Moyo became abusive. But in his original response he said Mugabe's public record would show that some of his worst deeds had occurred during the very early stages of his rule.

'I have in mind, for example, Gukurahundi, which to this day ranks as his darkest moment in power,' said Moyo. 'His quest for a one-party state came early rather than late.

'I believe that his character must have been formed during his childhood. I have not found anything from available information or his biography that paints a picture of a gregarious, wonderful fellow. Most of what we have suggests a person who has always been a loner, a recluse and an enigma. In this sense, what we have gotten all along is the real Mugabe.'

Tendai Dumbutshena suggested that Mugabe's greatest failure was his subordination of economic considerations to political expediency, saying any perceived transformation would have been imposed on Mugabe by external factors.

'Mugabe exhibited a fatal flaw in his leadership: the primacy, in his mind, of politics over economics. The result was that at the end of the 1980s, there was a government that lived beyond its means, with a sluggish economy not producing the wealth required to meet its commitments. Inevitably, it had to turn to the IMF for support.'

He said he had seen no fundamental change in Mugabe during his first twenty-five years in power. 'The only change was that in the 1990s the IMF and the World Bank imposed the Economic Structural Adjustment Programme (ESAP) on a reluctant government. Its half-hearted implementation and inherent weaknesses ensured that ultimately, it failed.

'I do not share the view that all was well until Mugabe underwent some transformation. Any government worth its salt sets its agenda in the first years of its reign. In the 1980s, an opportunity was missed to lay the foundation for sustained economic growth. Investors were discouraged by incessant talk about creation of a Marxist one-party state. Yet this was a time when companies were disinvesting from South Africa and looking to relocate to the second most developed economy in the region – Zimbabwe.'

Dumbutshena said Mugabe had concentrated on laying the foundation for a one-party state. The physical annihilation of PF-Zapu through Gukurahundi, the party's absorption into Zanu-PF through the Unity Accord and numerous amendments to the Lancaster House constitution had all been intended to pave the way for Mugabe's cherished dream, a one-party state.

Surprisingly – some would say predictably – Morgan Tsvangirai presented the most coherent analysis of his nemesis. Amid the emotion and euphoria of victory for the liberation struggle after ninety years of colonialism, many Zimbabweans had found little time to assess the true political character of Zanu-PF and of Mugabe and other leaders, he said.

'We were all in a celebratory mood, hoping to grasp the challenges and demands of a new era, a new beginning. In 1980, Mugabe was concerned with sprucing up his international image, which at the time was that of a rabid, bloodthirsty communist, hence all the talk of reconciliation and attempts at a non-racial society. He wanted to put on the mask of a statesman.

'There was no dramatic change to Mugabe's style of leadership. It is consistent with a man who loves power at any cost. The man appears to have always harboured a no-questions-to-authority and a life-presidency mentality. Coming out of a war, the people were denied the time to assess the competencies of their leaders in a free environment.'

Tsvangirai said signs of Mugabe's intolerance, hate, and political and economic mismanagement dated back to 1980. The government had started negotiating with the IMF for support almost immediately, then devalued the dollar by 20 per cent in 1982, before scrapping subsidies for workers altogether.

'Ironically, Smith had maintained these subsidies at the height of the war. Then a war was declared on PF-Zapu in 1982 and the top Zanu-PF leadership started to amass wealth with gay abandon, resulting in a face-saving but ineffectual Leadership Code in 1984.

'Mugabe's administration assumed office with immediate post-war problems of structure, authority and control. Through a series of executive interventions – remember Canaan Banana's presidential directive on black advancement in government and in the private sector – the white colonial administration was smashed overnight and replaced by a political system that became a major source of elite enrichment, corruption and a key barrier to change.'

The new system had entrenched sycophancy and political patronage and immediately fanned instability, Tsvangirai said, resulting in the disturbances in Matabeleland and parts of the Midlands.

'Do not forget the inflammatory speeches of the likes of Enos Nkala, the crossing of floors of characters like David Kwidini and Callistus Ndlovu and others. At that point, Mugabe's true colours became clearly visible. Dumiso Dabengwa and Lookout Masuku were arrested and detained for close on five years, despite having been acquitted by the courts. Masuku died a few days after his release from prison. Others, like William Kona, the PF-Zapu secretary for defence, were murdered. Nkomo was forced to flee for dear life. Ndabaningi Sithole was holed up in the United States for close on two years, fearing for his life at home. Muzorewa was harassed and arrested, but released without charge. Ian Smith was expelled from parliament, through a vote, yes, but for merely making statements while abroad criticising Mugabe and his regime.

'All this happened in the formative stages of our independence. So there was no dramatic change of character in Mugabe. The character remained consistent, starting with the detention of Mukudzei Mudzi, Henry Hamadziripi, Rugare Gumbo, Dzinashe Machingura and others in Mozambique during the war.

'The manner in which Mugabe treated Sithole, Chikerema and others, including the late Chief Justice Enoch Dumbutshena, showed a vindictive and callous politician, totally intolerant of diverse views in a diverse society whose ideals included the extension of basic freedoms, tolerance, equal opportunity and the development of a non-racial, non-ethnic society.'

Tsvangirai said Mugabe's new political system had merely replaced the colonial administration and adopted an agenda that was at variance with the expectations and aspirations of the majority of the people. The state apparatus had been staffed with partisan loyalists whose brief was to serve and save the ruling party, regardless of the national or liberation war agenda. The pattern had remained the same throughout.

'At the end of the first decade of independence, there was much public pressure on the system to adapt or die,' Tsvangirai said. 'Numerous challenges beckoned for attention, including a radical overhaul of the entire state structure and its institutions. Faced with such a challenge, instead of taking positive steps to entrench democracy, the system severed ties with the people; it broke ranks with the entire nation. The church, workers, students and peasants began to confront Mugabe, seeking answers as to the direction the revolution was taking. The revolution had clearly lost its way.

'To survive, Mugabe declared war against the people. But the church, trade unions and other civil society bodies refused to be cowed into submission. A standoff emerged; it continues to this day. This is the character of the man we face today.'

Tsvangirai said when Mugabe adopted ESAP as the new economic policy in 1990, workers and the poor had openly confronted the nationalists and challenged them on their earlier pronouncements and ideology. That had exposed Zanu-PF even further. Mugabe tried to negotiate with the workers, but when that failed to provide positive responses to the spirit of the liberation struggle, he opted for confrontation. The party's worker base had quickly slipped away.

'A bigger threat of losing a political base loomed large. The repressive pattern was extended to the student movement. Student leaders were arrested and charged. A new law was put in place restricting academic freedom. Student demonstrations were banned. The picture remains the same to this day.'

Through these actions, Mugabe had united the people against his regime, Tsvangirai said.

Opinion differed as to when Mugabe should have stepped down. The most generous was Dumbutshena, who suggested 1995, after fifteen years in power.

'It had become obvious that as Zimbabwe approached the twenty-first century in a rapidly changing world, Mugabe and his generation of leaders – Joshua Nkomo, Simon Muzenda, Joseph Msika and the rest – should have given way to younger leaders, more equipped to meet the challenge of modernising and industrialising the economy,' he said.

Instead, the country had continued under an ageing leadership that was more concerned about its past contributions than what future it could offer.

Tsvangirai was the most brutal. 'He should have retired after his failures during the first term of office led to the deaths of about 20 000 Zimbabweans in the Gukurahundi massacre. If that was not bad enough, Mugabe should have resigned when corruption in his regime was exposed by the *Chronicle* in what came to be known as Willowgate. If that was not enough, Mugabe should have resigned or retired after Patrick Kombayi was nearly killed by members of the secret service campaigning for his deputy, Muzenda.

'If that was still not enough, Mugabe should have gone when scandal after scandal unfolded in the nineties – the VIP housing scheme involving his wife Grace; the war veterans' disability fund; the land-for-the-*chefs* scandal of 1992–93; and the disbursement of gratuities to former guerrillas that led to the collapse of the Zimbabwe dollar in 1997.

'The list of cases and missed opportunities is endless.'

Moyo suggested that Mugabe had forfeited an opportunity to carve a niche for himself as Zimbabwe's respected elder statesman by not retiring in 1990.

'He really should have done that and he would be occupying a special position not only in our liberation struggle, but also in the history of our post-independence period,' he said. 'Now he has become synonymous with what's wrong with and in Zimbabwe. He has become the symbol and embodiment of utter failure and breathtaking ineptitude.'

Mawere endorsed the view that the president should have stepped down in 1990, pointing out that he had become an ideological anachronism.

'Personally,' he said, 'I do not subscribe to any left-wing ideology. My answer is, therefore, simple and straightforward. The left-wing ideology has been discredited universally. I am still to see any system that is as efficient and effective in addressing the needs of the poor as the capitalist system.

'To the extent that Mugabe is still clinging to the socialist mindset, I think he should have resigned when the former communist states of Europe saw the light.'

On the all-important issue of corruption, Moyo said Mugabe's leadership style had obviously fed into and nurtured corrupt practices. He had basically survived on the strength of patronage.

'That is always fertile breeding ground for corruption. I think Zimbabweans should brace themselves for horrible stories to be told about Mugabe in the coming years. He is not an angel at all, not a Julius Nyerere by any stretch of the imagination, and worse, he is not an intellectually honest person.'

Mawere said Mugabe presided over a 'generally corrupt' political system.

'You can compare the system to any socialist or communist system where the state is used for patronage. You have seen that Mugabe will not hesitate to use the state to settle personal or what he perceives to be national threats to his rule and this is typical of any state-driven system.'

Dumbutshena found no credible evidence that Mugabe was corrupt in the mould of Mobutu Sese Seko of Zaire or Omar Bongo of Gabon. 'His obsession was to concentrate power in his own hands. As his contemporaries fell by the wayside, they were replaced by younger people totally beholden to Mugabe. Justice minister Patrick Chinamasa is, perhaps, the most obnoxious example of this breed of young and unprincipled opportunists. Slowly, Mugabe imposed his will on the party and then on the nation.'

With hindsight, said Tsvangirai, it was not at all correct that Mugabe was an honest leader who surrounded himself with corrupt politicians.

'Competent, capable and honest leaders are able to see and distance themselves from corrupt politicians,' he pointed out. 'They are also able to take action to save the majority against corruption, even if the corrupt are family members or political friends. So I don't share that view.'

In my days as a teacher at Nyamaropa during the war of liberation, I witnessed and heard countless reports of gruesome murder and torture by Zanla guerrillas. I wondered then, and still question today, whether these acts of unmitigated violence were the spontaneous and unlawful decision of individuals or groups who would be punished if found out by the Zanla High Command, or whether, more ominously, the acts were committed within the framework of official policy formulated at headquarters in Maputo.

Zanu-PF and Mugabe were always intolerant of opposition and challenge. Dozens of guerrilla fighters were summarily executed after staging an uprising at Chifombo in eastern Zambia in 1975. Zanu-PF chairman Herbert Chitepo was assassinated in the same year because of rivalry within the party. While Mugabe had wrested power from Sithole, he would never tolerate any semblance of challenge or defiance of his own authority.

Suspected sell-outs were swiftly despatched by Zanla in the battle zones. Opponents to Mugabe's authority were imprisoned, tortured and killed in Mozambique. When Nkomo was perceived to be a challenge to Mugabe's authority after independence, an estimated 20 000 of his supporters were massacred. Zanu-PF unleashed violence against both PF-Zapu and Muzorewa's UANC during the 1985 election campaign, despite the fact that Muzorewa, in particular, had ceased to be a serious political threat to anyone by then.

When Edgar Tekere's Zimbabwe Unity Movement emerged ahead of the 1990 election, former Gweru mayor Patrick Kombayi was shot and left for dead by a CIO agent and a Zanu-PF activist. He was crippled for life. Kombayi had challenged Mugabe's deputy, Muzenda, for election in the Midlands capital. It is likely Kombayi's assailants were not acting directly on instructions from State House, but Mugabe nevertheless condoned their action. He used his presidential prerogative to pardon them when they were convicted and sentenced for attempted murder.

As with corruption, Mugabe rarely condemned violence.

His uncompromising and hateful speeches continually fuelled violence against his political opponents. When the white farmers were perceived to have influenced the black electorate to reject proposed constitutional reforms in February 2000, violence, retribution and dispossession were visited on them. In the face of the grave political challenge posed by the MDC, Zanu-PF unleashed wholesale violence on an unprecedented national scale.

Mugabe's treatment of Wilfred Mhanda or Dzinashe Machingura and other so-called dissidents in Mozambique serves as a typical example of how ruthlessly he has always dealt with his opponents. The Reverend Ndabaningi Sithole, Joshua Nkomo, Edgar Tekere, Eddison Zvobgo, James Chikerama, Enoch Dumbutshena, Dumiso Dabengwa, Lookout Masuku, Willie Musarurwa, Morgan Tsvangirai, Bishop Abel Muzorewa, Patrick Kombayi, Sir Garfield Todd, Dzikamai Mavhaire, Margaret Dongo, Chris Kuruneri, James Makamba and Jonathan Moyo would all have attested to Mugabe's vindictiveness.

It was Mugabe's intolerance, along with the insatiable greed of many of his senior lieutenants such as Nkala, Mnangagwa and the military top brass, that set Zimbabwe on the path to devastation and despair. Intolerance breeds violence, while greed begets corruption.

At no single point in his political career was Mugabe a man to brook opposition or challenge from any quarter. The farm invasions have to be seen in that context rather than as a premeditated, if belated, initiative to address the gross injustices of land ownership in colonial Rhodesia. The enactment of AIPPA, the arrest of local journalists, the expulsion of foreign correspondents and the general suppression of press freedom should be viewed in the same context.

The greatest lesson that Zimbabweans should have learned from Mugabe's autocratic rule is that never again can they permit a national leader to enjoy such unbridled power. Checks and balances on political power are the most essential component of any democracy.

The citizens of this once most beautiful country and extremely prosperous nation will hopefully also have learned that, ultimately, it is entirely their responsibility to determine their destiny. When the Zambians were fed up with suffering amid devastating shortages of essential commodities in 1991, they voted out the cause, Kenneth David Kaunda. Three years later, when the citizens of Malawi could no longer stomach dictatorship and abuse of power, they uprooted the problem – the geriatric Hastings Kamuzu Banda.

Resolute in their determination to restore self-esteem, dignity and national pride, neither the Zambians nor the Malawians cowered in fear while protesting that the South Africans and the entire Southern African Development Community should do more to rescue them. Nor did they seek salvation through the intervention of Britain or America.

The demise of the *Daily News* and the suppression of the media in general in the first quarter-century of independent Zimbabwe delivered the succinct message that without press freedom, there is little value to other freedoms. Zimbabweans need to learn to guard their freedoms jealously.

If ever there is another national cause requiring the citizens of Zimbabwe to make sacrifices, those who can must do so out of a sense of commitment and patriotism rather than any expectation of reward or compensation. President Robert Gabriel Mugabe was more than adequately compensated and rewarded for his sacrifice and contribution to the achievement of Zimbabwe's independence. So were most war veterans.

A total of more than twenty-five years of luxury in State House, while millions of Zimbabweans wallow in misery and poverty, is more than fair reward for ten years in detention and five years of living in the lap of luxury in Maputo, while some of those who suffer deprivation and indignity today engaged the enemy in the bush.

My own enthusiasm for the direction our post-independence revolution has taken is vastly diminished. For me, the revolution has totally lost direction. As I write, I am informed that our little family business is finally succumbing to the ravages of national economic stagnation. It never really prospered, but for fifteen years it kept the local population well supplied with essential commodities. The bottle store was the social hub of the community. Now the shelves are bare. When the wholesalers in Rusape have a little sugar, cooking oil, rice or soap, they ration purchases to one carton of a commodity per dealer. The bakeries have little bread. Above all, there is no transport because of fuel shortages. In June 2005, my son Tafi drove to Gwangwadza. He abandoned his truck there for two weeks due to lack of fuel. The supply of beer from the breweries is erratic. Few in the rural areas can afford to buy a 'scud' of Chibuku for Z$100 000. Every commodity is outrageously expensive. I am told the people are angry, but they speak only in whispers, while waiting for something to happen. Nobody, not even the MDC, seems to know what exactly should happen, or when.

We had invested a total of Z$25 000 when we started the business in 1989. We purchased the building, two paraffin deep freezes, two truckloads of stock and a beast for the butchery. In February 2006, the newly introduced Z$50 000 bank note was not enough to buy a loaf of bread. Meanwhile, the president blamed every one of Zimbabwe's ills on British prime minister Tony Blair. It worried me that he was beginning to sound as if he believed his own frequent outbursts.

I was forced to flee the country of my birth, abandoning everything I had worked for or built over the years. I was living comfortably. My family had last lived in an apartment in 1979, in Salisbury's then fashionable Glen Norah B Flats. When we left Zimbabwe in 2003, we had a lovely home in Harare's upmarket suburb of Highlands, another house at Gwangwadza and a home at Nyanga, complete with a fine orchard. On arrival at Harvard, our clock moved back many years and we took up residence in an apartment, comfortable enough by the standards of Cambridge, Massachusetts, but tiny compared with what we had in Harare.

Our loss was punishment for crimes that I did not commit.

In 2004, a woman from Zimbabwe died in Lowell, Massachusetts, a town forty miles north of Boston. She lived alone and her body lay in her apartment for two days before it was found. For three weeks she remained unburied, pending the arrival of her people from Harare. They never came. Visas to the United States are not easy to obtain, and an airline ticket from Harare to Boston at short notice presents an insurmountable challenge for the average Zimbabwean. Eventually, the woman's daughter arrived from Canada, where she had been granted asylum. Political refugees cannot easily travel outside their host countries. When we finally buried the woman, the small church in Lowell was packed to the rafters with Zimbabweans, most of them strangers who never knew her in life. As we huddled around the grave in the rain, strangers burying a compatriot among strangers in a distant cemetery, my thoughts drifted.

'Is President Mugabe aware this is what he has done to his people?' I mused.

In June 2005, an innocuous news item appeared in the press. Air Zimbabwe had a new board of directors. The chairman was Michael Bimha, a human resources practitioner I had known for many years. More significantly, he was a close relative of Grace Mugabe. Far more significant, for me, was the appointment as a director of one Phillip Mhike, my tormentor during the struggle for the independence of Zimbabwe. For a man who vowed to do everything possible to prevent a nationalist victory at the time, he had certainly prospered under his erstwhile foes after independence.

Of course, by 2005, the national airline routinely featured in news headlines such as, 'Air Zimbabwe plane impounded at Gatwick'; 'Fuel shortage grounds Air Zimbabwe' and 'IATA suspends Air Zimbabwe'. Meanwhile, three *Zimbabwe Independent* journalists were arrested for causing to be published a report that Mugabe had allegedly commandeered an Air Zimbabwe aeroplane, leaving paying and scheduled passengers stranded.

I suppose it was no longer an issue of great consequence who was in charge of the national airline's corporate affairs.

In the beginning, there was the Central African Airways Corporation, which served the three countries that made up the Federation of Rhodesia and Nyasaland. Following dissolution of the federation, Air Rhodesia was established in 1967. After the internal settlement in 1978, which saw the emergence of Abel Muzorewa as prime minister, the airline became Air Zimbabwe-Rhodesia.

At independence in April 1980, the national carrier became Air Zimbabwe, introducing services on the profitable London route on 2 April. As a mark of its steady growth, Air Zimbabwe took over the freight airline, Affretair, in 1983. The national airline was privatised in 1997.

In 1980, Air Zimbabwe operated a fleet of four Boeing 707s and two Vickers Viscount turbo-prop aircraft. These aged craft were phased out with the purchase of three Boeing 737s for short-haul routes and two Boeing 767 Extended Range aircraft to fly long distance to London, Frankfurt and Cyprus.

James Makamba, popular former disc jockey at the Rhodesian Broadcasting Corporation, was the middleman for the purchase of the 767 aircraft from Boeing, the Seattle-based manufacturer of commercial jetliners, military aircraft and satellites.

On the way to Canada to attend the 1987 Commonwealth Heads of Government Meeting, Mugabe's delegation landed at New York's JFK International. Makamba, then a little-known businessman, was waiting to whisk the entire presidential party, which included me as editor of the *Chronicle*, across North America to Seattle in a brand new Boeing 767. After spending a morning as Boeing's guests at its gigantic plant in the state of Washington, we proceeded to Vancouver.

Makamba spent the next few days on the sidelines of the biennial conference while Commonwealth leaders discussed strategies to end apartheid in South Africa, among other topics. After Mugabe spent the day attending to the rigours of world politics, Makamba no doubt enlightened him after hours on the finer points of the 767, the world's first twin-engine, wide-bodied long-haul airliner, pointing out many advantages over its rival. McDonnell Douglas, another US manufacturer, had offered Air Zimbabwe its tri-engine DC 10, an older-generation aircraft. Both Zambia Airways and Ghana Airways had added DC 10s to their fleets, and one of them flew regularly from the Zambian capital of Lusaka to New York, until Zambia Airways collapsed, never to fly again.

In 1987, the McDonnell Douglas representative in Harare was Joseph Mapondera, a dedicated socialite who never tired of telling all who cared to listen that Mugabe was his uncle. How Makamba and Mapondera came to be the agents of the world's largest airline manufacturers of the era, I could never fathom, but in order to brush aside the challenge posed by Mugabe's own clansman, Makamba must have been particularly talented. It was no secret, however, that he enjoyed the backing of Lonrho CEO Tiny Rowland, and, in fact, promoting the Boeing 767 was a sideline for Makamba, whose regular job was that of public relations executive with Lonrho Zimbabwe.

In due course, Air Zimbabwe acquired two Boeing 767 airliners, and Makamba became instantly prosperous. He entered into an extremely viable business partnership with Solomon Mujuru, also tremendously rich, after the latter's stint as commander of the Zimbabwe National Army.

Makamba never looked back until the fateful day in 2004, when he was arrested and held without bail for seven months after being accused of externalising funds. As soon as he was released, he skipped bail and fled to Johannesburg, abandoning the empire he had built since 1987. When I saw Makamba in London in November 2005, he looked somewhat bewildered, but nevertheless delighted to be on the better side of prison gates.

By the time Makamba escaped from Zimbabwe, Joyce Mujuru, wife of his former business partner, Solomon, had been appointed second vice-president. Solomon Tapfumaneyi Mujuru, then known as Rex Nhongo, had been instrumental in securing for Mugabe the position of Zanu-PF leader during the liberation struggle in Mozambique. By the time his wife became one of Mugabe's deputies, Mujuru was regarded in top Zanu-PF circles as the kingmaker of Zimbabwe.

At the time of my own flight to Johannesburg, Ursula and I had become young grandparents. Our granddaughter Chiedza was the love of our life. She was only two. After our sudden departure, we gradually became voices on the long-distance phone. Our children, Tafi and Isabel, were blessed with another child in 2003. They named him Geoffrey, after me.

'Should God summon me now,' I said to Ursula wistfully when we received the good news, 'I will go in peace.'

At the time of writing, Ursula had not seen her grandson. The circumstances of our existence make transatlantic journeys a luxury beyond reach. I was fortunate enough to travel to southern Africa alone in May 2004 and again in December 2005. On both occasions, while in Botswana, that blessed haven of peace, economic development and prosperity, Tafi and Isabel crossed the border to visit me in Gaborone, once sleepy and dusty, but now a bustling, modern metropolis. The city had become a haven for Zimbabwean economic and political refugees. I met my namesake for the first time in 2004 and saw him again in 2005.

While I played with my grandchildren in the lush gardens of the Holiday Inn, Tafi and Isabel went shopping. They bought rice, sugar, cooking oil and every other item that the average family purchases at the supermarket in Bulawayo or Mutare at the end of the month. Then Tafi took their truck to the garage for servicing, repairs and a set of new tyres. I was reminded anew of Zambians visiting Harare and Bulawayo on shopping sprees in the early days of Zimbabwe's independence. How arrogant it had been of Zimbabweans to ridicule their less prosperous neighbours then. How ironic that once proud Zimbabweans have become the target of xenophobes in southern Africa, their mushrooming numbers in countries such as Botswana, Namibia and South Africa resented by local residents against whom they compete for jobs and housing and healthcare and education.

Each time I bade my children and grandchildren farewell as they set out on their long drive back to Harare, tears welled up in my eyes.

Geoffrey will soon turn three, and has already built a small vocabulary. He learned to say 'Sekuru', Shona for grandfather, surprisingly early. Isabel's father, Geoffrey Bvumbi, is a regular visitor to their home, and occasionally, when we call from America, my heart sings when my grandson says, 'Allo, Sekulu Nyalota.' Meanwhile, life goes on.

Adversity, desolation and deprivation have become a way of life for most Zimbabweans. The little fellow has learned to endure such from an early age.

Zimbabwe is a land generously endowed with a vast array of natural resources, as well as a highly educated and hard-working population. The workforce is well qualified and highly skilled. Outside government there is no shortage of competent managerial skills. The majority of Zimbabweans are patriotic and law-abiding citizens.

The country boasts comprehensive agricultural, manufacturing, commercial and tourism sectors. It possesses the potential to rekindle international goodwill and attract foreign investment again. Driven by their courage and determination, and as masters of their own destiny, the nation will hopefully overcome the current situation of hardship to create a secure, bountiful and bright future for generations to come.

Hopefully, for Geoffrey Junior and his generation, Robert Mugabe will become just a distant, albeit painful, memory one day.

Select bibliography

Boynton, Graham. *Last Days in Cloud Cuckooland: Dispatches from White Africa*.
New York: Random House, 1997

Chan, Stephen. *Robert Mugabe: A Life of Power and Violence*. Ann Arbor: University
of Michigan Press, 2003

Chikuhwa, Jacob. *A Crisis of Governance: Zimbabwe*. New York: Algora
Publishing, 2004

Hill, Geoff. *The Battle for Zimbabwe: The Final Countdown*. Cape Town:
Zebra Press, 2003

———. *What Happens After Mugabe? Can Zimbabwe Rise from the Ashes?*
Cape Town: Zebra Press, 2005

Keeley, Robert V, Prosser Gifford, William E Schaufele, Jeffrey Davidow,
Pauline H Baker and Hugh P Elliot. *Perspectives on Negotiation – Negotiating
Zimbabwe's Independence*. Washington, DC: Department of State, 1986

Martin, David, and Phyllis Johnson. *The Struggle for Zimbabwe: The Chimurenga
War*. London: Faber and Faber, 1981

Meredith, Martin. *Our Votes, Our Guns: Robert Mugabe and the Tragedy of Zimbabwe*.
New York: Public Affairs, 2002

Nkomo, Joshua. *Nkomo: The Story of My Life*. Harare: Sapes Books, 2001

Sithole, Masipula. *Zimbabwe: Struggles within the Struggle*. Harare: Rujeko
Publishers, 1999

Smith, David, and Colin Simpson. *Mugabe*. Salisbury: Pioneer Head, 1981

Smith, Ian D. *The Great Betrayal*. London: Blake Publishing, 1997

Verrier, Anthony. *The Road to Zimbabwe, 1890–1980*. London: Jonathan Cape, 1986

White, Luise. *The Assassination of Herbert Chitepo: Text and Politics in Zimbabwe*.
Bloomington: Indiana University Press, 2003

Index